MARY ROBINSON:

SELECTED POEMS

MARY ROBINSON:
SELECTED POEMS

edited by Judith Pascoe

broadview literary texts

Canadian Cataloguing in Publication Data

Robinson, Mary, 1758-1800
    Mary Robinson : selected poems

(Broadview literary texts)
Includes bibliographical references.
ISBN 1-55111-201-9 (softcover) ISBN 1-55111-317-1 (hardcover)

I. Pascoe, Judith,   II. Title.   III. Series.
PR5233.R27A6 1999   821'.6   C99-930736-3

Broadview Press Ltd., is an independent, international publishing house,
incorporated in 1985.

North America:
P.O. Box 1243, Peterborough, Ontario, Canada K9J 7H5
3576 California Road, Orchard Park, NY 14127
TEL: (705) 743-8990; FAX: (705) 743-8353;
E-MAIL: customerservice@broadviewpress.com
United Kingdom: Turpin Distribution Services Ltd.,
Blackhorse Rd., Letchworth, Hertfordshire SG6 1HN
TEL: (1462) 672555; FAX: (1462) 480947; E-MAIL: turpin@rsc.org

Australia: St. Clair Press, P.O. Box 287, Rozelle, NSW 2039
TEL: (02) 818-1942; FAX: (02) 418-1923

www.broadviewpress.com
Broadview Press is grateful to Professor Eugene Benson for advice on
editorial matters for the Broadview Literary Texts series.

Broadview Press gratefully acknowledges the financial support of the
Ministry of Canadian Heritage through the Book Publishing Industry
Development Program.

Text design and composition by George Kirkpatrick

PRINTED IN CANADA
Canadä

For Stuart Curran,
who led the way

Contents

Lyrical Tales (1800)

Acknowledgements

Stuart Curran introduced me to Mary Robinson, advocated this edition, and shared his vision of a community of scholars, a vision so powerful that it sustains me still and always. While he would have edited Robinson's poems differently and, no doubt, better than I have here, I trust he will share my pleasure in seeing her poetry back in print.

In the final months of work on this edition, when my filing system was periodically breaking down and my memory was untrustworthy, Sharon Setzer opened her Robinson archives to me, sending e-mail messages, xeroxes, and shared insights flying between Raleigh, North Carolina, and Iowa City, Iowa. As usual, my husband Perry Howell read drafts, proofed poems, and stayed up late so I would not be working alone.

Along the way, I asked for help often and was grateful to receive assistance from Margaret Maison, Martin Levy, Jeannette Obstoj, Miriam Gilbert, Julie Shaffer, and Dan White. Bruce Barker-Benfield, Senior Assistant Librarian at the Bodleian Library, University of Oxford; Christopher Lloyd, Surveyor of The Queen's Pictures, The Royal Collection Trust; and Enid Foster, Librarian at the Garrick Club, kindly and helpfully responded to my queries. I am especially grateful to Lord Abinger for permission to reproduce in its entirety one of the Mary Robinson manuscript letters in his collection of Shelley and Godwin papers housed in the Bodleian Library, University of Oxford. Mary Wyly, senior librarian at the Newberry Library, transcribed lines for me from the Newberry's copy of the very rare 1793 *Poems*. I am also grateful to librarians and curators at the Wallace Collection, the British Library, the British Museum, the Library Company of Philadelphia, the Folger Shakespeare Library, the New York Public Library, and the University of Pennsylvania. The staff of both the special collections and the printing services departments at the University of Virginia Library, where Caroline Watson's engravings of Maria Cosway's illustrations for Robinson's "The Wintry Day" reside, were unfailingly helpful and obliging. Three research assistants, Thomas Pearson, Eun-Jung Yook, and William Ness, contributed to this project over the several years it was in the works and each was a model of patience and persistence. Barbara Conolly, my editor at Broadview, helped bring order to an unruly manuscript. Don LePan and Mical Moser provided enthusiastic support. I extend my sincere thanks to all who became caught up in this project.

Figure 1. George Romney, portrait of Mary Robinson, 1781.
(Reproduced by kind permission of the Trustees of the Wallace Collection, London.)

A Note on the Texts and Illustrations

Unless otherwise noted, the texts of Mary Robinson's poetry are drawn from the last edition over which the author exercised editorial control, with very occasional emendations when other versions of a poem suggest a printer's error or idiosyncrasy in the copy text. This means that the copy texts for the poems that follow are taken when possible from Robinson's 1775 *Poems*, her 1791 and 1793 *Poems*, the 1796 edition of *Sappho and Phaon*, and the 1800 *Lyrical Tales*. It is impossible to know which of the alterations to poems that took place in the 1806 *Poetical Works* can be attributed to Robinson and which were initiated by her daughter, another editor, or a typesetter. In the case of poems from the 1806 volume that were collected for the first time, but which appeared earlier in periodicals, I use the 1806 version unless I note otherwise. Although my decision to use versions of the poems over which Robinson exerted control would seem to dictate the use of periodical versions of all those poems from the 1806 edition that appeared in newspapers or magazines during Robinson's lifetime, the periodical variants frequently lack stanzas, a state of affairs which had more to do with the arbitrary space constraints of a newspaper editor than with any considered decision on Robinson's part. In several instances, though, I found compelling reasons to include a newspaper variant rather than the 1806 version of a poem, and I delineate these reasons in the first footnote to such a poem. In all cases, normalization of accidentals has been avoided, including spelling, punctuation, italicization, and capitalization. The long s and repeated quotation marks at the beginning of each line are modernized. I do not replicate the long bracket used to mark triple rhymes.

These editorial guidelines are followed in order to preserve the poems' original appearances, to let modern readers, as much as possible, see the poems as Robinson's contemporaries confronted them during the period of her greatest literary celebrity. An argument can be made for a different approach, especially in regard to poems from the 1791 and 1793 volumes, published at the height of the Della Cruscan rage. The argument, as set forth by a reviewer for the *English Review* goes as follows: "In every poem many words, and those too of no importance, are printed some in *Italics* and some in Capitals, without any apparent reason; except that, perhaps, the printer supposed that such variety adorned the page." One of Robinson's poems that exists in manuscript, while not distinguishing between the kinds of emphasis afforded by capitalization and italicization, convinced me that the emphatic nature of Robinson's printed poems, somewhat toned down in the 1806 edition, was a feature of her manuscript poems as well. Ultimately, I decided that the typographical idiosyncrasy of the Della Cruscan-era poems was revelatory and thus decided to retain it. In a few instances the 1806 texts provide corrections to typographical errors or clarifications of lines, and I incorporate these changes. A list of these corrections is provided on page 433.

The series of illustrations to Robinson's "The Wintry Day," which I use to divide the separate sections of this volume are Caroline Watson's engravings of drawings by Maria Cosway. Cosway was unacquainted with Robinson when she embarked on the series of drawings. Robinson noted in an 11 September 1800 letter to Jane Porter that she had received a flattering note from the artist who was at that point finishing the illustrations. The series of engravings were published by Rudolph Ackermann in September 1804. The note to "The Wintry Day" (pp. 340-341) provides information about the engravings as well. I am grateful to John Walker and Anne Mellor, whose separate essays on Cosway led me to the engravings which I previously knew only from brief mentions in the *Morning Post*.

Authorial notes to the poems are indicated by the insertion of Robinson's initials directly after a note as she gave it. Editorial notes, when necessary to augment Robinson's notes, follow the bracketed initials.

In the manuscript letters, reprinted in Appendix A, words or punctuation placed in brackets are my best guesses at illegible passages.

Illustrations

Figure 2. Joshua Reynolds, portrait of Mary Robinson, engraved by T. Burke for the
frontispiece to Robinson's *Poems* (1791).

Introduction

In a period of ten days in the summer of 1800, Mary Robinson translated Joseph Hager's *Picture of Palermo* from the German so that English readers could enjoy Hager's account of the pleasures of a Sicilian winter. In Robinson's translation, published by Richard Phillips before the year was out, the December fields are covered with May flowers and almond trees reach full bloom in mid-January. In January also, she translates, "ice is eaten at the coffee-houses in the evening; and the cold is not more felt with the doors and windows open than it is in Germany at the end of April."[1] In Robinson's England, by contrast, the cold had begun to set in. Although she had started the year being celebrated by Samuel Taylor Coleridge as "a woman of undoubted genius," by July she had narrowly escaped imprisonment for debt and was debilitated by an illness exacerbated by her intense bout of work on the Hager translation.[2]

Robinson's disciplined approach to this assignment in the midst of personal chaos is characteristic of her literary career as a whole. Between the publication of her 1791 *Poems* and her death on December 28, 1800, Mary Darby Robinson penned four further collections of poems, four novels, two political tracts, several essays, and literally countless (uncountable because they are so widely disseminated under multiple pseudonyms) individually published poems. Although Robinson's first collection of poems was published in 1775, the period of her greatest literary productivity paralleled the decade of the 1790s, making her the exact contemporary of the first generation of poets credited with ushering in a new literary movement. The reasons why Robinson has not, until very recently, been positioned alongside William Blake, Samuel Taylor Coleridge, and William Wordsworth in anthologies, academic courses, and scholarship devoted to the romantic era are not entirely specific to this woman writer. The failure of literary histories to acknowledge romanticism's debt to

---

1 Joseph Hager, *Picture of Palermo*. trans. Mary Robinson (London: R. Phillips, 1800) 7.

2 Samuel Taylor Coleridge to Robert Southey, 25 January 1800, *Collected Letters of Samuel Taylor Coleridge*, 6 vols., ed. Earl Leslie Griggs (Oxford: Clarendon Press, 1966-71) 1: 562.

Charlotte Smith or Joanna Baillie, Robinson's peers and co-innovators in the literary delineation of emotional extremes, suggests past critical standards inimical to female accomplishment. But Robinson's checkered history – especially her sensationalized liaison with the Prince of Wales in the early 1780s – has cast a long shadow over all her subsequent endeavours. Robinson the poet was also always Robinson the fallen woman. And the means she found of coping with that fact – her adoption of a retinue of alternate poetic identities coupled with her frank pursuit of commercial success – clash with the prevailing stereotype of the romantic poet with its emphasis on naturalness, authenticity, and spirituality.

Robinson's writings reflect the extent to which her poetry serves as a kind of cultural barometer of aesthetic change. Robinson's poems initiate or engage in her society's every literary preoccupation; she uses the Della Cruscan vogue as a springboard for her career as a poet of sensibility, contributes to the sonnet renaissance, and works changes upon the lyrical ballads of William Wordsworth in her own lyrical tales. Just as her poetry participates in the chief aesthetic innovations of the decade, it also chronicles the major news events of her day. In poems focusing on the death of Marie Antoinette or the discovery of the "Savage of Aveyron," Robinson turns the focal points of popular culture to literary advantage. These strategies contributed to Robinson's commercial success in her own time, and they make her work valuable as a window into her age.

Robinson's sonnet "Twilight" provides a preliminary glimpse of her poetic preoccupations and their place in the literary marketplace of the 1790s. Robinson writes:

> How placid is thy hour, O Twilight pale,
>   How soothingly sublime! Thy fragrant breath
> Steals o'er the flow'ry margin of the vale,
>   Cold as the Vestal's sigh, — and still as death.
> The western cliff, dim with expanding shade,
>   Scarce meets a gleamy star to point the way
>   Of wilder'd traveller, whose footsteps stray
> Along the sandy waste, or lonesome glade.
> Soft on the field flow'r falls the spangling dew,
>   'Till the young moon her silver wreath uprears

To crown the mountain's brow. The purpling hue
From the dark woody height now disappears;
  While nothing seems to breathe, save where the song
Of Philomel forlorn trills her dark haunts among.

The three chief locutions of the heading under which the poem was
published – "Original Sketches from Nature" – suggest attributes
conventionally used to yoke the work of Robinson's romantic peers:
a concern for originality or authenticity, an interest in the fragmen-
tary or unfinished, and a turning to nature for its restorative power.[3]
We recognize in Robinson's "wilder'd traveler" a counterpart of the
vagrant men and women who populate William Wordsworth's poems,
and we can characterize Robinson's subject, the moment of transition
between day and night, as a permutation of a romantic theme: the
heightened consciousness made possible by those moments when we
are caught between one state of being and another (for example, sleep
and wakefulness or life and death). Robinson's poem conjures up a
moment of poetic escape in the placid hour of twilight, but also, by its
end, allows for the intrusion of death in the "dark haunts" of the
nightingale, acknowledging in this way the failure of poetry to sustain
a transcendent gesture. It is a familiar kind of disappointment, fore-
shadowing, as it does, Wordsworth's undermining of his own grand
claims in "Lines composed a few miles above Tintern Abbey" ("If this
be but a vain belief"), and the dejected dreamers who populate John
Keats's poems (the loitering knight of "La Belle Dame sans Merci,"
for instance).

Although the poem situates itself within the "flow'ry margin of the
vale," it was published on the less ethereal pages of the *Morning Post* of
April 20, 1798, amid accounts of the seizure of the papers of the Lon-
don Corresponding Society (a radical organization suspected by the
government of treasonous activity) and of Twisleton's divorce bill,[4]
two items of news that had a bearing on Robinson, a writer of

---

3 On the centrality of the sketch in romantic-era culture, see Richard C. Sha, *The
   Visual and Verbal Sketch in British Romanticism* (Philadelphia: University of Pennsyl-
   vania Press, 1998).
4 Thomas J. Twisleton went before the House of Lords to request a divorce from
   Charlotte Anne Frances Wattell who had apparently pursued a stage career against
   her husband's wishes. Two of his poems are featured in *The Wild Wreath* (1804), an
   anthology edited by Robinson's daughter.

political tracts and an unhappily married woman. Robinson's publishing of her poems in a venue that was considered vulgar by many of her poetic peers – Wordsworth back-pedalled as fast as he could from his relatively slight involvement in newspaper writing[5] – underscores a motivating force of her writing: financial anxiety. The decorative extremes of "Twilight," the poem's allusions to "spangly dew" and "gleamy stars," are not a remote aesthete's poetic embroideries but rather, at least in part, a savvy writer's bows to an audience that enjoyed this form of poeticism.

Rather than demonstrating a steady evolution, Robinson's literary career presents a punctuated equilibrium as she took on disparate poetic identities: among them, the Della Cruscan Laura Maria, the tragic Sappho, the seductive Oberon, the acerbic Tabitha Bramble, and, finally, the late Mrs. Robinson. She came to a literary career by way of the stage; this fact and the sensational details of her entry into society help to explain the multiplicity of her poetic personae.

1. "I approached the audience"

By Robinson's own account in the posthumously published *Memoirs of the Late Mrs. Mary Robinson*, she was born Mary Darby in a house next to the Cathedral at Bristol and in front of the cloisters of St. Augustine's monastery "during a tempestuous night, on the twenty-seventh of November, 1758."[6] Robinson uses the meteorological moment to foreshadow the tumultuous events of her life: "Through life the tempest has followed my footsteps; and I have in vain looked for a short interval of repose from the perseverance of sorrow" (*Memoirs* 1: 4). She was the second surviving child of Nicholas and Hetty Darby.[7] An older brother, John, a merchant at Leghorn in Tuscany,

---

5   "Certain I am," he wrote to Daniel Stuart in 1838, "that the last thing that could have found its way into my thoughts would have been to enter into an engagement to write for any newspaper – and that I never did so." Wordsworth insisted in this same letter that those sonnets and pamphlets of his published by Stuart had not been financially remunerated. *The Letters of William and Dorothy Wordsworth*, ed. Ernest de Selincourt. *The Later Years, 1835-1839*. rev. Alan G. Hill (Oxford: Clarendon Press, 1982) 6: 590.

6   *Memoirs of the Late Mrs. Robinson, Written by Herself*, 4 vols. (London: R. Phillips, 1801) 1: 4. Hereafter cited in text as *Memoirs*.

7   William H. Whiteley identifies Robinson's father as Nicholas in his entry for the *Dictionary of Canadian Biography* (Toronto: Toronto University Press, 1979) 4: 194-

Italy, died in 1790; an older sister, Elizabeth, died of smallpox before the age of two. Of two younger brothers, William and George, only George survived childhood to become a merchant at Leghorn like his older brother.

Robinson describes herself as exhibiting a precocious inclination toward melancholy pursuits; she depicts her childhood self memorizing epitaphs and demonstrating a preference for mournful and touching melodies, such as Pope's "Elegy to the Memory of an Unfortunate Lady" (*Memoirs* 1: 14). According to her memoirs, she attended a boarding school run by the sisters of Hannah More, the writer famous for her poetry, political tracts, and moral essays. In a letter to the *Morning Post*, which had mistakenly reported her death on July 14, 1786, Robinson claimed to have been educated under More herself.[8]

The early childhood that Robinson described in bucolic terms was disrupted by her father's professional ambitions. A ship captain and merchant active in the Newfoundland fishing trade, Nicholas Darby embarked in 1765 on a scheme to establish seal, salmon and cod fishing camps on the southern coast of Labrador, a newly acquired British territory.[9] The enterprise came to an abrupt halt in 1767 when a band of Inuit killed three members of his crew, stole boats, and burnt equipment, quite possibly in a protest against what Robinson describes as her father's dream of "civilizing the Esquimaux Indians, in order to employ them in the extensive undertaking" (*Memoirs* 1: 18).

Darby's business failures coupled with his marital infidelity – he took a woman named Elenor on the trip to Labrador with him – resulted in the dissolution of the family's comfortable life in Bristol. He was forced to sell their home; Mrs. Darby, Mary, and George moved to London. Mary was placed in a Chelsea boarding school under the tutelage of Meribah Lorrington, a remarkable intellectual

---

95. He gives her mother's name as Hatty Vanacott. As Martin Levy has noted, Mrs. Darby signed her name as Hetty on the register of her daughter's marriage at St. Martin-in-the-Fields.

8   Robert D. Bass reprints the letter and the premature obituary that provoked it in his dual biography of Banastre Tarleton and Mary Robinson, *The Green Dragoon: The Lives of Banastre Tarleton and Mary Robinson* (London: Alvin Redman, 1957) 252–54. Hereafter cited in text.

9   Whiteley's dictionary entry on Robinson's father provides an account of his business affairs. *Dictionary of Canadian Biography* 4: 194–95.

but an alcoholic. Lorrington, according to the *Memoirs*, encouraged Mary Darby's literary efforts, some of which were compiled in her first published volume, the 1775 *Poems*. Lorrington's increasingly overt inebriation, however, led to Mary's removal to a boarding school at Battersea; she completed her education at Oxford-house, Marylebone. At this point her physical attributes won her an audience with David Garrick, the pre-eminent actor and theatre manager of the day.

As Mary Darby was coming under the theatrical tutelage of Garrick, she was also attracting public interest. She writes: "I now found myself an object of attention whenever I appeared at the theatre. I had been too often in public not to be observed; and it was buzzed about that I was the juvenile pupil of Garrick" (*Memoirs* 1: 54). Among Mary Darby's several suitors was a law clerk named Thomas Robinson who won over Mrs. Darby with his gifts of elegantly bound religious tomes and his assiduous attention first to her son George, then to Mary when they each contracted smallpox. Mary and Thomas were married in an April 12, 1773 ceremony at St. Martin-in-the-Fields. She was fourteen years old.

Thomas Robinson, who claimed to be the nephew and heir of a man of fortune, Thomas Harris of Tregunter, Wales, insisted that the marriage be kept secret until he completed his clerkship. Robinson was, in reality, the illegitimate son of the man he claimed was his uncle, and a ne'er-do-well of considerable, if charming, diabolism. The couple set up housekeeping in No. 13, Great Queen-street, and immersed themselves in the fashionable life, frequenting pleasure gardens like Vauxhall and Ranelagh, and the Pantheon Concert, "then the most fashionable assemblage of the gay and distinguished."[10] (See Figure 3.) A daughter, Maria Elizabeth, was born on October 18th, 1774.

Robinson's youthful beauty and keen fashion sense won her the attentions of the notorious womanizer Lord Lyttleton, among other

---

10 *Memoirs* 1:95. For fascinating accounts of the delights that visitors to London's pleasure gardens encountered, see Warwick Wroth, *The London Pleasure Gardens of the Eighteenth Century* (London: Macmillan and Co., Ltd., 1896); W. S. Scott, *Green Retreat: The Story of Vauxhall Gardens, 1661-1859* (London: Odhams Press Limited, 1955); and the chapter on pleasure resorts in E. Beresford Chancellor, *The XVIIIth Century in London: An Account of its Social Life and Arts* (London: B.T. Batsford Ltd., [1921]). Scott provides a detailed discussion of Rowlandson's "Vaux-hall" (Figure 3), identifying many of the individuals assembled in the crowd.

Figure 3. Thomas Rowlandson, *Vaux-Hall*, 1785. (By courtesy of the Yale Center for British Art, Paul Mellon Collection.) Mary Robinson is on the right side of the front row of revellers. She is bracketed by her husband Thomas Robinson (holding a cane) and the Prince of Wales.

and isn't he a clergyman?

suitors seemingly unfazed by her married status. It was Lyttleton, according to the *Memoirs*, who, surely out of self-interest, informed Robinson of her husband's mistress, a secret that proved to be just one in a complicated web of lies that underpinned the couple's existence and ultimately landed Thomas Robinson in prison for debt. Robinson's first volume of verse, the 1775 *Poems*, was released during the fifteen months he was imprisoned, and the topic of her second volume, *Captivity; a Poem, and Celadon and Lydia, a Tale* (1777), was inspired by this predicament. According to her own account, Robinson left the prison confines only to seek out the patronage of Georgiana, Duchess of Devonshire, a leading socialite. Thomas Robinson took the opportunity provided by her trips to enjoy the services of prostitutes.

Robinson had abandoned her theatrical ambitions for marriage, but her acting career was reinvigorated some three years later through the intervention of the actor William Brereton, the theatre manager and playwright Richard Brinsley Sheridan, and her old mentor Garrick.[11] The first volume of Robinson's 1801 *Memoirs* concludes with Robinson poised to greet her public as Shakespeare's Juliet:

> The theatre was crowded with fashionable spectators; the Green-room and Orchestra (where Mr. Garrick sat during the night) were thronged with critics. My dress was a pale pink satin, trimmed with crape, richly spangled with silver; my head was ornamented with white feathers, and my monumental suit, for the last scene, was white satin and completely plain; excepting that I wore a veil of the most transparent gauze, which fell quite to my feet from the back of my head, and a string of beads round my waist, to which was suspended a cross appropriately fashioned.
>
> When I approached the side wing my heart throbbed convulsively; I then began to fear that my resolution would fail, and I leaned upon the nurse's arm, almost fainting. Mr. Sheridan and several other friends encouraged me to proceed; and at

---

11 The most thorough accounts of Robinson's two-year stint on the stage are provided by Bass in *The Green Dragon* and by the entry on Robinson in Philip H. Highfill, Jr., Kalman A. Burnim, and Edward A. Langhans, *A Biographical Dictionary of Actors, Actresses, Musicians, Dancers, Managers and Other Stage Personnel in London, 1660-1800* (Carbondale: Southern Illinois University Press, 1973-93) 13: 30-47.

length, with trembling limbs and fearful apprehension, I
approached the audience. (*Memoirs* 1: 192)

A measured assessment of Robinson's performance in this role is pro-
vided by the prompter William Hopkins: "Juliet by Mrs Robinson – a
genteel Figure – a very tolerable first appearance and may do in
time."[12] Through the 1777-78, 1778-79, and 1779-80 seasons, Robin-
son's roles included Statira in Nathaniel Lee's *Alexander the Great*,
Amanda in Sheridan's *A Trip to Scarborough*, Fanny in George Colman's
The Clandestine Marriage (a role she performed while pregnant with
her second child, a daughter, Sophia, who died six weeks after her
birth in the spring of 1777), Ophelia in *Hamlet*, and Lady Macbeth.
She specialized in breeches parts, performing Viola in *Twelfth Night*,
Imogen in *Cymbeline*, Jacintha in Benjamin Hoadley's *The Suspicious
Husband*, and Rosalind in *As You Like It* (see Figure 4 for a depiction
of Robinson as Rosalind, although, unfortunately, this above-the-
shoulders portrait does not depict her page-boy trappings). The *Morn-
ing Chronicle* for May 27, 1780, enthused:

> Mrs. Robinson's Eliza [in Lady Craven's *The Miniature Picture*]
> does her infinite credit: she displays a degree of acting merit in
> the breeches scenes of the character, infinitely superior to any
> sample of professional talent she has before shown, and stands
> eminently distinguished from the other performers.[13]

Her performance in *The Miniature Picture* foreshadowed the
talismanic power another miniature associated with Robinson – that
of the Prince of Wales – would come to assume in public mythology.
The teenage George, Prince of Wales, was smitten with the twenty-
one-year-old Robinson as a result of seeing her act the role of Perdita
in the December 3, 1779 performance of *The Winter's Tale*, and he pro-
ceeded to pursue her with passionate letters, covert hand signals, and
the gift of his portrait in miniature.[14] The miniature was encased with

---

12 *A Biographical Dictionary of Actors, Actresses...* 13: 32.
13 Quoted in Bass 133.
14 Bass provides an account of a performance Robinson attended at the Opera House
    during which the Prince of Wales reportedly gestured meaningfully from his box
    in order to convince her that he was the author of the love letter signed "Florizel"
    that Lord Malden had delivered (128).

Figure 4. Johan Zoffany, portrait of Mary Robinson as Rosalind.
(By courtesy of the Garrick Club, London.)

a small paper heart on which was inscribed on opposing sides: "Je ne change qu'en mourant" and "Unalterable to my Perdita through life." Robinson ultimately succumbed to these blandishments, as well as to the promise of £20,000, payable upon the Prince's coming of age. The temptation must have been considerably heightened by her husband's promiscuity and impecuniousness.

Robinson's liaison with the Prince – which ended within a year when he abandoned her for Elizabeth Armistead – exposed her to social disgrace. One can see Robinson attempting to maintain a tenuous grasp on respectability in a letter she wrote as part of her financial dealings with the Prince in the immediate aftermath of the affair. Using love letters the Prince had written to Robinson as collateral against his pledge of £20,000, her negotiator, Lord Malden, sparred with the palace's representative, Colonel George Hotham, in an attempt to keep open the possibility of future financial support in the event that Robinson accepted Hotham's firm and final offer of £5,000 for the letters. Malden argues that Robinson was drawn into debt by an extravagance necessitated by her association with the Prince, and goes on to write:

> She still declares she cannot bear the idea held [within] Col. Hotham's letter, that the money therein mentioned is to be the consideration for the restitution of those papers and that she is to be precluded all hope of yr. R. Hs's future bounty. The idea she says shocks her, as it not only carries the strongest appearance of a price, put upon her conduct to yr. R. H. during the time of your attachment to her, but gives her reason to fear that she will be left wholly destitute and without income hereafter, which she trusts yr. R.Hs. does not intend should be the case.[15]

One witnesses here the delicate balance Robinson was trying to strike in her negotiations – even as she was in desperate need of ongoing financial support from the Prince, she was reluctant to have their relationship cast in mercenary rather than romantic terms.[16]

Robinson, already the subject of public fascination, became the butt of cruel caricatures and the debased heroine of a series of fictional accounts of her love affairs cast in pornographic terms. The 1784 *Memoirs of Perdita*, for instance, recounting her purported affair with Lord Malden, stages an elaborate pornographic tableau involving Robinson, a nest of ants, and a young gardener.[17] Before the published accounts of her purported sexual escapades reached this

---

15 Lord Malden to the Prince of Wales, 1781, Capell Ms. M275, Hertfordshire Record Office, England.
16 See her letter to John Taylor, Appendix A.
17 *Memoirs of Perdita* (London: G. Lister, 1784) 44-46.

extreme, Robinson left England in late 1781 to reside for two months in Paris, where she was apparently courted by the Duke of Chartres and the Duke of Lauzun, and also attracted the attention of Marie Antoinette, who requested the loan of Robinson's miniature of the Prince of Wales.[18] Robinson's intriguing account of this encounter in her *Memoirs* emphasizes her own queenly attire: her "pale green lustring train," her "tiffany petticoat" festooned with lilacs, the tasteful ornaments of Mademoiselle Bertin (the reigning milliner of the day).

Upon her return to London, Robinson became involved with Banastre Tarleton, a former officer in the 1st Regiment of the Dragoon Guards, one of the most prestigious regiments in the British army. Tarleton distinguished himself in the southern campaign of the American war of the Revolution by his ruthlessness (he became known in America as "Bloody Tarleton"). In 1783, on half-pay status from the British government, he absconded to the continent, seeking relief from his creditors. The married, twenty-three-year-old Robinson borrowed money on his behalf and took off after him. Robert Bass quotes contemporary news accounts that suggest that Robinson was pregnant and miscarried due to the rigors of the journey (224–25). Other accounts attribute her subsequent invalid status to what Robinson herself called a "violent rheumatism" brought on by expo-

---

18 Robinson published an account of the Duke de Lauzun (who at the time of his death was known under a different title) in the *Monthly Magazine* under the editorship of Richard Phillips, the publisher of her *Poetical Works* and *Memoirs*. See "Memoirs of the Late Duc de Biron," *Monthly Magazine* (Feb. 1, 1800): 43-46. Quite probably, the "Additional Anecdotes of Philip Egalité late Duke of Orleans, by one who knew him intimately" (the Duke of Orleans was known as the Duke of Chartres when Robinson first knew him) and the "Anecdotes of the late Queen of France, by the same," both published in the August 1, 1800 edition of the *Monthly Magazine*, were also penned by Robinson, who at this time was publishing her four-part "Present State of the Manners, Society, &c. &c. of the Metropolis of England" in that venue (see the *Monthly Magazine* for 1 August 1800, 1 September 1800, 1 October 1800, and 1 November 1800). Robinson confirms her authorship of the metropolis essays, which were signed "M.R." (as is the "Memoirs of the Late Duc de Biron") in a manuscript letter to Jane Porter where she corrects printing errors in the first essay. She writes: "Tell your brother to read my first paper on *"Society and manners in the metropolis of England"* page 35 of the Monthly Magazine but desire him to substitute the word *gust* for *Gusto* in Column 5. page 37. – There are also some other *press errors*; which you will see. –" Mary Robinson to Jane Taylor, August 5, 1800, Misc. Ms. 2290, The Carl H. Pforzheimer Collection of Shelley & His Circle; The New York Public Library; Astor, Lenox and Tilden Foundations.

sure to cold night air. The author of the 1804 *Eccentric Biography; or Memoirs of Remarkable Characters* writes:

> With the passion and zeal of generous minds, Mrs. Robinson, between one and two o'clock in the morning, threw herself into a post chaise to follow him [Tarleton], without sufficient precaution of dress against the cold, although it was the depth of winter, and the weather was very severe. She was agitated, and heated, by her apprehensions; and let down the glasses of the chaise; and, in that situation fell asleep. At the first stage, she was obliged to be carried into the inn, almost frozen; and from that hour, never recovered the entire use of her limbs.[19]

Whether as a result of exposure or, more plausibly, botched midwifery, Robinson spent much of the rest of her life severely crippled. Her correspondence provides graphic testimony to the humbling vicissitudes of her body's failures. In one particularly vivid account, she describes being tossed into a ceiling by a servant who was lifting her out of bed:

> Not a word, my dear Friend, to enquire after my poor head! Which not only narrowly escaped destruction; but has been these ten days almost [frantic] with torture! on the day of your departure my coachman, probably mistaking me for a truss of Hay, in lifting me out of the slanting room where I slept, forgot the low roof, or rather penthouse; and threw me with considerable violence, so high in his arms, that the top of my head absolutely cracked the ceiling.[20]

Still recovering a month later, Robinson writes to Jane Porter:

> Near a month confined to my bed, and every day expecting to prove that "there is another and a better world" — . I have

---

19 *Eccentric Biography; or Memoirs of Remarkable Characters* (1804), *British Biographical Archive*, ed. Paul Sieveking and Laureen Baillie (New York: D.G. Saur, 1984) fiche 939, grids 190-191.

20 Mary Robinson to James Marshall, September 10, 1800, [Abinger deposit] Dep. b. 215/2, The Bodleian Library, University of Oxford.

scarcely strength to thank you for your kind enquiries. My illness has indeed been so perilous, that I believe little hopes were entertained of my recovery. When my daughter received your letter I was in a state too terrible to describe. One blister on my shoulders, another on my head; – which with perpetual bleedings, with the lancet as well as with Leeches, have so reduced me that I am a mere spectre. My disease lay chiefly on my head; – and intermitting fever on the brain, – attended with other symptoms of the most alarming nature. –[21]

It is no wonder that Robinson turned to the use of the opium-based narcotic, laudanum, as a fence against pain. Martin Levy finds references to opium cropping up in several of Robinson's poems from the 1790s, such as "Invocation" ("From the POPPY I have ta'en / Mortal's BALM, and mortal's BANE!") and "Ode to Apathy" ("Thy poppy wreath shall bind my brows, / Dead'ning the sense of pain").[22] The most fascinating of Robinson's several allusions to laudanum usage occurs in the *Memoirs* where, in an account that anticipates (perhaps not coincidentally) Coleridge's 1816 preface to "Kubla Khan," the inspiration for her poem, "The Maniac," written in a delirium induced by "near eighty drops of laudanum," is described : "She lay, while dictating, with her eyes closed, apparently in the stupor which opium frequently produces, repeating like a person talking in her sleep."[23]

Robinson's relationship with Tarleton extended over fifteen years, during which time he won a seat in Parliament as the representative of Liverpool, in which capacity he was most noted for his opposition to William Wilberforce's campaign to abolish the slave trade, a

---

21 Mary Robinson to Jane Porter, October 15, 1800, Misc. Ms. 2293, The Carl H. Pforzheimer Collection of Shelley & His Circle; The New York Public Library; Astor, Lenox and Tilden Foundations.

22 Martin J. Levy, "Coleridge, Mary Robinson and *Kubla Khan*," *Charles Lamb Bulletin* ns 77 (1992): 156-66.

23 Coleridge took an interest in Robinson's chronic ailment, writing to Godwin on May 21, 1800: "I wish, I knew the particulars of her complaint. For [Humphrey] Davy has discovered a perfectly new Acid, by which he has restored the use of limbs to persons who had lost them for many years, (one woman 9 years) in cases of supposed Rheumatism. At all events, Davy says, it *can* do no harm, in Mrs Robinson's case – & if she will try it, he will make up a little parcel & write her a letter of *instructions* &c." *Collected Letters of Samuel Taylor Coleridge*, ed. Earl Leslie Griggs, 6 vols. (Oxford: Clarendon Press, 1966-71) 1: 589.

predictable stance for the representative of a slave port. Through these years, Robinson and her daughter gravitated from fashionable London addresses to resort areas in England and France where Robinson sought relief for her maladies in the waters of Bath or the hot mud baths of Aix-la-Chapelle. Her career as a writer was motivated by both artistic ambition and financial necessity. Through the intervention of the Whig leader Charles Fox in 1783, Robinson was granted a £500 annuity from the Prince of Wales. This sum coupled with Banastre Tarleton's military half pay of £341 per annum should have ensured a comfortable lifestyle, but the Prince's habitual dilatoriness in paying the annuity, Tarleton's gambling habit, and Robinson's fondness for expensive carriages and cutting-edge fashion all conspired to place her in a state of near constant financial desperation. According to Bass, her belongings were auctioned off in 1784 as a result of unpaid debt (238). And Robinson wrote to John Taylor in October 1794 of her plan to escape her creditors.[24]

Under arrest for debt in May 1800, Robinson refused to resist the action as a married woman and thus shift the burden of payment on to her wastrel husband to the peril of her creditors. Instead, according to her own account in a letter to Godwin:

> I therefore submit patiently ... I am too proud to borrow, while the arrears *now due* on my annuity from the Prince of Wales would doubly pay the sum for which I am arrested.[25]

The Prince's claim that there was no money at Carlton House to pay the £63 for which Robinson was in custody must have been particularly galling in light of the conspicuousness of his consumption (the decoration of Carlton House was his ongoing, expensive preoccupation). And despite Robinson's extraordinary literary productivity – she published two large collections of poetry and six full-scale novels in the course of seven years, in addition to plays, political tracts, and newspaper poems and essays – her literary earnings were often disap-

---

24 See Appendix A.
25 C. Kegan Paul prints part of this letter, dated May 30, 1800, in *William Godwin: His Friends and Contemporaries*, 2 vols. (London: Henry S. King & Co., 1876) 2: 34. The original letter is part of the Abinger deposit at The Bodleian Library, University of Oxford.

pointing. Jan Fergus and Janice Farrar Thaddeus's revealing research into publishing firm records shows Robinson clearing less than £10 over the course of her four and a half year relationship with Hookham and Carpenter. She fared better in the last three years of her life when she averaged approximately £150 per year in her business dealings with Longman.[26]

Robinson's last years were a period of great emotional turmoil due to the break up of her relationship with Banastre Tarleton and his subsequent marriage to Susan Priscilla Bertie, the illegitimate daughter of the Duke of Ancaster. This period was also, however, a time of poetic experimentation, perhaps necessitated by her increasingly high profile in the poetry columns of the *Morning Post*. She took over the position of poetry editor from Robert Southey at the end of 1799 and continued to publish her own poems in the newspaper, barely disguised behind such pseudonyms as Oberon, Laura Maria, and Tabitha Bramble. She was only lightly concealed because the London social scene was a small and gossipy realm where secrets had a very short shelf life, and Robinson, in the long run, always revealed her own disguises. She was justifiably proud of her poetic productivity. A "List of Poetical Pieces, Written between Dec. 1799 and Dec. 1800," published in the 1801 *Memoirs of the Late Mrs. Robinson*, provides an impressive account of the seventy-four poems Robinson penned in the last year of her life.

Among the more fascinating aspects of Robinson's life is her relationship with her daughter Maria Elizabeth, who, relegated to the background of Robinson's *Memoirs* and other biographical accounts, comes across as a dutiful helpmate to her mother. Life as the daughter of a socially notorious and physically incapacitated woman could not have been easy. Maria Elizabeth, by necessity, played a large role in her mother's medical treatment. That she had her own artistic ambitions is evidenced by her 1794 novel, *The Shrine of Bertha*, but also, indirectly, in her efforts to see her mother's three-volume *Poetical Works* into print in the years after Robinson's death in 1800. (A three-volume collection had been heralded in an advertisement at the end of Robinson's 1799 novel, *The False Friend*.) In a letter to the book-selling firm of Cadell and Davies in June of 1804, Maria Elizabeth

---

26 Jan Fergus and Janice Farrar Thaddeus, "Women, Publishers, and Money, 1790-1820," *Studies in Eighteenth-Century Culture* 17 (1987): 196-97.

Robinson writes: "I have the whole of her MSS, in my possession, as arranged by *herself*, for Publication, a very few weeks previous to her death: – and [*left*] *to me* to Publish by *her own express commands.*" She also communicates her desire to put her mother's work in someone else's hands: "I have at this time, in hand; several matters of importance to myself – which would make the toil of bringing out a work on my own account, very inconvenient if not impracticable."[27] The "several matters of importance" may have included a volume of her own poems, for which she was actively seeking a publisher in August of 1805. Writing to Cadell and Davies, she described the volume as resembling in size and "form[ing] a very good companion for" *The Wild Wreath*, an anthology of her mother's and others' poetry published the year before. The proposed volume never made its way into print.[28]

Mary Robinson spent the last months of her life at Englefield Green, near Old Windsor, in a cottage that Eliza Fenwick described in a letter to her friend Mary Hays:

> Mrs Robinson's Cottage stands aloof from the grander dwellings of Lady Shuldam, Lord Uxbridge & Mrs. Freemantle. Its front windows look over St Ann's Hill, the retreat of Mr Fox, & from the back we are sheltered by the tall trees of the forest.
>
> Mrs Robinson has displayed great taste in the fitting up of her cottage; the papers of the rooms in a particular degree are beautifully appropriated to the building & situation. The furniture is perhaps more ornamental than I should chuse for myself, but still it is elegant & quiet – nothing gaudy nor ill

---

27 Maria Elizabeth Robinson to Messrs. Cadell and Davies, June 18, 1804, Manuscript letter, Private Collection.

28 The rest of Maria Elizabeth's life is a cipher with two tantalizing clues. The first is the inclusion in the 1804 *Wild Wreath* of engravings from drawings by "Mrs. B. Tarleton" (presumably Susan Priscilla Tarleton) as well as poems by "Susan." Did Maria Elizabeth forge or maintain a friendly relationship with the Tarletons after her mother's death? More important is the identity and ultimate whereabouts of the Miss Weale who dined at Old Windsor with William Godwin in the days after Mary Robinson's death and who possibly resurfaced in the will which Maria Elizabeth signed in August of 1801 and which was "Proved at London 3 Nov 1818 before the Worshipful Samuel Rush." She designates Elizabeth Weale, "now residing with me," as her heir. The trail of any extant Robinson manuscript materials passed down by her daughter runs cold with Weale.

placed.... I may congratulate myself on being the guest of a woman whose powers of pleasing, ever varied & graceful, are united to quick feeling & generosity of temper.[29]

She died on December 26, 1800, at the age of forty-two. The writer of the Robinson entry in the 1804 *Eccentric Biography; or, Memoirs of Remarkable Female Characters* reports: "On the body being opened, by the express wish of the physicians who attended her, *the immediate cause* of her death was found to be an accumulation of water on the chest, together with six large stones contained in the gall bladder."[30] William Godwin attended the body to the cemetery. Coleridge melodramatically espoused his objection to Maria Elizabeth Robinson's plan to include one of his poems in a tribute volume that would include works by Thomas Moore and Monk Lewis – "I have a wife, I have sons, I have an infant Daughter – what excuse could I offer to my own conscience if by suffering my name to be connected with those of Mr Lewis, or Mr Moore, I was the *occasion* of their reading the Monk, or the wanton poems of Thomas Little Esqre?"[31] But he was sincerely moved by her mother's death ("I can not think of your Mother without Tears"),[32] leaving a fragmentary poetic tribute to her memory:

> O'er her pil'd grave the gale of evening sighs;
> And flowers will grow upon it's grassy Slope.
> I wipe the dimming Water from mine eyes –
> Ev'n in the cold Grave dwells the Cherub Hope![33]

2. "a world of Talents, drawn into a small but brilliant circle"

With the publication of her 1791 and 1793 volumes of poems, Robinson went a long way toward establishing a new identity for

29 *Fate of the Fenwicks: Letters to Mary Hays (1798-1828)*, ed. A.F. Wedd (London: Methuen & Co., Ltd. 1927) 10.

30 *Eccentric Biography; or, Memoir of Remarkable Female Characters* (1804), *British Biographical Archive* fiche 939, grid 193. This account is based on Robinson's *Memoirs*.

31 December 27, 1802, *Collected Letters of Samuel Taylor Coleridge*, 2: 905.

32 December 27, 1802, *Collected Letters of Samuel Taylor Coleridge*, 2: 904.

33 Samuel Taylor Coleridge to Thomas Poole, February 1, 1801, *Collected Letters of Samuel Taylor Coleridge*, 2: 669.

herself as a poet, but without, it must be acknowledged, cutting herself entirely free of the sensational streamers of her past life. A reviewer for the *Gentleman's Magazine* foregrounded her association with a group of individuals "comprehending almost the whole circle of Rank, Fortune, and Fashion of this Country," and suggested that had Robinson been less blessed with "beauty and captivating manners," "her poetical taste might have been confined in its influence."[34] The subscriber list prefacing the 1791 *Poems* was headed up by the Prince of Wales and thus inevitably drew attention to her sexual history. Still, even this skeptical reviewer came around to admitting "without the smallest hesitation, that they [the poems] are generally elegant, harmonious, and correct; a spirit of pensiveness pervades them all; and Nature, on various occasions, seems to have asserted her rights by inspiring some very delicate and charming sentiments."[35] In this assessment, the *Gentleman's Magazine* encapsulated the grudgingly positive response to Robinson's poems in literary journals.[36] Contemporary reviewers, nearly to a person, noted the plaintive aspect of her verse and admired, as Coleridge was to do, her metrical ingenuity.

The more negative responses to her poetry are interesting for the way in which they use Robinson's poetry to fulminate against a "new species of Poetry." The reviewer for the *Critical Review* wrote:

Within a very few years, a race of versifiers has sprung up, determined to claim at least the merit of novelty in expression, in unusual figure and striking combination. Rejecting the accustomed modes of description and phraseology, these fastidious writers seem fond of introducing uncommon terms and ideas, to provoke attention and excite admiration.[37]

Robinson's poetry is seen as the epitome of Della Cruscan verse and the Della Cruscan school is portrayed as the culturally dominant poetic coterie of the moment. However extreme Della Cruscran

---

34 *Gentleman's Magazine* 61 (1791): 560.
35 *Gentleman's Magazine* 61 (1791): 561.
36 For a listing of reviews for each of Robinson's published volumes, see William S. Ward's invaluable bibliographies, *Literary Reviews in British Periodicals, 1789-1797* (New York: Garland, 1979) and *Literary Reviews in British Periodicals, 1798-1820* (New York: Garland, 1972).
37 Rev. of *Poems* (1791), by Mary Robinson, *Critical Review* ns 2 (July 1791): 309.

poetry may have seemed in its reliance on flowery description and emotional high jinks — features that have made it easy for twentieth-century literary historians to ignore or deride it — it also clearly loomed as a threat to be reckoned with. When Dorothy Wordsworth, in 1800, bemoaned the similarity between the titles of William Wordsworth's *Lyrical Ballads* and Robinson's *Lyrical Tales*, it could have been either an aesthetic association — Robinson's link to Della Cruscanism — or a biographical association — Robinson's scandalous past — from which she saw the need to distance William's work.[38]

It is probably impossible to overplay the role of Robinson's affair with the Prince of Wales in her later literary and social reception. The proliferation of biographical treatments of Robinson, including reprints of her memoirs, scurrilous versions of her letters, and novelistic treatments of her life, all encourage the conflation of writer and royal mistress. It has been all too possible, however, to underplay Robinson's other, more creatively influential liaisons, such as her friendship with William Godwin, to whom she was introduced by Robert Merry in 1796. Godwin's manuscript diary notes an initial appointment with Robinson on February 9, 1796 ("tea Mrs. Robinson's"), an engagement which is followed by a steady stream of teas, dinners, and other social calls that dominate Godwin's social calendar through July of that year, dwindling off and then resuming with even greater frequency in the beginning of 1800.[39] Mary Shelley counted Robinson among "several women to whose society he [Godwin] was exceedingly partial, and who were all distinguished for personal attractions and talents." She notes that Godwin "to the end of his life ... considered [Robinson] as the most beautiful woman he had ever seen, but though he admired her so greatly, their acquaintance

---

38 Dorothy Wordsworth wrote: "My brother William is going to publish a second Edition of the Lyrical Ballads with a second volume. He intends to give them the title of 'Poems by W. Wordsworth' as Mrs. Robinson has claimed the title and is about publishing a volume of *Lyrical Tales*. This is a great objection to the former title, particularly as they are both printed at the same press and Longman is the publisher of both the works." Dorothy Wordsworth to Mrs. John Marshall, September 1800, *The Letters of William and Dorothy Wordsworth*, ed. Ernest de Selincourt. *The Early Years, 1787-1805*, rev. Chester L. Shaver (Oxford: Clarendon Press, 1967) 1: 297.

39 William Godwin Ms. diary, Vol. VII [Abinger deposit] Dep. e. 202, The Bodleian Library, University of Oxford.

scarcely attained intimate friendship."[40] Godwin's visits with Robinson tapered off during the period of his growing involvement with and marriage to Mary Wollstonecraft – Robinson later complained of his neglect, exaggerating somewhat the duration of his absence from her social gatherings: "Two years elapsed after your marriage, and I never saw you! – This circumstance I did not fail to feel, – though I felt it in silence."[41] But since many of Godwin's visits to Robinson took place in the company of Banastre Tarleton, it seems unlikely that his attraction to her was primarily a physical one. His reading schedule, duly noted in his manuscript diary, suggests an intellectual and sustained engagement. Between his first recorded meeting with Robinson and her funeral at Old Windsor, Godwin read his way through *Angelina* (February to March, 1796), Maria Elizabeth Robinson's *The Shrine of Bertha* (October, 1796), "Robinson on Women," (presumably her *Thoughts on the Condition of Women* [June, 1800]), and *Lyrical Tales* (December, 1800). In August 1801 Godwin was reading the posthumously published *Memoirs of the Late Mrs. Robinson*.[42]

Robinson, who addressed Godwin in her letters to him as "my dear Philosopher," was clearly bent on proving herself an intellectual equal and disavowing her image as a frivolous social butterfly. She writes of the few individuals she has discovered in her journey through life "whose minds and sentiments, whose feelings and affections, have been such as [she] almost instinctively idolise[s]," and of her failure to be accepted in the circles of those she admires.[43] She addresses Godwin as a "tutor of the *mind*" as well as "an associate of the *soul*," encouraging him to visit her at the cottage at Englefield Green, Surrey, an intimacy she refused to extend to Godwin's new acquaintance John Philpot Curran, apparently responding to some perceived or anticipated social slight. In a letter in which she explains this refusal, she alludes to another man she will not admit into her

---

40 Qtd. in *Shelley and his Circle*, ed. Kenneth Neill Cameron, 2 vols. (Cambridge: Harvard University Press, 1961), 1: 180.

41 Mary Robinson to William Godwin, August 28, 1800, [Abinger deposit] Dep. b. 215/2, The Bodleian Library, University of Oxford.

42 Godwin Ms. diary, Vols. VII, VIII, and X [Abinger deposit] Dep. e. 202-203 and Dep. e. 205, The Bodleian Library, University of Oxford.

43 Mary Robinson to William Godwin, August 24, 1800, [Abinger deposit] Dep. b. 215/2, The Bodleian Library, University of Oxford. The letter is reprinted in its entirety in Appendix A.

home, writing, "[A]s I was placed in so *awkward* a situation yesterday when *waiting* in the high-road, and as *he* did not there *desire* to be presented *to me*, I now cannot suffer it —"[44]

Indeed, the most poignant testimony to Robinson's liminal social position, her status as an object of admiration and pity at best or envy and malicious gossip at worst, is provided by the manuscript diary in which Jane Porter describes her guarded response to the news of Robinson's demise. When Robinson's death was announced at a dinner party Porter attended in the company of Mrs. Crespigny, Porter felt compelled to disavow any knowledge of her good friend and so suffered in a silent welter of grief and guilt.[45] She writes:

> Obliged as I was to conceal the shock, which this intelligence gave to me, I bore up very composedly, till after the company had dined. Then finding, that in spite of Mrs. Crespigny's penetration, (for to her sense enquiries, I had denied my knowledge of Mrs Robinson,) I must be overcome, I pleaded a nervous head-ache, and made that an excuse for the tears which poured down my cheeks. Oh! how did it cut my heart, that I was thus forced to hide a regret which I thought laudable! I one moment despised myself, for being ashamed to avow feelings, which I could not condemn; and the next, I excused myself, from the conviction that it was only a prudence due to my sister and myself, not to publish a conduct, which however guiltless, would draw on us the disrespect of many of our friends, and most likely the scandal of the whole world.[46]

---

44 Mary Robinson to William Godwin, 2 September 1800, [Abinger deposit] Dep. c. 507, The Bodleian Library, University of Oxford.

45 The lengthy entry devoted to Mrs. Crespigny in *Public Characters* does not reveal her first name, although it does identify her as the author of a "highly-praised novel called the *Pavilion*, which, though published without Mrs. Crespigny's name, is well known to be the production of her leisure moments." *The Pavilion*, by Mary De Crespigny, was published at the Minerva Press in 1796. The *Public Characters* entry also notes: "She has long been considered as the patroness of talent, and the benefactress of those in distress. Some of the most admired names in the two London theatres, as well as the opera-house, obtained their earliest celebrity in consequence of her notice; and many well-known literary characters received their first distinctions from her pen." *Public Characters*, 4th ed. (1799-1809), *British Biographical Archive*, fiche 282, grid 084 .

46 Jane Porter Ms. Diary, 1801, Mb15, f. 2, Folger Shakespeare Library, Washington, D.C.

Porter went on to write a memorial to Robinson which she intended for publication in a monthly magazine, but was warned against carrying out this plan by her sister, who feared that Porter would not be able to conceal her authorship of the piece, particularly from the curious Mrs. Crespigny who, according to Porter, warned that if an association between Porter and Robinson became known, "all the world would cut me – that she must drop me that I should be shunned by all decent people." Given the social repercussions, it is all the more fascinating that Porter is moved to record her close affiliation with Robinson:

> When I find, that my violent-candour, is hurrying me into the powers of calumny, I will remember Mrs Robinson! That I admired her talents, that I pitied her sufferings, that I loved her virtues, that I forgot her errors, as I hope Heaven will forget mine; that I visited her, that I wrote to her, that she called me her "sweet Friend!" And yet, that I could, when taxed with it, deny that we were acquainted! I ought not have accepted her friendship, when I was afraid to assert it.[47]

But Porter did assert it, through a series of visits and letters, and despite Robinson's mistrust of female friendship, which she candidly revealed to Porter in August of her last year of life, writing:

> If I did not enter into the true spirit of Friendship for my own Sex, it is because I have almost universaly found that Sex unkind and hostile towards *me*. I have seen the most miserable and degrading [reserve], the most contemptible *traits* of false delicacy, glaring through the thin veil of artificial virtue. I have found those women the most fastidiously severe, whose own lives have been marked by *private follies* and *assumed propriety*. The women whom I have most admired, have been the least prone to condemn, while they have been themselves the most *blameless*. – Of this distinguished class I consider you.[48]

---

47 Jane Porter Ms. Diary, 1801, Mb15, ff. 2–3, Folger Shakespeare Library, Washington, D.C.

48 Mary Robinson to Jane Porter, August 27, 1800, Misc. Ms. 2295, Carl H. Pforzheimer Collection of Shelley & His Circle; New York Public Library; Astor, Lenox and Tilden Foundations.

Robinson's distrust of her female contemporaries may have been a result of her less than cordial relationship with Hannah Cowley who apparently suggested one of Robinson's poems was written by a man.[49] And Robinson's idolatrous enthusiasm for Sarah Siddons – she praised her extravagantly in a letter to John Taylor and sent her poems – met no return from an actress intent on maintaining an impeccable character. Siddons wrote to Taylor:

> If she is half as amiable as her writings, I shall long for the *possibility* of being acquainted with her. I say the *possibility*, because one's whole life is one continual sacrifice of inclinations, which to indulge, however laudable or innocent, would draw down the malice and reproach of those prudent people who never do ill ... The charming and beautiful Mrs. Robinson: I pity her from the bottom of my soul.[50]

Given Robinson's status as the poster girl for unfettered female passion, it is not surprising that her friend Jane Porter took the tack she did in her unpublished posthumous tribute to her friend, framed as a letter from one unidentified lady to another. Porter's "Character of the late Mrs Robinson, who is usually stiled the British Sappho. Extracted from a letter to a lady" is a redemptive exercise, aimed at garnering for Robinson a respectability she did not possess in her

49 See the note to "To the Muse of Poetry," a poem Robinson claims was called forth "by an illiberal and unjust attack" by a rival poetess. *The Poetical Works of the Late Mrs. Mary Robinson* (London: Richard Phillips, 1806) 1: 187. See also the note to James Boaden's "To Mrs. Robinson," one of the tribute poems included in Robinson's *Poetical Works*: "This little Poem was occasioned by a most malignant un-womanly attack on the *authenticity* of Mrs. Robinson's productions, by a *Sister Poet*, whose name we forbear to mention." In an epigraph to his poem, Boaden quotes a variation of some lines from Cowley's poem "To Della Crusca." A version of Cowley's poem which omits the two lines that call Robinson's authorship into question was published in the *British Album* (London: J. Bell, 1790) 2: 144-48. I am grateful to Sharon Setzer for calling my attention to this literary fracas, and for identifying the offending Cowley poem.

50 Quoted in J. Fitzgerald Molloy's introduction to *Memoirs of Mary Robinson* (London: Gibbings and Company, 1895) xiv. For a more detailed discussion of Siddons in relation to romantic writers, see Julie A. Carlson, *In the Theatre of Romanticism: Coleridge, Nationalism, Women* (New York: Cambridge University Press, 1994) and Judith Pascoe, *Romantic Theatricality: Gender, Poetry, and Spectatorship* (Ithaca: Cornell University Press, 1997).

lifetime. Porter provides an exculpatory reading of Robinson's liaison with the Prince, depicting her as a "lovely Magdalen" most noted for self-sacrifice ("I have known her for a length of time confine her food to vegetables, that she might afford a more nourishing repast for the tables of the poor"). Porter's memorial ends with Robinson sitting "in rapture before the throne of God."[51]

Robinson used a combination of great charm and name-dropping to overcome social reservations in many of her female contemporaries. Her letter to the novelist Elizabeth Gunning, whose mother had recently died, is a model in this regard. Robinson, with no prior acquaintance with Gunning, invites her for an extended stay at Englefield Cottage, writing:

> Your Genius, your amiable and inestimable virtues have so often been the themes of admiration, when I have conversed with my sweet and lovely friends, the Misses Porter ... I have a small hovel of a Cottage, here: would a change of scenery, would the aids of Books, music, conversation and affectionate attentions ... in the smallest degree alienate your mind from the severity of filial regret? ... My humble fortune precludes the enjoyment of Splendours; but all that Sympathy, all that a fervent admiration of *genius* and *virtue* can bestow, – shall be *yours*.[52]

Robinson, whose own mother had died in 1793, a loss she felt intensely, was sincerely moved by Gunning's loss, which she dwelled on as well in letters to Jane Porter. But she also delighted in gathering around her a coterie of the most gifted artists and writers of her time. She writes to Porter in September 1800:

> Oh! Heavens! if a Select Society could be formed, – a little Colony of Mental [powers], – a world of Talents, drawn into a small but brilliant circle, – what a splendid Sunshine would it

---

51 Jane Porter, "Character of the late Mrs Robinson," Misc. Ms. 2296, The Carl H. Pforzheimer Collection of Shelley & His Circle; The New York Public Library; Astor, Lenox and Tilden Foundation.

52 Mary Robinson to Miss Gunning, August 31, 1800, Misc. Ms. 2291, Carl H. Pforzheimer Collection of Shelley & His Circle; The New York Public Library; Astor, Tilden and Lenox Foundation.

display; and how deeply in gloom would it throw all the unin-
teresting vapid scenery of Human life! Visionary idea! It
can never be! The malignant Spirit of contention, – the
Demons Envy, Calumny, and Vanity, led on by the Imp Caprice,
and the phantom Imagination, would interrupt the harmony of
Souls....[53]

Robinson came close to achieving her dream of an Elysian coterie at
Old Windsor. She writes to Samuel Jackson Pratt in August 1800 of
her distinguished guests:

> I am still tormented with ill health, but I have had my Cottage
> perpetually full of visitors ever since I came to it: and some
> charming literary characters, – *authoresses* – &ccc. I wish you
> would come and see us; – I expect the Miss Porters, the beauti-
> ful Sisters of the painter of —— the Seringapatam Picture with
> their mother. I have had Mrs Fenwick, the elegant authoress of
> "*Secresy*" and her daughter here, this month past – . Tomorrow
> I expect Godwin – and his Philanthropic friend, Mr Marshall:
> they will only stay a day or two. I shall see Mrs Parsons here
> soon; and I regret that I was not in town when Mrs Bennett
> called upon me....[54]

Robinson's dream of a "world of Talents, drawn into a small but
brilliant circle" prefigures Samuel Taylor Coleridge's idealist notion of

---

53 Mary Robinson to Jane Porter, September 11, 1800, Misc. Ms. 2292, Carl H.
   Pforzheimer Collection of Shelley & His Circle; The New York Public Library;
   Astor, Tilden and Lenox Foundation.
54 31 August 1800, *Shelley and His Circle*, ed. Kenneth Neill Cameron (Cambridge,
   MA: Harvard University Press, 1961) 1: 231. Jane Porter would become famous as
   the author of *The Scottish Chiefs* (1810). Eliza Fenwick was the author of *Secresy; or,
   The Ruin on the Rock* (1795). James Marshall was Godwin's friend and the translator
   of Volney's *Ruins of Empire*. See William St. Clair, *The Godwins and the Shelleys* (Lon-
   don: Faber & Faber, 1989). Mrs. Parsons was most likely Mrs. Eliza Parsons, the
   author of *The History of Miss Meredith, A Novel* (1790), *Ellen and Julia* (1793), and
   Lucy, a Novel (1794), among other works. Mrs. Bennet was probably Agnes Maria
   Bennet, the author of *The Beggar Girl and Her Benefactors* (1797), *Agnes de Courci, a
   Domestic Tale* (1789), and *Ellen, Countess of Castle Howel, a Novel* (1794). William S.
   Ward's *Literary Reviews in British Periodicals, 1789-1797* and *Literary Reviews in British
   Periodicals, 1798-1820* are the sources of information for these surmises.

a "clerisy," and the failed plan of Coleridge and Robert Southey to establish a self-contained society of like-minded intellectuals on the banks of the Susquehanna River in Pennsylvania. Robinson, even before she moved to Englefield Green, came closer than they to realizing her utopian vision, including in her London soirées the likes of Edmund Burke, Joshua Reynolds, and Richard Brinsley Sheridan. The connection between Coleridgean and Robinsonian ideals is probably not coincidental, given their co-membership in the remarkable circle of friends and acquaintances recorded in Godwin's diary, as well as their mutual admiration, expressed through an exchange of poems in the *Morning Post* (see Appendix B). Godwin notes having tea at Robinson's in the company of Coleridge on January 15, 1800; after that date, Coleridge and Robinson dine together on January 18th and February 22.[55]

Godwin's diary provides tantalizing hints, although no hard evidence of an actual meeting between Robinson and Charlotte Smith, arguably the two most distinguished women poets of the 1790s.[56] Robinson quotes from the preface to Smith's *Elegiac Sonnets* in the preface to her own sonnet sequence, *Sappho and Phaon*. Her interest in initiating a more intimate association with Smith seems evident in Robinson's publication of a poem expressing sympathy for Smith's familial travail (see "Sonnet to Mrs. Charlotte Smith, on Hearing That Her Son Was Wounded at the Siege of Dunkirk," p. 290).

Perhaps the most intriguing connection, however, between Robinson and another woman writer is the line of influence suggested by Charlotte Dacre's "To the Shade of Mary Robinson," published in the first volume of Dacre's 1805 *Hours of Solitude*.[57] Dacre claims in the poem not to have known Robinson while she was living, but portrays herself as Robinson's soul sister, as having a "heart form'd to love" her, and one which "responsive had beat" to Robinson's own. This poem

---

55 Godwin Ms. diary, Vol. IX [Abinger deposit] Dep. e. 204, The Bodleian Library, University of Oxford.

56 According to one of his diary notations, Godwin first met Smith in 1796, the same year in which he made the acquaintance of Robinson. His relationship with Smith, as it can be traced through abbreviated allusions to dinners and teas in his diary, runs a parallel course to his relationship with Robinson.

57 I am grateful to Adriana Craciun for drawing my attention to this poem by reprinting it in an appendix to her edition of Dacre's *Zofloya* (Peterborough, Ontario: Broadview Press, 1997) 275-76.

overtly signifies the influence that Robinson cast over the volume as a whole. The similarities between Dacre's poems and Robinson's, especially the poems published in *Lyrical Tales*, are multiple and telling. Dacre's "The Murderer" recalls Robinson's "The Haunted Beach," Dacre's "The Poor Negro Sadi" conjures up Robinson's "The Lascar" and "The Negro Girl," and Dacre's "Maniac" and "The Musing Maniac" resemble Robinson's "The Maniac."

Robinson's proliferating pseudonyms may have suggested Dacre's strategy of writing under a double pseudonym.[58] Robinson may have served as a model as well for Dacre's novelistic stock in trade, the wild, impassioned heroine. This possibility is bolstered by Robinson's scandalous link to Dacre's father, John King, an association immortalized in King's 1781 *Letters to a Certain Israelite, and His Answers to Them*.[59] King carried out an extortion scheme, ultimately publishing letters Robinson had written to him interspersed with fake and much more damning epistles.[60] The *Letters to a Certain Israelite* was, of course, only one of a flurry of titillating epistolary publications attributed to Robinson, which all acted to charge her person with a sexual *frisson*. In its exploration of female sexual passion, Dacre's 1806 novel, *Zofloya; or, The Moor*, participates in what was arguably the major literary preoccupation of British women novelists writing in the 1790s. Elizabeth Inchbald's *A Simple Story*, Mary Hays's *The Memoirs of*

---

58 She published *Hours of Solitude* as the work of "Charlotte Dacre, better known by the name of Rosa Matilda," but she was the daughter of John King (b. Jacob Rey, 1753-1824) and the wife of Nicholas Byrne, and so her real name was first Charlotte King and then Charlotte Byrne.

59 Lucyle Werkmeister identifies King as the "Certain Israelite" in *A Newspaper History of England 1792-1793* (Lincoln: University of Nebraska Press, 1967) 33.

60 In her book manuscript, "Mary Robinson: Woman of Letters," Sharon Setzer traces the public portrayal of Robinson's altercation with King through advertisements and news accounts published in the *Morning Herald* and *Morning Post* in March of 1781. An advertisement which appeared in the *Morning Herald* on March 23 noted that "Specimens of the original letters are left with the Publisher. Fielding. No. 23 Pater-noster Row," an account which is supported by this notice in the March 25 *Morning Post* : "The noble Paramour [presumably Lord Malden] of the celebrated Perditta and the fair dame herself, on Monday evening made a bold push to recover *certain letters*, upon the originality of which a *certain book* has lately been published; but the attempt was abortive; the publisher would not surrender, but challenged the demandant to the *Chapter coffee-house*, there to decide his right. The *attic regions of Pater-noster Row* were in an uproar, but, the amorous pair were obliged to retreat without the objects of their wishes."

Emma Courtney, Mary Wollstonecraft's *Maria* – all use sexual passion as plot motivation. That all of these women are linked to Robinson through friendship – or, in the case of Inchbald, through Godwin – is probably not coincidental. Tellingly, Robinson's most direct treatment of sexual passion, her "Ode to Rapture" (p. 138), published in the *Oracle* and in the 1793 *Poems*, was not reprinted in the 1806 *Poetical Works*.

3. "Pale Moon! thou Spectre of the Sky"

Robinson's *Memoirs*, begun two years before she died in 1800, attempts to construct a beatific self. Like her friend Jane Porter's "Character," the text reveals a redemptive project in its earnest and frequent interjections. "Ah! how little has the misjudging world known of what has passed in my mind," Robinson writes, predicting, "Probably these pages will be read, when the hand that writes them moulders in the grave; when that God who judges all hearts will know how innocent I was of the smallest conjugal infidelity" (*Memoirs* 1: 82 and 121). But Robinson also portrays herself as singled out from birth, born in the middle of a storm on the site of an old monastery, of which she writes, "A spot more calculated to inspire the soul with mournful meditation can scarcely be found amidst the monuments of antiquity" (*Memoirs* 1: 3). "The early propensities of my life," she writes, "were tinctured with romantic and singular characteristics" (*Memoirs* 1: 11-12). Her development is marked by moments in which she is uniquely at one with the world around her, struck by the sublimity of Westminster Abbey, or "inspired with a pensive melancholy" by a "romantic space of scenery" (*Memoirs* 1: 87). She writes of a stay near the foot of Sugar-loaf, "a stupendous mountain":

> Here I enjoyed the sweet repose of solitude: here I wandered about woods entangled by the wild luxuriance of nature, or roved upon the mountain's side, while the blue vapours floated round its summit. O, God of Nature! Sovereign of the universe of wonders! in those interesting moments how fervently did I adore thee! (*Memoirs* 1: 141)

If Robinson's depictions of herself as uniquely chosen, as finding in solitude a special connection with a cosmic force, seem familiar, it is because we recognize in these passages the standard tropes of romantic autobiography. When Wordsworth recalls his childhood in *The Prelude*, he depicts himself as one of those "favored being[s]" for whom spirits of nature "do open out the clouds / As at the touch of lightning, seeking him / With gentle visitation."[61] Robinson, punctuating her *Memoirs* with heightened moments of escape into nature, conjures up Wordsworth's "fleeting moods / of shadowy exaltation."[62]

The alternate constructions of herself which Robinson offers in the *Memoirs* are, of course, aligned with two different self-promotional projects. The first, and the one to which friends like Porter contributed, was an attempt to claim for Robinson a position she did not hold while alive, that of respectable woman. The second, which is evidenced materially by the body of poetry Robinson wrote, particularly in the last ten years of her life, represents an effort to secure Robinson's status as an artist. Although Robinson's literary career flowered in the 1790s, it is important to remember that she published her first volumes of poems, *Poems* (1775) and *Captivity, a Poem. And Celadon, A Tale* (1777), in the 1770s. Robinson's poetic career, like that of Anna Aikin Barbauld, the poet she claimed as her poetic ideal in the *Memoirs*,[63] has its origins in the so-called graveyard poets of the mid-eighteenth century, poets like Edward Young, author of *Night Thoughts on Life, Death, and Immortality*; Thomas Gray, most famous for his "Elegy in a Country Churchyard"; and Robert Blair, author of *The Grave*. In fact, lines from these poets' works, along with lines from works by William Cowper, Mark Akenside, and Thomas Warton the younger (Robinson quotes from his ode, "The Suicide") are interpolated into Robinson's 1796 novel, *Hubert de Sevrac*, providing a suggestive glimpse of her reading habits. Robinson was arguably *the* poet of sensibility. As a reviewer of her *Memoirs* noted, "She labours to touch the feelings and to melt the heart of the reader."[64] Her work makes

---

61 William Wordsworth, "The Two-Part *Prelude* of 1799," *The Prelude 1799, 1805, 1850*, ed. Jonathan Wordsworth, M.H. Abrams, and Stephen Gill (New York: W.W. Norton & Co., 1979) 1.70–73.

62 Wordsworth 2.361–62.

63 Robinson writes of being presented with the works of Miss Aikin (Barbauld was Aikin's married name): "I read them with rapture; I thought them the most beautiful Poems I had ever seen, and considered the woman who could invent such poetry, as the most to be envied of human creatures." *Memoirs* 1: 102.

apparent romanticism's debt to a cult of sensibility that advanced, and was advanced by, the works of women authors.[65]

Robinson's juvenile volume of 1775 (published when she was seventeen, but including poems she had written years earlier), provides a glimpse of what would become her primary poetic concerns. Her multiple forays into the pastoral mode (represented in this volume by "A Pastoral Elegy," p.67), in which she laments the faithlessness of the shepherd Damon, are harbingers of her later poetic stock in trade: the evocation of human loss. Her sympathy for the fate of a captive bird in "The Linnet's Petition" (which is possibly modeled after Barbauld's "The Mouse's Petition") demonstrates an early concern with social and political inequity, which she went on to explore at greater length in poems that address the cruelty of the slave trade (p.69). And her "Letter to a Friend on Leaving Town" (p.72), with its rejection of the amusements afforded by London pleasure gardens like Vauxhall and Ranelagh, anticipates the social critique she would advance as "Horace Juvenal," the pseudonymous author of the satirical *Modern Manners* (1793), and as "Tabitha Bramble" in the pages of the *Morning Post* near the end of her life.

The vogue for Della Cruscan poetry began when poems from *The Florence Miscellany* (1785), a volume of poems contrived by Robert Merry, Hester Thrale Piozzi, Bertie Greatheed, and William Parsons during their sojourns in Italy, were reprinted in English newspapers and inspired similar efforts by Robinson and Hannah Cowley, among others.[66] Robinson, using the pseudonym Laura Maria, came between Robert Merry's "Della Crusca" and Hannah Cowley's "Anna Matilda," who had been carrying out a verse dalliance in the pages of the *World*. First in the *World*, and then in the rival upstart paper the *Oracle*, Robinson published poems that embodied a Della Cruscan aesthetic predicated on emotional and ornamental excess.

Among the more charming of Robinson's experiments in the

---

64 *Monthly Review* 36 (Dec. 1801): 345.

65 The connection is also made explicit in the review of Robinson's *Poetical Works* published in the 1806 *Annual Review* (see Appendix C).

66 On the Della Cruscan phenomenon, see Jerome J. McGann, "The Literal World of the English Della Cruscans," *The Poetics of Sensibility: A Revolution in Poetic Style* (Oxford: Clarendon Press, 1996) 74-93. See also Pascoe, "'That fluttering, tinselled crew': Women Poets and Della Cruscanism," *Romantic Theatricality: Gender, Poetry, and Spectatorship*, 68-94.

Della Cruscan mode are her "Fairy Rhymes" with their miniaturized treatment of these thematic and stylistic conventions. Possibly inspired by Henry Fuseli's erotic representations of the fairies in *Midsummer Night's Dream* for John Boydell's Shakespeare Gallery, which opened in Pall Mall in 1790, Robinson poetically enacts the amours of Titania and Oberon. In "Oberon's Invitation to Titania," Robinson writes:

> Come, come, my pretty love, and sip
>   The dew that from each herb is flowing;
> And let the insects round thy lip
>   With envy hover while 'tis glowing!
> Beneath a spring-flow'r's bell we'll sing,
> While southern gales shall fragrance bring.
>   . . .
> I've made thee, love, a canopy
>   Of tulips tinted rich – a cluster
> Of golden cups is waving nigh,
>   Bath'd in the moon-beams' dewy lustre!
> The softest turf shall be our floor,
>   With twinkling dew-drops spangled o'er! (p.344-45)

With its invention of this Keatsian floral retreat and its sensual minuteness, Oberon's address to Titania is more fully realized than his long suffering consort's response in "Titania's Answer to Oberon," in which the fairy queen's mistrust of her suitor's advances is set forth in somewhat less vivid terms ("Inconstant! ev'ry fairy knows / Thy love is like the gale that blows!" [p.345]) This attention to floral decor was precisely the kind of poetic charm that invoked critical derision from the reviewer for the *English Review*. Faulting Robinson's 1791 *Poems* in terms that were critical commonplaces of the response to Della Cruscan poetry, the reviewer wrote:

> We cannot help regretting that the fair writer has too often imitated the new school of poets, which has lately appeared amongst us, and which sacrifices nature, simplicity, and passion, to luxuriant and ill-placed description, and to a load of imagery, and ornament of every kind. We are suffocated by the sweets of

these poets, and dazzled by the glare of their tinsel. With them the rage of passion, the moanings of love, the scream of despair, all must be *pretty*.[67]

Far from being an occasional votary of Della Crusca, Robinson fully participated, even fueled, the Della Cruscan enthusiasm with poems like "Ode to the Muse" (p.76), and "Ode to Della Crusca" (p.85), both published in her 1791 *Poems*.

In his analysis of Robinson's *Sappho and Phaon* (1796), Jerome McGann points out that the poetry of sensibility, as represented by this sonnet sequence, is "a pre-eminent intellectual force, and the emblem of whatever social and philosophical advancement the present age can claim for itself." McGann reads Robinson's sonnets and their preface as a poetic manifesto aimed at "restructuring the philosophy of literature in terms of the feelings and the passions" so that strong passion and emotion are not opposed to artistic power and integrity.[68] Countering the Mary Wollstonecraft of the *Vindication of the Rights of Woman* (but not necessarily Wollstonecraft the novelist), Robinson insists on coupling passion and reason, sensibility and political consciousness.

Given this yoking, a discontinuity between the thematic concerns of Della Cruscan poetry and the political events of the late 1780s and early 1790s, the period in which this mode of verse flourished, cannot be assumed. The political turmoil resulting from George III's lapses into mental illness and, on the other side of the English Channel, the storming of the Bastille, is not entirely without reference in Robinson's 1791 volume of poems, which includes "Ainsi va le Monde." In this ringing paean to a freedom capable of rejuvenating a moribund national poetry, Robinson writes:

> Thro' all the scenes of Nature's varying plan,
> Celestial Freedom warms the breast of man;
> Led by her daring hand, what pow'r can bind
> The boundless efforts of the lab'ring mind.

---

67 *English Review* 19 (1792): 42-43.
68 Jerome J. McGann, *The Poetics of Sensibility: A Revolution in Literary Style,* 102 and 104.

The god-like fervour, thrilling thro' the heart,
Gives new creation to each vital part;
Throbs rapture thro' each palpitating vein,
Wings the rapt thought, and warms the fertile brain;
. . .
To her the sounds of melody belong,
She wakes the raptures of the Poet's song ... (p.108-109)

In the period between the publication of the 1791 and 1793 vol-
umes, Robinson, stopping at Calais in July 1792 en route to Spa, Flan-
ders, barely escaped the general arrest that restrained all British
subjects in France. Her references to the events in France are more
frequent and sustained in the later volume, and her response more
nuanced. Robinson equivocates, for instance, in her poetic treatment
of Marie Antoinette. Whether by virtue of her prior association with
the French queen during Robinson's charmed Parisian encounter a
decade before, or because her cognizance of gender inequities ran
deeper than her awareness of class-based suffering, Robinson turns
Marie Antoinette, republican symbol of aristocratic corruption, into a
martyr figure. Writing of the French queen in "Marie Antoinette's
Lamentation, in her Prison of the Temple," Robinson emphasizes
Marie Antoinette's status as a grieving mother, recreating the queen's
response to her sleeping children:

When I behold my darling INFANTS sleep,
    Fair spotless blossoms, deck'd in op'ning charms,
Why do I start aghast, and wildly weep,
    And madly snatch them to my eager arms?
Ah me! because my sense, o'erwhelm'd with dread,
    Views the sweet CHERUBS ON THEIR FUNERAL BED! (p.135)

In dwelling on the French queen in this intimate maternal tableau,
Robinson counters pornographic propaganda which accused the
queen of incestuous relations with her son.[69] Here, as Sharon Setzer
argues convincingly in the case of *The Natural Daughter*, Robinson "is

---

69 On the pamphlet campaign against Marie Antoinette, see Lynn Hunt, "The Many
   Bodies of Marie Antoinette: Political Pornography and the Problem of the Femi-

more concerned with the gender politics that aligned Jacobins and anti-Jacobins than with the party politics that divided them."[70] Setzer shows how Robinson "collapses distinctions between ideological fathers of the French Revolution and biological fathers of ostensibly respectable English families" (532-33). In the Marie Antoinette poems and in the 1791 tract *Impartial Reflections on the Present Situation of the Queen of France,* Robinson presents the French queen as first and foremost a wronged woman and thus ignores her status as an avatar of aristocratic frivolity. Or, rather, Robinson, who brought dress fashions first worn by the French queen to England, was charmed rather than repulsed by the queen's glittering persona, and was able to support both the French queen and the general tenets of French radicalism.

Similarly, Robinson seems to have managed to sustain a fifteen-year relationship with Banastre Tarleton, an outspoken proponent of the slave trade, while dramatizing the horrors of slavery in her poems. As Moira Ferguson points out, Robinson published attacks on the institution of slavery throughout the 1770s, 1780s, and 1790s. For example, in "Captivity, A Poem," published in 1777, she made use of her experience in debtors' prison by reference to a variety of forms of captivity including slavery.[71] In poems like *The Progress of Liberty* and "The Negro Girl" (p.234), Robinson empathized particularly with female slaves and, in so doing, "anticipated future anti-slavery arguments about their sexually jeopardized lives."[72] Her opposition to the slave trade may well have been sincere, but the plight of "The Negro Girl," Zelma, who watches her companion Draco drown shackled in a slave ship struck by lightning, allows Robinson to take her favorite theme – love's loss – to its most emotionally fraught and theatrically vivid extreme.

The largest segment of the selection of Robinson's poetry which follows is devoted to the *Lyrical Tales,* the last collection of poems she published in her lifetime and her "favorite offspring."[73] As is clear

nine in the French Revolution," *Eroticism and the Body Politic,* ed. Lynn Hunt (Baltimore: Johns Hopkins University Press, 1991) 108-130. See also Chantal Thomas, *La reine scélérate: Marie-Antoinette dans les pamphlets* (Paris: Seuil, 1989).

70 Sharon M. Setzer, "Romancing the Reign of Terror: Sexual Politics in Mary Robinson's *Natural Daughter," Criticism* 39 (1997): 532.

71 Moira Ferguson, *Subject to Others: British Women Writers and Colonial Slavery, 1670-1834* (New York: Routledge, 1992) 175-176.

72 Ferguson 177.

from her promotion of one of Wordsworth's lyrical ballads which was reprinted in the poetry column of the *Morning Post* (then under her editorship), Robinson was much taken with Wordsworth's 1798 volume. An April 2, 1800 introduction to "The Mad Mother" reports:

> We have been so much captivated with the following beautiful piece, which appears in a small volume LYRICAL BALLADS, that we are tempted to transgress the rule we have laid down for ourselves [i.e. to only publish original poetry]. Indeed, the whole collection, with the exception of the first piece, which appears manifestly to have been written by a different hand, is a tribute to genuine nature.[74]

When Robinson submitted her own *Lyrical Tales* to publishers, she acknowledged her debt to Wordsworth in a postscript where she noted: "The volume will consist of Tales, serious and gay, on a variety of subjects in the manner of Wordsworth's Lyrical ballads."[75] It is important as well, however, to be reminded of Wordsworth's borrowings of popular poetic subjects from the pages of the newspapers and magazines in which Robinson's work was so prominently featured.[76]

The inclusion here of the *Lyrical Tales* in its entirety makes it possible to do poem-by-poem comparisons of, for example, Wordsworth's "We are Seven" and Robinson's "All Alone," or Coleridge's "Rime of the Ancient Mariner" and Robinson's "Golfre." Such comparisons not only underscore Robinson's poetic affinity with Wordsworth and Coleridge, but also the ways in which her project diverged from theirs. Stuart Curran, reading the *Lyrical Tales* in the context of both *Lyrical Ballads* and Robert Southey's more overtly political "English Eclogues," claims that Robinson's poems are invested with a "more urgent sense ... of the stark contingency of human desire."[77] Certainly in Robinson's rewriting of "We are Seven," her replacement of the fey

---

73 She wrote, "I have also [something] at Bristol (in the beautiful press of Biggs and Cottle) a volume of Lyrical Tales; my favorite offspring." To Miss Porter, 27 August 1800, Misc. 2295; Carl H. Pforzheimer Collection of Shelley & His Circle; New York Public Library; Astor, Lenox and Tilden Foundation. See Appendix A for complete letter.

74 *Morning Post* 2 April 1800.

75 Mary Robinson, letter to unknown publisher, June 17, 1800, Garrick Club, London.

76 See Robert Mayo's "The Contemporaneity of the *Lyrical Ballads*," *PMLA* 69 (1954): 486–522.

child, who plays and sups by her siblings' graves, with a boy whose catalogue of deprivation – of father, mother, baby goat, family dog, cottage – makes the little girl Wordsworth describes seem perhaps a little too charming.

Robinson juxtaposes tales of abjection with humorous tales, but the humor is of a dark variety predicated on over-controlling women who receive their come-uppance. The Granny Grey, in the poem of that name, is beaten by villagers who mistake her for "a fierce, ill-omen'd crabbed bird" who has been

> Pinching, like fairies, harmless lasses,
> And shewing Imps, in looking-glasses. (p.269)

The poem mocks and ultimately punishes the old woman for her prurient interest in others' affairs ("she made / Scandal her pleasure – and her trade"), but in doing so it invests in the power of tale-telling. The tale that Granny's nemesis William tells about an old gray owl turns "cheeks of Oker, chalky pale," and finally leads to Granny's position as the focus of mocking village lore:

> 'Till to her home the GRANNY came,
> Where, to confirm the tale of shame,
> Each rising day they went, in throngs,
> With ribbald jests, and sportive songs. (p.270)

Granny gives in to William's desire to marry her granddaughter, and the poem ends with a nod toward the ongoing circulation of this tale:

> And should this TALE, fall in the way
> Of LOVERS CROSS'D, or GRANNIES GREY, –
> Let them confess, 'tis made to prove –
> The *wisest heads*, – TOO WEAK FOR LOVE! (p.270)

Stripped of the glamorous trappings of her own celebrity status, Robinson proceeded to critique the inequities and inanities of her

---

77 Stuart Curran, "Mary Robinson's *Lyrical Tales* in Context," *Re-Visioning Romanticism: British Women Writers, 1776-1837*, ed. Carol Shiner Wilson and Joel Haefner (Philadelphia: University of Pennsylvania Press, 1994) 26.

culture.[78] While poems like the last one seem to mock female tale tellers, it is worth noting that the putative author of the poem – Robinson first published it in the *Morning Post* as the offering of Tabitha Bramble – is a figure who, emboldened by her age and crone status, casts a jaundiced eye on the lifestyles of the rich and famous. In one of her first poems written under this sobriquet, Robinson refers to herself as a poor spinster and makes reference to Matthew Bramble, lest anyone miss the connection to Tobias Smollett's *The Expedition of Humphry Clinker* (1771).[79] As Margaret Higonnet notes, Robinson "often invokes a kind of two-class system of oppressor and oppressed, of "Great and Small," spendthrifts and forsaken poor."[80] Her final geographic stationing near Old Windsor – in a cottage within the demesne of Windsor Castle, the Prince of Wales's occasional residence – enhanced her sense of identification with the lowly side of that binary. "The Poor, Singing Dame," with its depiction of the "neat little Hovel" near an old castle whose turrets "frown'd on the poor simple dwelling," can be read autobiographically with Robinson in the role of the old Dame who persistently and merrily sings to the great annoyance of the surly Lord of the Castle who has her carted off to prison where she dies.[81] Enhancing the identification between Robinson and her singing heroine is the fact that the dame's first name is belatedly revealed in a stanza which can be read as a revenge fantasy:

---

78 Betsy Bolton, comparing Robinson's work to the *Lyrical Ballads*, writes: "Darby Robinson's 'Tales' also demand to be read on more than one level at a time, but rather than contrasting an event with the response to that event, she models for the reader two opposing stances: that of hypocritical innocence, and that of knowing cynicism. The moralizing conclusions of the tales repeatedly disrupt the naïveté they ostensibly support, to promulgate instead a mode of social cynicism, especially in cases of sexual impropriety." "Romancing the Stone: 'Perdita' Robinson in Wordsworth's London," *ELH* 64 (1997): 742.

79 "Tabitha Bramble, to Her Cousins in Scotland. Ode the Third," *Morning Post* 25 Dec. 1797. Robinson's appropriation of the name of Tabitha Bramble may have been inspired by the fact that her brother owned a villa near Pisa that had formerly belonged to Smollett. Robinson mentions this fact in a manuscript letter, dated October 14, 1794, that is now in the Folger Shakespeare Library.

80 Margaret Higonnet, "Social Archetypes and Lyric Structure," American Conference on Romanticism, January 23, 1998.

81 I am grateful for Sharon Setzer's suggestion of this reading of "The Poor, Singing Dame" as self-portraiture.

The Lord of the Castle, from that fatal moment
　　When poor Singing MARY was laid in her grave,
Each night was surrounded by Screech-owls appalling,
　　Which o'er the black turrets their pinions would wave!
On the ramparts that frown'd on the river, swift flowing,
　　They hover'd, still hooting a terrible song,
When his windows would rattle, the Winter blast blowing,
　　They would shriek like a ghost, the dark alleys among! (p.192)

Robinson is comical on the vagaries of contemporary clothing fashion, a subject she knew intimately. Commenting on women's haberdashery in a poem first published in the *Morning Post* of December 28, 1799, Tabitha Bramble writes of:

　　A bowl of straw to deck the head,
　　　　Like porringer unmeaning;
　　A bunch of *poppies,* flaming red,
　　　　With tawdry ribbands, streaming. (p.362)

Likening women's hats to dishes, Robinson exposes the "unmeaning" dictates of fashion and the unwitting women and men (see "Modern Male Fashions" [p.360]) enslaved by them.

Robinson's later poems are noteworthy as well for their metrical ingenuity, the aspect of her poetry that attracted Coleridge's attention.[82] In a letter to Southey in which he entreated the then editor of the *Annual Anthology* to publish Robinson's "Jasper," Coleridge commented:

There was a poem of her's in this Morning's paper which both

82　Earl Leslie Griggs provides a detailed account of the Coleridge/Robinson artistic engagement in his "Coleridge and Mrs. Mary Robinson," *Modern Language Notes* 45 (1930): 90-95. David V. Erdman details the cooperative efforts of a number of scholars to find the missing copy of Coleridge's "The Apotheosis, or the Snow-Drop," written in response to Robinson's "Ode to the Snow-Drop" in "Lost Poem Found: The cooperative pursuit & recapture of an escaped Coleridge 'sonnet' of 72 lines," *Bulletin of the New York Public Library* 65 (1961): 249-268. Martin Levy, Susan Luther, Daniel Robinson, and Lisa Vargo all make significant contributions to our understanding of the Robinson/Coleridge relationship. See Bibliography for full citations and Appendix B for Coleridge poems.

in metre and matter pleased me much – She overloads every thing; but I never knew a human Being with so *full* a mind – bad, good, & indifferent, I grant you, but full, & overflowing. This Poem I *asked* for you, because I thought the meter stimulating – & some of the Stanzas really *good* – The first line of the 12th would of itself redeem a worse Poem.[83]

Southey perhaps shared Coleridge's admiration for the line – "Pale Moon! thou Spectre of the Sky" – from Robinson's "Jasper." In any event, he published "Jasper" along with "The Haunted Beach" in the 1800 *Annual Anthology*. Of the latter poem, Coleridge wrote:

[I]t falls off sadly to the last – wants Tale – & Interest; but the Images are new & very distinct – that 'silvery carpet' is so *just*, that it is unfortunate it should *seem* so bad – for it is *really* good – but the Metre – ay! that Woman has an Ear.[84]

The poetic exchange Coleridge and Robinson carried out in the pages of the *Morning Post* (see Appendix B) provides one register of their poetic kinship. The metrical parallels between Robinson's "The Savage of Aveyron" and Coleridge's "Kubla Khan" provide another. Robinson's "To the Poet Coleridge," published October 17, 1800, in the *Morning Post*, serves notice, with its allusions to a sunny dome and caves of ice, that she had read Coleridge's poem in manuscript.[85] But the opening lines of Robinson's "The Savage of Aveyron," a poem inspired by the feral child who was discovered in the woods of southern France, and whose plight was featured prominently in British newspapers, shows how Robinson internalized the idiosyncratic meter of Coleridge's incantatory poem. Robinson writes:

'Twas in the mazes of a wood,

---

83 January 25, 1800, *Collected Letters of Samuel Taylor Coleridge*, 1: 562. Robinson's "The Poor Singing Dame" appeared in the *Morning Post* 25 January 1800.

84 Coleridge to Robert Southey, February 18, 1800, *Collected Letters of Samuel Taylor Coleridge*, 1: 576.

85 See Daniel Robinson's reading of Robinson's "To the Poet Coleridge" for a detailed analysis of the way Robinson appropriated and revised aspects of "Kubla Khan." "From 'Mingled Measure' to 'Ecstatic Measures': Mary Robinson's Poetic Reading of 'Kubla Khan,'" *Wordsworth Circle* 26 (1995): 4-7.

The lonely wood of AVERYON,
   I heard a melancholy tone: –
      It seem'd to freeze my blood!
A torrent near was flowing fast,
And hollow was the midnight blast
As o'er the leafless woods it past,
      While terror-fraught I stood!
O! mazy woods of AVERYON!
   O! wilds of dreary solitude!
Amid thy thorny alleys rude
   I thought myself alone! (p.332-33)

Robinson's poem, with its narrative of the savage child's history, departs fairly dramatically from Coleridge's enigmatic fragment poem. But in its replication of Coleridge's mazy measure and fraught tone, "The Savage of Aveyron" shows Robinson's studied craftsmanship and persistent emotional intensity.

Robinson and Coleridge may have taught each other some new metrical tricks, but musicality had been a hallmark of her poetry long before the two became acquaintances. Robinson wrote an operetta which was performed in conjunction with *Macbeth* on April 30, 1778, inspiring mixed reviews (and resulting in the publication of *The Songs, Chorusses, &c. in the Lucky Escape*). She was trying to see an opera entitled *Kate of Aberdeen* into production in 1793.[86] If many of Robinson's poems were not written with the explicit intention that they be set to music, it quickly became obvious that they were easily adapted to a musical performance. The *Morning Post* contains several notices of the actress Dorothy Jordan's efforts to set Robinson's poems to music.[87] Little trace remains of these forays into the world of musical theatre, but one has only to read a poem like "Stanzas.

---

86   A notice in the *Oracle* of March 23, 1793 reports: "Mrs. ROBINSON's opera is said to breathe that spirit of LOYALTY, which would at this period render it highly popular. Why is it not produced? It would have been in a better channel, had she presented it to Covent-Garden Theatre, for a variety of reasons." Bass reports that the *Oracle* made earlier reference to the opera, noting on July 30, 1792, that Robinson would be bringing out her newly composed opera at Drury Lane in about two months (320).

87   See the notice in the January 27, 1800 *Morning Post*: "Mrs. JORDAN has composed a beautiful air to the elegant lines of SAPPHO which appeared in this paper a few days ago." On February 8, 1800, the *Post* confirms: "The Poem of Sappho, set to music

Written Between Dover and Calais, in July, 1792" to appreciate Robinson's lyric talents. The poem begins:

> BOUNDING BILLOW, cease thy motion,
> Bear me not so swiftly o'er!
> Cease thy roaring, foamy OCEAN!
> I will tempt thy rage no more. (p.132)

With its reference to a severed love relationship, the poem also, of course, provides yet another demonstration of what contemporary reviewers considered Robinson's greatest poetic strength: the authentic evocation of human loss. The fact that Robinson was fixed in the public imagination as "Perdita" (the lost one), jilted lover of the Prince of Wales's "Florizel," validated her numerous poetic adieus to love. But her ability to evocatively suggest reluctance in the face of the ocean's "bounding," to delineate the exact balance of attraction and revulsion produced by a failed love affair, furthered her claim to being the poet of love gone wrong.

Jane Porter, in her unpublished "Character of the late Mrs Robinson," recalls the period of Robinson's French conquests in the early 1780s, writing:

> She now dedicated all her time to the culture of her understanding. And in that epoch of her life, when her loveliness shone in its brightest perfection, instead of receiving the Nobles of the French Court, who all crowded to pay her homage, she secluded herself within her closet; and for hours, and days, and weeks, has remained there, studying how to become wiser and better. At this time, (and every Englishman who was then at Paris, must know it;) her society was sought by the first literary characters, male and female, in that country. Even Antionette [sic] herself used to say, "Send for the lovely Mrs Robinson. Let me look at her again, and hear her speak, before I go to sleep!"[88]

---

by Mrs. JORDAN, is from the pen of Mrs. Robinson." The *Post* had published a poem entitled "To Henry" and attributed to Sappho on January 11th.

88 Jane Porter, "Character of the Late Mrs. Robinson," Misc. Ms. 2296; Carl H. Pforzheimer Collection of Shelley & His Circle; Astor, Lenox and Tilden Foundation.

While Robinson never entirely eschewed the pleasures of society, she did spend a great deal of her life at work in her closet (as a small, private room was then called). Before she died, she had arranged her poems for the collected works eventually published in 1806. This exercise suggests her awareness of her poetry as a substantial accomplishment and her hopes for posthumous recognition as a significant literary figure. The most distinctive feature of her verse – her stylistic and thematic heterogeneousness – confuses any effort to make the story of romanticism a simple tale. But then we know from Robinson's lyrical tales the perils of being a tale teller.

Is it in mansions rich and gay
On downy beds, or couches warm,
That Nature owns the Wintry Day,
And shrinks to hear the howling storm?

                                        Ah! no!

Figure 5. Mezzotint engraving after Maria Cosway, illustration No. 1 for "The Wintry Day,"
1804. (By courtesy of the Special Collections Department, University of Virginia Library.)

Mary Darby Robinson: A Brief Chronology

1758	Born Mary Darby, 27 November 1758, in Bristol to Nicholas and Hetty Darby.
Mid-1760s	Attends boarding school run by the sisters of Hannah More.
1767	Nicholas Darby suffers failure of his Newfoundland fishing scheme.
1768	Mrs. Darby, Mary, and her brother George move to London.
1773	Introduced to David Garrick. Marriage to Thomas Robinson at St. Martin-in-the-Fields on 12 April.
1774	Birth of Maria Elizabeth Robinson on 18 October.
1775	Publication of *Poems*. Thomas Robinson imprisoned for debt in Fleet Prison from 3 May 1775 to 3 August 1776. Mary befriended by Georgiana, Duchess of Devonshire.
1776	Debut performance as Juliet in Shakespeare's *Romeo and Juliet* on 10 December.
1777	Birth of second daughter, Sophia, who died at six weeks old. Visits Bath and Bristol. Publication of *Captivity, A Poem; and Celadon, A Tale*.
1779	Performance as Perdita in *The Winter's Tale* on 3 December is attended by the Prince of Wales (later George IV). Liaison with the Prince commences soon after.
1781	Estranged from Prince and mired in debt. Leaves England for Paris. Encounter with Marie Antoinette.
1782	Living in Berkeley Square, London. Begins fifteen-year-long relationship with Banastre Tartleton.
1783	Pursues Tarleton to the Continent. Trip results in lingering disability.
1784	Charlotte Smith publishes first edition of *Elegiac Sonnets, and Other Essays*. Robinson's possessions auctioned off to satisfy debt.
1786-87	Visits Germany. Her father dies on 5 December 1786 at age 62. Robinson returns to London by way of Paris in early 1787.
1788-89	Publishes as "Laura Maria" in the *World*, then the *Oracle*.

1791	Publication of *Poems*.
1792	French royal family imprisoned. Publication of *Vancenza, or, The Dangers of Credulity*. To Spa, Flanders, with her mother and daughter in July. Delayed in Calais because of inability to travel through war-torn Flanders. Leaves Calais for England on 2 September, narrowly avoiding an *arrêt* which restrained British subjects in France.
1793	Execution of Louis XVI and Marie Antoinette. Robinson publishes *Modern Manners* (attributed to "Horace Juvenal"), *A Monody to the Memory of the Late Queen of France*, second volume of *Poems*, and *Sight, The Cavern of Woe, and Solitude*. Death of Mrs. Darby on 6 August.
1794	State trials of London Corresponding Society members accused of treasonous activity end in acquittals. Robinson's *Nobody*, a satire of female gamesters starring Mrs. Jordan, is staged at Drury Lane on 29 November and is hissed by the audience.
1796–97	*Sappho and Phaon. In A Series of Legitimate Sonnets* published in 1796. *Walsingham, or, The Pupil of Nature* published in 1797.
1798	Begins her *Memoirs* on 14 January. Banastre Tartleton marries Susan Priscilla Bertie on 17 December.
1799	Publishes *The False Friend* and *The Natural Daughter*. Becomes poetry editor for the *Morning Post* under the general editorship of Daniel Stuart.
1800	Publication of *Lyrical Tales* on 20 November. Translation of Joseph Hager's *Picture of Palermo*. Death at Englefield Cottage, Englefield Green, Surrey, on 26 December.

MARY ROBINSON: SELECTED POEMS

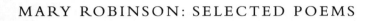

FROM *POEMS* (1775)

A PASTORAL ELEGY[1]

I

YE nymphs, ah! give ear to my lay,
   Your pastime I prithe' give o'er,
For Damon the youthful and gay,
   Is gone, — and our joys are no more.
That Shepherd so blithsome and fair,   5
   Whose truth was the pride of the plains,
Has left us alas! in despair,
   For no such a Shepherd remains.

II

His life was a compound of joy,
   Pure innocence guided each thought,   10
No envy his bliss cou'd annoy,
   For with virtue his bosom was fraught.
He scorn'd to deceive or betray,
   Fair truth ever dwelt in his sight,
He always was blithsome and gay,   15
   And to please was his only delight.

III

In the shade when reclin'd on his crook,
   To hear his melodious strains,
My flocks I have often forsook,
   To wander alone on the plains.   20
Each bird did attend on the spray,[2]

---

1 The pastoral mode originated with the Greek Theocritus who wrote poems about
the lives of Sicilian shepherds in the third century B.C. Virgil imitated Theocritus
in his Latin *Eclogues*, which established the lasting conventions of this form: shep-
herds, shepherdesses, and other country folk in an idealized natural setting. In the
pastoral elegy, a particularly enduring variant of the pastoral mode, the death of a
fellow shepherd is mourned.
2 Collective term for slender twigs.

The zephers[1] did play on the trees,
Sweet harmony join'd the soft lay,
    And whisper'd his praise in each breeze.

IV

25 My lambkins are straying far wide,
        The lilly reclines her fair head,
    My crook is with scorn thrown aside,
        For alas! my sweet Shepherd is dead.
    I will riffle the jessamin[2] bow'rs
30   To deck the green turf on his breast,
    With myrtle and sweet scented flow'rs,
        My Damon's cold grave shall be dress'd.

V

    While Eglantine sheds a perfume,
        Or peace is Pastora's[3] desire,
35 While the cowslip continues to bloom,
        Or the rose is adorn'd with a brier.
    While the lambkins shall graze on the plain,
        Or the nightingale warble its lay,
    As long as old time shall remain,
40   His memory ne'er shall decay.

VI

    But alas! the lov'd youth is no more,
        Each stream shall repeat the sad sound,
    Each Shepherd the loss shall deplore,
        And his fate thro' the grove shall resound.
45 Since truth like my Damon's must yield,
        To death, that invincible foe,
    Ye swains,[4] ah! make virtue your shield,
        Nor tremble to meet the dire blow.

---

1 Zephyrs: gentle breezes.
2 Variant form of jasmine, a climbing shrub with fragrant white flowers. The flowers
   of the myrtle, eglantine, and cowslip plants mentioned in the lines that follow are all
   known for their sweet fragrances.
3 Female shepherdess.
4 Shepherd or countryman.

THE LINNET'S PETITION

I

As STELLA sat the other day,
   Beneath a myrtle shade,
A tender bird in plaintive notes,
   Address'd the pensive maid.

II

Upon a bough in gaudy cage,   5
   The feather'd warbler hung,
And in melodious accents thus,
   His fond petition sung.

III

"Ah! pity my unhappy fate,
   And set a captive free,   10
So may you never feel the loss,
   Of peace, or liberty.

IV

With ardent pray'r and humble voice,
   Your mercy now I crave,
Your kind compassion and regard,   15
   My tender life to save.

V

Ah! wherefore am I here confin'd,
   Ah! why does fate ordain,
A life so innocent as mine,
   Should end in grief and pain.   20

VI

I envy every little bird,
   That warbles gay and free,
The meanest of the feather'd race,
   Is happier far than me.

VII

25

Sweet liberty by heaven sent,
    From me, alas! is torn,
And here without a cause confin'd,
    A captive doom'd I mourn.

VIII

When bright Aurora's[1] silver rays,
    Proclaim the rising morn,
And glitt'ring dew drops shine around,
    Or gild the flow'ring thorn.

30

IX

When every bird except myself,
    Went forth his mate to see,
I always tun'd my downy throat,
    To please, and gladden thee.

35

X

Beneath thy window each new day,
    And in the myrtle bow'r,
I strove to charm thy list'ning ear,
    With all my little pow'r.

40

XI

Ah! what avails this gaudy cage,
    Or what is life to me,
If thus confin'd, if thus distress'd,
    And robb'd of liberty.

XII

I who the greatest fav'rite was
    Of all the feather'd race,
Think, Stella think, the pain I feel,
    And pity my sad case.

45

---

1   Roman goddess of the dawn.

XIII

While here condemn'd to sure despair,
    What comfort have I left,   50
Or how can I this fate survive,
    Of every joy bereft.

XIV

My harmless life was ever free,
    From mischief and from ill,
My only wish on earth to prove,   55
    Obedient to your will.

XV

Then pity my unhappy fate,
    And set a captive free,
So may you never feel the loss,
    Of peace, or liberty."   60

XVI

On Stella's breast compassion soon,
    Each tender feeling wrought,
Resolv'd to give him back with speed,
    That freedom which he sought.

XVII

With friendly hand she ope'd the cage,   65
    By kindred pity mov'd,
And sympathetic joys divine,
    Her gentle bosom prov'd.

XVIII

When first she caught the flutt'ring thing,
    She felt strange extasy,   70
But never knew so great a bliss,
    As when she set him free.

LETTER TO A FRIEND ON LEAVING TOWN

GLADLY I leave the town, and all its care,
For sweet retirement, and fresh wholsome air,
Leave op'ra, park, the masquerade, and play,
In solitary groves to pass the day.
5   Adieu, gay throng, luxurious vain parade,
Sweet peace invites me to the rural shade,
No more the Mall,¹ can captivate my heart,
No more can Ranelagh,² one joy impart.
Without regret I leave the splendid ball,
10 And the inchanting shades of gay Vauxhall,³
Far from the giddy circle now I fly,
Such joys no more, can please my sicken'd eye.
The town's alluring scenes no more can charm,
Nor dissipation my fond breast alarm;
15 Where vice and folly has each bosom fir'd,
And what is most absurd, — is most admir'd.
Alas! what diff'rence 'twixt the town bred fair,
And the blith maid who breaths the purer air.
Whose life is innocent, whose thoughts are clear,
20 Whose soul is gentle, and whose heart sincere.
Bless'd with her swain, she wants no greater joy,
Nor fears inconstancy, her bliss can cloy,
No anxious fears invade her tranquil breast,
The peaceful mansion of content and rest.
25 But rich in every virtue, void of art,
She feels those joys, truth only can impart.

---

1 A pedestrian walkway in St. James's Park and a popular place for fashionable
strollers to see and be seen.
2 A pleasure garden in the Chelsea area of London. It was known for firework dis-
plays, garden concerts, masquerades, and balls.
3 Vauxhall Gardens, located in Lambeth near the Thames, was a summer resort
(whereas Ranelagh was chiefly patronised during the winter). Its grounds extended
about twelve acres and its amusements included lamp-lit walkways, gardens studded
with statues, and a Rotunda featuring popular musical performances and painting
exhibitions. When Robinson attended Vauxhall as a young woman it was known as
a place where people of all classes rubbed shoulders. See W. S. Scott, *Green Retreats:
The Story of Vauxhall Gardens 1661-1859* (London: Odhams Press, [1955]) 30. See Fig-
ure 3 for Thomas Rowlandson's depiction of Vauxhall, in which Mary Robinson is
featured in the right front row.

View the gay courtly dame, and mark her face,
Where art supply's fair nature's nobler place,
Luxurious pleasures, all her days divide,
And fashion taints, bright beauty's greatest pride.   30
Each action has its fixt and settled rule,
Eyes, limbs, and features, are all put to school.
Beaux without number, daily round her swarm,
And each with fulsome flatt'ry try's to charm.
Till, like the rose, which blooms but for an hour,   35
Her face grown common, loses all its power.
Each idle coxcomb[1] leaves the wretched fair,
Alone to languish, and alone despair,
To cards, and dice, the slighted maiden flies,
And every fashionable vice apply's,   40
Scandal and coffee, pass the morn away,
At night a rout,[2] an opera, or a play;
Thus glide their life, partly through inclination,
Yet more, because it is the reigning fashion.
Thus giddy pleasures they alone pursue,   45
Merely because, they've nothing else to do;
Whatever can afford their hearts delight,
No matter if the thing be wrong, or right;
They will pursue it, tho' they be undone,
They see their ruin, — still they venture on.   50
Prudence they hate, grave wisdom they despise,
And laugh at those who teach them to be wise.
Pleas'd they embark upon the dangerous tide,
And with the fashionable current glide;
Till fate has every wish and purpose cross'd,   55
Their health, their beauty, and their fortune loss'd:
No art their wanted youth can then repair,
Abandon'd to remorse, and keen despair,
Repentant sighs, their wretched bosom wound,
And happiness, alas! no more is found.   60
In some sequester'd shade alone they stray,
And pensive waste, the solitary day.

---

1   Vain or showy person; a fop.
2   A large evening party or reception; a fashionable gathering.

Till fate relieves the wretched maid from grief,
And death affords, a long and last relief.
65   These are the follies that engage the mind,
And taint the principles, of half mankind,
Then wonder not my friend, that I can leave,
Those transient pleasures, only born to grieve.
Those short liv'd shadows of a fleeting day,
70   Those idle customs of the rich and gay.
Henceforth, retirement, is my chosen seat,
Far from the insolent, the vain, the great.
Sweet solitude, ah! welcome to my breast,
And with thee welcome, sweet content, and rest;
75   Farewell ambition, source of every pain,
Farewell pale malice, and thy hateful train:
Farewell black calumny, no more thy dart,
Shall force one sigh, or wound my placid heart.
My future days, shall with sweet peace abound,
80   By friendship, virtue, and experience crown'd.

'Tis on the bleak and barren heath,
Where mis'ry feels the shaft of death,
As to the dark and freezing grave,
Her children (not a friend to save) Unheeded go!

Figure 6. Mezzotint engraving after Maria Cosway, illustration No. 2 for "The Wintry Day," 1804. (By courtesy of the Special Collections Department, University of Virginia Library.)

FROM *POEMS* (1791)

ODE TO THE MUSE

O, LET me seize thy pen sublime
That paints, in melting dulcet rhyme,
The glowing pow'r, the magic art,
Th' extatic raptures of the Heart;
5   Soft Beauty's timid smile serene,
The dimples of Love's sportive mien;
The sweet descriptive tale to trace;
To picture Nature's winning grace;
To steal the tear from Pity's eye;
10   To catch the sympathetic sigh;
O teach me, with swift light'nings force
To watch wild passion's varying course;
To mark th' enthusiast's vivid fire,
Or calmly touch thy golden lyre,
15   While gentle Reason mildly sings
Responsive to the trembling strings.

    SWEET Nymph, enchanting Poetry!
I dedicate my mind to Thee.
Oh! from thy bright Parnassian[1] bow'rs
20   Descend, to bless my sombre hours;
Bend to the earth thy eagle wing,
And on its glowing plumage bring
Blithe FANCY, from whose burning eye
The young ideas sparkling fly;
25   O, come, and let us fondly stray,
Where rosy Health shall lead the way,
And soft FAVONIUS[2] lightly spread
A perfum'd carpet as we tread;
Ah! let us from the world remove,
30   The calm forgetfulness to prove,

---

1   Parnassus: mountain in central Greece, sacred to Apollo and the Muses.
2   The west wind, also known as Zephyr.

Which at the still of evening's close,
Lulls the tir'd peasant to repose;
Repose, whose balmy joys o'er-pay
The sultry labours of the day.

And when the blue-ey'd dawn appears,   35
Just peeping thro' her veil of tears;
Or blushing opes her silver gate,
And on its threshold, stands elate,
And flings her rosy mantle far
O'er every loit'ring dewy star;   40
And calls the wanton breezes forth,
And sprinkles diamonds o'er the earth;
While in the green-wood's shade profound,
The insect race, with buzzing sound
Flit o'er the rill,[1] — a glitt'ring train,   45
Or swarm along the sultry plain.
Then in sweet converse let us rove,
Where in the thyme-embroider'd grove,
The musky air its fragrance pours
Upon the silv'ry scatter'd show'rs;   50
To hail soft Zephyr, as she goes
To fan the dew-drop from the rose;
To shelter from the scorching beam,
And muse beside the rippling stream.

Or when, at twilight's placid hour,   55
We stroll to some sequester'd bow'r;
And watch the haughty Sun retire
Beneath his canopy of fire;
While slow the dusky clouds enfold
Day's crimson curtains fring'd with gold;   60
And o'er the meadows faintly fly
Pale shadows of the purpling sky:
While softly o'er the pearl-deck'd plain,
Cold Dian[2] leads the sylvan train;

---

1   A small stream.
2   Diana: goddess of the moon.

65　　　In mazy dance and sportive glee,
　　　SWEET MUSE, I'll fondly turn to thee;
　　　And thou shalt deck my couch with flow'rs,
　　　And wing with joy my silent hours.

　　　·When Sleep, with downy hand, shall spread
70　　A wreath of poppies round my head;
　　　Then, FANCY, on her wing sublime,
　　　Shall waft me to the sacred clime
　　　Where my enlighten'd sense shall view,
　　　Thro' ether realms of azure hue,
75　　That flame, where SHAKESPEARE us'd to fill,
　　　With matchless fire, his "golden quill."[1]
　　　While, from its point bright Genius caught
　　　The wit supreme, the glowing thought,
　　　The magic tone, that sweetly hung
80　　About the music of his tongue.
　　　Then will I skim the floating air,
　　　On a light couch of gossamer,
　　　While with my wonder-aching eye,
　　　I contemplate the spangled sky,
85　　And hear the vaulted roof repeat
　　　The song of Inspiration sweet;
　　　While round the winged cherub train,
　　　Shall iterate the aëry strain:
　　　Swift, thro' my quiv'ring nerves shall float
90　　The tremours of each thrilling note;
　　　And every eager sense confess
　　　Extatic transport's wild excess:
　　　'Till, waking from the glorious dream,
　　　I hail the morn's refulgent beam.

1　The phrase "golden quill" has a number of possible poetic precedents, including
　　William Shakespeare's Sonnet 85 ("comments of your praise, richly compil'd,/
　　Reserve their character with golden quill"), Edmund Spenser's sonnet "The world
　　that cannot deeme of worthy things" ("Deepe in the closet of my parts entyre, /
　　her worth is written with a golden quill"), and Hannah Cowley's paean to Della
　　Crusca, "The Pen," which begins: "O! seize again thy golden quill, / And with its
　　point my bosom thrill." *The Poetry of Anna Matilda* (London: John Bell, 1788) 14.

Dear Maid! of ever-varying mien,   95
Exulting, pensive, gay, serene,
Now, in transcendent pathos drest,
Now, gentle as the turtle's breast;[1]
Where'er thy feath'ry steps shall lead,
To side-long hill, or flow'ry mead;   100
To sorrow's coldest, darkest cell,
Or where, by Cynthia's[2] glimm'ring ray,
The dapper fairies frisk and play
About some cowslip's golden bell;
And, in their wanton frolic mirth,   105
Pluck the young daisies from the earth,
To canopy their tiny heads,
And decorate their verdant beds;
While to the grass-hopper's shrill tune,
They quaff libations to the moon,   110
From acorn goblets, amply fill'd
With dew, from op'ning flow'rs distill'd
Or when the lurid tempest pours,
From its dark urn, impetuous show'rs,
Or from its brow's terrific frown,   115
Hurls the pale murd'rous lightnings down;
To thy enchanting breast I'll spring,
And shield me with thy golden wing.

Or when amidst ethereal fire,
Thou strik'st thy DELLA CRUSCAN lyre,[3]   120
While round, to catch the heavenly song,
Myriads of wond'ring seraphs throng:
Whether thy harp's empassioned strain
Pours forth an OVID's[4] tender pain;

---

1 Turtle-dove.
2 Latin name for Diana, goddess of the moon.
3 Della Crusca was the pen name of Robert Merry (1755-98), one of a number of
   poets associated with a school of poetry (of which Robinson's early odes serve as
   examples) renowned for its extravagant emotionalism and its ornamental descrip-
   tions.
4 Ovid, a Roman poet who lived from 43 B.C.-A.D.18, was banished by the emper-
   or Augustus to Tomis, a port on the extreme confines of the Roman empire. In

Or in PINDARIC[1] flights sublime
Re-echoes thro' the starry clime;
Thee I'll adore; transcendent guest,
And woo thee to my burning breast.

But, if thy magic pow'rs impart
One soft sensation to the heart,
If thy warm precepts can dispense
One thrilling transport o'er my sense;
Oh! keep thy gifts, and let me fly,
In APATHY's cold arms to die.

ODE TO MELANCHOLY

SORC'RESS of the Cave profound!
Hence, with thy pale and meagre train,
Nor dare my roseate bow'r profane,
Where light-heel'd mirth despotic reigns,
Slightly bound in feath'ry chains,
And scatt'ring blisses round.

Hence, to thy native Chaos — where
Nurs'd by thy haggard Dam, DESPAIR,
Shackled by thy numbing spell,
Mis'ry's pallid children dwell;
Where, brooding o'er thy fatal charms,
FRENZY rolls the vacant eye;
Where hopeless LOVE, with folded arms,
Drops the tear, and heaves the sigh;
Till cherish'd Passion's tyrant sway
Chills the warm pulse of Youth, with premature decay.

O, fly Thee to some Church-yard's gloom,
Where beside the mould'ring tomb,

---

works such as the *Tristria* ("Sorrows") and *Epistulae ex Ponto* ("Letters from the Black Sea"), he made a series of pathetic pleas to the emperor, although to no avail.

1 Pindar (*c.*522–*c.*442 B.C.) was a Greek choral lyrist, particularly acclaimed for his odes, written to praise or glorify their subjects.

Restless Spectres glide away,
Fading in the glimpse of Day;   20
Or, where the Virgin ORB of Night,[1]
Silvers o'er the Forest wide,
Or across the silent tide,
Flings her soft, and quiv'ring light:
Where, beneath some aged Tree,   25
Sounds of mournful Melody
Caught from the NIGHTINGALE's enamour'd Tale,
Steal on faint Echo's ear, and float upon the gale.

DREAD POW'R! whose touch magnetic leads
O'er enchanted spangled meads,   30
Where by the glow-worm's twinkling ray,
Aëry Spirits lightly play;
Where, around some Haunted Tow'r,
Boding Ravens wing their flight,
Viewless, in the gloom of Night,   35
Warning oft the luckless hour;
Or, beside the Murd'rer's bed,
From thy dark, and morbid wing,
O'er his fev'rish, burning head,
Drops of conscious anguish fling;   40
While freezing HORROR's direful scream,
Rouses his guilty soul from kind oblivion's dream.

Oft, beneath the witching Yew,[2]
The trembling MAID, steals forth unseen;
With true-love wreaths, of deathless green,   45
Her Lover's grave to strew;
Her downcast Eye, no joy illumes,
Nor on her Cheek, the soft Rose blooms;
Her mourning Heart, the victim of thy pow'r,
Shrinks from the glare of Mirth, and hails the MURKY HOUR.   50

---

1   The moon.
2   The yew is often planted in cemeteries and is symbolic of sadness.

O, say what FIEND first gave thee birth,
    In what fell Desart wert thou born;
    Why does thy hollow voice, forlorn,
        So fascinate the Sons of Earth;
55   That once encircled in thy icy arms,
    They court thy torpid touch, and doat upon thy Charms?

HATED IMP, — I brave thy Spell,
    REASON shuns thy barb'rous sway;
    Life, with mirth should glide away,
60   Despondency, with guilt should dwell;
    For conscious TRUTH's unruffled mien,
Displays the dauntless Eye, and patient smile serene.

ODE TO THE NIGHTINGALE[1]

SWEET BIRD OF SORROW! — why complain
    In such soft melody of Song,
That ECHO, am'rous of thy Strain,
    The ling'ring cadence doth prolong?
5   Ah! tell me, tell me, why,
    Thy dulcet Notes ascend the sky.
    Or on the filmy vapours glide
    Along the misty mountain's side?
    And wherefore dost Thou love to dwell,
10   In the dark wood and moss-grown cell,
    Beside the willow-margin'd stream —
    Why dost Thou court wan Cynthia's beam?
    Sweet Songstress — if thy wayward fate
    Hath robb'd Thee of thy bosom's mate,
15   Oh, think not thy heart-piercing moan
        Evap'rates on the breezy air,
        Or that the plaintive Song of Care

---

1   According to myth, the nightingale's song is sweetest because it is saddest. Procne
    (or Philomela, depending on the account), who was changed into a nightingale by
    the gods, can never forget the son she killed. In this poem, the nightingale's song
    commemorates the loss of a mate, not a child.

Steals from THY Widow'd Breast alone.
Oft have I heard thy mournful Tale,
On the high Cliff, that o'er the Vale   20
Hangs its dark brow, whose awful shade
Spreads a deep gloom along the glade:
Led by its sound, I've wander'd far,
Till crimson evening's flaming Star
On Heav'n's vast dome refulgent hung,   25
And round ethereal vapours flung;
And oft I've sought th' HYGEIAN MAID,[1]
In rosy dimpling smiles array'd,
Till, forc'd with every HOPE to part,
Resistless Pain subdued my Heart.   30

Oh then, far o'er the restless deep
    Forlorn my poignant pangs I bore,
Alone in foreign realms to weep,
        Where ENVY's voice could taunt no more.
I hop'd, by mingling with the gay,   35
To snatch the veil of Grief away;
I hop'd, amid the joyous train,
To break Affliction's pond'rous chain;
VAIN was the Hope — in vain I sought
The placid hour of careless thought,   40
Where Fashion wing'd her light career,
    And sportive Pleasure danc'd along,
    Oft have I shunn'd the blithsome throng,
To hide th' involuntary tear,
    For e'en where rapt'rous transports glow,   45
From the full Heart the conscious tear will flow.
When to my downy couch remov'd,
    FANCY recalled my wearied mind
    To scenes of FRIENDSHIP left behind,
Scenes still regretted, still belov'd!   50
Ah, then I felt the pangs of Grief
Grasp my warm Heart, and mock relief;

---

1   Hygea: goddess of health.

My burning lids Sleep's balm defied,
And on my fev'rish lip imperfect murmurs died.

55   Restless and sad — I sought once more
     A calm retreat on BRITAIN's shore;
    Deceitful HOPE, e'en there I found
     That soothing FRIENDSHIP's specious name
    Was but a short-liv'd empty sound,
60   And LOVE a false delusive flame.

    Then come, Sweet BIRD, and with thy strain,
    Steal from my breast the thorn of pain;
    Blest solace of my lonely hours,
    In craggy caves and silent bow'rs;
65   When HAPPY Mortals seek repose,
    By Night's pale lamp we'll chaunt our woes,
    And, as her chilling tears diffuse
    O'er the white thorn their silv'ry dews,
    I'll with the lucid boughs entwine
70   A weeping Wreath, which round my Head
    Shall by the waning Crescent shine,
     And light us to our leafy bed. —
    But, ah! nor leafy beds nor bow'rs
    Fring'd with soft MAY's enamell'd flow'rs,
75   Nor pearly leaves, nor Cynthia's beams,
    Nor smiling Pleasure's shad'wy dreams,
    Sweet BIRD, not e'en THY melting Strains —
Can calm the Heart, where TYRANT SORROW REIGNS.

ODE TO DELLA CRUSCA[1]

ENLIGHTEN'D Patron of the sacred Lyre!
Whose ever-varying, ever-witching song
    Revibrates on the heart
    With magic thrilling touch,
Till ev'ry nerve, with quiv'ring throb divine,   5
In madd'ning tumults, owns thy wond'rous pow'r;
    For well thy dulcet notes
    Can wind the mazy song,
In labyrinth of wild fantastic form;
Or with empassion'd pathos woo the soul   10
    With sounds more sweetly mild,
    Than SAPPHO's[2] plaint forlorn,
When bending o'er the wave she sung her woes,
While pitying ECHO[3] hover'd o'er the deep,
    Till in their coral caves,   15
    The tuneful NEREIDES[4] wept.
Ah! whither art thou flown? where pours thy song?
The model and the pride of British bards!
    Sweet STAR of FANCY's orb,
    "O, tell me, tell me, where?"   20
Say, dost thou waste it on the viewless air
That bears it to the confines of high Heav'n?
    Or does it court the meed
    Of proud pre-eminence?
Or steals it o'er the glitt'ring Sapphire wave,   25
Calming the tempest with its silver sounds?
    Or does it charm to love

---

1   See note 3 on page 79.
2   Sappho (fl. ca. 610 - ca. 580 B.C.): an accomplished Greek poet whose persona Robinson adopted. Robinson became known as "the British Sappho" even before she wrote a series of sonnets based on Sappho's tragic love affair with Phaon.
3   A nymph who was punished by the goddess Hera for chattering too much while Hera was trying to spy on Zeus in his love affairs. Hera thought Echo was trying to help Zeus and so she decreed that the nymph would only be able to repeat the final syllables of others' speeches.
4   Nereids: sea-deities, the daughters of Nereus and Doris, and the granddaughters of Oceanus. They are sometimes said to personify the waves of the sea.

The fond believing maid?
Or does it hover o'er the ALPINE steep,
30   Or softly breathing under myrtle shades,
           With SYMPATHY divine,
           Solace the child of woe?
Where'er thou art, Oh! let thy gentle strain
Again with magic pow'r delight mine ear,
35   Untutor'd in the spells,
           And mysteries of song.
Then, on the margin of the deep I'll muse,
And bless the rocking bark[1] ordain'd to bear
           My sad heart o'er the wave,
40   From this ungrateful isle;
When the wan queen of night, with languid eye,
Peeps o'er the mountain's head, or thro' the vale
           Illumes the glassy brook,
           Or dew-besprinkled heath,
45   Or with her crystal lamp, directs the feet
Of the benighted TRAV'LLER, cold, and sad,
           Thro' the long forest drear,
           And pathless labyrinth,
To the poor PEASANT's hospitable cot,
50   For ever open to the wretch forlorn;
           O, then I'll think on THEE,
           And iterate thy strain,
And chaunt thy matchless numbers o'er and o'er,
And I will court the sullen ear of night,
55   To bear the rapt'rous sound,
           On her dark shad'wy wing,
To where encircled by the sacred NINE,[2]
Thy LYRE awakes the never-dying song!
           Now, BARD admir'd, farewell!
60   The white sail flutters loud,
The gaudy streamers lengthen in the gale,
Far from my native shore I bend my way;
           Yet, as my aching eye

---

1   Small ship.
2   The nine Muses, divine singers whose hymns delighted the gods.

Shall view the less'ning cliff,
'Till its stupendous head shall scarce appear   65
Above the surface of the swelling deep;
    I'll snatch a ray of hope,
    For HOPE's the lamp divine
That lights and vivifies the fainting soul,
With extacies beyond the pow'rs of song!   70
    That ere I reach those banks
    Where the loud TIBER[1] flows,
Or milder ARNO[2] slowly steals along,
To the soft music of the summer breeze,
    The wafting wing of TIME   75
    May bear this last ADIEU,
This wild, untutor'd picture of the heart,
To HIM, whose magic verse INSPIR'D THE STRAIN.

LINES TO HIM WHO WILL UNDERSTAND THEM[3]

THOU art no more my bosom's FRIEND;
Here must the sweet delusion end,
That charm'd my senses many a year,
Thro' smiling summers, winters drear. —
O, FRIENDSHIP! am I doom'd to find   5
Thou art a phantom of the mind?
A glitt'ring shade, an empty name,
An air-born vision's vap'rish flame?
And yet, the dear DECEIT so long
Has wak'd to joy my matin song,   10
Has bid my tears forget to flow,

---

1   The river that runs through Rome.
2   A river that flows through Florence and Pisa on its way to the Mediterranean.
3   First published in the *World* on October 31, 1788, under the pen name of Laura, the
    poem is apparently addressed to Banastre Tarleton who was, at that time, campaign-
    ing for the Liverpool seat in Parliament. The poem is incorporated into the second
    volume of Robinson's 1801 *Memoirs* surrounded by the following contextual infor-
    mation: "Conversing one evening with Mr. Richard Burke [Son of the celebrated
    Edmund Burke (M.R.)], respecting the facility with which modern poetry was
    composed, Mrs. Robinson repeated nearly the whole of those beautiful lines, which

Chas'd ev'ry pain, sooth'd ev'ry woe;
That TRUTH, unwelcome to my ear,
Swells the deep sigh, recalls the tear,
15   Gives to the sense the keenest smart,
Checks the warm pulses of the Heart,
Darkens my FATE and steals away
Each gleam of joy thro' life's sad day.

BRITAIN, FAREWELL! I quit thy shore,
20   My native Country charms no more;
No guide to mark the toilsome road;
No destin'd clime; no fix'd abode;
Alone and sad, ordain'd to trace
The vast expanse of endless space;
25   To view, upon the mountain's height,
Thro' varied shades of glimm'ring light,
The distant landscape fade away
In the last gleam of parting day: —
Or, on the quiv'ring lucid stream,
30   To watch the pale moon's silv'ry beam;
Or when, in sad and plaintive strains
The mournful PHILOMEL¹ complains,

---

were afterward given to the public, addressed — '*To him who will understand them.*'...
This *improvisatoré* produced in her auditor not less surprise than admiration, when
solemnly assured by its author that this was the first time of its being repeated. Mr.
Burke entreated her to commit the poem to writing, a request which was readily
complied with. Mrs. Robinson had afterwards the gratification of finding this
offspring of her genius inserted in The Annual Register, with a flattering encomi-
um from the pen of the eloquent and ingenious editor" [The Right Honourable
Edmund Burke, at that time conductor of The Annual Register (M.R.)](2:116 and
120-121).

1   In mythology, Philomela was the sister-in-law of Tereus who, according to one ver-
sion of the story, raped her and cut out her tongue so that she could not reveal to
his wife Procne what he had done. Philomela managed to communicate with Proc-
ne through a tapestry she wove. To punish Tereus, Procne killed their son Itys, and
served him to her husband in a stew. When Tereus discovered what had happened,
he set out in pursuit of the sisters, but they were rescued by the gods who changed
them into birds. Procne became a nightingale (a bird noted for its beautiful song)
and Philomela became a swallow (a bird that makes only twittering noises). In
some versions of this story, the roles are reversed; this perhaps explains why poets
have come to associate the name Philomela with the nightingale.

In dulcet notes bewails her fate,
And murmurs for her absent mate;
Inspir'd by SYMPATHY divine,   35
I'll weep her woes — FOR THEY ARE MINE.
Driven by my FATE, where'er I go
O'er burning plains, o'er hills of snow,
Or on the bosom of the wave,
The howling tempest doom'd to brave,   40
Where'er my lonely course I bend,
Thy image shall my steps attend;
Each object I am doom'd to see,
Shall bid remembrance PICTURE THEE.

   Yes; I shall view thee in each FLOW'R,   45
That changes with the transient hour:
Thy wand'ring Fancy I shall find
Borne on the wings of every WIND:
Thy wild impetuous passions trace
O'er the white wave's tempestuous space: 50
In every changing season prove
An emblem of thy wav'ring LOVE.

   Torn from my country, friends, and you,
The World lies open to my view;
New objects shall my mind engage;   55
I will explore th' HISTORIC page;
Sweet POETRY shall soothe my soul;
PHILOSOPHY each pang controul:
The MUSE I'll seek, her lambent fire
My soul's quick senses shall inspire;   60
With finer nerves my heart shall beat,
Touch'd by Heaven's own PROMETHEAN[1] heat;
ITALIA's gales shall bear my song
In soft-link'd notes her woods among;
Upon the blue hill's misty side,   65

---

1   Prometheus stole fire from the sun and gave it to mortals against the wishes of
    Zeus. Zeus punished Prometheus by binding him to a rock and sending an eagle to
    peck at his liver, which would continually regenerate itself.

Thro' trackless desarts waste and wide,
O'er craggy rocks, whose torrents flow
Upon the silver sands below.
Sweet Land of MELODY! 'tis thine
70   The softest passions to refine;
Thy myrtle groves, thy melting strains,
Shall harmonize and soothe my pains.
Nor will I cast one thought behind,
On foes relentless, FRIENDS unkind;
75   I feel, I feel their poison'd dart
Pierce the life-nerve within my heart;
'Tis mingled with the vital heat,
That bids my throbbing pulses beat;
Soon shall that vital heat be o'er,
80   Those throbbing pulses beat no more!
No — I will breathe the spicy gale;
Plunge the clear stream, new health exhale;
O'er my pale cheek diffuse the rose,
And drink OBLIVION to my woes.

LINES INSCRIBED
TO P. DE LOUTHERBOURG, Esq. R.A.

ON SEEING HIS VIEWS IN SWITZERLAND, &C. &C.[1]

WHERE on the bosom of the foamy RHINE,
In curling waves the rapid waters shine;
Where tow'ring cliffs in awful grandeur rise,
And midst the blue expanse embrace the skies;
5   The wond'ring eye beholds yon craggy height,
Ting'd with the glow of Evening's fading light:
Where the fierce cataract swelling o'er its bound,

---

1   Philippe Jacques de Loutherbourg (1740-1812), painter and Royal Academician, earned a reputation as a painter of wild romantic landscapes in the manner of Salvator Rosa. From the early 1770s to the mid-1780s, he was the chief designer of scenery at Drury Lane Theatre. He exhibited a painting entitled "View in Switzerland" at the Royal Academy in 1791. A similar painting, "Falls of the Rhine at Schaffhausen," was exhibited at the Royal Academy in 1788.

Bursts from its source, and dares the depth profound.
On ev'ry side the headlong currents flow,
Scatt'ring their foam like silv'ry sands below: 10
From hill to hill responsive echoes sound,
Loud torrents roar, and dashing waves rebound:
Th' opposing rock, the azure stream divides
The white froth tumbling down its sparry[1] sides;
From fall to fall the glitt'ring channels flow,   15
'Till lost, they mingle in the Lake below.
Tremendous spot! amid thy views sublime,
The mental sight ethereal realms may climb,
With wonder rapt the mighty work explore,
Confess TH' ETERNAL's pow'r! and pensively adore!   20

    ALL VARYING NATURE! oft the outstretch'd eye
Marks o'er the WELKIN's[2] brow the meteor fly:
Marks, where the COMET with impetuous force,
O'er Heaven's wide concave, skims its fiery course:
While on the ALPINE steep thin vapours rise,   25
Float on the blast — or freeze amidst the skies:
Or half congeal'd in flaky fragments glide
Along the gelid mountain's breezy side;
Or, mingling with the waste of yielding snow,
From the vast height in various currents flow.   30

    Now pale-ey'd MORNING, at thy soft command,
O'er the rich landscape spreads her dewy hand:
Swift o'er the plain the lucid rivers fly,
Imperfect mirrors of the dappled sky:
On the fring'd margin of the dimpling tide,   35
Each od'rous bud, by FLORA's[3] pencil dy'd,
Expands its velvet leaves of lust'rous hue,
Bath'd in the essence of celestial dew:
While from the METEOR to the simplest FLOW'R,
Prolific Nature! we behold thy pow'r!   40

---

1   Studded with crystals.
2   Welkin: poetic term for sky.
3   Goddess of flowers.

Yet has mysterious Heaven with care consign'd
Thy noblest triumphs to the human mind;
MAN feels the proud pre-eminence impart
Intrepid firmness to his swelling heart;
45   Creation's lord! where'er HE bends his way,
The torch of REASON spreads its godlike ray.

    As o'er SICILIAN sands the Trav'ller roves,
Feeds on its fruits, and shelters in its groves,
Sudden amidst the calm retreat he hears
50   The pealing thunders in the distant spheres;
He sees the curling fumes from ETNA[1] rise,
Shade the green vale, and blacken all the skies.
Around his head the forked lightnings glare,
The vivid streams illume the stagnant air:
55   The nodding hills hang low'ring o'er the deep,
The howling winds the clust'ring vineyards sweep;
The cavern'd rocks terrific tremours rend;
Low to the earth the tawny forests bend:
While *He*, an ATOM in the direful scene,
60   Views the wild CHAOS, wond'ring, and serene;
Tho' at his feet sulphureous rivers roll,
No touch of terror shakes his conscious soul:
His MIND! enlighten'd by PROMETHEAN rays
Expanding, glows with intellectual blaze!

65   Such scenes, long since, th' immortal POET[2] charm'd,
His MUSE enraptur'd, and his FANCY warm'd:
From them he learnt with magic eye t' explore
The dire ARCANUM[3] of the STYGIAN[4] shore!
Where the departed spirit trembling, hurl'd
70   "With restless violence round the pendent world,"[5]

---

1   Mount Aetna is a volcano on the east coast of Sicily in Italy. It is the highest and
    most active European volcano.
2   John Milton (1608–74).
3   A mystery or profound secret.
4   Stygian refers to the river Styx, one of the rivers that separate the underworld, or
    realm of the dead, from the world above.
5   Shakespeare's *Measure for Measure*, [M.R.] 3.i.125.

On the swift wings of whistling whirlwinds flung,
Plung'd in the wave, or on the mountain hung.

   While o'er yon cliff the ling'ring fires of day,
In ruby shadows faintly glide away;
The glassy source that feeds the CATARACT's stream   75
Bears the last image of the solar beam:
Wide o'er the Landscape Nature's tints disclose,
The softest picture of sublime repose;
The sober beauties of EVE's hour serene,
The scatter'd village, now but dimly seen,   80
The neighb'ring rock, whose flinty brow inclin'd,
Shields the clay cottage from the northern wind:
The variegated woodlands scarce we view,
The distant mountains ting'd with purple hue:
Pale twilight flings her mantle o'er the skies,   85
From the still lake, the misty vapours rise;
Cold show'rs, descending on the western breeze,
Sprinkle with lucid drops the bending trees,
Whose spreading branches o'er the glade reclin'd,
Wave their dank leaves, and murmur to the wind.   90

   Such scenes, O LOUTHERBOURG! thy pencil fir'd,
Warm'd thy great mind, and every touch inspir'd:
Beneath thy hand the varying colours glow,
Vast mountains rise, and crystal rivers flow:
Thy wond'rous Genius owns no pedant rule,   95
Nature's thy guide, and Nature's works thy school:
Pursue her steps, each rival's art defy,
For while she charms, THY NAME shall never die.

THE ADIEU TO LOVE[1]

LOVE, I renounce thy tyrant sway,
   I mock thy fascinating art,
MINE, be the calm unruffled day,
   That brings no torment to the heart;
The tranquil mind, the noiseless scene,
Where FANCY, with enchanting mien,
Shall in her right-hand lead along
The graceful *patroness of Song*;
Where HARMONY shall softly fling
Her light tones o'er the dulcet string;
And with her magic LYRE compose
Each pang that throbs, each pulse that glows;
Till her resistless strains dispense,
The balm of blest INDIFFERENCE.

Love, I defy thy vaunted pow'r!
In still Retirement's sober bow'r
I'll rest secure; — no fev'rish pain
Shall dart its hot-shafts thro' my brain,
No start'ling dreams invade my mind
No spells my stagnate pulses bind;
No jealous agonies impart
Their madd'ning poisons to my heart;
But sweetly lull'd to placid rest,
The sensate tenant of my breast
Shall one unshaken course pursue,
Such as thy vot'ries never knew. —

Sweet SOLITUDE! pure Nature's child,
Fair pensive daughter of the wild;
Nymph of the Forest; thee I press
My weary sick'ning soul to bless;
To give my heart the dear repose,

---

1   This poem was not reprinted in Robinson's *Poetical Works*. Perhaps either Robinson
or her daughter wanted distance from the persona of this poem, with her allusions
to a life in the thrall of passion.

That smiles unmov'd at transient woes;
That shelter'd from Life's trivial cares,
Each calm delicious comfort shares;
While conscious rectitude of mind,   35
Blends with each thought a bliss refin'd,
And scorning fear's soul-chilling pow'r,
Dares court REFLECTION's dang'rous hour,
To scrutinize with cautious art,
Each hidden channel of the heart. —   40

    Ah, gentle maiden, let me stray,
Where Innocence for ever gay,
Shall lead me to her loveliest bow'rs
And crown my brow with thornless flow'rs;
And strew the weedy paths of time   45
With Resignation's balm sublime;
While Rosy SPRING, shall smiling haste,
On light steps o'er the dewy waste,
Eager her brightest gems to shed
Around my verdant perfum'd bed;   50
And in her train the glowing hours
Shall bathe their wings in scented show'rs;
And shake the fost'ring drops to earth,
To nurse meek blossoms into birth;
And when autumnal zephyrs fly   55
Sportive, beneath the sapphire sky,
Or in the stream their pinions lave,[1]
Or teach the golden sheaves to wave;
I'll watch the ruby eye of day
In awful lustre glide away,   60
And closing sink to transient rest,
On panting Ocean's pearly breast.

    O SOLITUDE! how blest the lot
Of her who shares thy silent cot!
Who with celestial peace, pursues   65

---

1 Pinions being laved are wings being washed.

The pensive wand'rings of the MUSE;
To stray unseen where'er she leads,
O'er grassy hills and sunny meads,
Or at the still of Night's cold noon
70   To gaze upon the chilly Moon,
While PHILOMELA's mournful Song
Meanders fairy haunts among,
To tell the hopeless LOVER's ear,
That SYMPATHY's FOND BIRD is near;
75   Whose note shall soothe his aching heart,
Whose grief shall emulate his smart;
And by its sadly proud excess,
Make every pang he suffers less;
For oft in passion's direst woes,
80   The veriest wretch can yield repose;
While from the voice of kindred grief,
We gain a sad, but kind relief.

AH LOVE! thou barb'rous fickle boy,
Thou semblance of delusive joy,
85   Too long my heart has been thy slave:
For thou hast seen me wildly rave,
And with impetuous frenzy haste,
Heedless across the thorny waste,
And drink the cold dews, ere they fell
90   On my bare bosom's burning swell;
When bleak the wintry whirlwinds blew;
And swift the sultry meteors flew;
Yes, thou hast seen me, tyrant pow'r,
At freezing midnight's witching hour,
95   Start from my couch, subdu'd, oppres'd,
While jealous anguish wrung my breast,
While round my eager senses flew,
Dark brow'd Suspicion's wily crew,
Taunting my soul with restless ire,
100   That set my pulsate brain on fire.
What didst thou then? Inhuman Boy!
Didst thou not paint each well-feign'd joy,

Each artful smile, each study'd grace
That deck'd some sordid rival's face;
Didst thou not feed my madd'ning sense   105
With Love's delicious eloquence,
While on my ear thy accents pour'd
The voice of him my soul ador'd,
His rapt'rous tones — his strains divine,
And all those vows that once were mine.   110
But mild Reflection's piercing ray,
Soon chas'd the fatal dream away,
And with it all my rending woes,
While in its place majestic rose
The Angel TRUTH! — her stedfast mien   115
Bespoke the conscious breast serene;
Her eye more radiant than the day
Beam'd with persuasion's temper'd ray;
Sweet was her voice, and while she sung
    Myriads of Seraphs hover'd round,   120
    Eager to iterate the sound,
That on her heav'n-taught accents hung.
Wond'ring I gaz'd! my throbbing breast,
Celestial energies confest;
Transports, before unfelt, unknown,   125
Throng'd round my bosom's tremb'ling throne,
While ev'ry nerve with rapture strange,
Seem'd to partake the blissful change.

    Now with unmov'd and dauntless Eye,
I mark thy winged arrows fly;   130
No more thy baneful spells shall bind
The purer passions of my mind;
No more, false Love, shall jealous fears
Inflame my cheek with scalding tears;
Or shake my vanquish'd sense, or rend   135
    My aching heart with poignant throes,
Or with tumultuous fevers blend,
    Self-wounding, visionary woes. —
No more I'll waste the midnight hour

140 In expectation's silent bow'r;
And musing o'er thy transcripts dear,
Efface their sorrows with a tear.
No more with timid fondness wait
Till morn unfolds her glitt'ring gate,
145 When thy lov'd song's seraphic sound,
Wou'd on my quiv'ring nerves rebound
With proud delight; — no more thy blush
Shall o'er my cheek unbidden rush,
And scorning ev'ry strong controul,
150 Unveil the tumults of my soul.
No more when in retirement blest,
Shalt thou obtrude upon my rest;
And tho' encircled with delight,
Absorb my sense, obscure my sight,
155 Give to my eye the vacant glance,
The mien that marks the mental trance;
The fault'ring tone — the sudden start,
The trembling hand, the bursting heart;
The devious step, that strolls along
160 Unmindful of the gazing throng;
The feign'd indiff'rence prone to chide;
That blazons[1] — what it seeks to hide.

Nor do I dread thy vengeful wiles,
Thy soothing voice, thy winning smiles,
165 Thy trick'ling tear, thy mien forlorn,
Thy pray'r, thy sighs, thy oaths I scorn;
No more on ME thy arrows show'r,
Capricious Love — I BRAVE THY POW'R.

---

1   Blazon: to publish or announce in a way that draws attention.

STANZAS TO FLORA[1]

LET OTHERS wreaths of ROSES twine
With scented leaves of EGLANTINE;
Enamell'd buds and gaudy flow'rs,
The pride of FLORA's painted bow'rs;
Such common charms shall ne'er be wove   5
Around the brows of him I LOVE.

Fair are their beauties for a day,
But swiftly do they fade away;
Each PINK sends forth its choicest sweet
AURORA's[2] warm embrace to meet;   10
And each inconstant breeze, that blows,
Steals essence from the musky ROSE.

Then lead me, FLORA, to some vale,
Where, shelter'd from the fickle gale,
In modest garb, amidst the gloom,   15
The constant MYRTLE[3] sheds perfume;
And hid secure from prying eyes,
In spotless beauty BLOOMS and DIES.

And should its velvet leaves dispense
No pow'rful odours to the sense;   20
Should no proud tints of gaudy hue
With dazz'ling lustre pain the view;
Still shall its verdant boughs defy
The northern blast, and wintry sky.

Ah, VENUS! should this hand of mine   25
Steal from thy tree a wreath divine,
Assist me, while I fondly bind

---

1   Flora is the personification of nature's power to produce flowers. She is the goddess
    of flowers in mythology.
2   Roman goddess of the dawn.
3   An emblem of love because of its association with Venus, the goddess of love and
    beauty.

Two Hearts, by holy FRIENDSHIP join'd;
Thy cherish'd branches then shall prove,
30   Sacred to TRUTH, as well as LOVE.

OBERON TO THE QUEEN OF THE FAIRIES[1]

"My OBERON, with ev'ry sprite
That gilds the vapours of the night,
Shall dance and weave the verdant ring
With joy that mortals thus can sing;
And when thou sigh'st MARIA's name,
And mourn'st to feel a hopeless flame,
Eager they'll catch the tender note
Just parting from thy tuneful throat,
And bear it to the careless ear
Of her who scorn'd a lover's tear."

Queen of the Fairies to Il Ferito
ORACLE, June 2, 1790

SWEET MAB![2] at thy command I flew
O'er glittering floods of midnight dew,
O'er many a silken violet's head,
Unpress'd by vulgar mortal tread;
5   Eager to execute thy will,
I mounted on the ZEPHYR's wing,
And bid her whisp'ring tongue be still,
Nor thro' the air its murmurs fling.

Cold CYNTHIA hid her silver bow[3]
10   Beneath her azure spangled vest;

---

1   This poem was first published in the *Oracle* of June 3, 1790, the day after the poem
entitled "Queen of the Fairies to Il Ferito" from which Robinson quotes in the
epigraph. Oberon was one of Robinson's pen names, apparently inspired by the
king of the fairies in Shakespeare's *A Midsummer Night's Dream*.
2   Queen Mab, "the fairies' midwife," is described in a fanciful speech Mercutio makes
to Romeo in *Romeo and Juliet*, Act 1, Scene 4.
3   Cynthia: alternate name for Diana or Artemis, the huntress (hence the silver bow),
who was born at Mount Cynthus in Delos. She is associated with the moon.

No gentle ray my wand'rings blest,
Save the small night-worm's twinkling glow.
Upon the budding thorn I found
A veil of gossamer, which bound
My tiny head; — about my waist   15
    A scarf of magic pow'r I threw,
With many a crystal dew-drop grac'd,
    And deck'd with leaves of various hue.

    Thus, gaily dress'd, I reach'd the grove,
Where, like the Paphian Queen of Love[1]   20
Upon a bank of lillies fair
MARIA[2] slept; the am'rous air
Snatch'd nectar from her balmy lips,
Sweeter than haughty JUNO[3] sips,
When GANYMEDE[4] her goblet fills   25
With juice, the citron bud distills.

    Her breast was whiter than the down
That on the RING-DOVE's bosom grows;
Her cheek, more blushing than the rose
    That blooms on FLORA's May-day crown!   30
Beneath her dark and "fringed lid,"
I spy'd LOVE's glittering arrows hid;
I listen'd to the dulcet song
That trembled on her tuneful tongue;
And, "IL FERITO"[5] was the sound   35
The babbling echo whisper'd round:
The blissful moment swift I caught,
    And to the maiden's slumb'ring thought

---

1 Paphos is a city of Cyprus sacred to Aphrodite or Venus, the goddess of love and
    beauty.
2 Maria was the name of Robinson's daughter.
3 Zeus's wife and sister. She is most often depicted punishing the many women Zeus
    fell in love with. She was the goddess married women looked to for help.
4 A cupbearer to the gods. He was a beautiful young Trojan prince who was seized by
    Zeus's eagle and carried up to Olympus.
5 Della Crusca [M.R.]. This pseudonym of Robert Merry translates from the Italian
    as "the wounded man."

Pictur'd the graces of his mind,
His taste, his eloquence refin'd!
His polish'd manners sweetly mild!
His soft poetic warblings wild!
His warm impassion'd verse, that fills
The soul with Love's extatic thrills.

I mark'd the blush upon her cheek,
Her spotless bosom's language speak;
I mark'd the tear of pity roll,
Sweet emblem of her feeling soul:
I heard the sympathetic sigh

Upon her lips vermilion die.
When busy LOVE too eager sped
His light steps near the charmer's bed;
His pinions[1] rustling thro' the air
Awoke the trembling spotless fair;

Swiftly her radiant eyes unclose,
When, on my filmy wing I rose
Sweet MAB the rapt'rous tale to bear,
To "IL FERITO's" GRATEFUL EAR.

SONNET.

WRITTEN AMONG THE RUINS OF AN ANCIENT CASTLE IN GERMANY, IN THE YEAR 1786

Ye mould'ring walls where Titian colours[2] glow'd,
And the soft minstrel's echo charm'd the ear;
Alas! how chang'd your dreary haunts appear,
The solitary Screech-owl's dark abode.

---

1   Wings.
2   Tiziano Vecellio (c. 1477-1578), known as Titian, was an Italian painter who domi-
    nated Venetian art during its greatest era. He was known for his distinctive use of
    colour, first the employment of primary blues and reds, and, later in his career,
    yellows and pale shades as he began to juxtapose related rather than contrasting
    hues.

Where in yon gothic hall fair forms divine,   5
    Trip'd with light heel, or swam with graceful ease;
Now clasping ivy round the columns twine,
    And loathsome weeds infect the midnight breeze.

Those turrets wasting in the northern blast,
    No more with burnish'd radiance proudly glow,   10
But in small fragments on the pavement cast,
    Heap the wild ruin on the plain below;
Mingling with dust thy mighty roofs are laid,
So MAN, the grandest work of Heav'n, SHALL FADE.

AINSI VA LE MONDE[1]

O THOU, to whom superior worth's allied,
Thy Country's honour — and the Muses' pride;
Whose pen gives polish to the varying line
That blends instruction with the song divine;
Whose fancy, glancing o'er the hostile plain,   5
Plants a fond trophy o'er the mighty slain;[2]

---

1 "So goes the world." The 1791 version of the poem, reprinted here, has the follow-
ing inscription above the title: "As a Tribute of Esteem and Admiration this Poem is
inscribed to ROBERT MERRY, Esq. A.M. Member of the Royal Academy at Flo-
rence, and Author of the Laurel of Liberty, and the Della Crusca Poems." The ver-
sion of the poem in the 1806 edition has two subheadings: "Inscribed to a Friend"
and "Written at the beginning of the French Revolution." The poem was published
independently by John Bell in 1790 in an edition that was attributed to Laura Maria
(one of Robinson's pen names) and dedicated to Robert Merry. The poem was
reprinted in Robinson's 1791 *Poems* and in the posthumous *Memoirs* (1801) which
includes the following note: "In 1791, Mrs. Robinson produced her quarto poem,
entitled 'Ainsi va le Monde.' This work, containing three hundred and fifty lines,
was written in twelve hours, as a reply to Mr. Merry's 'Laurel of Liberty,' which was
sent to Mrs. Robinson on a Saturday; on the *Tuesday following* the answer was *com-
posed and given to the public*" (2: 127). In the version of the poem printed in the 1806
Poetical Works, the two mentions of Merry within the poem are erased.

2 See the elegy written on the plains of Fontenoy, by Robert Merry, Esq. [M.R.].
"Elegy, written on the Plain of Fontenoy" appeared in the *New Annual Register* for
1788, with "Stanzas to Della Crusca, occasioned by the above Elegy." Both poems
were reprinted from *The Poetry of Anna Matilda* (1788). Della Crusca and Anna
Matilda were pseudonyms for Robert Merry and Hannah Cowley.

Or to the daisied lawn directs its way,
Blithe as the songstress of returning day;
Who deign'd to rove where twinkling glow-worms lead
10   The tiny legions o'er the glitt'ring mead;
Whose liquid notes in sweet meand'rings flow,
Mild as the murmurs of the Bird of Woe;
Who gave to Sympathy its softest pow'r,
The charm to wing Affliction's sable hour;
15   Who in *Italia's* groves, with thrilling song,
Call'd mute attention from the minstrel throng;
Gave proud distinction to the Poet's name,
And claim'd, by modest worth, the wreath of fame——
Accept the Verse thy magic harp inspires,
20   Nor scorn the Muse that kindles at its fires.

O, justly gifted with the Sacred Lyre,
Whose sounds can more than mortal thoughts inspire,
Whether its strings HEROIC measures move,
Or lyric numbers charm the soul to love;
25   Whether thy fancy "pours the varying verse"
In bow'rs of bliss, or o'er the plumed hearse;
Whether of patriot zeal, or past'ral sports,
The peace of hamlets, or the pride of courts:
Still Nature glows in ev'ry classic line——
30   Still Genius dictates — still the verse is *thine*.

Too long the Muse, in ancient garb array'd,
Has pin'd neglected in oblivion's shade;
Driv'n from the sun-shine of poetic fame,
Stripp'd of each charm she scarcely boasts a name:
35   Her voice no more can please the vapid throng,
No more loud Paeans consecrate her song,
Cold, faint, and sullen, to the grove she flies,
A faded garland veils her radiant eyes:
A with'ring laurel on her breast she wears,
40   Fann'd by her sighs, and spangled with her tears;
From her each fond associate early fled,
She mourn'd a MILTON lost, a SHAKSPERE dead:

Her eye beheld a CHATTERTON[1] oppress'd,
A famish'd OTWAY[2] — ravish'd from her breast;
Now in their place a flutt'ring form appears,   45
Mocks her fall'n pow'r, and triumphs in her tears:
A flippant, senseless, aëry, thing, whose eye
Glares wanton mirth, and fulsome ribaldry.
While motley mumm'ry holds her tinsel reign,
SHAKSPERE might write, and GARRICK[3] act in vain: 50
True Wit recedes, when blushing Reason views
This spurious offspring of the banish'd Muse.

    The task be thine to check the daring hand
That leads fantastic folly o'er the land;
The task be thine with witching spells to bind   55
The feath'ry shadows of the fickle mind;
To strew with deathless flow'rs the dreary waste;
To pluck the weeds of vitiated taste;
To cheer with smiles the Muse's glorious toil,
And plant perfection on her native soil: 60
The Arts, that thro' dark centuries have pin'd,
Toil'd without fame, in sordid chains confin'd,
Burst into light with renovated fire,
Bid Envy shrink, and Ignorance expire.
No more prim KNELLER's simp'ring beauties vie,   65
Or LELY's genius droops with languid eye:[4]

---

1   Thomas Chatterton (1752-70), famous for carrying out an elaborate literary hoax,
the fabrication of the works of antique poets, most notably the "Rowley
Romance," purported to be the work of a fifteenth-century monk. He died impov-
erished, a suicide.

2   Thomas Otway (1652-85), a dramatist famous for plays such as *The Orphan* and
Venice Preserved. Like Chatterton, he died young, in poverty.

3   David Garrick (1717-79) was the most distinguished actor and theatre manager of
the late eighteenth century. He also gave Robinson her first role on the stage, cast-
ing her as Juliet in his production of Shakespeare's *Romeo and Juliet*.

4   Sir Godfrey Kneller (1646-1723), a painter noted for his portraits of aristocratic
subjects. He painted a series of twelve portraits of "Beauties" for Queen Mary, wife
of King William III; these were in imitation of a similar series carried out by Sir
Peter Lely (1618-80) for the Duchess of York. Lely was famous for the voluptuous-
ness of his female portraits. They were celebrated by Pope who wrote in his "First
Epistle of the Second Book of Horace, Imitated": "Lely on animated canvas stole, /
The sleepy eye that spoke the melting soul."

No more prepost'rous figures pain the view,
Aliens to Nature, yet to Fancy true,
The wild chimeras of capricious thought,
70 Deform'd in fashion, and with errors fraught;
The gothic phantoms sick'ning fade away,
And native Genius rushes into day.

REYNOLDS,[1] 'tis thine with magic skill to trace
The perfect semblance of exterior grace;
75 Thy hand, by Nature guided, marks the line
That stamps perfection on the form divine.
'Tis thine to tint the lip with rosy die,
To paint the softness of the melting eye;
With auburn curls luxuriantly display'd,
80 The ivory shoulders polish'd fall to shade;
To deck the well-turn'd arm with matchless grace,
To mark the dimpled smile on Beauty's face:
The task is thine, with cunning hand to throw
The veil transparent on the breast of snow:
85 The Statesman's thought, the Infant's cherub mien,
The Poet's fire, the Matron's eye serene,
Alike with animated lustre shine
Beneath thy polish'd pencil's touch divine.
As BRITAIN's Genius glories in thy Art,
90 Adores thy virtues, and reveres thy heart,
Nations unborn shall celebrate thy name,
And waft thy mem'ry on the wings of Fame.

Oft when the mind, with sick'ning pangs oppress'd,
Flies to the Muse, and courts the balm of rest,
95 When Reason, sated with life's weary woes,
Turns to *itself* — and finds a blest repose,

---

1 Sir Joshua Reynolds (1723-92) painted several portraits of Mary Robinson, as well
as famous paintings of her contemporaries Banastre Tarleton, the Prince of Wales,
and David Garrick. Reynolds was the first president of the Royal Academy, found-
ed in 1768. In that capacity, he gave a series of lectures which were published serial-
ly through the 1770s and 1780s and are known collectively as *Discourses*. Robinson
published a monody on the death of Reynolds, and a letter he wrote to her was
included in the collection of tribute poems published in the *Memoirs* 4:191-192.

A gen'rous pride that scorns each petty art,
That feels no envy rankling in the heart,
No mean deceit that wings its shaft at *Fame*,
Or gives to pamper'd *Vice* a pompous *Name*;   100
Then, calm reflection shuns the sordid crowd,
The senseless chaos of the *little* proud,
Then, indignation stealing through the breast,
Spurns the pert tribe in flimsy greatness drest;
Who, to their native nothingness consign'd,   105
Sink in contempt — nor leave a trace behind.
Then Fancy paints in visionary gloom,
The sainted shadows of the laurel'd tomb,[1]
The Star of Virtue glist'ning on each breast,
Divine insignia of the spirit blest!   110
Then MILTON smiles serene, a beauteous shade,
In worth august — in lust'rous fires array'd.
Immortal SHAKSPERE gleams across the sight,
Rob'd in ethereal vest of radiant light.
Wing'd Ages picture to the dazzled view   115
Each mark'd perfection — of the sacred few,
POPE, DRYDEN, SPENSER, all that Fame shall raise,
From CHAUCER's gloom — till MERRY's lucid days:
Then emulation kindles fancy's fire,
The glorious throng poetic flights inspire;   120
Each sensate bosom feels the god-like flame,
The cherish'd harbinger of future fame.
Yet timid genius, oft in conscious ease,
Steals from the world, content the few to please:
Obscur'd in shades, the modest Muse retires,   125
While sparkling vapours emulate her fires.
The proud enthusiast shuns promiscuous praise,
The Idiot's smile condemns the Poet's lays.
Perfection wisely courts the lib'ral few,
The voice of kindred genius must be true.   130

---

1   Robinson follows this reference to the "sainted shadows of the laurel'd tomb" with
    a roster of England's poets: John Milton (1608-74), Alexander Pope (1688-1744),
    John Dryden (1631-1700), Edmund Spenser (1552-99), Geoffrey Chaucer (1340-
    1400), and Robert Merry (1755-98).

But empty witlings sate the public eye
With puny jest and low buffoonery,
The buzzing hornets swarm about the great,
The poor appendages of pamper'd state;
135   The trifling, flutt'ring insects of a day
Flit near the sun, and glitter in its ray;
Whose subtle fires with charms magnetic burn,
Where every servile fool *may* have his turn.
Lull'd in the lap of indolence, they boast
140   Who best can fawn — and who can flatter most;
While with a cunning arrogance they blend
Sound without sense — and wit that stabs a friend;
Slanders oblique — that check ambition's toil,
The pois'nous weeds, that mark the barren soil.
145   So the sweet blossoms of salubrious spring
Thro the lone wood their spicy odours fling;
Shrink from the sun, and bow their beauteous heads
To scatter incense o'er their native beds,
While coarser flow'rs expand with gaudy ray,
150   Brave the rude wind, and mock the burning day.

     Ah! gentle Muse, from trivial follies turn,
Where Patriot souls with god-like passions burn;
Again to MERRY dedicate the line,
So shall the envied boast of taste be thine;
155   So shall thy song to glorious themes aspire,
"Warm'd with a spark" of his transcendent fire.

     Thro' all the scenes of Nature's varying plan,
Celestial Freedom warms the breast of man;
Led by her daring hand, what pow'r can bind
160   The boundless efforts of the lab'ring mind.
The god-like fervour, thrilling thro' the heart,
Gives new creation to each vital part;
Throbs rapture thro' each palpitating vein,
Wings the rapt thought, and warms the fertile brain;
165   To her the noblest attributes of Heav'n,
Ambition, valour, eloquence, are giv'n.

She binds the soldier's brow with wreaths sublime,
From her, expanding reason learns to climb,
To her the sounds of melody belong,
She wakes the raptures of the Poet's song;   170
'Tis god-like Freedom bids each passion live,
That truth may boast, or patriot virtue give;
From her, the Arts enlighten'd splendours own,
She guides the peasant — She adorns the throne;
To mild Philanthropy extends her hand,   175
Gives Truth pre-eminence, and Worth command;
Her eye directs the path that leads to Fame,
Lights Valour's torch, and trims the glorious flame;
She scatters joy o'er Nature's endless scope,
Gives strength to Reason — extacy to Hope;   180
Tempers each pang Humanity can feel,
And binds presumptuous Power with nerves of steel;
Strangles each tyrant Phantom in its birth,
And knows no title — but SUPERIOR WORTH.

    Enlighten'd Gallia![1] what were all your toys,   185
Your dazzling splendours — your voluptuous joys?
What were your glitt'ring villas — lofty tow'rs,
Your perfum'd chambers, and your painted bow'rs?
Did not insidious *Art* those gifts bestow,
To cheat the prying eye — with tinsel show?   190
Yes; luxury diffus'd her spells to bind
The deep researches of the restless mind;
To lull the active soul with witching wiles,
To hide pale Slav'ry in a mask of smiles:
The tow'ring wings of reason to restrain,   195
And lead the victim in a flow'ry chain:
Cold Superstition favour'd the deceit,
And e'en Religion lent her aid to cheat, —
When warlike LOUIS,[2] arrogant and vain,
Whom *worth* could never hold, or *fear* restrain;   200
The soul's last refuge, in repentance sought,

---

1   France.
2   Louis XIV [M.R.]. King of France from 1643 to 1715.

An artful MAINTENON[1] absolv'd each fault;
She who had led his worldly steps astray,
Now, "smooth'd his passage to the realms of day!"[2]
205   O, monstrous hypocrite! — who vainly strove
By pious fraud, to win a people's love;
Whose coffers groan'd with reliques from the proud,
The pompous off'rings of the venal crowd,
The massy hecatombs of dire disgrace,
210   To purchase titles, or secure a place. —
And yet — so sacred was the matron's fame,
Nor truth, nor virtue, dar'd assail her name;
None could approach but with obsequious breath,
To *smile* was TREASON — and to *speak* was DEATH.
215   In meek and humble garb, she veil'd command,
While helpless millions shrunk beneath her hand.
And when Ambition's idle dream was o'er,
And art could blind, and beauty charm no more;
She, whose luxurious bosom spurn'd restraint,
220   Who liv'd the slave of passion — died a saint![3]

What were the feelings of the hapless throng,
By threats insulted, and oppress'd with wrong?
While grasping avarice, with skill profound,
Spread her fell snares, and dealt destruction round;
225   Each rising sun some new infringement saw,
While pride was consequence — and pow'r was law;
A people's suff'rings hop'd redress in vain,
Subjection curb'd the tongue that *dar'd* complain.
Imputed guilt each virtuous victim led
230   Where all the fiends their direst mischiefs spread;

1   Françoise D'Aubigné, Marquise de Maintenon (1635-1719), was the governess of
     Louis XIV's illegitimate children by the Marquise de Montespan. She was secretly
     married to Louis XIV after the death of the Queen, Marie Thérèse. She was a
     devout Catholic and the religious intolerance of the King's later years is often
     attributed to her influence.
2   From Alexander Pope's "Eloisa to Abelard." The dying Eloisa exclaims: "Thou,
     Abelard! the last sad office pay, / And smooth my passage to the realms of day."
3   Madame de Maintenon died a perfect devotee at the convent of St. Cyr [M.R.].

Where, thro' long ages past, with watchful care,
THY TYRANTS, GALLIA, nurs'd the witch DESPAIR.
Where in her black BASTILE[1] the harpy fed
On the warm crimson drops, her fangs had shed;
Where recreant malice mock'd the suff'rer's sigh,   235
While regal lightnings darted from her eye. —
Where deep mysterious whispers murmur'd round,
And death stalk'd sullen o'er the treach'rous ground.
O DAY — transcendent on the page of Fame!
When from her Heav'n, insulted *Freedom* came;   240
Glancing o'er earth's wide space, her beaming eye
Mark'd the dread scene of impious slavery,
Warm'd by her breath, the vanquish'd, trembling race,
Wake from the torpid slumber of disgrace;
Rous'd by oppression, *Man* his birth-right claims,   245
O'er the proud battlements red vengeance flames;
Exulting thunders rend the turbid skies; —
In sulph'rous clouds the gorgeous ruin lies! —
The angel, PITY, now each cave explores,
Braves the chill damps, and fells the pond'rous doors,   250
Plucks from the flinty walls the clanking chains,
Where many a dreadful tale of woe remains,
Where many a sad memorial marks the hour,
That gave the *rights of man* to *rav'nous pow'r*;
Now snatch'd from death, the wond'ring wretch shall prove   255
The rapt'rous energies of social love;
Whose limbs each faculty denied — whose sight
Had long resign'd all intercourse with light;
Whose wasted form the humid earth receiv'd,
Who numb'd with anguish — scarcely felt he *liv'd*;   260
Who when the midnight bell assail'd his ears,
From fev'rish slumbers woke — to drink his tears:
While slow-consuming grief each sense enthrall'd,
'Till *Hope* expir'd, and *Valour* shrunk — appall'd:
Where veil'd suspicion lurk'd in shrewd disguise,   265

---

1   The Bastille was a French state prison attacked and captured on July 14, 1789, the
    moment conventionally cited as the beginning of the French Revolution.

While eager vengeance op'd her thousand eyes;
While the hir'd slave, the fiend of wrath, design'd
To lash, with scorpion scourges, human-kind —
Dragg'd with ingenious pangs, the tardy hour,
270   To feed the rancour of *insatiate Pow'r.*

   Blest be the favor'd delegates of Heav'n,
To whose illustrious souls the task was giv'n
To wrench the bolts of tyranny — and dare
The petrifying confines of despair;
275   With Heav'n's own breeze to chear the gasping breath,
And spread broad sun-shine in the caves of death.

   What is the charm that bids mankind disdain
The Tyrant's mandate, and th' Oppressor's chain;
What bids exulting Liberty impart
280   Extatic raptures to the Human Heart;
Calls forth each hidden spark of glorious fire,
Bids untaught minds to valiant feats aspire;
What gives to Freedom its supreme delight?
'Tis Emulation, Instinct, Nature, Right.

285   When this revolving Orb's first course began,
Heav'n stamp'd divine pre-eminence on man;
To him it gave the intellectual mind,
Persuasive Eloquence and Truth refin'd;
Humanity to harmonize his sway,
290   And calm Religion to direct his way;
Courage to tempt Ambition's lofty flight,
And Conscience to illume his erring sight.
Who shall the nat'ral Rights of Man[1] deride,
When Freedom spreads her fost'ring banners wide?
295   Who shall contemn the heav'n-taught zeal that throws
The balm of comfort on a Nation's woes?
That tears the veil from superstition's eye,

---

1   Thomas Paine's 1791 *Rights of Man*, a response to Edmund Burke's 1790 *Reflections on the Revolution in France*, was adopted as a manifesto by British sympathizers with the French Revolution. Robinson's poem first appeared in 1790.

Bids despots tremble, scourg'd oppression die?
Wrests hidden treasure from the sordid hand,
And flings profusion o'er a famish'd land? —   300
Nor yet, to GALLIA are her smiles confin'd,
She opes her radiant gates to *all mankind*;
Sure on the peopled earth there cannot be
A foe to Liberty — that dares be free.
Who that has tasted bliss will e'er deny   305
The magic power of thrilling extacy?
Who that has breath'd Health's vivifying breeze,
Would tempt the dire contagion of Disease?
Or prodigal of joy, his birth-right give
In shackled slavery — a wretch to live?   310

  Yet let Ambition hold a temp'rate sway,
When Virtue rules — 'tis Rapture to obey;
Man can but reign his transitory hour,
And *love* may bind — when *fear* has lost its pow'r.
Proud may he be who nobly acts his part,   315
Who boasts the empire of each subject's heart,
Whose worth, exulting millions shall approve,
Whose richest treasure — IS A NATION'S LOVE.

  Freedom — blithe Goddess of the rainbow vest,
In dimpled smiles and radiant beauties drest,   320
I court thee from thy azure-spangled bed
Where Ether floats about thy winged head;
Where tip-toe pleasure swells the choral song,
While gales of odour waft the Cherub throng;
On every side the laughing loves prepare   325
Enamel'd wreaths to bind thy flowing hair:
For thee the light-heel'd graces fondly twine,
To clasp thy yielding waist, a zone divine!
Venus for thee her crystal altar rears,
Deck'd with fresh myrtle — gemm'd with lovers' tears;   330
Apollo strikes his lyre's rebounding strings,[1]

---

1 Apollo, sometimes known as the sun god, is represented in Greek poetry as the
master musician who plays on a golden lyre.

Responsive notes divine Cecilia sings,[1]
The tuneful sisters prompt the heavenly choir,
335 Thy temple glitters with Promethean fire.
The sacred Priestess in the centre stands,
She strews the sapphire floor with flow'ry bands.
See! from her shrine electric incense rise;
Hark! "Freedom" echoes thro' the vaulted skies.
340 The Goddess speaks! O mark the blest decree, —
TYRANTS SHALL FALL — TRIUMPHANT MAN BE FREE!

---

1   St. Cecilia, a famous martyr, is the patron saint of church music. She is often represented playing an organ.

Is it in chambers silken drest,
At tables which profusions heap,
Is it on pillow soft to rest,
In dreams of long & balmy sleep?
                              Ah! no!

Figure 7. Mezzotint engraving after Maria Cosway, illustration No. 3 for "The Wintry Day,"
1804. (By courtesy of the Special Collections Department, University of Virginia Library.)

FROM *POEMS* (1793)

SIGHT[1]

INSCRIBED TO JOHN TAYLOR, ESQ.[2]

O THOU! all wonderful, all glorious Pow'r!
That through the SOUL diffusest light sublime,
And bidst it see th' omnipotence of God!
O SIGHT! to man the vivifying lamp,
5   That, darting through the intellectual maze,
Giv'st to each rising thought the living ray!
As the PROMETHEAN[3] touch awoke THAT source
Whose glory warms the PLANETARY world;
So THE SUPREME illum'd the VISUAL ORB,
10   To mark his works, and wonder at his pow'r!

Transcendent gift! but for thy light divine,
Oh! what a chaos were the mind of MAN!
Compos'd of atoms, exquisitely fine,
Each moving in a dark obstructed sphere,
15   Forlorn, and undelighted! for to him
Whose eye ne'er drank the widely beaming ray,
What are the wonders of the starry worlds;
Creation's fair domain, its gems, its hues,
And all its bright diversity of charms?
20   What are his faculties, his passions, thoughts?
HE labours through a wilderness obscure,
Each OTHER sense awaken'd; wanting still

---

1   Published in 1793 in *Sight, The Cavern of Woe, and Solitude* (London: Evans and Becket) and in *Poems* that same year.

2   John Taylor (1757-1832) served as eye doctor to George III and George IV. He later turned to journalism and became editor of the *Morning Post* in 1787. He was a friend of Robinson, whom he mentioned in his 1832 *Records of My Life*. The chatty letters she wrote to him, printed in the *Catalogue of the Collection of Autograph Letters and Historical Documents, Formed between 1865 and 1882 by A. Morrison*, edited by A. W. Thibaudeau (London: Strangeways and Sons, 1891), suggest a warm and friendly relationship. See Appendix A.

3   Prometheus gave the gift of fire to humankind.

THAT SENSE DIVINE, which gives to each its charm;
The earth, to HIM, a solitary speck,
For ever mournful, and for ever drear!   25

   Oblivion horrible! to know no change;
Nor light from darkness! nor the human form,
The image of perfection infinite!
To fashion various phantoms of the brain,
By each amus'd, and yet by each deceiv'd!   30
To roll the aching eye, alas! in vain,
And still to find a melancholy blank
Of years, and months, and days, and ling'ring hours,
All dark alike, eternally obscure!
To such a wretch! whose brightest hour of bliss   35
Is but the shadow of a waking dream,
The sleep of DEATH, with all its start'ling fears,
Would teem with prospects of ELYSIUM![1]
For what is *sleep*, but temporary *death*;
Sealing up all the windows of the soul,   40
And binding ev'ry sense in torpid chains?
Yet, only for a time the spell controuls,
And soothing visions gild the transient gloom;
For every active faculty of mind
Springs from the numbing apathy of sleep   45
With renovated lustre and delight!
But HE who knows ONE unenlighten'd void,
ONE dreary night, unbless'd with cheerful dreams,
Lives in the midst of Death; and, when he sleeps,
Feeds a perpetual solitude of woe,   50
Without one ray to dissipate its gloom.

   Then what to him avails the varying year,
The orient morn, or evening's purple shade,
That robes Creation in a garb of rest?
WHAT all the beauties of the vast expanse,   55
The tint cerulean,[2] or the vaulted arch

---

1   The realm of the blessed after death.
2   A shade of blue.

Of Heaven's eternal dome! Can FANCY paint,
With all the vivid magic of her pow'r,
The spangling legions of the sphery plains;
60   The gaudy-vested SUMMER's saffron glow,
When proudly gilded by its parent SUN,
As through the flaming Heav'ns his dazzling car,
Burnish'd with sparkling light, sheds liquid gold
O'er seas ethereal; while the breezes stay
65   To kiss the fainting flow'rs, whose silky heads
Inclining, fade beneath their with'ring touch?
Can FANCY give the rainbow's lustre pure
To the cold vacuum of the sightless eye?
Insensible to colours, space, or form,
70   Stumbling and fearful, through a desart shade,
MAN gropes forlorn, and lab'ring like the MOLE
He feels the vivifying glow divine;
But, 'midst the blaze of radiance infinite,
An isolated being, wanders still,
75   Sad, unillum'd, disconsolate, and lost!

        Nor yet alone the misery extreme
Of the dread gloom opake involves his mind;
The longing for that SOMETHING yet unknown,
Whose pow'r he feels, diffusing its warm touch
80   O'er ev'ry sensate nerve! that POW'R which marks
The varying seasons in their varying forms,
That tells him there is YET a sense untry'd,
Ungratified, yet fraught with heavenly bliss,
Distracts beyond the certitude of pain,
85   Chills the expanding source of mental joy,
And deadens all the faculties of man!

        AH! woe too exquisite for human thought!
Of mortal miseries, the DREAD supreme!
How can the soul its energies sustain,
90   When REASON's crystal gates are clos'd in night,
And cold Oblivion hovers o'er the mind?
What are the horrors of the dungeon's gloom,

The bolts of steel, or the flint-fretted roof,
The temporary spells that shut the wretch
From the bland glories of effulgent day? 95
While HOPE comes smiling on the wings of TIME,
And the small crevice in his loathsome cell,
That promises a glimm'ring stream of light,
Bids him look forward to the coming joy!
What are the self-created, anxious fears, 100
That, thronging round the midnight traveller,
Give to his straining eye, fantastic forms,
And fill imagination's boundless scope
With shad'wy hosts, scaring his startled mind;
While silence reigns despotic o'er the plain; 105
Save where the BIRD OF SOLITUDE salutes
The melancholy hour, and pours, alone,
Her love-bewailing song; yet HOPE beguiles,
Nor quits him as he strays, 'till the wan MOON,
Peering in silv'ry panoply of light, 110
Sails placidly sublime through the still air,
And scatters round her imitative day!
But the unvarying cloud of deepest night!
The blank *perpetual* of the sightless orb!
The mournful CHAOS of the darken'd brain! 115
No HOPE can animate, no THOUGHT illume;
ALL is eternal solitude profound,
A dreadful SHADE; that mocks each other sense,
And plunges Reason in its WORST ABYSS!

And yet, in such a mind, so whelm'd in gloom, 120
The fine affections of the Soul still live!
The melancholy void is subject still
To the sweet magic of seraphic sounds;
The soothing eloquence of sacred song;
The whisp'ring gale, that mourns declining day; 125
Or Philomela's[1] soul-subduing strain,
That woos lone Echo, from her viewless seat,

---

1   Philomela: the nightingale.

To sail aërial-thron'd upon the breeze!
The lulling murmurs of the wand'ring stream;
130   The ever rippling rill;[1] the cataract fierce;
The lowing herds; and the small drowsy tones,
That, from the insect myriads, hum around;
The love-taught minstrelsy of plumed throats;
The dulcet strains of gentle Consolation!
135   But most of all, to THAT LOV'D VOICE, whose thrill,
Rushing impetuous through each throbbing vein,
Dilates the wond'ring mind, and frees its pow'rs
From the cold chains of icy apathy
To all the vast extremes of bliss and pain!
140   For, to THAT VOICE ADOR'D, his quiv'ring pulse
Responsive beats! he marks its *ev'ry* tone,
And finds in *each* a sympathetic balm!
Ill-fated wretch! HE knows not the sweet *sense*
That feeds upon the magic of a smile!
145   That drinks the poison of the murd'rous eye,
Or rushes, in an extacy of bliss,
To snatch the living roses from the cheek!
HE knows not what it is to trace each charm,
That plays about the symmetry of form,
150   And heightens ev'ry timid *blushing* grace,
More lovely, from the wonder it commands!
He never mark'd the soul-expressive tear!
The undescribable and speaking glance,
That promises unutterable bliss!
155   Then what to HIM avails the ruby lip,
Or the rich lustre of the silky waves,
That half conceal the azure tinctur'd eye,
As golden clouds rush on the morning star,
And glow, exulting, o'er its milder ray!

160   O glorious SIGHT! sublimest gift of God!
Expansive source of intellectual bliss!
By thee we climb to Immortality,
Through all the rugged paths of tedious life!

---

1 A small stream.

THY nerve shoots forth a light ineffable,
That marks the fount of SCIENCE, and reveals 165
The many-winding paths of wisdom's maze!
Thou canst within thy narrow vortex grasp
The outstretch'd OCEAN, and the LANDSCAPE wide,
Diversified with craggy cliffs, whose heads
Hang fearfully sublime, half veil'd in clouds, 170
O'er the low valley's solitary breast!
'Tis thine, upon the mountain's dizzy edge,
To ponder on the wonders of the SKY!
Or bending o'er the margin, trace below,
The world of mingling atoms, less'ning still 175
As the dread cavity grows more profound;
Till woods, and lakes, and scatter'd villages,
And stately palaces, and lofty spires,
Fade in the deep impenetrable gloom!
THOU canst avert the storm that gathers round, 180
And bids thee seek the hospitable roof
Where meek PHILANTHROPY unfolds her store!
'Tis THINE to contemplate the gorgeous SUN
In all its majesty of living light,
Flaming, despotic, o'er unnumber'd WORLDS! 185
'TIS THINE to mark the snowy-vested plains,
That, like the glitt'ring stores of Avarice,
Dazzle and chill the wretched wand'rer's soul!
Or 'midst the wreck of Nature, still secure,
Gaze, where the black'ning tempest, bursting round, 190
Tears the young branches from the parent trunk,
And strips the forest of its loftiest pride!

And YET! so wonderfully form'd to meet
The cutting blast, the winged light'ning's glare,
The painful radiance of the scorching Sun; 195
To watch the midnight taper's glimm'ring flame
O'er the long studious page, or pore intent
Upon the fine-wrought mysteries that lurk
In art mechanical! to trace the stars
Through all their devious labyrinths of air; 200
To plunge amidst the foamings of the deep;

Or pour the copious torrents from that spring
By pity cherish'd in the human breast!
YET so alive is ev'ry wond'rous part,
205   In *each complete*, in ALL PRE-EMINENT!
So exquisitely delicate each nerve,
So subject to destruction and to pain,
That the minutest particle of dust,
Almost invisible to that it meets,
210   Obstructs its pow'rs, and o'er the visual ray
Rolls a huge mass of AGONIZING SHADE!
Such are the horrors, such the pangs acute,
That shroud the DARKEN'D EYE, whose mortal sense,
Consign'd to one unbless'd and mournful night,
215   Can by ETERNAL DAY alone be cur'd!
Where the dim shade shall vanish from its beams,
And bathing in a sea of endless light,
The renovated ORB, awoke from DEATH,
Shall snatch its rays FROM IMMORTALITY!

THE MANIAC[1]

AH! WHAT ART THOU, whose eye-balls roll
Like *Heralds* of the wand'ring soul,
While down thy cheek the scalding torrents flow?
Why does that agonizing shriek
5   The mind's unpitied anguish speak?
O tell me, THING FORLORN! and let me share thy woe.

---

1   In Robinson's *Memoirs*, an account of the composition of "The Maniac" is given as
an example of "the facility and rapidity with which she composed" (2: 129).
According to this account, Robinson witnessed an elderly man being hurried on
by a crowd of people who pelted him with mud and stones. Inspired by "mad
Jemmy," as the man was known, and under the influence of eighty drops of lau-
danum, Robinson dictated "The Maniac" "faster than it could be committed to
paper." In an account that anticipates the composition story of Coleridge's "Kubla
Khan," Robinson's daughter (the putative author of the last section of Robinson's
Memoirs) writes:

She lay, while dictating, with her eyes closed, apparently in the stupor which
opium frequently produces, repeating like a person talking in her sleep. This

Why dost thou rend thy matted hair,
And beat thy burning bosom bare?
Why is thy lip so parch'd? thy groan so deep?
    Why dost thou fly from cheerful light,   10
    And seek in caverns mid-day night,
And cherish thoughts untold, and banish gentle sleep?

Why dost thou from thy scanty bed
Tear the rude straw to crown thy head,
And nod with ghastly smile, and wildly sing?   15
    While down thy pale distorted face,
    The crystal drops each other chase,
As though thy brain were drown'd in ONE ETERNAL SPRING?

Why dost thou climb yon craggy steep,
    That frowns upon the clam'rous deep,   20
And howl, responsive to the waves below?
    Or on the margin of the rock
    Thy SOV'REIGN ORB exulting mock,
And waste the freezing night in pacing to and fro?

Why dost thou strip the fairest bow'rs,   25
    To dress thy scowling brow with flow'rs,
And fling thy tatter'd garment to the wind?
    Why madly dart from cave to cave,
    Now laugh and sing, then weep and rave,
And round thy naked limbs fantastic fragments bind?   30

Why dost thou drink the midnight dew,
    Slow trickling from the baneful YEW,
Stretch'd on a pallet of sepulchral stone;
    While, in her solitary tow'r,

affecting performance, produced in circumstances so singular, does no less cred-
it to the genius than to the heart of the author.
    On the ensuing morning Mrs. Robinson had only a confused idea of what
had past, nor could be convinced of the fact till the manuscript was produced.
She declared, that she had been dreaming of mad Jemmy throughout the night,
but was perfectly unconscious of having been awake while she composed the
poem, or of the circumstances narrated by her daughter. (2: 132)

35   The *Minstrel of the witching hour*
Sits half congeal'd with fear, to hear thy dismal moan?

    Thy form upon the cold earth cast,
    Now grown familiar with the blast,
Defies the biting FROST and scorching SUN:
40   ALL SEASONS are alike to THEE;
    Thy sense, unchain'd by Destiny,
Resists, with dauntless pride, ALL MISERIES BUT ONE!

    Fix not thy steadfast gaze on me,
    SHRUNK ATOM of MORTALITY!
45   Nor freeze my blood with thy distracted groan;
    Ah! quickly turn those eyes away,
    They fill my soul with dire dismay!
For dead and dark they seem, and almost chill'd to STONE!

    Yet, if thy precious senses stray,
50   Where REASON scorns to lend a ray,
Or if DESPAIR SUPREME usurps her throne,
    Oh! let me all thy sorrows know;
    With THINE my mingling tear shall flow,
And I will share thy pangs, and make thy griefs my OWN.

55   Hath LOVE unlock'd thy feeling breast,
    And stol'n from thence the balm of rest?
Then far away, on purple pinions[1] borne,
    Left only keen *regret* behind,
    To tear with poison'd fangs thy mind,
60   While barb'rous MEM'RY lives, and bids thee HOPELESS MOURN?

    Does FANCY, to thy straining arms,
    Give the false NYMPH in all her charms,
And with her airy voice beguile thee so,
    That Sorrow seems to pass away,
65   Till the blithe harbinger of day
Awakes thee from thy dream, and yields thee back to woe?

---

1 Wings.

Say, have the bonds of FRIENDSHIP fail'd,
    Or JEALOUS pangs thy mind assail'd;
While black INGRATITUDE, with ranc'rous tooth,
    Pierc'd the fine fibres of thy heart,   70
    And fest'ring every sensate part,
Dim'd with contagious breath, the crimson glow of youth?

    Or has stern FATE, with ruthless hand,
    Dash'd on some wild untrodden strand
Thy little BARK, with all thy fortunes fraught;   75
    While THOU didst watch the stormy night
    Upon some bleak rock's fearful height,
Till thy hot brain consum'd with desolating THOUGHT?

    Ah! WRETCH FORLORN, perchance thy breast,
    By the cold fangs of AVARICE press'd,   80
Grew hard and torpid by her touch profane;
    Till FAMINE pinch'd thee to the bone,
    And MENTAL torture MADE thee own
THAT THING THE MOST ACCURS'D, who drags her ENDLESS CHAIN!

    Or say, does flush'd AMBITION's wing   85
    Around thy fev'rish temples fling
Dire incense, smoking from th' ensanguin'd plain,
    That drain'd from bleeding warriors' hearts,
    Swift to thy shatter'd sense imparts
The VICTOR's savage joy, that thrills through ev'ry vein?   90

    Does not the murky gloom of night
    Give to thy view some murd'rous SPRITE,
Whose POIGNARD¹ gleams along thy cell forlorn;
    And when the SUN expands his ray,
    Dost thou not shun the jocund day,   95
And mutter curses deep, and *hate* the ruddy MORN?

---

1   A dagger.

And YET the MORN on rosy wing
Could ONCE to THEE its raptures bring,
And Mirth's enliv'ning song delight thine ear!
100   While HOPE thine eye-lids could unclose,
From the sweet slumbers of repose,
To TELL THEE LOVE's gay throng of tender joys were NEAR!

Or hast thou stung with poignant smart,
The ORPHAN's and the WIDOW's heart,
105   And plung'd them in cold POVERTY's abyss;
While CONSCIENCE, like a VULTURE stole,
To feed upon thy tortur'd soul,
And tear each BARB'ROUS SENSE from TRANSITORY BLISS?

Or hast thou seen some gentle MAID,
110   By thy deluding voice betray'd,
Fade like a flow'r, slow with'ring with remorse?
And didst thou THEN refuse to save
Thy VICTIM from an early grave,
Till at thy feet she lay, a pale and ghastly CORSE?

115   OH! TELL ME, tell me all thy pain;
Pour to mine ear thy frenzied strain,
And I will share thy pangs, and soothe thy woes!
POOR MANIAC! I will dry thy tears,
And bathe thy wounds, and calm thy fears,
120   And with soft PITY's balm ENCHANT THEE TO REPOSE.

A FRAGMENT,

SUPPOSED TO BE WRITTEN NEAR THE TEMPLE, AT PARIS, ON THE NIGHT BEFORE THE EXECUTION OF LOUIS XVI[1]

Now MIDNIGHT spreads her sable vest
   With starry rays, light-tissu'd o'er;
Now from the Desart's thistled breast
   The chilling dews begin to soar;
The OWL shrieks from the tott'ring TOW'R,   5
Dread *watch-bird* of the *witching hour*!
   Spectres, from their charnel cells,
   Cleave the air with hideous yells!
   Not a GLOW-WORM ventures forth
   To *gild* his little *speck* of earth!   10
In wild despair Creation seems to wait,
While HORROR stalks abroad, to deal the shafts of FATE!

To yonder damp and dreary Cave,
From black OBLIVION's silent wave,
   Borne on *Desolation*'s wings,   15
   DEATH his poison'd chalice brings!
Wide beneath the turbid sky,
Fierce REBELLION's banners fly!
   Sweeping to her iron den
   The agonizing hearts of men!   20
There, in many a ghastly throng,
Blood-stain'd Myriads glide along,
While each above his crest a FAULCHION[2] rears,
Imbu'd with TEPID GORE, or drench'd with SCALDING TEARS!

Beneath yon TOW'R, (whose grated cell   25
   Entombs the fairest child of earth,
AUGUST, in MISERY, as in BIRTH!)

---

1   Louis XVI was executed on January 21, 1793. The Temple was a thirteenth-century monastery in Paris in which the king and his family were imprisoned from August 10, 1792, until their executions.
2   A sword.

The troops of PANDIMONIUM[1] dwell!
Night and day the Fiends conspire
30   To glut their desolating ire!
I RE that feeds on human woe;
That, *smiling*, deals the murd'rous blow;
And as the hopeless VICTIM dies,
Fills with shouts the threat'ning skies;
35 Nor trembles, lest the vengeful light'ning's glare
Should blast their recreant arms, and SCATTER THEM TO AIR!

Round the deep entrenchments stand
Bold AMBITION's giant band;
Beneath, insidious MALICE creeps;
40   And keen REVENGE, that never sleeps;
While dark SUSPICION hovers near,
Stung by the dastard scorpion, FEAR!
R EASON, shrinking from her gaze,
Flies the scene in wild amaze;
45   While trembling PITY dies to see
The barb'rous Sons of ANARCHY
Drench their unnatural hands in regal blood,
While patriot Virtue sinks beneath the whelming flood!

HARK! the petrifying shriek
50   Breaks, from yonder TURRET bleak!
The lofty TOWER returns the sound,
Echoing through its base profound!
The rising MOON, with paly light,
Faintly greets the aching sight
55   With many a gliding CENTINEL,
Whose *shadow* would his steps repel!
Whose *soul*, convuls'd with conscious woe,
Pants for the MORNING's purple glow;
The *purple glow* that cheers his breast,
60 And gives his startled MIND a SHORT-LIV'D HOUR OF REST!

---

1   Pandemonium is an assembly of devils. The term is used by Milton in *Paradise Lost*
1.756 and 10.424.

But when shall MORN's effulgent light
The HAPLESS SUFFERER's glance invite?
When shall the breath of rosy day
Around the INFANT VICTIMS play?
When will the vivifying ORB   65
The tears of WIDOW'D LOVE absorb?
See! see! the palpitating breast
By all the weeping Graces drest,
Now dumb with grief, now raving wild,
Bending o'er each with'ring child,   70
The ONLY treasures spar'd by savage ire,
The fading shadows of their MURDER'D SIRE!

The SERAPH HOPE, with transient light,
Illumes the dreary shade of night;
Suspends a while the frenzy'd shriek,   75
The slow-pac'd tear of Suff'rance meek;
But soon the DEMON WRATH appears,
Who braves the touch of mortal fears!
His flaming sword, with hideous glare,
Proves the dire signal of DESPAIR!   80
Retiring HOPE beholds, subdu'd,
The fatal mandate sign'd with blood,
WITH KINDRED BLOOD! OH! HORRIBLE AND BASE,
To stigmatize with shame, a LONG, ILLUSTRIOUS RACE!

Oh, FANCY! spread thy powerful wing;   85
From HELL's polluted confines spring!
Quit, quit the cell where MADNESS lies,
With wounded breast, and starting eyes!
The RUTHLESS FIENDS have done their worst,
They triumph in the DEED ACCURS'D!   90
See, her veil OBLIVION throws
O'er THE LAST of HUMAN WOES!
The Royal STOLE, with many a crimson stain,
Closes from every eye the scene of pain,

95   While from afar the WAR SONG[1] dins the ear,
    And drowns the dying groan,[2] which ANGELS WEEP TO HEAR!

STANZAS.

WRITTEN AFTER SUCCESSIVE NIGHTS OF MELANCHOLY DREAMS

YE airy PHANTOMS, by whose pow'r
  Night's curtains spread a deeper shade;
Who, prowling in the murky hour,
  The weary sense with spells invade;
5   Why round the fibres of my brain,
    Such desolating miseries fling,
And, with new scenes of mental pain,
Chase from my languid eye, sleep's balm-dispensing wing?

Ah! why, when o'er the darken'd globe
10   All NATURE's children sink to rest —
Why, wrapp'd in horror's ghastly robe,
  With shad'wy hand assail my breast?
Why conjure up a tribe forlorn,
  To menace, where I bend my way?
15   Why round my pillow plant the thorn,
    Or fix the DEMONS dire, in terrible array?

Why, when the busy day is o'er —
  A day, perhaps, of *tender thought* —
Why bid my eager gaze explore
20   New prospects, with new anguish fraught?
Why bid my madd'ning sense descry
  The FORM, in silence I adore?
His magic smile! his murd'rous eye!
Then bid me wake to prove, the fond illusion o'er!

---

1   *Ca ira* [M.R.]. Translated idiomatically, this song title becomes "we'll make it." It
    became associated with violence and hatred of the aristocracy because a refrain
    added to the original version called for the hanging of aristocrats from lampposts.
2   The *last* insult offered to the expiring Monarch! [M.R.]

When, fev'rish with the throbs of pain,   25
    And bath'd with many a trickling tear,
I close my cheated eyes again,
    Despair's wild bands are hov'ring near;
Now, borne upon the yelling blast,
    O'er craggy PEAKS I bend my flight;   30
Now, on the yawning OCEAN cast,
I plunge unfathom'd depths, amid the shades of night!

Or, borne upon the billow's IRE,
    O'er the vast waste of waters drear,
Where shipwreck'd MARINERS expire,   35
    No friend their dying plaints to hear,
I view far off the craggy cliff,
    Whose white top mingles with the skies;
While, at its base the shatter'd SKIFF,
Wash'd by the foaming wave, in many a fragment lies.   40

Oft, when the MORNING's gaudy beams
    My lattice gild with sparkling light,
O'erwhelm'd with agonizing dreams,
    And bound in spells of FANCIED NIGHT,
I start, convulsive, wild, distraught!   45
    By some pale MURD'RER's poignard[1] press'd,
Or by the grinning PHANTOM caught,
Wake from the madd'ning grasp with horror-freezing breast!

Then, down my cold and pallid cheek,
    The mingling tears of joy and grief,   50
The soul's tumultuous feelings speak,
    And yield the struggling heart relief;
I smile to KNOW the danger PAST!
    But soon the radiant moment flies;
SOON is the transient DAY o'ercast,   55
And hope steals trembling from my languid eyes!

---

1   A dagger

If THUS, for MOMENTS of repose,
    Whole HOURS of mis'ry I must know;
If, when each sunny day shall close,
60   I must each gleam of PEACE forego!
If, for one LITTLE MORN OF MIRTH,
    This breast must feel long nights of pain;
OH! LIFE, thy joys are nothing worth;
Then let me sink to rest — AND NEVER WAKE AGAIN!

STANZAS.

WRITTEN BETWEEN DOVER AND CALAIS, IN JULY, 1792[1]

BOUNDING BILLOW, cease thy motion;
    Bear me not so swiftly o'er!
Cease thy roaring, foamy OCEAN!
    I will tempt thy rage no more.

5   Ah! within my bosom beating,
    Varying passions wildly reign!
LOVE, with proud resentment meeting;
    Throbs by turns, of joy and pain!

JOY, that far from foes I wander,
10   Where their ARTS can reach no more;
PAIN, that woman's heart grows fonder,
    When the dream of bliss is o'er!

LOVE, by fickle fancy banish'd,
    Spurn'd by HOPE, indignant flies!

---

1 Robinson wrote this poem while travelling to Spa, a town in Flanders famous for its mineral springs, with her mother and daughter. According to the *Memoirs*, "She longed once more to experience the friendly greeting and liberal kindness, which even her acknowledged talents had in her native country failed to procure.... In the midst of the depressing feelings which Mrs. Robinson experienced, in once more becoming a wanderer from her home, she courted the inspiration of the muse, and soothed, by the following beautiful stanzas, the melancholy sensations that oppressed her heart" (2: 133-34). According to Robert Bass, Robinson was visited in Calais by her husband who wanted to introduce his daughter to his brother, a

Yet, when love and hope are vanish'd, 15
  Restless MEM'RY never dies!

FAR I go! where FATE shall lead me,
  FAR across the troubled deep!
Where no stranger's ear shall heed me;
  Where no eye for ME shall weep. 20

PROUD has been my fatal passion!
  PROUD my injur'd heart shall be!
While each thought and inclination
  Proves that heart was form'd for THEE!

Not one SIGH shall tell my story; 25
  Not one TEAR my cheek shall stain!
SILENT grief shall be my glory;
  GRIEF that stoops not to COMPLAIN!

Let the bosom, prone to ranging,
  Still, by ranging, seek a cure! 30
MINE disdains the thought of changing,
  Proudly destin'd to ENDURE!

Yet ere far from all I treasur'd,
  * * * * * * * *![1] ere I bid adieu,
Ere my days of pain are measur'd 35
  Take the song that's STILL thy due!

YET believe, no servile passions
  Seek to charm thy wand'ring mind;
Well I know thy inclinations,
  Wav'ring as the passing wind! 40

---

distinguished officer in the British navy who, newly returned from the East Indies,
offered to take her into his home. In this way, Maria Elizabeth would have been
afforded a respectability she was denied while living with her mother. The offer
was rejected. Robinson turned back from Calais on 2 September 1792, narrowly
escaping arrest as a British subject (Bass 318-322).

1 Banastre Tarleton. The version of this poem that appears in Robinson's *Poetical
Works* has a "T" at the beginning of the string of asterisks.

I have lov'd thee! DEARLY lov'd thee!
   Through an age of worldly woe!
How ungrateful I have prov'd thee,
   Let my mournful exile show!

45   TEN long years of anxious sorrow,
   Hour by hour, I counted o'er;
Looking forward 'till to morrow,
   Every day I lov'd thee more!

POW'R and SPLENDOUR could not charm me;
50   I no joy in WEALTH could see;
Nor could threats or fears alarm me —
   Save THE FEAR of losing THEE!

When the storms of fortune press'd thee,
   I have sigh'd to hear *thee* sigh!
55   Or when sorrows dire distress'd thee,
   I have bid those sorrows fly!

Often hast thou smiling told me,
   WEALTH and POW'R were trifling things,
While LOVE, smiling to behold me,
60   Mock'd cold TIME's destructive wings.

When with THEE, what ills could harm me?
   THOU couldst every pang assuage!
Now, ALAS! what HOPE shall charm me?
   Every moment seems an age!

65   FARE THEE WELL, ungrateful Rover!
   Welcome GALLIA's[1] hostile shore;
Now, the breezes waft me over;
   Now we part — TO MEET NO MORE!

---

1   France.

MARIE ANTOINETTE'S LAMENTATION,

IN HER PRISON OF THE TEMPLE[1]
Written in March, 1793

When on my bosom EVENING's ruby light
    Through my THRICE-GRATED window warmly glows,
Why does the cheerful ray offend my sight,
    And with its lustre mock my weary woes?
Alas! because on my sad breast appears   5
A dreadful record — WRITTEN WITH MY TEARS!

When awful MIDNIGHT, with her EBON wand,
    Charms Nature's poorest, meanest child to peace,
Why cannot I, one little hour command,
    When gentle sleep may bid my anguish cease?   10
Alas! because, where'er I lay my head,
A dreary couch I find, WITH MANY A THORN O'ERSPREAD.

When the SUN, rising in the Eastern skies,
    Awakes the feather'd race to songs divine,
Why does remembrance picture to these eyes   15
    The jocund MORN OF LIFE, that once was mine?
Alas! because, in sorrow doom'd to mourn,
I ne'er shall see THAT BLISSFUL MORN RETURN!

When I behold my darling INFANTS sleep,
    Fair spotless blossoms, deck'd in op'ning charms,   20
Why do I start aghast, and wildly weep,
    And madly snatch them to my eager arms?
Ah me! because my sense, o'erwhelm'd with dread,
Views the sweet CHERUBS ON THEIR FUNERAL BED!

---

1   Marie Antoinette was imprisoned from August 10, 1792 until her execution on
    October 16, 1793. She had two living children at the time of her imprisonment,
    Louis XVII and Marie Thérèse. She was accused of having incestuous relations with
    her son, who contracted tuberculosis of the bones while incarcerated in the Temple
    and died there in 1795 at the age of ten.

25 Why, when they ope their eyes to gaze on ME,
    And fondly press me in their dear embrace,
Hang on my neck, or clasp my trembling knee,
    Why do MATERNAL SORROWS drench my face?
Alas! because inhuman hands unite,
30 To tear from my fond soul ITS LAST DELIGHT!

OH, FELL BARBARITY! yet spare a while
    The sacred treasures of my throbbing breast;
Oh, spare their infant hearts, untouch'd by guile,
    And let a WIDOW'D MOTHER's darlings rest!
35 Though you have struck your faulchions at the ROOT,
Oh! give the tender BRANCHES TIME TO SHOOT!

The lightning, by the angry tempest cast,
    Strikes at the lofty PINE, and lays it low;
While the small FLOWRET 'scapes the deadly blast,
40   A while its od'rous breath around to throw!
Then let distracted GALLIA's LILIES[1] bloom,
Though but to deck with sweets A DUNGEON's GLOOM!

O my poor INNOCENTS! all bath'd in tears,
    Like with'ring FLOWRETS, wash'd with CHILLING dew!
45 SLEEP ON! nor heed a frantic mother's fears;
    The SAVAGE TIGERS will not injure YOU!
Your HARMLESS bosoms not a CRIME can know,
Scarce born to GREATNESS — ERE CONSIGN'D TO WOE!

When left forlorn, dejected, and alone,
50   Imperfect sounds my pensive soul annoy;
I hear in every distant mingling tone,
    The merry BELLS — the boist'rous SONGS of JOY!
Ah! then I contemplate my loathsome CELL,
    Where MEAGRE GRIEF and SCOWLING HORROR DWELL!

---

1 The fleur-de-lis, or lily flower: a symbol of the French crown and part of the
French coat of arms until 1830. The lily signifies purity.

The RABBLE's din, the TOCSIN's fateful sound[1] —   55
    The CANNON thund'ring through the vaulted sky —
The curling smoke, in columns rising round,
    Which from my IRON LATTICE I descry,
Rouse my LETHARGIC MIND! I shriek in vain;
My TYRANT JAILOR only mocks my pain!   60

Yet bear thy woes, my SOUL, with proud disdain;
    Meet the keen lance of DEATH with stedfast eye:
Think on the GLORIOUS TIDE that fills each VEIN,
    And throbbing bids ME tremble not, TO DIE!
YET, shall I from my FRIENDLESS CHILDREN part?   65
Oh! all the MOTHER RUSHES TO MY HEART!

Where'er I turn, a thousand ills appear:
    Arm'd at all points, in terrible array
PALE, HOOD-WINK'D MURDER, ever lurking near,
    And COWARD CRUELTY, that shuns the DAY!   70
See! see! they pierce, with many a recreant sword,
The mangled bosom OF MY BLEEDING LORD![2]

OH, DREADFUL THOUGHT! OH, AGONY SUPREME!
    When will the sanguinary scene be o'er?
When will my SOUL, in sweet OBLIVION's dream,   75
    Fade from this ORB, to some more peaceful shore?
When will the CHERUB PITY break the snare,
And snatch ONE VICTIM from the LAST DESPAIR?

---

1 A tocsin is a bell used to sound an alarm. Normally sounded upon the birth or
   death of a sovereign, it served during the Revolution as an announcement of insur-
   rection.
2 Robinson seems to be influenced here by Burke's famous treatment of the French
   royal couple in his 1790 *Reflections of the Revolution in France* where he writes of the
   "band of cruel ruffians and assassins" who "rushed into the chamber of the queen,
   and pierced with an hundred strokes of bayonets and poniards the bed, from which
   this persecuted woman had but just time to fly almost naked." He also writes:
   "I thought ten thousand swords must have leaped from their scabbards to avenge
   even a look that threatened her with insult." Edmund Burke, *Reflections on the Revo-
   lution in France* (London: J. M. Dent & Sons, 1960) 68–69 and 73. See also Robin-
   son's "A Fragment, Supposed to Be Written Near the Temple, at Paris, on the Night
   Before the Murder of Louis XVI" (p. 127).

ODE TO RAPTURE

> BLISS *goes but to a certain bound;*
> *Beyond, 'tis* AGONY.
>
> Mrs. Greville's "Ode to Indifference"[1]

NATURE, with colours heav'nly pure!
Her proudest attributes display'd!
ALL that could fascinate, allure,
Inspire, or soothe, her skill essay'd;
5   She trac'd the PASSIONS; at command,
Each yielded to her potent hand!
LOVE! PITY! HOPE! by turns she drew;
To each, she found her pencil true!
Till RAPTURE, darting o'er her sight,
10   Inspir'd her glowing breast, with NEW AND
                   FIERCE DELIGHT.

    NATURE, astonish'd at her charms,
Her bosom fill'd with wild alarms,
Then seiz'd her magic pencil, gay,
15   Dipp'd in the RAINBOW's brightest ray!
She trac'd the BLUSH, the speaking EYE!
The snowy BOSOM, beating high!
Yet o'er the languid FORM,
Extatic! tender! timid! warm!
20   A SWEET CONFUSION seem'd to steal,
    SUCH as NATURE's pencil faint,
    Trembling try'd, but COULD NOT PAINT;
Yet, such as SHE ALONE COULD FEEL!

    Now, wond'ring at the work she made,
25   She thus address'd the beauteous shade,
With throbbing pulses! quiv'ring sighs!
And fond, adoring eyes!
"Fairest offspring of the sky!
Swift, to mortal regions fly;

---

1   Frances Greville (c. 1726–89) was a celebrated beauty and wit. Her "Ode to Indifference" was widely anthologized.

Go, in all thy softness dress'd;
Soothe the sensate yielding breast!
And show thy magic THRILL was giv'n,
To prove on EARTH, a transient HEAV'N."

As NATURE SPOKE, half madd'ning at the view,
The glowing Phantom fainter grew;
Till, like a METEOR, glimm'ring through a shade,
TOO EXQUISITE TO LAST! the FLEETING FORM DECAY'D.

STANZAS TO A FRIEND,

WHO DESIRED TO HAVE MY PORTRAIT

My PORTRAIT you desire! and why?
To keep a shade on Mem'ry's eye?
    What bliss can REASON prove,
To gaze upon a senseless frame!
On looks eternally the SAME,
    And lips that NEVER move?

Perhaps, when silent, you will say,
Those lips no anger can betray;
    But, fix'd, in smiles remain;
Those eyes, so gentle, can impart
No keen reproach to wound the heart,
    No glance of cold disdain!

You'll say, this FORM may quickly fade;
One hour in glowing health array'd,
    The next, perchance, 'tis lost!
But, cherish'd by the PAINTER's skill,
And AGE may see it blooming still,
    As Evergreens in frost.

But what are features? what is form?
To combat life's tempestuous storm?
    Can they TIME's pinions bind?

TRUTH whispers, No! Then take, my FRIEND,
The LASTING sketch, which I here send,
   The PICTURE of MY MIND!

25   A BARD has told us long ago,
'Tis difficult ourselves to know:
   That BARD was conscious grown;
And when he scrutiniz'd HIS HEART,
Where ENVY lurk'd in ev'ry part,
30   Scarce thought it was HIS OWN!

RELIGION says, to be forgiv'n,
We all should own our crimes to Heav'n,
   And picture each transgression:
And thus, my follies to repair,
35   For well I KNOW I have my share,
   I make this frank CONFESSION.

Nor PEDANT dull, nor CYNIC cold,
I blush not freely to unfold
   The feelings of my breast;
40   My FAULTS I OWN — my VIRTUES KNOW;
To EDUCATION half I owe,
   And NATURE did the rest.

E'en from the early days of youth,
I've blessed the sacred voice of TRUTH;
45   And Candour is my pride:
I always SPEAK what I BELIEVE;
I know not if I CAN deceive;
   Because I NEVER TRIED.

I'm often serious, sometimes gay;
50   Can laugh the fleeting hours away,
   Or weep — for OTHERS' woe;
I'm PROUD! THIS fault YOU cannot blame,
Nor does it tinge my cheek with shame;
   YOUR FRIENDSHIP MADE ME SO!

I'm odd, eccentric, fond of ease; 55
Impatient; difficult to please:
   AMBITION fires my breast!
Yet not for wealth, or titles vain;
Let but the LAUREL deck MY strain,[1]
   And, dullness, take the rest. 60

In temper quick, in friendship nice;
I doat on GENIUS, shrink from vice,
   And scorn the flatt'rer's art!
With penetrating skill can see,
Where, mask'd in sweet simplicity, 65
   Lies hid the treach'rous heart.

If ONCE betray'd, I SCARCE forgive:
And though I pity ALL that live,
   And mourn for ev'ry pain;
Yet never could I court the Great, 70
Or worship FOOLS, whate'er their state;
   For falsehood I disdain!

I'm JEALOUS, for I fondly LOVE;
No feeble flame my heart can prove;
   Caprice ne'er dimm'd its fires: 75
I blush, to see the human MIND,
For nobler, prouder claims design'd,
   The slave of low desires!

Reserv'd in manner, where unknown;
A little OBSTINATE, I own, 80
   And apt to form opinion:
Yet, ENVY never broke my rest,
Nor could SELF-INT'REST bow my breast
   To FOLLY's base dominion.

---

1   The laurel wreath was an emblem of distinction in poetry.

85   No gaudy trappings I display;
        Nor meanly plain, nor idly gay;
            Yet sway'd by Fashion's rule:
        For SINGULARITY, we find,
        Betrays, to ev'ry reasoning mind,
90   The PEDANT or the FOOL.

        I fly the rich, the sordid crowd,
        The little great, the vulgar proud,
            The ignorant and base:
        To sons of GENIUS homage pay,
95   And own their sov'reign right to sway,
            LORDS of the HUMAN RACE!

        When COXCOMBS[1] tell me I'm DIVINE,
        I plainly see the weak design,
            And mock a tale so common:
100   Howe'er the flatt'ring strain may flow,
        My FAULTS, alas! too plainly show
            I'm but a MORTAL WOMAN!

        Such is my PORTRAIT; now believe;
        My pencil never can deceive,
105   And know me what I paint;
        Taught in AFFLICTION's rigid school,
        I act from PRINCIPLE, not RULE,
            No SINNER, yet no SAINT.

        Now contemplate a picture true;
110   With KINDNESS ev'ry VIRTUE view;
            And all that's WRONG explore:
        If YOU the brightest tints defend,
        The darkest shades I'll TRY to mend;
            The WISEST CAN NO MORE!

---

1   Coxcomb: A foolish, conceited, showy person.

'Tis in the rushy hut obscure
Where poverty's low sons endure,
And scarcely daring to repine
On a straw pallet mute recline.
                        O'erwhelm'd with woe!

Figure 8. Mezzotint engraving after Maria Cosway, illustration No. 4 for "The Wintry Day,"
1804. (By courtesy of the Special Collections Department, University of Virginia Library.)

SAPPHO AND PHAON (1796)

SAPPHO AND PHAON. IN A SERIES OF LEGITIMATE SONNETS,
WITH THOUGHTS ON POETICAL SUBJECTS, AND ANECDOTES
OF THE GRECIAN POETESS (1796)

PREFACE

It must strike every admirer of poetical compositions, that the modern sonnet, concluding with two lines, winding up the sentiment of the whole, confines the poet's fancy, and frequently occasions an abrupt termination of a beautiful and interesting picture; and that the ancient, or what is generally denominated, the LEGITIMATE SONNET, may be carried on in a series of sketches, composing, in parts, one historical or imaginary subject, and forming in the whole a complete and connected story.

With this idea, I have ventured to compose the following collection; not presuming to offer them as imitations of PETRARCH,[1] but as specimens of that species of sonnet writing, so seldom attempted in the English language; though adopted by that sublime Bard, whose Muse produced the grand epic of Paradise Lost, and the humbler effusion, which I produce as an example of the measure to which I allude, and which is termed by the most classical writers, the *legitimate sonnet*.

> O Nightingale, that on yon bloomy spray
>   Warblest at eve, when all the woods are still,
>   Thou with fresh hope the lover's heart dost fill,
> While the jolly hours lead on propitious May.
> Thy liquid notes that close the eye of day
>   First heard before the shallow cuccoo's bill,
>   Portend success in love; O if Jove's will

---

1 The Petrarchan sonnet, named after the fourteenth-century Italian poet, Petrarch, is composed of fourteen iambic pentameter lines. It consists of two main parts: an octave (eight lines) rhyming *a b b a a b b a* and a sestet (six lines) rhyming *c d e c d e* or some other variation (such as *c d c d c d*, as in the sonnet by Milton which follows).

Have link'd that amorous power to thy soft lay,
    Now timely sing, ere the rude bird of hate
Foretel my hopeless doom in some grove nigh,
    As thou from year to year hast sung too late
For my relief, yet hadst no reason why:
    Whether the Muse, or Love call thee his mate,
Both them I serve, and of their train am I.[1]

To enumerate the variety of authors who have written sonnets of
all descriptions, would be endless; indeed few of them deserve notice:
and where, among the heterogeneous mass of insipid and laboured
efforts, sometimes a bright gem sheds lustre on the page of poesy, it
scarcely excites attention, owing to the disrepute into which sonnets
are fallen. So little is rule attended to by many, who profess the art
of poetry, that I have seen a composition of more than thirty lines,
ushered into the world under the name of Sonnet, and that, from the
pen of a writer, whose classical taste ought to have avoided such a
misnomer.

Doctor Johnson describes a Sonnet, as "a short poem, consisting of
fourteen lines, of which the rhymes are adjusted by a particular rule."
He further adds, "It has not been used by any man of eminence since
MILTON."[2]

---

1   This sonnet, composed by Milton around 1629, is an example of a Petrarchan son-
net.
2   Since the death of Doctor Johnson a few ingenious and elegant writers have com-
posed sonnets, according to the rules described by him: of their merits the public
will judge, and the *literati* decide. The following quotations are given as the opinions
of living authors, respecting the legitimate sonnet.

> The little poems which are here called Sonnets, have, I believe, no very just
> claim to that title: but they consist of fourteen lines, and appear to me no
> improper vehicle for a single sentiment. I am told, and I read it as the opinion of
> very good judges, that the legitimate sonnet is ill calculated for our language.
> The specimens Mr. Hayley has given, though they form a strong exception,
> prove no more, than that the difficulties of the attempt vanish before uncommon
> powers.
>
>   *Mrs. C. Smith's Preface to her Elegiac Sonnets*

Likewise in the preface to a volume of very charming poems, (among which are
many *legitimate sonnets*) by Mr. William Kendall, of Exeter, the following opinion is
given of the Italian rhythm, which constitutes the legitimate sonnet: he describes it
as —

Sensible of the extreme difficulty I shall have to encounter, in offering to the world a little wreath, gathered in that path, which, even the best poets have thought it dangerous to tread; and knowing that the English language is, of all others, the least congenial to such an undertaking, (for, I believe, that the construction of this kind of sonnet was originally in the Italian, where the vowels are used almost every other letter,) I only point out the track where more able pens may follow with success; and where the most classical beauties may be adopted, and drawn forth with peculiar advantage.

Sophisticated sonnets are so common, for every rhapsody of rhyme, from six lines to sixty comes under that denomination, that the eye frequently turns from this species of poem with disgust. Every school-boy, every romantic scribbler, thinks a sonnet a task of little difficulty. From this ignorance in some, and vanity in others, we see the monthly and diurnal publications abounding with ballads, odes, elegies, epitaphs, and allegories, the non-descript ephemera from the heated brains of self-important poetasters, all ushered into notice under the appellation of SONNET!

I confess myself such an enthusiastic votary of the Muse, that any innovation which seems to threaten even the least of her established rights, makes me tremble, lest that chaos of dissipated pursuits which has too long been growing like an overwhelming shadow, and menacing the lustre of intellectual light, should, aided by the idleness of some, and the profligacy of others, at last obscure the finer mental powers, and reduce the dignity of talents to the lowest degradation.

As poetry has the power to raise, so has it also the magic to refine. The ancients considered the art of such importance, that before they led forth their heroes to the most glorious enterprizes, they animated

---

A chaste and elegant model, which the most enlightened poet of our own country disdained not to contemplate. Amidst the degeneracy of modern taste, if the studies of a Milton have lost their attraction, legitimate sonnets, enriched by varying pauses, and an elaborate recurrence of rhyme, still assert their superiority over those tasteless and inartificial productions, which assume the name, without evincing a single characteristic of distinguishing modulation. [M.R.]

Samuel Johnson defined the sonnet in his *Dictionary of the English Language*. Charlotte Smith's *Elegiac Sonnets and Other Poems* was published in ever expanding editions between 1784 and 1797. She dedicated the series to William Hayley (1745-1820), poet and friend of William Cowper and William Blake, as well as of Smith herself. For the prefaces to all the editions, see *The Poems of Charlotte Smith*, ed. Stuart Curran (New York: Oxford University Press, 1993).

them by the recital of grand and harmonious compositions. The wisest scrupled not to reverence the invocations of minds, graced with the charm of numbers: so mystically fraught are powers said to be, which look beyond the surface of events, that an admired and classical writer,[1] describing the inspirations of the MUSE, thus expresses his opinion:

> So when remote futurity is brought
> Before the keen inquiry of her thought,
> A terrible sagacity informs
> The Poet's heart, he looks to distant storms,
> He hears the thunder ere the tempest low'rs,
> And, arm'd with strength surpassing human pow'rs,
> Seizes events as yet unknown to man,
> And darts his soul into the dawning plan.
> Hence in a Roman mouth the graceful name
> Of Prophet and of Poet was the same,
> Hence British poets too the priesthood shar'd,
> And ev'ry hallow'd druid — was a bard.

That poetry ought to be cherished as a national ornament, cannot be more strongly exemplified than in the simple fact, that, in those centuries when the poets' laurels have been most generously fostered in Britain, the minds and manners of the natives have been most polished and enlightened. Even the language of a country refines into purity by the elegance of numbers: the strains of WALLER[2] have done more to effect that, than all the labours of monkish pedantry, since the days of druidical mystery and superstition.

Though different minds are variously affected by the infinite diversity of harmonious effusions, there are, I believe, very few that are wholly insensible to the powers of poetic compositions. Cold must that bosom be, which can resist the magical versification of Eloisa to Abelard;[3] and torpid to all the more exalted sensations of the soul is

---

1   Cowper [M.R.]. The excerpt that follows is from William Cowper's *Table Talk*, written in 1781, lines 492-503.
2   Edmund Waller (1606-87), poet noted for his successful use of the couplet form and the smoothness of his verse. "Go, lovely rose" is probably his best known poem.
3   Most likely a reference to Alexander Pope's *Eloisa to Abelard* (1717).

that being, whose ear is not delighted by the grand and sublime effusions of the divine Milton! The romantic chivalry of Spencer vivifies the imagination; while the plaintive sweetness of Collins soothes and penetrates the heart.[1] How much would Britain have been deficient in a comparison with other countries on the scale of intellectual grace, had these poets never existed! yet it is a melancholy truth, that here, where the attributes of genius have been diffused by the liberal hand of nature, almost to prodigality, there has not been, during a long series of years, the smallest mark of public distinction bestowed on literary talents. Many individuals, whose works are held in the highest estimation, now that their ashes sleep in the sepulchre, were, when living, suffered to languish, and even to perish, in obscure poverty: as if it were the peculiar fate of genius, to be neglected while existing, and only honoured when the consciousness of inspiration is vanished for ever.

The ingenious mechanic has the gratification of seeing his labours patronized, and is rewarded for his invention while he has the powers of enjoying its produce. But the Poet's life is one perpetual scene of warfare: he is assailed by envy, stung by malice, and wounded by the fastidious comments of concealed assassins. The more eminently beautiful his compositions are, the larger is the phalanx he has to encounter; for the enemies of genius are multitudinous.

It is the interest of the ignorant and powerful, to suppress the effusions of enlightened minds: when only monks could write, and nobles read, authority rose triumphant over right; and the slave, spell-bound in ignorance, hugged his fetters without repining. It was then that the best powers of reason lay buried like the gem in the dark mine; by a slow and tedious progress they have been drawn forth, and must, ere long, diffuse an universal lustre: for that era is rapidly advancing, when talents will tower like an unperishable column, while the globe will be strewed with the wrecks of superstition.

As it was the opinion of the ancients, that poets possessed the powers of prophecy, the name was consequently held in the most unbounded veneration. In less remote periods the bard has been publicly distinguished; princes and priests have bowed before the majesty of genius: Petrarch was crowned with laurels, the noblest diadem, in

---

1 Edmund Spenser (1552?-99); William Collins (1721-59).

the Capitol of Rome: his admirers were liberal; his cotemporaries were just; and his name will stand upon record, with the united and honourable testimony of his own talents, and the generosity of his country.

It is at once a melancholy truth, and a national disgrace, that this Island, so profusely favored by nature, should be marked, of all enlightened countries, as the most neglectful of literary merit! and I will venture to believe, that there are both POETS and PHILOSO-PHERS, now living in Britain, who, had they been born in any *other* clime, would have been honoured with the proudest distinctions, and immortalized to the latest posterity.

I cannot conclude these opinions without paying tribute to the talents of my illustrious countrywomen; who, unpatronized by courts, and unprotected by the powerful, persevere in the paths of literature, and ennoble themselves by the unperishable lustre of MENTAL PRE-EMINENCE!¹

TO THE READER

The story of the LESBIAN MUSE,² though not new to the classical reader, presented to my imagination such a lively example of the human mind, enlightened by the most exquisite talents, yet yielding to the destructive controul of ungovernable passions, that I felt an

---

1   With her reference to those who are "unpatronized by courts," Robinson may be casting a barb at the Prince of Wales who was often remiss in paying the annuity she was promised from him in the aftermath of their affair. The "illustrious countrywomen" to whom she refers would surely include the women writers Robinson counted among her own friends who included the novelists Jane Porter, Eliza Fenwick, Eliza Parsons, and Agnes Maria Bennet.

2   Sappho (fl. ca.610-ca.580 B.C.). Very little is known about her life, although there are numerous legends associated with her. She was a native of Lesbos, an island in Asia Minor, and was probably born in either Eresus or Mytilene. She ran an academy for unmarried women where beauty and grace were greatly valued. Her poetry, very little of which survives, is noted for its personal emotiveness. According to legend, she fell hopelessly in love with Phaon, a young boatman, and, when their affair ended, leaped to her death from a cliff. Although this story was immortalized by the Roman poet Ovid in his *Heroides*, it is unsubstantiated. Several centuries after her death, Sappho became the target of jokes about promiscuity and lesbianism. Mary Robinson was known as the "English Sappho," a double-edged designation connoting both poetic gifts and passionate abandon, well before 1796 when she published the sonnet series which underscored the association.

irresistible impulse to attempt the delineation of their progress; mingling with the glowing picture of her soul, such moral reflections, as may serve to excite that pity, which, while it proves the susceptibility of the heart, arms it against the danger of indulging a too luxuriant fancy.

The unfortunate lovers, Heloise and Abeilard; and, the supposed platonic, Petrarch and Laura, have found panegyrists in many distinguished authors.[1] OVID and POPE have celebrated the passion of Sappho for Phaon; but their portraits, however beautifully finished, are replete with shades, tending rather to depreciate than to adorn the Grecian Poetess.[2]

I have endeavoured to collect, in the succeeding pages, the most liberal accounts of that illustrious woman, whose fame has transmitted to us some fragments of her works, through many dark ages, and for the space of more than two thousand years. The merit of her compositions must have been indisputable, to have left all cotemporary female writers in obscurity; for it is known, that poetry was, at the period in which she lived, held in the most sacred veneration; and that those who were gifted with that divine inspiration, were ranked as the first class of human beings.

Among the many Grecian writers, Sappho was the unrivalled poetess of her time: the envy she excited, the public honours she received, and the fatal passion which terminated her existence, will, I trust, create that sympathy in the mind of the susceptible reader, which may render the following poetical trifles not wholly uninteresting.

MARY ROBINSON
St. James's Place,
1796.

---

1   Pierre Abélard (1079-1142/4) was a famous philosopher who became the tutor of Héloïse. They became lovers and were secretly married. When Héloïse's uncle thought that Abélard had reneged on his marriage vows, he sent her to a nunnery and had Abélard attacked in his sleep and castrated. Alexander Pope's *Eloisa to Abelard* was published in 1717. Francesco Petrarch (1304-74) was an Italian poet. In verses which expressed his love for Laura, Petrarch also told the story of the development of his soul.

2   In the fifteenth of Ovid's *Heroides*, Sappho addresses Phaon. Pope's translation of Ovid's epistle, "Sapho to Phaon," was published in 1712.

ACCOUNT OF SAPPHO

SAPPHO, whom the ancients distinguished by the title of the TENTH MUSE, was born at Mytilene in the island of Lesbos, six hundred years before the Christian era.[1] As no particulars have been transmitted to posterity, respecting the origin of her family, it is most likely she derived but little consequence from birth or connections. At an early period of her life she was wedded to Cercolus, a native of the isle of Andros; he was possessed of considerable wealth, and though the Lesbian Muse is said to have been sparingly gifted with beauty, he became enamoured of her, more perhaps on account of mental, than personal charms. By this union she is said to have given birth to a daughter; but Cercolus leaving her, while young, in a state of widowhood, she never after could be prevailed on to marry.

The Fame which her genius spread even to the remotest parts of the earth, excited the envy of some writers who endeavoured to throw over her private character, a shade, which shrunk before the brilliancy of her poetical talents. Her soul was replete with harmony; that harmony which neither art nor study can acquire; she felt the intuitive superiority, and to the Muses she paid unbounded adoration.

The Mytilenians held her poetry in such high veneration, and were so sensible of the honour conferred on the country which gave her birth, that they coined money with the impression of her head; and at the time of her death, paid tribute to her memory, such as was offered to sovereigns only.

The story of Antiochus has been related as an unequivocal proof of Sappho's skill in discovering, and powers of describing the passions of the human mind. That prince is said to have entertained a fatal affection for his mother-in-law Stratonice; which, though he endeavoured to subdue it's influence, preyed upon his frame, and after many ineffectual struggles, at length reduced him to extreme danger. His physicians marked the symptoms attending his malady, and found them so exactly correspond with Sappho's delineation of the tender passion, that they did not hesitate to form a decisive opinion on the cause, which had produced so perilous an effect.

---

1   The nine Muses were divine singers whose hymns delighted the gods. Lesbos is in the northern part of the Grecian archipelago.

That Sappho was not insensible to the feelings she so well described, is evident in her writings: but it was scarcely possible, that a mind so exquisitely tender, so sublimely gifted, should escape those fascinations which even apathy itself has been awakened to acknowledge.

The scarce specimens now extant, from the pen of the Grecian Muse, have by the most competent judges been esteemed as the standard for the pathetic, the glowing, and the amatory.[1] The ode, which has been so highly estimated, is written in a measure distinguished by the title of the Sapphic.[2] POPE made it his model in his juvenile production, beginning —

Happy the man — whose wish and care — [3]

Addison was of opinion, that the writings of Sappho were replete with such fascinating beauties, and adorned with such a vivid glow of sensibility, that, probably, had they been preserved entire, it would have been dangerous to have perused them.[4] They possessed none of the artificial decorations of a feigned passion; they were the genuine effusions of a supremely enlightened soul, labouring to subdue a fatal enchantment; and vainly opposing the conscious pride of illustrious fame, against the warm susceptibility of a generous bosom.

Though few stanzas from the pen of the Lesbian poetess have darted through the shades of oblivion: yet, those that remain are so exquisitely touching and beautiful, that they prove beyond dispute the taste, feeling, and inspiration of the mind which produced them. In

---

1   At the time Robinson was writing, the known works of Sappho consisted of an ode to Aphrodite, a poem which begins "Peer of the gods he seems to me," and miscellaneous fragments.

2   The Sapphic verse form consists of three lines of eleven syllables each and a fourth line of five syllables. There are three spondees in each line with variations in the fourth and eleventh syllables of the first three lines, and in the last syllable of the fourth line.

3   Alexander Pope produces a variation of the Sapphic stanza in his "Ode on Solitude" which begins:
          Happy the man, whose wish and care
          A few paternal acres bound,
          Content to breathe his native air,
          In his own ground.

4   See Joseph Addison's *Spectator*, essay number 223, 15 November 1711.

examining the curiosities of antiquity, we look to the perfections, and not the magnitude of those reliques, which have been preserved amidst the wrecks of time: as the smallest gem that bears the fine touches of a master, surpasses the loftiest fabric reared by the labours of false taste, so the precious fragments of the immortal Sappho, will be admired, when the voluminous productions of inferior poets are mouldered into dust.

When it is considered, that the few specimens we have of the poems of the Grecian Muse, have passed through three and twenty centuries, and consequently through the hands of innumerable translators: and when it is known that Envy frequently delights in the base occupation of depreciating merit which it cannot aspire to emulate; it may be conjectured, that some passages are erroneously given to posterity, either by ignorance or design. Sappho, whose fame beamed round her with the superior effulgence which her works had created, knew that she was writing for future ages: it is not therefore natural that she should produce any composition which might tend to tarnish her reputation, or to lessen that celebrity which it was the labour of her life to consecrate. The delicacy of her sentiments cannot find a more eloquent advocate than in her own effusions; she is said to have commended in the most animated panegyric, the virtues of her brother Lanychus; and with the most pointed and severe censure, to have contemned the passion which her brother Charaxus entertained for the beautiful Rhodope. If her writings were, in some instances, too glowing for the fastidious refinement of modern times; let it be her excuse, and the honour of her country, that the liberal education of the Greeks was such, as inspired them with an unprejudiced enthusiasm for the works of genius: and that when they paid adoration to Sappho, they idolized the MUSE, and not the WOMAN.

I shall conclude this account with an extract from the works of the learned and enlightened ABBE BARTHELEMI; at once the vindication and eulogy of the Grecian Poetess.[1]

SAPPHO undertook to inspire the Lesbian women with a taste for literature; many of them received instructions from her, and

---

1   Jean-Jacques Barthélemy (1716-95) was a classical scholar who achieved popular success with his *Le Voyage du jeune Anacharsis en Grèce* (1788).

foreign women increased the number of her disciples. She loved them to excess, because it was impossible for her to love otherwise; and she expressed her tenderness in all the violence of passion: your surprize at this will cease, when you are acquainted with the extreme sensibility of the Greeks; and discover, that amongst them the most innocent connections often borrow the impassioned language of love.

A certain facility of manners, she possessed; and the warmth of her expressions were but too well calculated to expose her to the hatred of some women of distinction, humbled by her superiority; and the jealousy of some of her disciples, who happened not to be the objects of her preference. To this hatred she replied by truths and irony, which completely exasperated her enemies. She repaired to Sicily, where a statue was erected to her; it was sculptured by SILANION, one of the most celebrated staturists of his time. The sensibility of SAPPHO was extreme! she loved PHAON, who forsook her; after various efforts to bring him back, she took the leap of Leucata,[1] and perished in the waves!

Death has not obliterated the stain imprinted on her character; for ENVY, which fastens on ILLUSTRIOUS NAMES, does not expire; but bequeaths her aspersions to that calumny which NEVER DIES.

Several Grecian women have cultivated POETRY, with success, but none have hitherto attained to the excellence of SAPPHO. And among other poets, there are few, indeed, who have surpassed her.

---

1   Leucata was a promontory of Epirus, on the top of which stood a temple dedicated to Apollo. From this promontory despairing lovers threw themselves into the sea, with an idea that, if they survived, they should be cured of their hopeless passions. The Abbé Barthelemi says, that, "many escaped, but others having perished, the custom fell into disrepute; and at length was wholly abolished." — *Vide Travels of Anacharsis the Younger* [M.R.].

SAPPHO AND PHAON

FLENDUS AMOR MEUS EST; ELEGEÏA FLEBILE CARMEN;
NON FACIT AD LACRYMAS BARBITOS ULLA MEAS.

OVID[1]

Love taught my tears in sadder notes to flow,
And tun'd my heart to elegies of woe.

POPE[2]

SONNET INTRODUCTORY

FAVOUR'D by Heav'n are those, ordain'd to taste
   The bliss supreme that kindles fancy's fire;
   Whose magic fingers sweep the muses' lyre,
In varying cadence, eloquently chaste!
Well may the mind, with tuneful numbers grac'd,   5
   To Fame's immortal attributes aspire,
   Above the treach'rous spells of low desire,
That wound the sense, by vulgar joys debas'd.
   For thou, blest POESY! with godlike pow'rs
To calm the miseries of man wert giv'n;   10
   When passion rends, and hopeless love devours,
By mem'ry goaded, and by frenzy driv'n,
   'Tis thine to guide him 'midst Elysian[3] bow'rs,
And shew his fainting soul, — a glimpse of Heav'n.

SONNET II

HIGH on a rock, coeval[4] with the skies,
   A Temple stands, rear'd by immortal pow'rs
   To Chastity divine! ambrosial flow'rs

---

1 Ovid, *Heroides*, XV, lines 7-8. Harold Isbell translates the lines as:
       But I weep and tears fit well the elegy —
       a lyre cannot bear the weight of tears.
                    Heroides (New York: Penguin Books, 1990).
2 Pope's translation of Ovid's lines in "Sappho and Phaon" (1712).
3 In Greek mythology, Elysium is the realm of the blessed after death.
4 Coeval means of the same age.

Twining round icicles, in columns rise,
Mingling with pendent gems of orient dyes!
  Piercing the air, a golden crescent tow'rs,
  Veil'd by transparent clouds; while smiling hours
Shake from their varying wings — celestial joys!
  The steps of spotless marble, scatter'd o'er
With deathless roses arm'd with many a thorn,
  Lead to the altar. On the frozen floor,
Studded with tear-drops petrified by scorn,
  Pale vestals[1] kneel the Goddess to adore,
While Love, his arrows broke, retires forlorn.

SONNET III

TURN to yon vale beneath, whose tangled shade
  Excludes the blazing torch of noon-day light,
  Where sportive Fawns,[2] and dimpled Loves invite,
The bow'r of Pleasure[3] opens to the glade:
Lull'd by soft flutes, on leaves of violets laid,
  There witching beauty greets the ravish'd sight,
  More gentle than the arbitress of night
In all her silv'ry panoply array'd!
  The birds breathe bliss! light zephyrs kiss the ground,
Stealing the hyacinth's divine perfume;
  While from pellucid[4] fountains glitt'ring round,
Small tinkling rills[5] bid rival flow'rets bloom!
  HERE, laughing Cupids bathe the bosom's wound;
THERE, tyrant passion finds a glorious tomb!

---

1 Vestal Virgins tended the altar fire at the temple of Vesta in Rome. Vesta was the Roman goddess of the hearth fire.
2 Young deer. Fawn is also an early spelling of faun so Robinson could be referring to the Roman gods of fields and herds, satyr figures which are part man and part goat.
3 See the Bower of Bliss in Edmund Spenser's *The Faerie Queene*, 2.12.69–87.
4 Extremely clear.
5 Small streams.

SONNET IV

WHY, when I gaze on Phaon's beauteous eyes,
 Why does each thought in wild disorder stray?
 Why does each fainting faculty decay,
And my chill'd breast in throbbing tumults rise?
Mute, on the ground my Lyre neglected lies,   5
 The Muse forgot, and lost the melting lay;
 My down-cast looks, my faultering lips betray,
That stung by hopeless passion, — Sappho dies!
 Now, on a bank of Cypress[1] let me rest;
Come, tuneful maids, ye pupils of my care,   10
 Come, with your dulcet numbers soothe my breast;
And, as the soft vibrations float on air,
 Let pity waft my spirit to the blest,
To mock the barb'rous triumphs of despair!

SONNET V

O! How can LOVE exulting Reason quell!
 How fades each nobler passion from his gaze!
E'en Fame, that cherishes the Poet's lays,
That fame, ill-fated Sappho lov'd so well.
Lost is the wretch, who in his fatal spell   5
 Wastes the short Summer of delicious days,
 And from the tranquil path of wisdom strays,
In passion's thorny wild, forlorn to dwell.
 O ye! who in that sacred Temple smile
Where holy Innocence resides enshrin'd;   10
 Who fear not sorrow, and who know not guile,
Each thought compos'd, and ev'ry wish resign'd;
 Tempt not the path where pleasure's flow'ry wile
In sweet, but pois'nous fetters, holds the mind.

---

1   The cypress is associated with mourning and funerals.

SONNET VI

Is it to love, to fix the tender gaze,
    To hide the timid blush, and steal away;
    To shun the busy world, and waste the day
In some rude mountain's solitary maze?
5   Is it to chant *one* name in ceaseless lays,
    To hear no words that other tongues can say,
    To watch the pale moon's melancholy ray,
To chide in fondness, and in folly praise?
    Is it to pour th' involuntary sigh,
10   To dream of bliss, and wake new pangs to prove;
    To talk, in fancy, with the speaking eye,
Then start with jealousy, and wildly rove;
    Is it to loath the light, and wish to die?
For these I feel, — and feel that they are Love.

SONNET VII

COME, Reason, come! each nerve rebellious bind,
    Lull the fierce tempest of my fev'rish soul;
    Come, with the magic of thy meek controul,
And check the wayward wand'rings of my mind:
5   Estrang'd from thee, no solace can I find,
    O'er my rapt brain, where pensive visions stole,
    Now passion reigns and stormy tumults roll —
So the smooth Sea obeys the furious wind!
    In vain Philosophy unfolds his store,
10   O'erwhelm'd is ev'ry source of pure delight;
    Dim is the golden page of wisdom's lore;
All nature fades before my sick'ning sight:
    For what bright scene can fancy's eye explore,
'Midst dreary labyrinths of mental night?

SONNET VIII

WHY, through each aching vein, with lazy pace
    Thus steals the languid fountain of my heart,
    While, from its source, each wild convulsive start
Tears the scorch'd roses from my burning face?
In vain, O Lesbian Vales! your charms I trace;   5
    Vain is the poet's theme, the sculptor's art;
    No more the Lyre[1] its magic can impart,
Though wak'd to sound, with more than mortal grace!
    Go, tuneful maids, go bid my Phaon prove
That passion mocks the empty boast of fame;   10
    Tell him no joys are sweet, but joys of love,
Melting the soul, and thrilling all the frame!
    Oh! may th' ecstatic thought his bosom move,
And sighs of rapture, fan the blush of shame!

SONNET IX

YE, who in alleys green and leafy bow'rs,
    Sport, the rude children of fantastic birth;
    Where frolic nymphs, and shaggy tribes of mirth,
In clam'rous revels waste the midnight hours;
Who, link'd in flaunting bands of mountain flow'rs,   5
    Weave your wild mazes o'er the dewy earth,
    Ere the fierce Lord of Lustre rushes forth,
And o'er the world his beamy radiance pours!
    Oft has your clanking cymbal's madd'ning strain,
Loud ringing through the torch-illumin'd grove,   10
    Lur'd my lov'd Phaon from the youthful train,
Through rugged dells, o'er craggy rocks to rove;
    Then how can she his vagrant heart detain,
Whose Lyre throbs only to the touch of Love?

---

1 Sappho wrote songs that were accompanied by the lyre.

SONNET X

DANG'ROUS to hear, is that melodious tongue,
   And fatal to the sense those murd'rous eyes,
   Where in a sapphire sheath, Love's arrow lies,
Himself conceal'd the crystal haunts among!
5   Oft o'er that form, enamour'd have I hung,
   On that smooth cheek to mark the deep'ning dyes,
   While from that lip the fragrant breath would rise,
That lip, like Cupid's bow with rubies strung!
   Still let me gaze upon that polish'd brow,
10   O'er which the golden hair luxuriant plays;
   So, on the modest lily's leaves of snow
The proud Sun revels in resplendent rays!
   Warm as his beams this sensate heart shall glow,
Till life's last hour, with Phaon's self decays!

SONNET XI

O! Reason! vaunted Sov'reign of the mind!
   Thou pompous vision with a sounding name!
   Can'st thou the soul's rebellious passions tame?
Can'st thou in spells the vagrant fancy bind?
5   Ah, no! capricious as the wav'ring wind
   Are sighs of Love that dim thy boasted flame,
   While Folly's torch consumes the wreath of fame,
And Pleasure's hands the sheaves of Truth unbind.
   Press'd by the storms of Fate, hope shrinks and dies;
10   Frenzy darts forth in mightiest ills array'd;
   Around thy throne destructive tumults rise,
And hell-fraught jealousies, thy rights invade!
   Then, what art thou? O! Idol of the wise!
A visionary theme! — a gorgeous shade!

SONNET XII

Now, o'er the tessellated[1] pavement strew
   Fresh saffron, steep'd in essence of the rose,
   While down yon agate[2] column gently flows
A glitt'ring streamlet of ambrosial dew!
My Phaon smiles! the rich carnation's hue,   5
   On his flush'd cheek in conscious lustre glows,
   While o'er his breast enamour'd Venus throws
Her starry mantle of celestial blue!
   Breathe soft, ye dulcet flutes, among the trees
Where clust'ring boughs with golden citron twine,   10
   While slow vibrations, dying on the breeze,
Shall soothe his soul with harmony divine!
   Then let my form his yielding fancy seize,
And all his fondest wishes, blend with mine.

SONNET XIII

Bring, bring to deck my brow, ye Sylvan girls,[3]
   A roseate wreath; nor for my waving hair
   The costly band of studded gems prepare,
Of sparkling crysolite[4] or orient pearls:
Love, o'er my head his canopy unfurls,   5
   His purple pinions[5] fan the whisp'ring air;
   Mocking the golden sandal, rich and rare,
Beneath my feet the fragrant woodbine curls.[6]
   Bring the thin robes, to fold about my breast,
White as the downy swan; while round my waist   10
   Let leaves of glossy myrtle bind the vest,
Not idly gay, but elegantly chaste!

---

1   Composed of small blocks of variously coloured material to form a mosaic effect.
2   A precious stone with colours arranged in bands or blended in clouds.
3   Sylvan girls inhabit the woods or forest; spirits of the forest.
4   A precious yellow-green stone.
5   Wings.
6   The woodbine is another name for the common honeysuckle, a climbing plant
   with a fragrant yellow flower. It is also a more general name for a variety of climb-
   ing plants.

Love scorns the nymph in wanton trappings drest;
And charms the most conceal'd, are doubly grac'd.

SONNET XIV

COME, soft Aeolian harp, while zephyr plays[1]
    Along the meek vibration of thy strings,
    As twilight's hand her modest mantle brings,
Blending with sober grey, the western blaze!
O! prompt my Phaon's dreams with tend'rest lays,
    Ere night o'ershade thee with its humid wings,
    While the lorn Philomel[2] his sorrow sings
In leafy cradle, red with parting rays!
    Slow let thy dulcet tones on ether glide,[3]
So steals the murmur of the am'rous dove;
    The mazy legions swarm on ev'ry side,
To lulling sounds the sunny people move!
    Let not the wise their little world deride,
The smallest sting can wound the breast of Love.

SONNET XV

NOW, round my favour'd grot[4] let roses rise,
    To strew the bank where Phaon wakes from rest;
    O! happy buds! to kiss his burning breast,
And die, beneath the lustre of his eyes!
Now, let the timbrels echo to the skies,
    Now damsels sprinkle cassia[5] on his vest,
    With od'rous wreaths of constant myrtle drest,
And flow'rs, deep tinted with the rainbow's dyes!
    From cups of porphyry[6] let nectar flow,

1   An Aeolian harp is a stringed instrument that produces musical sounds upon exposure to a current of air, in this case, upon exposure to zephyrs, or soft breezes. Aeolus is the Greek god of winds.
2   Philomel (or Philomela) is a name given to the nightingale.
3   Ether is air or, more specifically, the divine air breathed by the gods.
4   Poetic shorthand for grotto, a picturesque cave.
5   A fragrant shrub.
6   A beautiful purple stone.

Rich as the perfume of Phoenicia's vine!   10
   Now let his dimpling cheek with rapture glow,
   While round his heart love's mystic fetters twine;
   And let the Grecian Lyre its aid bestow,
In songs of triumph, to proclaim him mine!

SONNET XVI

DELUSIVE Hope! more transient than the ray
   That leads pale twilight to her dusky bed,
   O'er woodland glen, or breezy mountain's head,
Ling'ring to catch the parting sigh of day.
Hence with thy visionary charms, away!   5
   Nor o'er my path the flow'rs of fancy spread;
   Thy airy dreams on peaceful pillows shed,
And weave for thoughtless brows, a garland gay.
   Farewell low vallies; dizzy cliffs, farewell!
Small vagrant rills that murmur as ye flow: 10
   Dark bosom'd labyrinth and thorny dell;
The task be mine all pleasures to forego;
   To hide, where meditation loves to dwell,
And feed my soul, with luxury of woe!

SONNET XVII

LOVE steals unheeded o'er the tranquil mind,
   As Summer breezes fan the sleeping main,[1]
   Slow through each fibre creeps the subtle pain,
'Till closely round the yielding bosom twin'd.
Vain is the hope the magic to unbind,   5
   The potent mischief riots in the brain,
   Grasps ev'ry thought, and burns in ev'ry vein,
'Till in the heart the Tyrant lives enshrin'd.
   Oh! Victor strong! bending the vanquish'd frame;
Sweet is the thraldom that thou bids't us prove!   10
   And sacred is the tear thy victims claim,

---

[1] An open expanse of land or sea.

For blest are those whom sighs of sorrow move!
Then nymphs beware how ye profane my name,
Nor blame my weakness, till like me ye love!

SONNET XVIII

WHY art thou chang'd? O Phaon! tell me why?
   Love flies reproach, when passion feels decay;
   Or, I would paint the raptures of that day,
When, in sweet converse, mingling sigh with sigh,
5   I mark'd the graceful languor of thine eye
     As on a shady bank entranc'd we lay:
     O! Eyes! whose beamy radiance stole away
As stars fade trembling from the burning sky!
    Why art thou chang'd? dear source of all my woes!
10 Though dark my bosom's tint, through ev'ry vein
     A ruby tide of purest lustre flows,
Warm'd by thy love, or chill'd by thy disdain;
    And yet no bliss this sensate Being knows;
Ah! why is rapture so allied to pain?

SONNET XIX

FAREWELL, ye coral caves, ye pearly sands,
   Ye waving woods that crown yon lofty steep;
   Farewell, ye Nereides[1] of the glitt'ring deep,
Ye mountain tribes, ye fawns, ye sylvan bands:
5   On the bleak rock your frantic minstrel stands,
     Each task forgot, save that, to sigh and weep;
     In vain the strings her burning fingers sweep,
No more her touch, the Grecian Lyre commands!
    In Circe's[2] cave my faithless Phaon's laid,
10 Her daemons dress his brow with opiate flow'rs;
     Or, loit'ring in the brown pomgranate[3] shade,

---

1   Nymphs of the sea, daughters of Nereus, the Old Man of the Sea, and Doria, a
    daughter of the Ocean.
2   A witch in Homer's *Odyssey* who serves a banquet to Odysseus's men and trans-
    forms them into animals.
3   Pomegranate.

Beguile with am'rous strains the fateful hours;
    While Sappho's lips, to paly ashes fade,
And sorrow's cank'ring worm her heart devours!

SONNET XX

OH ! I could toil for thee o'er burning plains;
    Could smile at poverty's disastrous blow;
    With thee, could wander 'midst a world of snow,
Where one long night o'er frozen Scythia[1] reigns.
Sever'd from thee, my sick'ning soul disdains   5
    The thrilling thought, the blissful dream to know,
    And can'st thou give my days to endless woe,
Requiting sweetest bliss with cureless pains?
    Away, false fear! nor think capricious fate
Would lodge a daemon in a form divine!   10
    Sooner the dove shall seek a tyger mate,
Or the soft snow-drop round the thistle twine;
    Yet, yet, I dread to hope, nor dare to hate,
Too proud to sue! too tender to resign!

SONNET XXI

WHY do I live to loath the cheerful day,
    To shun the smiles of Fame, and mark the hours
    On tardy pinions move, while ceaseless show'rs
Down my wan cheek in lucid currents stray?
My tresses all unbound, nor gems display,   5
    Nor scents Arabian! on my path no flow'rs
    Imbibe the morn's resuscitating pow'rs,
For one blank sorrow, saddens all my way!
    As slow the radiant Sun of reason rose,[2]

---

1   The name given by the ancient Greeks to an area around the Black Sea coast of
Russia and the Caucasus mountains.

2   Sex mihi natales ierant, cum lecta parentis
                    Ante diem lacrymas ossa bibere meas.
                    Arsit inops frater, victus meretricis amore;
                    Mistaque cum turpi damna pudore tulit. *Ovid* [M.R.]
Harold Isbell translates these lines as follows:

Through tears my dying parents saw it shine;
A brother's frailties,[1] swell'd the tide of woes, —
And, keener far, maternal griefs were mine!
Phaon! if soon these weary eyes shall close,
Oh! must that task, that mournful task, be thine?

SONNET XXII

WILD is the foaming Sea! The surges roar!
And nimbly dart the livid lightnings round!
On the rent rock the angry waves rebound;
Ah me! the less'ning bark is seen no more!
Along the margin of the trembling shore,
Loud as the blast my frantic cries shall sound,
My storm-drench'd limbs the flinty fragments wound,
And o'er my bleeding breast the billows pour!
Phaon! return! ye winds, O! waft the strain
To his swift bark; ye barb'rous waves forbear!
Taunt not the anguish of a lover's brain,
Nor feebly emulate the soul's despair!
For howling winds, and foaming seas, in vain
Assail the breast, when passion rages there!

SONNET XXIII

To Aetna's scorching sand my Phaon flies![2]
False Youth! can other charms attractive prove?
Say, can Sicilian loves thy passions move,
Play round thy heart, and fix thy fickle eyes,

Only six birthdays had come and gone for me when I swept up my father's bones, dead too soon, and let them drink my young tears. Caught up with a whore, untrained in loving ways, my innocent brother bore the foulest shame and suffered the greatest loss.
    "XV: Sappho to Phaon," *Heroides* (New York: Penguin Books, 1990) 135.
1 Sappho purportedly had a brother Charaxos who squandered his money on the courtesan Rhodope.
2 Arva Phaon celebrat diversa Typhoidos Ætnæ. [M.R.] Line 11 of Ovid's *Heroides* XV. Isbell translates this line paired with Robinson's annotation to line 10 of her poem as: "The fields where you are now, on the slopes of Typhoeus' Aetna, Phaon,

While in despair the Lesbian Sappho dies? 5
　　Has Spring for thee a crown of poppies wove,
　　Or dost thou languish in th' Idalian grove,[1]
Whose altar kindles, fann'd by Lover's sighs?
　　Ah! think, that while on Aetna's shores you stray,
A fire, more fierce than Aetna's, fills my breast;[2] 10
　　Nor deck Sicilian nymphs with garlands gay,
While Sappho's brows with cypress wreaths are drest;
　　Let one kind word my weary woes repay,
Or, in eternal slumbers bid them rest.

SONNET XXIV

O THOU! meek Orb![3] that stealing o'er the dale
　　Cheer'st with thy modest beams the noon of night!
　　On the smooth lake diffusing silv'ry light,
Sublimely still, and beautifully pale!
What can thy cool and placid eye avail, 5
　　Where fierce despair absorbs the mental sight,
　　While inbred glooms the vagrant thoughts invite,
To tempt the gulph where howling fiends assail?
　　O, Night! all nature owns thy temper'd pow'r;
Thy solemn pause, thy dews, thy pensive beam; 10
　　Thy sweet breath whisp'ring in the moonlight bow'r,
While fainting flow'rets kiss the wand'ring stream!
　　Yet, vain is ev'ry charm! and vain the hour,
That brings to madd'ning love, no soothing dream!

---

　　are far away but no less subject than I to the flames that come by storm." *Heroides*
　　133. Aetna is the highest active volcano in Europe; it is located in eastern Sicily.
1　Idalium: a town in Cyprus where Aphrodite was worshipped.
2　Me calor Ætnæo non minor igne coquit. *Ovid* [M.R.]. See note 2 on page 168.
3　The moon.

SONNET XXV

Cans't thou forget, O! Idol of my Soul!
   Thy Sappho's voice, her form, her dulcet Lyre!
   That melting ev'ry thought to fond desire,
Bade sweet delirium o'er thy senses roll?
5   Cans't thou, so soon, renounce the blest control
   That calm'd with pity's tears love's raging fire,
   While Hope, slow breathing on the trembling wire,
In every note with soft persuasion stole?
   Oh! Sov'reign of my heart! return! return!
10 For me no spring appears, no summers bloom,
   No Sun-beams glitter, and no altars burn!
The mind's dark winter of eternal gloom,
   Shews 'midst the waste a solitary urn,
A blighted laurel, and a mould'ring tomb!

SONNET XXVI

Where antique woods o'er-hang the mountain's crest,
   And mid-day glooms in solemn silence lour,[1]
   Philosophy, go seek a lonely bow'r,
And waste life's fervid noon in fancied rest.
5   Go, where the bird of sorrow weaves her nest,
   Cooing, in sadness sweet, through night's dim hour;
   Go, cull the dew-drops from each potent flow'r
That med'cines to the cold and reas'ning breast!
   Go, where the brook in liquid lapse steals by,
10 Scarce heard amid'st the mingling echoes round,
   What time, the moon fades slowly down the sky,
And slumb'ring zephyrs moan, in caverns bound:
   Be these thy pleasures, dull Philosophy!
Nor vaunt the balm, to heal a lover's wound.

---

1   To frown or scowl.

SONNET XXVII

OH! ye bright Stars! that on the Ebon fields
    Of Heav'n's vast empire, trembling seem to stand;
    'Till rosy morn unlocks her portal[1] bland,
Where the proud Sun his fiery banner wields!
To flames, less fierce than mine, your lustre yields,   5
    And pow'rs more strong my countless tears command;
    Love strikes the feeling heart with ruthless hand,
And only spares the breast which dullness shields.
    Since, then, capricious nature but bestows
The fine affections of the soul, to prove   10
    A keener sense of desolating woes,
Far, far from me the empty boast remove;
    If bliss from coldness, pain from passion flows,
Ah! who would wish to feel, or learn to love?

SONNET XXVIII

WEAK is the sophistry, and vain the art
    That whispers patience to the mind's despair!
    That bids reflection bathe the wounds of care,
While Hope, with pleasing phantoms, soothes their smart!
For mem'ry still, reluctant to depart   5
    From the dear spot, once rich in prospects fair,
    Bids the fond soul enamour'd linger there,
And its least charm is grateful to the heart!
    He never lov'd, who could not muse and sigh,
Spangling the sacred turf with frequent tears,   10
    Where the small rivulet, that ripples by,
Recalls the scenes of past and happier years,
    When, on its banks he watch'd the speaking eye,
And one sweet smile o'erpaid an age of fears!

---

1 A door or entrance.

SONNET XXIX

FAREWELL, ye tow'ring Cedars, in whose shade,
 Lull'd by the Nightingale, I sunk to rest,
 While spicy breezes hover'd o'er my breast
To fan my cheek, in deep'ning tints array'd;
5 While am'rous insects, humming round me, play'd,
 Each flow'r forsook, of prouder sweets in quest;
 Of glowing lips, in humid fragrance drest,
That mock'd the Sunny Hybla's vaunted aid![1]
 Farewell, ye limpid rivers! Oh! farewell!
10 No more shall Sappho to your grots repair;
 No more your white waves to her bosom swell,
Or your dank weeds, entwine her floating hair;
 As erst, when Venus in her sparry cell[2]
Wept, to behold a brighter goddess there!

SONNET XXX

O'ER the tall cliff that bounds the billowy main
 Shad'wing the surge that sweeps the lonely strand,
 While the thin vapours break along the sand,
Day's harbinger unfolds the liquid plain.
5 The rude Sea murmurs, mournful as the strain
 That love-lorn minstrels strike with trembling hand,
 While from their green beds rise the Syren band[3]
With tongues aërial to repeat my pain!
 The vessel rocks beside the pebbly shore,
10 The foamy curls its gaudy trappings lave;
 Oh! Bark propitious! bear me gently o'er,
Breathe soft, ye winds; rise slow, O! swelling wave!
 Lesbos; these eyes shall meet thy sands no more:
I fly, to seek my Lover, or my Grave!

---

1 Hybla is a town on the slopes of Mt. Aetna famous for its herbs and scented honey.
2 Venus is the goddess of love and beauty. A sparry cell is studded with crystals.
3 Sirens are mythological sea demons, remarkable musicians who lured sailors to
   destruction with their beautiful songs.

SONNET XXXI

FAR o'er the waves my lofty Bark shall glide,
  Love's frequent sighs the flutt'ring sails shall swell,
  While to my native home I bid farewell,
Hope's snowy hand the burnish'd helm shall guide!
Tritons[1] shall sport amidst the yielding tide,   5
  Myriads of Cupids round the prow shall dwell,
  And Venus,[2] thron'd within her opal shell,
Shall proudly o'er the glitt'ring billows ride!
  Young Dolphins,[3] dashing in the golden spray,
Shall with their scaly forms illume the deep   10
  Ting'd with the purple flush of sinking day,
Whose flaming wreath shall crown the distant steep;
  While on the breezy deck soft minstrels play,
And songs of love, the lover soothe to sleep!

SONNET XXXII

BLEST as the Gods! Sicilian Maid is he,[4]
  The youth whose soul thy yielding graces charm;
  Who bound, O! thraldom sweet! by beauty's arm,
In idle dalliance fondly sports with thee!
Blest as the Gods! that iv'ry throne to see,   5
  Throbbing with transports, tender, timid, warm!
  While round thy fragrant lips light zephyrs swarm,
As op'ning buds attract the wand'ring Bee!
  Yet, short is youthful passion's fervid hour;
Soon, shall another clasp the beauteous boy;   10
  Soon, shall a rival prove, in that gay bow'r,
The pleasing torture of excessive joy!

---

1 Triton was a god of the sea whose trumpet was a great shell.
2 Venus or Aphrodite was the goddess of love and beauty. She was said to have sprung
   from the foam of the sea. She is often depicted riding on a shell.
3 The dolphin was sacred to Apollo, the god of light and truth who plays on a golden
   lyre.
4 Vide Sappho's Ode [M.R.]. Robinson's first line quotes the first line of Sappho's
   homoerotic fragment known in English as "To a Beloved Girl" or "Peer of the
   Gods."

The Bee flies sicken'd from the sweetest flow'r;
The lightning's shaft, but dazzles to destroy!

SONNET XXXIII

I WAKE! delusive phantoms hence, away!
    Tempt not the weakness of a lover's breast;
    The softest breeze can shake the halcyon's nest,[1]
And lightest clouds o'er cast the dawning ray!
5   'Twas but a vision! Now, the star of day
    Peers, like a gem on Aetna's[2] burning crest!
    Welcome, ye Hills, with golden vintage drest;
Sicilian forests brown, and vallies gay!
    A mournful stranger, from the Lesbian Isle,
10 Not strange, in loftiest eulogy of Song!
    She, who could teach the Stoic's cheek to smile,[3]
Thaw the cold heart, and chain the wond'ring throng,
    Can find no balm, love's sorrows to beguile;
Ah! Sorrows known too soon! and felt too long!

SONNET XXXIV

VENUS! to thee, the Lesbian muse shall sing,
    The song, which Myttellenian youths[4] admir'd,
    When Echo, am'rous of the strain inspir'd,
Bade the wild rocks with madd'ning plaudits ring!
5   Attend my pray'r! O! Queen of rapture! bring
    To these fond arms, he, whom my soul has fir'd;
    From these fond arms remov'd, yet, still desir'd,
Though love, exulting, spreads his varying wing!
    Oh! source of ev'ry joy! of ev'ry care!
10 Blest Venus! Goddess of the zone divine!

---

1   The mythological Alcyone and her drowned husband Ceyx were transformed into
    birds. Halcyon days are those days when the ocean is perfectly still and calm, puta-
    tively during the period in which Halycon is brooding over her nest. The charm is
    broken when the young birds are hatched.
2   The highest active volcano in Europe.
3   The Stoic school of Greek philosophers was characterized by austerity.
4   Youths from Mytilene, reportedly the birthplace of Sappho.

To Phaon's bosom, Phaon's victim bear;
So shall her warmest, tend'rest vows be thine!
For Venus, Sappho shall a wreath prepare,
And Love be crown'd, immortal as the Nine![1]

SONNET XXXV

WHAT means the mist opake that veils these eyes;
Why does yon threat'ning tempest shroud the day?
Why does thy altar, Venus, fade away,
And on my breast the dews of horror rise?
Phaon is false! be dim, ye orient Skies,   5
And let black Erebus[2] succeed your ray;
Let clashing thunders roll, and lightnings play;
Phaon is false! and hopeless Sappho dies!
"Farewell! my Lesbian love, you might have said,"
Such sweet remembrance had some pity prov'd,   10
"Or coldly thus, farewell, Oh! Lesbian maid!"[3]
No task severe, for one so fondly lov'd!
The gentle thought had sooth'd my wand'ring shade,
From life's dark valley, and its thorns remov'd!

SONNET XXXVI

LEAD me, Sicilian Maids, to haunted bow'rs,
While yon pale moon displays her faintest beams
O'er blasted woodlands, and enchanted streams,
Whose banks infect the breeze with pois'nous flow'rs.
Ah! lead me, where the barren mountain tow'rs,   5

---

1   The nine Muses.
2   The son of Chaos (the primeval void). His name usually refers to the darkest depths
    of the underworld.
3   Pope.

> Si tam certus eras hinc ire, modestius isses,
> Et modo dixisses Lesbi puella, vale. *Ovid* [M.R.]

Robinson signals her debt to Alexander Pope, who wrote:

> Farewel *my* Lesbian *Love*! you might have said,
> Or coldly thus, *Farewel oh* Lesbian *Maid*!
>
> *Sappho to Phaon*, lines 113-14

Where no sounds echo, but the night-owl's screams,
　Where some lone spirit of the desert gleams,
And lurid horrors wing the fateful hours!
　Now goaded frenzy grasps my shrinking brain,
10　Her touch absorbs the crystal fount of woe!
　My blood rolls burning through each gasping vein;
　Away, lost Lyre! unless thou cans't bestow
　A charm, to lull that agonizing pain,
Which those who never lov'd, can never know!

SONNET XXXVII

WHEN, in the gloomy mansion of the dead,
　This with'ring heart, this faded form shall sleep:
　When these fond eyes, at length shall cease to weep,
And earth's cold lap receive this fev'rish head:
5　Envy shall turn away, a tear to shed,
　And Time's obliterating pinions sweep
　The spot, where poets shall their vigils keep,
To mourn and wander near my freezing bed!
　Then, my pale ghost, upon th' Elysian shore,
10　Shall smile, releas'd from ev'ry mortal care;
　While, doom'd love's victim to repine no more,
My breast shall bathe in endless rapture there!
　Ah! no! my restless shade would still deplore,
Nor taste that bliss, which Phaon did not share.

SONNET XXXVIII

OH Sigh! thou steal'st, the herald of the breast,
　The lover's fears, the lover's pangs to tell;
　Thou bid'st with timid grace the bosom swell,
Cheating the day of joy, the night of rest!
5　Oh! lucid Tears! with eloquence confest,
　Why on my fading cheek unheeded dwell,
　Meek, as the dew-drops on the flowret's bell
By ruthless tempests to the green-sod prest.
　Fond sigh be hush'd! congeal, O! slighted tear!

Thy feeble pow'rs the busy Fates control!
  Or if thy crystal streams again appear,
Let them, like Lethe's,[1] to oblivion roll:
  For Love the tyrant plays, when hope is near,
And she who flies the lover, — chains the soul!

SONNET XXXIX

PREPARE your wreaths, Aonian maids divine,[2]
  To strew the tranquil bed where I shall sleep;
  In tears, the myrtle and the laurel steep,
And let Erato's hand[3] the trophies twine.
No parian marble,[4] there, with labour'd line,
  Shall bid the wand'ring lover stay to weep;
  There holy silence shall her vigils keep,
Save, when the nightingale such woes as mine
  Shall sadly sing; as twilight's curtains spread,
There shall the branching lotos widely wave,[5]
  Sprinkling soft show'rs upon the lily's head,
Sweet drooping emblem for a lover's grave!
  And there shall Phaon pearls of pity shed,
To gem the vanquish'd heart he scorn'd to save!

SONNET XL

ON the low margin of a murm'ring stream,
  As rapt in meditation's arms I lay;
  Each aching sense in slumbers stole away,
While potent fancy form'd a soothing dream;

---

1 The river of forgetfulness in Hades.
2 Aonia was a region of ancient Boeotia that contained the mountains Helicon and Cithaeron, sacred to the Muses or "Aonian maids."
3 Erato was one of the nine Muses. She was the Muse of lyric poetry, especially love poetry.
4 Parian marble came from the island of Paros (between Greece and Turkey) and was highly valued among the ancients for statuary. The Parian Chronicle, a document inscribed on marble and outlining Greek history, alludes to Sappho fleeing from Mytilene and sailing to Sicily.
5 In Homer's *Odyssey* Odysseus encounters on his travels the land of the lotus-eaters. Eating lotus results in the loss of the desire to return home.

SAPPHO AND PHAON (1796)   177

O'er the Leucadian deep,[1] a dazzling beam
Shed the bland light of empyrean[2] day!
But soon transparent shadows veil'd each ray,
While mystic visions sprang athwart the gleam!
Now to the heaving gulf they seem'd to bend,
And now across the sphery regions glide;
Now in mid-air, their dulcet voices blend,
"Awake! awake!" the restless phalanx cried,
"See ocean yawns the lover's woes to end;
Plunge the green wave, and bid thy griefs subside."

SONNET XLI

YES, I will go, where circling whirlwinds rise,
Where threat'ning clouds in sable grandeur lour;
Where the blast yells, the liquid columns pour,
And madd'ning billows combat with the skies!
There, while the Daemon of the tempest flies
On growing pinions through the troublous hour,
The wild waves gasp impatient to devour,
And on the rock the waken'd Vulture cries!
Oh! dreadful solace to the stormy mind!
To me, more pleasing than the valley's rest,
The wood land songsters, or the sportive kind,
That nip the turf, or prune the painted crest;
For in despair alone, the wretched find
That unction[3] sweet, which lulls the bleeding breast!

SONNET XLII

OH! can'st thou bear to see this faded frame,
Deform'd and mangled by the rocky deep?
Wilt thou remember, and forbear to weep,

---

1 Leucadia: one of the Ionian islands off the west coast of Greece. The temple of
   Apollo was on a promontory at the end of the island. According to legend, lovers
   who threw themselves off this cliff into the sea would be cured of their infatuation.
2 Associated with the highest heaven, the abode of God and angels.
3 An ointment.

My fatal fondness, and my peerless fame?
Soon o'er this heart, now warm with passion's flame,   5
    The howling winds and foamy waves shall sweep;
    Those eyes be ever clos'd in death's cold sleep,
And all of Sappho perish, but her name!
Yet, if the Fates suspend their barb'rous ire,
If days less mournful, Heav'n designs for me!   10
    If rocks grow kind, and winds and waves conspire,
    To bear me softly on the swelling sea;
        To Phoebus[1] only will I tune my Lyre,
"What suits with Sappho, Phoebus suits with thee!"[2]

SONNET XLIII

WHILE from the dizzy precipice I gaze,
    The world receding from my pensive eyes,
    High o'er my head the tyrant eagle flies,
Cloth'd in the sinking sun's transcendent blaze!
The meek-ey'd moon, 'midst clouds of amber plays   5
    As o'er the purpling plains of light she hies,[3]
    Till the last stream of living lustre dies,
And the cool concave owns her temper'd rays!
So shall this glowing, palpitating soul,
    Welcome returning Reason's placid beam,   10
        While o'er my breast the waves Lethean roll,
    To calm rebellious Fancy's fev'rish dream;
        Then shall my Lyre disdain love's dread control,
And loftier passions, prompt the loftier theme!

---

1 Phoebus Apollo is the god of light and truth, a beautiful figure who plays on a golden lyre.
2 Pope. Grata lyram posui tibi Phœbe, poëtria Sappho: / Convenit illa mihi, convenit illa tibi. *Ovid*. [M.R.] Robinson acknowledges Alexander Pope as the source of her line (Pope's *Sappho and Phaon*, line 216) and quotes lines from Ovid's *Heroides* which Isbell translates as follows: "Phoebus, the grateful poetess, Sappho, brings a lyre, a gift proper to us both." "Sappho to Phaon," *Heroides*, trans. Harold Isbell (New York: Penguin Books, 1990) 139.
3 Hastens.

SONNET XLIV. CONCLUSIVE

HERE droops the muse! while from her glowing mind,
   Celestial Sympathy, with humid eye,
   Bids the light Sylph[1] capricious Fancy fly,
Time's restless wings with transient flow'rs to bind!
For now, with folded arms and head inclin'd,
   Reflection pours the deep and frequent sigh,
   O'er the dark scroll of human destiny,
Where gaudy buds and wounding thorns are twin'd.
   O! Sky-born VIRTUE! sacred is thy name!
And though mysterious Fate, with frown severe,
   Oft decorates thy brows with wreaths of Fame,
Bespangled o'er with sorrow's chilling tear!
   Yet shalt thou more than mortal raptures claim,
The brightest planet of th' ETERNAL SPHERE!

FINIS

---

1   An imaginary being who inhabits the air.

Is it to haunt in warm attire?
To laugh & feast & dance & sing,
To crowd around the blazing fire,
And make the roof with revels ring?
                                    Ah! no!

Figure 9. Mezzotint engraving after Maria Cosway, illustration No. 5 for "The Wintry Day,"
1804. (By courtesy of the Special Collections Department, University of Virginia Library.)

ALL ALONE

I

Ah! wherefore by the Church-yard side,
  Poor little LORN ONE, dost thou stray?
Thy wavy locks but thinly hide
  The tears that dim thy blue-eye's ray;
And wherefore dost thou sigh, and moan,
And weep, that thou art left alone?

II

Thou art not left alone, poor boy,
  The Trav'ller stops to hear thy tale;
No heart, so hard, would thee annoy!
  For tho' thy mother's cheek is pale
And withers under yon grave stone,
Thou art not, Urchin, left alone.

III

I know thee well! thy yellow hair
  In silky waves I oft have seen;
Thy dimpled face, so fresh and fair,
  Thy roguish smile, thy playful mien
Were all to me, poor Orphan, known,
Ere Fate had left thee — all alone!

IV

Thy russet coat is scant, and torn,
  Thy cheek is now grown deathly pale!
Thy eyes are dim, thy looks forlorn,
  And bare thy bosom meets the gale;
And oft I hear thee deeply groan,
That thou, poor boy, art left alone.

V

Thy naked feet are wounded sore   25
  With naked thorns, that cross thy daily road;
The winter winds around thee roar,
  The church-yard is thy bleak abode;
Thy pillow now, a cold grave stone —
And there thou lov'st to grieve — alone!   30

VI

The rain has drench'd thee, all night long;
  The nipping frost thy bosom froze;
And still, the yew-tree shades among,
  I heard thee sigh thy artless woes;
I heard thee, till the day-star shone   35
In darkness weep — and weep alone!

VII

Oft have I seen thee, little boy,
  Upon thy lovely mother's knee;
For when she liv'd — thou wert her joy,
  Though now a mourner thou must be!   40
For she lies low, where yon grave-stone
Proclaims, that thou art left alone.

VIII

Weep, weep no more; on yonder hill
  The village bells are ringing, gay;
The merry reed, and brawling rill[1]   45
  Call thee to rustic sports away.
Then wherefore weep, and sigh, and moan,
A truant from the throng — alone?

IX

"I cannot the green hill ascend,
  I cannot pace the upland mead;   50
I cannot in the vale attend,
  To hear the merry-sounding reed:

---

1   A small stream.

For all is still, beneath yon stone,
   Where my poor mother's left alone!

X

55   I cannot gather gaudy flowers
   To dress the scene of revels loud —
I cannot pass the ev'ning hours
   Among the noisy village croud —
For, all in darkness, and alone
60   My mother sleeps, beneath yon stone.

XI

See how the stars begin to gleam
   The sheep-dog barks, 'tis time to go; —
The night-fly hums, the moonlight beam
   Peeps through the yew-trees' shadowy row —
65   It falls upon the white grave-stone,
   Where my dear mother sleeps alone. —

XII

O stay me not, for I must go
   The upland path in haste to tread;
For there the pale primroses grow
70   They grow to dress my mother's bed. —
They must, ere peep of day, be strown,
Where she lies mould'ring all alone.

XIII

My father o'er the stormy sea
   To distant lands was borne away,
75   And still my mother stay'd with me
   And wept by night and toil'd by day.
And shall I ever quit the stone
Where she is left, to sleep alone.

XIV

My father died, and still I found
80   My mother fond and kind to me;

I felt her breast with rapture bound
  When first I prattled on her knee —
And then she blest my infant tone
And little thought of yon grave-stone.

XV

No more her gentle voice I hear,   85
  No more her smile of fondness see;
Then wonder not I shed the tear
  She would have DIED, to follow me!
And yet she sleeps beneath yon stone
And I STILL LIVE — to weep alone.   90

she seems angry here, or just unbearably sad, she's gone & now alone

XVI

The playful kid, she lov'd so well
  From yon high clift was seen to fall;
I heard, afar, his tink'ling bell —
  Which seem'd in vain for aid to call —
I heard the harmless suff'rer moan,   95
And griev'd that he was left alone.

XVII

Our faithful dog grew mad, and died,
  The lightning smote our cottage low —
We had no resting-place beside
  And knew not whither we should go —
For we were poor, — and hearts of stone   100
Will never throb at mis'ry's groan.

like the grave

XVIII

My mother still surviv'd for me,
  She led me to the mountain's brow,
She watch'd me, while at yonder tree   105
  I sat, and wove the ozier bough;[1]
And oft she cried, "fear not, MINE OWN!
Thou shalt not, BOY, be left ALONE."

---

1 A species of willow with pliant branches that were used for basket work.

XXI

The blast blew strong, the torrent rose
 And bore our shatter'd cot away;
And, where the clear brook swiftly flows —
 Upon the turf at dawn of day,
When bright the sun's full lustre shone,
I wander'd, FRIENDLESS — and ALONE!"

XX

Thou art not, boy, for I have seen
 Thy tiny footsteps print the dew.
And while the morning sky serene
 Spread o'er the hill a yellow hue,
I heard thy sad and plaintive moan,
Beside the cold sepulchral stone.

XXI

And when the summer noontide hours
 With scorching rays the landscape spread,
I mark'd thee, weaving fragrant flow'rs
 To deck thy mother's silent bed!
Nor, at the church-yard's simple stone,
Wert, thou, poor Urchin, left alone.

XXII

I follow'd thee, along the dale
 And up the woodland's shad'wy way:
I heard thee tell thy mournful tale
 As slowly sunk the star of day:
Nor, when its twinkling light had flown,
Wert thou a wand'rer, all alone.

XXIII

"O! yes, I was! and still shall be
 A wand'rer, mourning and forlorn;
For what is all the world to me —
 What are the dews and buds of morn?
Since she, who left me sad, alone
In darkness sleeps, beneath yon stone!

XXIV

No brother's tear shall fall for me,
    For I no brother ever knew;   140
No friend shall weep my destiny
    For *friends* are scarce, and *tears* are few;
None do *I* see, save on this stone
Where I will stay, and weep alone!

[margin, handwritten: very powerful]

XXV

My Father never will return,   145
    He rests beneath the sea-green wave;
I have no kindred left, to mourn
    When I am hid in yonder grave!
Not one! to dress with flow'rs the stone; —
Then — surely, I AM LEFT ALONE!"   150

THE MISTLETOE,

A CHRISTMAS TALE

A FARMER's WIFE, both young and gay,
And fresh as op'ning buds of May;
Had taken to herself, a Spouse,
And plighted many solemn vows,
That she a faithful mate would prove,   5
In meekness, duty, and in love!
That she, despising joy and wealth,
Would be, in sickness and in health,
His only comfort and his Friend —
But, mark the sequel, — and attend!   10

[margin, handwritten: a a b b, all 8]

This Farmer, as the tale is told —
Was somewhat cross, and somewhat old!
His, was the wintry hour of life,
While summer smiled before his wife;
A contrast, rather form'd to cloy   15
The zest of matrimonial joy!

[margin, handwritten: he is old, she young]

'Twas Christmas time, the peasant throng
Assembled gay, with dance and Song:
The Farmer's Kitchen long had been
20 Of annual sports the busy scene;
The wood-fire blaz'd, the chimney wide
Presented seats, on either side;
Long rows of wooden Trenchers, clean,
Bedeck'd with holly-boughs, were seen;
25 The shining Tankard's foamy ale
Gave spirits to the Goblin tale,
And many a rosy cheek — grew pale.

It happen'd, that some sport to shew
The ceiling held a MISTLETOE.
30 A magic bough, and well design'd
To prove the coyest Maiden, kind.
A magic bough, which DRUIDS old
Its sacred mysteries enroll'd;[1]
And which, or gossip Fame's a liar,
35 Still warms the soul with vivid fire;
Still promises a store of bliss
While bigots snatch their Idol's kiss.

This MISTLETOE was doom'd to be
The talisman of Destiny;
40 Beneath its ample boughs we're told
Full many a timid Swain grew bold;
Full many a roguish eye askance
Beheld it with impatient glance,
And many a ruddy cheek confest,
45 The triumphs of the beating breast;
And many a rustic rover sigh'd
Who ask'd the kiss, and was denied.

---

1   The ancient Celtic druids ritualistically cut the oak mistletoe on the sixth night of
     the moon with a golden sickle. It was caught in a white cloth so as not to allow it
     to touch the ground. It was offered up to the gods along with two white bulls.
     Mistletoe is still ceremonially plucked in Celtic and Scandinavian countries on
     Midsummer Eve.

First MARG'RY smil'd and gave her Lover
A Kiss; then thank'd her stars, *'twas over!*
Next, KATE, with a reluctant pace,   50
Was tempted to the mystic place;
Then SUE, a merry laughing jade[1]
A dimpled yielding blush betray'd;
While JOAN her chastity to shew
Wish'd "the bold knaves would serve *her* so,"   55
She'd "teach the rogues such wanton play!"
And well she could, she knew the way.

The FARMER, mute with jealous care,
Sat sullen, in his wicker chair;
Hating the noisy gamesome host   60
Yet, fearful to resign his post;
He envied all their sportive strife
But most he watch'd his blooming wife,
And trembled, lest her steps should go,
Incautious, near the MISTLETOE.   65

Now HODGE, a youth of rustic grace
With form athletic; manly face;
On MISTRESS HOMESPUN turn'd his eye
And breath'd a soul-declaring sigh!
Old HOMESPUN, mark'd his list'ning Fair   70
And nestled in his wicker chair;
HODGE swore, she might his heart command —
The pipe was dropp'd from HOMESPUN's hand!

HODGE prest her slender waist around;
The FARMER check'd his draught, and frown'd!   75
And now beneath the MISTLETOE
'Twas MISTRESS HOMESPUN's turn to go;
Old Surly shook his wicker chair,
And sternly utter'd — "*Let her dare!*"

---

1   A derogatory term for a female, similar to minx or hussy.

HODGE, to the FARMER's wife declar'd
Such husbands never should be spar'd;
Swore, they deserv'd the worst disgrace,
That lights upon the wedded race;
And vow'd — that night he would not go
Unblest, beneath the MISTLETOE.

The merry group all recommend
An harmless Kiss, the strife to end:
"Why not?" says MARG'RY, "who would fear,
A dang'rous moment, once a year?"
SUSAN observ'd, that "ancient folks
Were seldom pleas'd with youthful jokes;"
But KATE, who, till that fatal hour,
Had held, o'er HODGE, unrivall'd pow'r,
With curving lip and head aside
Look'd down and smil'd in conscious pride,
Then, anxious to conceal her care,
She humm'd — "*what fools some women are!*"

Now, MISTRESS HOMESPUN, sorely vex'd,
By pride and jealous rage perplex'd,
And angry, that her peevish spouse
Should doubt her matrimonial vows,
But, most of all, resolved to make
An envious rival's bosom ache;
Commanded Hodge to let her go,
Nor lead her to the Mistletoe;
"Why should you ask it o'er and o'er?"
Cried she, "*we've been there twice before!*"

'Tis thus, to check a rival's sway,
That Women oft themselves betray;
While VANITY, alone, pursuing,
They rashly prove, their own undoing.

THE POOR, SINGING DAME

Beneath an old wall, that went round an old Castle,
    For many a year, with brown ivy o'erspread;
A neat little Hovel, its lowly roof raising,
    Defied the wild winds that howl'd over its shed:
The turrets, that frown'd on the poor simple dwelling,   5
    Were rock'd to and fro, when the Tempest would roar,
And the river, that down the rich valley was swelling,
    Flow'd swiftly beside the green step of its door.

The Summer Sun, gilded the rushy-roof slanting,
    The bright dews bespangled its ivy-bound hedge   10
And above, on the ramparts, the sweet Birds were chanting,
    And wild buds thick dappled the clear river's edge.
When the Castle's rich chambers were haunted, and dreary,
    The poor little Hovel was still, and secure;
And no robber e'er enter'd, nor goblin nor fairy,   15
    For the splendours of pride had no charms to allure.

The Lord of the Castle, a proud, surly ruler,
    Oft heard the low dwelling with sweet music ring:
For the old Dame that liv'd in the little Hut chearly,
    Would sit at her wheel, and would merrily sing: 20
When with revels the Castle's great Hall was resounding,
    The Old Dame was sleeping, not dreaming of fear;
And when over the mountains the Huntsmen were bounding
    She would open her wicket,[1] their clamours to hear.

To the merry-ton'd horn, she would dance on the threshold,   25
    And louder, and louder, repeat her old Song:
And when Winter its mantle of Frost was displaying
    She caroll'd, undaunted, the bare woods among:
She would gather dry Fern, ever happy and singing,
    With her cake of brown bread, and her jug of brown beer,   30
And would smile when she heard the great Castle-bell ringing,
    Inviting the Proud — to their prodigal chear.

---

1   A small door or gate.

Thus she liv'd, ever patient and ever contented,
    Till Envy the Lord of the Castle possess'd,
35   For he hated that Poverty should be so chearful,
      While care could the fav'rites of Fortune molest;
He sent his bold yeoman with threats to prevent her,
    And still would she carol her sweet roundelay;
At last, an old Steward, relentless he sent her —
40   Who bore her, all trembling, to Prison away!

Three weeks did she languish, then died, broken-hearted,
    Poor Dame! how the death-bell did mournfully sound!
And along the green path six young Bachelors bore her,
    And laid her, for ever, beneath the cold ground!
45   And the primroses pale, 'mid the long grass were growing,
    The bright dews of twilight bespangled her grave
And morn heard the breezes of summer soft blowing
    To bid the fresh flow'rets in sympathy wave.

The Lord of the Castle, from that fatal moment
50   When poor Singing MARY was laid in her grave,
Each night was surrounded by Screech-owls appalling,
    Which o'er the black turrets their pinions would wave!
On the ramparts that frown'd on the river, swift flowing,
    They hover'd, still hooting a terrible song,
55   When his windows would rattle, the Winter blast blowing,
    They would shriek like a ghost, the dark alleys among!

Whenever he wander'd they followed him crying,
    At dawnlight, at Eve, still they haunted his way!
When the Moon shone across the wide common, they hooted,
60   Nor quitted his path, till the blazing of day.
His bones began wasting, his flesh was decaying,
    And he hung his proud head, and he perish'd with shame;
And the tomb of rich marble, no soft tear displaying,
    O'ershadows the grave, of THE POOR SINGING DAME!

· this story
is almost like
fable-like

MISTRESS GURTON'S CAT,

A DOMESTIC TALE

OLD MISTRESS GURTON had a Cat,
   A Tabby, loveliest of the race,
Sleek as a doe, and tame, and fat
   With velvet paws, and whisker'd face;
The Doves of VENUS not so fair,   5
   Nor JUNO's Peacocks[1] half so grand
As MISTRESS GURTON's Tabby rare,
   The proudest of the purring band;
So dignified in all her paces —
She seem'd, a pupil of the Graces!   10
There never was a finer creature
In all the varying whims of Nature!

All liked Grimalkin,[2] passing well!
Save MISTRESS GURTON, and, 'tis said,
She oft with furious ire would swell,   15
When, through neglect or hunger keen,
Puss, with a pilfer'd scrap, was seen,
Swearing beneath the pent-house[3] shed:
For, like some fav'rites, she was bent
On all things, yet with none content;   20
And still, whate'er her place or diet,
She could not pick her bone, in quiet.

Sometimes, new milk GRIMALKIN stole,
And sometimes — over-set the bowl!
For over eagerness will prove,   25
Oft times the bane of what we love;
And sometimes, to her neighbor's home,
GRIMALKIN, like a thief would roam,
Teaching poor Cats, of humbler kind,

---

1   Doves are sacred to Venus; peacocks are sacred to Juno.
2   A name associated with an old female cat; it was also contemptuously applied to a
jealous old woman.
3   A small building attached to a main one.

30   For high example sways the mind!
Sometimes she paced the garden wall,
Thick guarded by the shatter'd pane,
And lightly treading with disdain,
Fear'd not Ambition's certain fall!
35   Old China broke, or scratch'd her Dame
And brought domestic friends to shame!
And many a time this Cat was curst,
Of squalling, thieving things, the worst!
Wish'd Dead! and menac'd with a string,
40   For Cats of such scant Fame, deserv'd to swing!

One day, report, for ever busy,
Resolv'd to make Dame Gurton easy;
A Neighbour came, with solemn look,
And thus, the dismal tidings broke.
45   "Know you, that poor GRIMALKIN died
Last night, upon the pent-house side?
I heard her for assistance call;
I heard her shrill and dying squall!
I heard her, in reproachful tone,
50   Pour, to the stars, her feeble groan!
Alone, I heard her piercing cries —
With not a Friend, to close her Eyes!

Poor Puss! I vow it grieves me sore,
Never to see thy beauties more!
55   Never again to hear thee purr,
To stroke thy back, of Zebra fur;
To see thy em'rald eyes — so bright,
Flashing around their lust'rous light
Amid the solemn shades of night!

60   Methinks I see her pretty paws —
As gracefully she paced along;
I hear her voice, so shrill, among
The chimney rows! I see her claws,
While, like a Tyger, she pursued
65   Undauntedly the pilf'ring race;

I see her lovely whisker'd face
When she her nimble prey subdued!
And then, how she would frisk, and play,
And purr the Evening hours away:
Now stretch'd beside the social fire;   70
Now on the sunny lawn, at noon,
Watching the vagrant Birds that flew,
Across the scene of varied hue,
To peck the Fruit. Or when the Moon
Stole o'er the hills, in silv'ry suit,   75
How would she chaunt her lovelorn Tale
  Soft as the wild Eolian Lyre![1]
'Till ev'ry brute, on hill, in dale,
  Listen'd with wonder mute!"

"O! Cease!" exclaim'd DAME GURTON, straight,   80
"Has my poor Puss been torn away?
Alas! how cruel is my fate,
How shall I pass the tedious day?
Where can her mourning mistress find
So sweet a Cat? so meek! so kind!   85
So keen a mouser, such a beauty,
So orderly, so fond, so true,
That every gentle task of duty
The dear, domestic creature knew!
Hers, was the mildest tend'rest heart!   90
She knew no little *cattish* art;
Not cross, like *fav'rite Cats*, was she
But seem'd the queen of Cats to be!
I cannot live — since doom'd, alas! to part
From poor GRIMALKIN kind, the darling of my heart!"   95

And now DAME GURTON, bath'd in tears,
With a black top-knot vast, appears:
Some say that a black gown she wore,
As many oft have done before,
For Beings, valued less, I ween,   100

---

1 The Aeoliean harp, named after Aeolus, Greek god of the winds, is a stringed
instrument that produces sounds upon exposure to a current of air.

Than this, of Tabby Cats, the fav'rite Queen!
But lo! soon after, one fair day,
Puss, who had only been a roving —
Across the pent-house took her way,
105   To see her Dame, so sad, and loving;
Eager to greet the mourning fair
She enter'd by a window, where
A China bowl of luscious cream
Was quiv'ring in the sunny beam.

110   Puss, who was somewhat tired and dry,
And somewhat fond of bev'rage sweet;
Beholding such a tempting treat,
Resolved its depth to try.
She saw the warm and dazzling ray
115   Upon the spotless surface play:
She purr'd around its circle wide,
And gazed, and long'd, and mew'd and sigh'd!
But Fate, unfriendly, did that hour controul,
She overset the cream, and smash'd the gilded bowl!

120   As MISTRESS GURTON heard the thief,
         She started from her easy chair,
And, quite unmindful of her grief,
         Began aloud to swear!
"Curse that voracious beast!" she cried,
125   "Here SUSAN, bring a cord —
         I'll hang the vicious, ugly creature —
         The veriest plague e'er form'd by nature!"
And MISTRESS GURTON kept her word —
         And Poor GRIMALKIN — DIED!

130   Thus, often, we with anguish sore
The *dead*, in clam'rous grief deplore;
Who, were they once *alive* again
Would meet the sting of cold disdain!
For FRIENDS, whom trifling faults can sever,
Are *valued most*, WHEN LOST FOR EVER!

THE LASCAR[1]
In Two Parts

I

"Another day, Ah! me, a day
     Of dreary Sorrow is begun!
And still I loathe the temper'd ray,
     And still I hate the sickly Sun!
Far from my Native Indian shore,   5
I hear our wretched race deplore;
I mark the smile of taunting Scorn,
And curse the hour, when I was born!
I weep, but no one gently tries
To stop my tear, or check my sighs;   10
For, while my heart beats mournfully,
Dear Indian home, I sigh for Thee!

II

Since, gaudy Sun! I see no more
     Thy hottest glory gild the day;
Since, sever'd from my burning shore,   15
     I waste the vapid hours away;
O! darkness come! come, deepest gloom!
Shroud the young Summer's op'ning bloom;
Burn, temper'd Orb, with fiercer beams
This northern world! and drink the streams   20
That thro' the fertile vallies glide
To bathe the feasted Fiends of Pride!
Or, hence, broad Sun! extinguish'd be!
For endless night encircles Me!

III

What is, to me, the City gay?   25
     And what, the board profusely spread?
I have no home, no rich array,
     No spicy feast, no downy bed!

---

1 An East Indian sailor.

I, with the dogs am doom'd to eat,
30 To perish in the peopled street,
To drink the tear of deep despair;
The scoff and scorn of fools to bear!
I sleep upon a bed of stone,
I pace the meadows, wild — alone!
35 And if I curse my fate severe,
Some Christian Savage mocks my tear!

IV

Shut out the Sun, O! pitying Night!
   Make the wide world my silent tomb!
O'ershade this northern, sickly light,
40   And shroud me, in eternal gloom!
My Indian plains, now smiling glow,
There stands my Parent's hovel low,
And there the tow'ring aloes rise
And fling their perfumes to the skies!
45 There the broad palm Trees covert lend,
There Sun and Shade delicious blend;
But here, amid the blunted ray,
Cold shadows hourly cross my way!

V

Was it for this, that on the main[1]
50   I met the tempest fierce and strong,
And steering o'er the liquid plain,
      Still onward, press'd the waves among?
Was it for this, the LASCAR brave
Toil'd, like a wretched Indian Slave;
55 Preserv'd your treasures by his toil,
And sigh'd to greet this fertile soil?
Was it for this, to beg, to die,
   Where plenty smiles, and where the Sky
Sheds cooling airs; while fev'rish pain,
60 Maddens the famish'd LASCAR's brain?

---

1   An expanse of water.

VI

Oft, I the stately Camel led,
  And sung the short-hour'd night away;
And oft, upon the top-mast's head,
  Hail'd the red Eye of coming day.
The Tanyan's[1] back my mother bore;   65
And oft the wavy Ganges'[2] roar
Lull'd her to rest, as on she past —
'Mid the hot sands and burning blast!
And oft beneath the Banyan tree[3]
She sate and fondly nourish'd me;   70
And while the noontide hour past slow,
I felt her breast with kindness glow.

VII

Where'er I turn my sleepless eyes,
  No cheek so dark as mine, I see;
For Europe's Suns, with softer dyes   75
  Mark Europe's favour'd progeny!
Low is my stature, black my hair,
The emblem of my Soul's despair!
My voice no dulcet cadence flings,
To touch soft pity's throbbing strings!   80
Then wherefore cruel Briton, say,
Compel my aching heart to stay?
To-morrow's Sun — may rise, to see —
The famish'd LASCAR, blest as thee!"

VIII

The morn had scarcely shed its rays   85
  When, from the City's din he ran;
For he had fasted, four long days,

---

1 Tanyan: variant spelling of Tanghan, a native horse of Tibet and Bhutan, a strong
   little pony.
2 A river in the north of India that was held sacred by Hindus who sought to wash
   away their sins in its waters.
3 An Indian tree, remarkable for the way in which its branches drop shoots to the
   ground, which then take root and support their parent branches.

And faint his Pilgrimage began!
The LASCAR, now, without a friend, —
Up the steep hill did slow ascend;
Now o'er the flow'ry meadows stole,
While pain, and hunger, pinch'd his Soul;
And now his fev'rish lip was dried,
And burning tears his thirst supply'd,
And, ere he saw the Ev'ning close,
Far off, the City dimly rose!

IX

Again the Summer Sun flam'd high
    The plains were golden, far and wide;
And fervid was the cloudless sky,
    And slow the breezes seem'd to glide:
The gossamer, on briar and spray,
Shone silv'ry in the solar ray;
And sparkling dew-drops, falling round
Spangled the hot and thirsty ground;
The insect myriads humm'd their tune
To greet the coming hour of noon,
While the poor LASCAR Boy, in haste,
Flew, frantic, o'er the sultry waste.

X

And whither could the wand'rer go?
    Who would receive a stranger poor?
Who, when the blasts of night should blow,
    Would ope to him the friendly door?
Alone, amid the race of man,
The sad, the fearful alien ran!
None would an Indian wand'rer bless;
None greet him with the fond caress;
None feed him, though with hunger keen
He at the Lordly gate were seen,
Prostrate, and humbly forc'd to crave
A shelter, for an Indian Slave.

XI

The noon-tide Sun, now flaming wide,
  No cloud its fierce beam shadow'd o'er,
But what could worse to him betide
  Than begging, at the proud man's door?
For clos'd and lofty was the gate,   125
And there, in all the pride of State,
A surly Porter turn'd the key,
A man of sullen soul was he —
His brow was fair; but in his eye
Sat pamper'd scorn, and tyranny;   130
And, near him, a fierce mastiff stood,
Eager to bathe his fangs in blood.

XII

The weary LASCAR turn'd away,
  For trembling fear his heart subdued,
And down his cheek the tear would stray,   135
  Though burning anguish drank his blood!
The angry Mastiff snarl'd, as he
Turn'd from the house of luxury;
The sultry hour was long, and high
The broad-sun flamed athwart the sky —   140
But still a throbbing hope possess'd
The Indian wand'rer's fev'rish breast,
When from the distant dell a sound
Of swelling music echo'd round.

XIII

It was the church-bell's merry peal;   145
  And now a pleasant house he view'd:
And now his heart began to feel
  As though, it were not quite subdu'd!
No lofty dome, shew'd loftier state,
No pamper'd Porter watch'd the gate,   150
No Mastiff, like a tyrant stood,
Eager to scatter human blood;
Yet the poor Indian wand'rer found,

E'en where Religion smil'd around —
155   That tears had little pow'r to speak
When trembling, on a sable cheek!

XIV

With keen reproach, and menace rude,
    The LASCAR Boy away was sent;
And now again he seem'd subdu'd,
160   And his soul sicken'd, as he went.
Now, on the river's bank he stood;
Now, drank the cool refreshing flood;
Again his fainting heart beat high;
Again he rais'd his languid eye;
165   Then, from the upland's sultry side,
Look'd back, forgave the wretch, and sigh'd!
While the proud PASTOR bent his way
To preach of CHARITY — and PRAY!

Part Second

I

The LASCAR Boy still journey'd on,
170   For the hot Sun, HE well could bear,
And now the burning hour was gone,
    And Evening came, with softer air!
The breezes kiss'd his sable breast,
While his scorch'd feet the cold dew prest;
175   The waving flow'rs soft tears display'd,
And songs of rapture fill'd the glade;
The South-wind quiver'd, o'er the stream
Reflecting back the rosy beam,
While, as the purpling twilight clos'd,
180   On a turf bed — the Boy repos'd!

II

And now, in fancy's airy dream,
    The LASCAR Boy his Mother spied;
And, from her breast, a crimson stream
    Slow trickled down her beating side:

And now he heard her wild, complain,   185
As loud she shriek'd — but shriek'd in vain!
And now she sunk upon the ground,
The red stream trickling from her wound,
And near her feet a murd'rer stood,
His glitt'ring poniard[1] tipp'd with blood!   190
And now, "farewell, my son!" she cried,
Then clos'd her fainting eyes — and died!

III

The Indian Wand'rer, waking, gaz'd
   With grief, and pain, and horror wild;
And tho' his fev'rish brain was craz'd,   195
   He rais'd his eyes to Heav'n, and smil'd!
And now the stars were twinkling clear,
And the blind Bat was whirling near;
And the lone Owlet shriek'd, while He
Still sate beneath a shelt'ring tree;   200
And now the fierce-ton'd midnight blast
Across the wide heath, howling past,
When a long cavalcade he spied
By torch-light near the river's side.

IV

He rose, and hast'ning swiftly on,   205
   Call'd loudly to the Sumptuous train, —
But soon the cavalcade was gone —
   And darkness wrapp'd the scene again.
He follow'd still the distant sound;
He saw the lightning flashing round;   210
He heard the crashing thunder roar;
He felt the whelming torrents pour;
And, now beneath a shelt'ring wood
He listen'd to the tumbling flood —
And now, with falt'ring, feeble breath,   215
The famish'd LASCAR, pray'd for Death.

---

1   A dagger.

V

And now the flood began to rise
   And foaming rush'd along the vale;
The LASCAR watch'd, with stedfast eyes,
    The flash descending quick and pale;
220   And now again the cavalcade
Pass'd slowly near the upland glade; —
But HE was dark, and dark the scene,
The torches long extinct had been;
225   He call'd, but, in the stormy hour,
His feeble voice had lost its pow'r,
'Till, near a tree, beside the flood,
A night-bewilder'd Trav'ller stood.

VI

The LASCAR now with transport ran
230   "Stop! stop!" he cried — with accents bold;
The Trav'ller was a fearful man —
   And next his life he priz'd his gold! —
He heard the wand'rer madly cry;
He heard his footsteps following nigh;
235   He nothing saw, while onward prest,
Black as the sky, the Indian's breast;
Till his firm grasp he felt, while cold
Down his pale cheek the big drop roll'd;
Then, struggling to be free, he gave —
240   A deep wound to the LASCAR Slave.

VII

And now he groan'd, by pain opprest,
   And now crept onward, sad and slow:
And while he held his bleeding breast,
   He feebly pour'd the plaint of woe!
245   "What have I done?" the LASCAR cried —
"That Heaven to me the pow'r denied
To touch the soul of man, and share
A brother's love, a brother's care?
Why is this dingy form decreed

To bear oppression's scourge and bleed? —   250
Is there a GOD, in yon dark Heav'n,
And shall such monsters be forgiv'n?

VIII

Here, in this smiling land we find
  Neglect and mis'ry sting our race;
And still, whate'er the LASCAR's mind,   255
  The stamp of sorrow marks his face!"
He ceas'd to speak; while from his side
Fast roll'd life's swiftly-ebbing tide,
And now, though sick and faint was he,
He slowly climb'd a tall Elm tree,   260
To watch, if, near his lonely way,
Some friendly Cottage lent a ray,
A little ray of chearful light,
To gild the LASCAR's long, long night!

IX

And now he hears a distant bell,   *sound*   265
  His heart is almost rent with joy!
And who, but such a wretch can tell,
  The transports of the Indian Boy?
And higher now he climbs the tree,
And hopes some shelt'ring Cot to see;   270
Again he listens, while the peal
Seems up the woodland vale to steal;
The twinkling stars begin to fade,
And dawnlight purples o'er the glade —
And while the sev'ring vapours flee,   275
The LASCAR Boy looks chearfully!   *cold vs. hot*

X

And now the Sun begins to rise
  Above the Eastern summit blue;
And o'er the plain the day-breeze flies,
  And sweetly bloom the fields of dew!   280
The wand'ring wretch was chill'd, for he

Sate, shiv'ring in the tall Elm tree;
And he was faint, and sick, and dry,
And bloodshot was his fev'rish eye;
285 And livid was his lip, while he
Sate silent in the tall Elm tree —
And parch'd his tongue; and quick his breath,
And his dark cheek, was cold as Death!

XI

And now a Cottage low he sees,
290   The chimney smoke, ascending grey,
Floats lightly on the morning breeze
   And o'er the mountain glides away.
And now the Lark, on flutt'ring wings,
Its early Song, delighted sings;
295 And now, across the upland mead,
The Swains[1] their flocks to shelter lead;
The shelt'ring woods, wave to and fro;
The yellow plains, far distant, glow;
And all things wake to life and joy,
300   All! but the famish'd Indian Boy!

XII

And now the village throngs are seen,
   Each lane is peopled, and the glen
From ev'ry op'ning path-way green,
   Sends forth the busy hum of men.
305 They cross the meads, still, all alone,
They hear the wounded LASCAR groan!
Far off they mark the wretch, as he
Falls, senseless, from the tall Elm tree!
Swiftly they cross the river wide
310 And soon they reach the Elm tree's side,
But, ere the sufferer they behold,
His wither'd Heart, is DEAD, — *and* COLD!

---

1   Shepherds or countrymen.

THE WIDOW'S HOME

Close on the margin of a brawling brook
That bathes the low dell's bosom, stands a Cot;
O'ershadow'd by broad Alders. At its door
A rude seat, with an ozier canopy
Invites the weary traveller to rest.   5
'Tis a poor humble dwelling; yet within,
The sweets of joy domestic, oft have made
The long hour not unchearly, while the Moor
Was covered with deep snow, and the bleak blast
Swept with impetuous wing the mountain's brow!   10

On ev'ry tree of the near shelt'ring wood
The minstrelsy of Nature, shrill and wild,
Welcomes the stranger guest, and carolling
Love-songs, spontaneous, greets him merrily.
The distant hills, empurpled by the dawn   —love thus   15
And thinly scatter'd with blue mists that float
On their bleak summits dimly visible,
Skirt the domain luxuriant, while the air
Breathes healthful fragrance. On the Cottage roof
The gadding Ivy, and the tawny Vine   20
Bind the brown thatch, the shelter'd winter-hut
Of the tame Sparrow, and the Red-breast bold.

There dwells the Soldier's Widow! young and fair
Yet not more fair than virtuous. Every day
She wastes the hour-glass, waiting his return, —   25
And every hour anticipates the day,
(Deceiv'd, yet cherish'd by the flatt'rer hope)
When she shall meet her Hero. On the Eve
Of Sabbath rest, she trims her little hut
With blossoms, fresh and gaudy, still, herself   30
The queen-flow'r of the garland! The sweet Rose
Of wood-wild beauty, blushing thro' her tears.

One little Son she has, a lusty Boy,
The darling of her guiltless, mourning heart,
35   The only dear and gay associate
Of her lone widowhood. His sun-burnt cheek
Is never blanch'd with fear, though he will climb
The broad oak's branches, and with brawny arm
Sever the limpid wave. In his blue eye
40   Beams all his mother's gentleness of soul;
While his brave father's warm intrepid heart
Throbs in his infant bosom. 'Tis a wight[1]
Most valourous, yet pliant as the stem
Of the low vale-born lily, when the dew
45   Presses its perfum'd head. Eight years his voice
Has chear'd the homely hut, for he could lisp
Soft words of filial fondness, ere his feet
Could measure the smooth path-way.
                                    On the hills
50   He watches the wide waste of wavy green
Tissued with orient lustre, till his eyes
Ache with the dazzling splendour, and the main,
Rolling and blazing, seems a second Sun!
And, if a distant whitening sail appears,
55   Skimming the bright horizon while the mast
Is canopied with clouds of dappled gold,
He homeward hastes rejoicing. An old Tree
Is his lone watch-tow'r; 'tis a blasted Oak
Which, from a vagrant Acorn, ages past,
60   Sprang up, to triumph like a Savage bold
Braving the Season's warfare. There he sits
Silent and musing the still Evening hour,
'Till the short reign of Sunny splendour fades
At the cold touch of twilight. Oft he sings;
65   Or from his oaten pipe, untiring pours
The tune mellifluous which his father sung,
When HE could only listen.

---

1   Archaic term for a human being.

                        On the sands
That bind the level sea-shore, will he stray,
When morn unlocks the East, and flings afar   70
The rosy day-beam! There the boy will stop
To gather the dank weeds which ocean leaves
On the bleak strand, while winter o'er the main
Howls its nocturnal clamour. There again
He chaunts his Father's ditty. Never more   75
Poor mountain minstrel, shall thy bosom throb
To the sweet cadence! never more thy tear
Fall as the dulcet breathings give each word
Expression magical! Thy Father, Boy,
Sleeps on the bed of death! His tongue is mute,   80
His fingers have forgot their pliant art,
His oaten pipe will ne'er again be heard
Echoing along the valley! Never more
Will thy fond mother meet the balmy smile
Of peace domestic, or the circling arm   85
Of valour, temper'd by the milder joys
Of rural merriment. His very name
Is now forgotten! for no trophied tomb
Tells of his bold exploits; such heraldry
Befits not humble worth: For pomp and praise   90
Wait in the gilded palaces of Pride
To dress Ambition's Slaves. Yet, on his grave,
The unmark'd resting place of Valour's Sons,
The morning beam shines lust'rous; the meek flow'r
Still drops the twilight tear, and the night breeze   95
Moans melancholy music!
                        Then, to ME,
O! dearer far is the poor Soldier's grave,
The Widow's lone and unregarded Cot,
The brawling Brook, and the wide Alder-bough,   100
The ozier Canopy, and plumy choir,
Hymning the Morn's return, than the rich Dome
Of gilded Palaces! and sweeter far —
O! far more graceful! far more exquisite,
The Widow's tear bathing the living rose,   105

Than the rich ruby, blushing on the breast,
Of guilty greatness. Welcome then to me —
The WIDOW'S LOWLY HOME: The Soldier's HEIR;
The proud inheritor of Heav'n's best gifts —
110   The mind unshackled — and the guiltless Soul!

THE SHEPHERD'S DOG

I

A Shepherd's Dog there was; and he
    Was faithful to his master's will,
For well he lov'd his company,
    Along the plain or up the hill;
5   All Seasons were, to him, the same
Beneath the Sun's meridian flame;
Or, when the wintry wind blew shrill and keen,
Still the Old Shepherd's Dog, was with his Master seen.

II

His form was shaggy clothed; yet he
10   Was of a bold and faithful breed;
And kept his master company
    In smiling days, and days of need;
When the long Ev'ning slowly clos'd,
When ev'ry living thing repos'd,
15   When e'en the breeze slept on the woodlands round,
The Shepherd's watchful Dog, was ever waking found.

III

All night, upon the cold turf he
    Contented lay, with list'ning care;
And though no stranger company,
20   Or lonely traveller rested there;
Old Trim was pleas'd to guard it still,
For 'twas his aged master's will; —
And so pass'd on the chearful night and day,
'Till the poor Shepherd's Dog, was very old, and grey.

IV

Among the villagers was he   25
   Belov'd by all the young and old,
For he was chearful company,
   When the north-wind blew keen and cold;
And when the cottage scarce was warm,
While round it flew, the midnight storm,   30
When loudly, fiercely roll'd the swelling tide —
The Shepherd's faithful Dog, crept closely by his side.

V

When Spring in gaudy dress would be,
   Sporting across the meadows green,
He kept his master company,   35
   And all amid the flow'rs was seen;
Now barking loud, now pacing fast,
Now, backward he a look would cast,
And now, subdu'd and weak, with wanton play,
Amid the waving grass, the Shepherd's Dog would stay.   40

VI

Now, up the rugged path would he
   The steep hill's summit slowly gain,
And still be chearful company,
   Though shiv'ring in the pelting rain;
And when the brook was frozen o'er,   45
Or the deep snow conceal'd the moor,
When the pale moon-beams scarcely shed a ray,
The Shepherd's faithful Dog, would mark the dang'rous way.

VII

On Sunday, at the old Yew Tree,
Which canopies the church-yard stile,   50
Forc'd from his master's company,
   The faithful TRIM would mope awhile;
For then his master's only care
Was the loud Psalm, or fervent Pray'r,

55   And, 'till the throng the church-yard path retrod,
     The Shepherd's patient guard, lay silent on the sod.

VIII

    Near their small hovel stood a tree,
      Where TRIM was ev'ry morning found —
    Waiting his master's company,
60   And looking wistfully around;
    And if, along the upland mead,[1]
    He heard him tune the merry reed,
    O, then! o'er hedge and ditch, thro' brake and briar,
    The Shepherd's dog would haste, with eyes that seem'd on fire.

IX

65   And now he pac'd the valley, free,
      And now he bounded o'er the dew,
    For well his master's company
      Would recompence his toil he knew;
    And where a rippling rill[2] was seen
70   Flashing the woody brakes between,
    Fearless of danger, thro' the lucid tide,
    The Shepherd's eager dog, yelping with joy, would glide.

X

    Full many a year, the same was he
      His love still stronger every day,
75   For, in his master's company,
      He had grown old, and very grey;
    And now his sight grew dim: and slow
    Up the rough mountain he would go,
    And his loud bark, which all the village knew,
80   With ev'ry wasting hour, more faint, and peevish grew.

XI

    One morn, to the low mead went he,
      Rous'd from his threshold-bed to meet

---

1   Meadow.
2   A small stream.

A gay and lordly company!
    The Sun was bright, the air was sweet;
Old TRIM was watchful of his care,   85
His master's flocks were feeding there,
And, fearful of the hounds, he yelping stood
Beneath a willow Tree, that wav'd across the flood.

XII

Old TRIM was urg'd to wrath; for he
    Was guardian of the meadow bounds;   90
And, heedless of the company,
    With angry snarl attack'd the hounds!
Some felt his teeth, though they were old,
For still his ire was fierce and bold,
And ne'er did valiant chieftain feel more strong   95
Than the Old Shepherd's dog, when daring foes among.

XIII

The Sun was setting o'er the Sea,
    The breezes murmuring sad, and slow,
When a gay lordly company,
    Came to the Shepherd's hovel low;   100
Their arm'd associates stood around
The sheep-cote fence's narrow bound,
While its poor master heard, with fix'd despair,
That TRIM, his friend, deem'd MAD, was doom'd to perish there!

XIV

The kind old Shepherd wept, for he   105
    Had no such guide, to mark his way,
And kneeling pray'd the company,
    To let him live, his little day!
"For many a year my Dog has been
The only friend these eyes have seen;   110
We both are old and feeble, he and I —
Together we have liv'd, together let us die!"

XV

Behold his dim, yet speaking eye!
    Which ill befits his visage grim
115 He cannot from your anger fly,
    For slow and feeble is old TRIM!
He looks, as though he fain[1] would speak,
His beard is white — his voice is weak —
He is NOT MAD! O! then, in pity spare
120 The only watchful friend, of my small fleecy care!"

XVI

The Shepherd ceas'd to speak, for He
    Leant on his maple staff, subdu'd;
While pity touch'd the company,
    And all, poor TRIM with sorrow view'd:
125 Nine days, upon a willow bed
Old TRIM was doom'd to lay his head,
Oppress'd and sever'd from his master's door,
Enough to make him MAD — were he not so before!

XVII

But not forsaken yet, was he,
130   For ev'ry morn, at peep of day,
To keep his old friend company,
    The lonely Shepherd bent his way:
A little boat, across the stream,
Which glitter'd in the sunny beam,
135 Bore him, where foes no longer could annoy,
Where TRIM stood yelping loud, and ALMOST MAD with joy!

XVIII

Six days had pass'd and still was he
    Upon the island left to roam,
When on the stream a wither'd tree
140   Was gliding rapid midst the foam!
The little Boat now onward prest,
Danc'd o'er the river's bounding breast,

---

1 Gladly or willingly.

Till dash'd impetuous, 'gainst the old tree's side,
The Shepherd plung'd and groan'd, then sunk amid the tide.

XIX

Old TRIM, now doom'd his friend to see   145
  Beating the foam with wasted breath,
Resolv'd to bear him company,
  E'en in the icy arms of death;
Soon with exulting cries he bore
His feeble master to the shore,   150
And, standing o'er him, howl'd in cadence sad,
For, fear and fondness, now, had nearly made him MAD.

XX

Together, still their flocks they tend,
  More happy than the proudly great;
The Shepherd has no other friend —   155
  No Lordly home, no bed of state!
But on a pallet, clean and low,
They hear, unmov'd, the wild winds blow,
And though they ne'er another spring may see,
The Shepherd, and his Dog, are chearful company.   160

THE FUGITIVE

OFT have I seen yon Solitary Man
Pacing the upland meadow. On his brow
Sits melancholy, mark'd with decent pride,
As it would fly the busy, taunting world,
And feed upon reflection. Sometimes, near   5
The foot of an old Tree, he takes his seat
And with the page of legendary lore
Cheats the dull hour, while Evening's sober eye
Looks tearful as it closes. In the dell
By the swift brook he loiters, sad and mute,   10
Save when a struggling sigh, half murmur'd, steals
From his wrung bosom. To the rising moon,
His eye rais'd wistfully, expression fraught,

He pours the cherish'd anguish of his Soul,
Silent yet eloquent: For not a sound
That might alarm the night's lone centinel,
The dull-eyed Owl, escapes his trembling lip,
Unapt[1] in supplication. He is young,
And yet the stamp of thought so tempers youth,
That all its fires are faded. What is He?
And why, when morning sails upon the breeze,
Fanning the blue hill's summit, does he stay
Loit'ring and sullen, like a Truant boy,
Beside the woodland glen; or stretch'd along
On the green slope, watch his slow wasting form
Reflected, trembling, on the river's breast?

His garb is coarse and threadbare, and his cheek
Is prematurely faded. The check'd tear,
Dimming his dark eye's lustre, seems to say,
"This world is now, to me, a barren waste,
A desart, full of weeds and wounding thorns,
And I am weary: for my journey here
Has been, though short, but chearless." Is it so?
Poor Traveller! Oh tell me, tell me all —
For I, like thee, am but a Fugitive
An alien from delight, in this dark scene!

And, now I mark thy features, I behold
The cause of thy complaining. Thou art here
A persecuted Exile! one, whose soul
Unbow'd by guilt, demands no patronage
From blunted feeling, or the frozen hand
Of gilded Ostentation. Thou, poor PRIEST!
Art here, a Stranger, from thy kindred torn —
Thy kindred massacred! thy quiet home,
The rural palace of some village scant,
Shelter'd by vineyards, skirted by fair meads,
And by the music of a shallow rill

15

20

25

30

35

40

45

---

1   The youth could be unapt, or unsuited for, supplication. Though "rapt" seems the
more likely word here, it is "unapt" in every version of the poem.

Made ever chearful, now thou hast exchang'd
For stranger woods and vallies.
                                    What of that!   50
Here, or on torrid desarts; o'er the world
Of trackless waves, or on the frozen cliffs
Of black Siberia, thou art not alone!
For there, on each, on all, The Deity
Is thy companion still! Then, exiled Man!   55
Be chearful as the Lark that o'er yon hill
In Nature's language, wild, yet musical,
Hails the Creator! nor thus, sullenly
Repine, that, through the day, the sunny beam
Of lust'rous fortune gilds the palace roof,   60
While thy short path, in this wild labyrinth,
Is lost in transient shadow.
                                    Who, that lives,
Hath not his portion of calamity?
Who, that feels, can boast a tranquil bosom?   65
The fever, throbbing in the Tyrant's veins
In quick, strong language, tells the daring wretch
That He is mortal, like the poorest slave
Who wears his chain, yet healthfully suspires.
The sweetest Rose will wither, while the storm   70
Passes the mountain thistle. The bold Bird,
Whose strong eye braves the ever burning Orb,
Falls like the Summer Fly, and has at most,
But his allotted sojourn. Exiled Man!
Be chearful! Thou art not a fugitive!   75
All are thy kindred — all thy brothers, here —
The hoping — trembling Creatures — of *one* God!

THE HAUNTED BEACH

Upon a lonely desart Beach
    Where the white foam was scatter'd,
A little shed uprear'd its head
    Though lofty Barks were shatter'd.
The Sea-weeds gath'ring near the door,   5

A sombre path display'd;
And, all around, the deaf'ning roar,
Re-echo'd on the chalky shore,
   By the green billows made.

Above, a jutting cliff was seen
   Where Sea Birds hover'd, craving;
And all around, the craggs were bound
   With weeds — for ever waving.
And here and there, a cavern wide
   Its shad'wy jaws display'd;
And near the sands, at ebb of tide,
A shiver'd mast was seen to ride
   Where the green billows stray'd.

And often, while the moaning wind
   Stole o'er the Summer Ocean,
The moonlight scene was all serene,
   The waters scarce in motion:
Then, while the smoothly slanting sand
   The tall cliff wrapp'd in shade,
The Fisherman beheld a band
Of Spectres, gliding hand in hand —
   Where the green billows play'd.

And pale their faces were, as snow,
   And sullenly they wander'd:
And to the skies with hollow eyes
   They look'd as though they ponder'd.
And sometimes, from their hammock shroud,
   They dismal howlings made,
And while the blast blew strong and loud
The clear moon mark'd the ghastly croud,
   Where the green billows play'd!

And then, above the haunted hut
   The Curlews screaming hover'd;
And the low door with furious roar
   The frothy breakers cover'd.

10

15

20

25

30

35

40

218   MARY ROBINSON

For, in the Fisherman's lone shed
　　A MURDER'D MAN was laid,
With ten wide gashes in his head
And deep was made his sandy bed
　　Where the green billows play'd.

A Shipwreck'd Mariner was he,
　　Doom'd from his home to sever;
Who swore to be thro' wind and sea
　　Firm and undaunted ever!
And when the wave resistless roll'd,
　　About his arm he made
A packet rich of Spanish gold,
And, like a British sailor, bold,
　　Plung'd, where the billows play'd!

The Spectre-band, his messmates brave
　　Sunk in the yawning ocean,
While to the mast he lash'd him fast
　　And brav'd the storm's commotion.
The winter moon, upon the sand
　　A silv'ry carpet made,
And mark'd the Sailor reach the land,
And mark'd his murd'rer wash his hand
　　Where the green billows play'd.

And since that hour the Fisherman
　　Has toil'd and toil'd in vain!
For all the night, the moony light
　　Gleams on the specter'd main!
And when the skies are veil'd in gloom,
　　The Murd'rer's liquid way
Bounds o'er the deeply yawning tomb,
And flashing fires the sands illume,
　　Where the green billows play!

Full thirty years his task has been,
　　Day after day more weary;
For Heav'n design'd, his guilty mind

45

50

55

60

65

70

75

Should dwell on prospects dreary.
Bound by a strong and mystic chain,
   He has not pow'r to stray;
But, destin'd mis'ry to sustain,
He wastes, in Solitude and Pain —
   A loathsome life away.

[handwritten marginalia:] She is examining the power guilt

OLD BARNARD,

A MONKISH TALE

OLD BARNARD was still a lusty hind,
Though his age was full fourscore;
   And he us'd to go
   Thro' hail and snow,
   To a neighb'ring town,
   With his old coat brown,
To beg, at his GRANDSON's door!

OLD BARNARD briskly jogg'd along,
When the hail and snow did fall;
   And, whatever the day,
   He was always gay,
   Did the broad Sun glow,
   Or the keen wind blow,
While he begg'd in his GRANDSON's Hall.

His GRANDSON was a Squire, and he
Had houses, and lands, and gold;
   And a coach beside,
   And horses to ride,
   And a downy bed
   To repose his head,
And he felt not the winter's cold.

Old BARNARD had neither house nor lands,
Nor gold to buy warm array;
   Nor a coach to carry,

His old bones weary 25
Nor beds of feather
In freezing weather,
To sleep the long nights away.

But BARNARD a quiet conscience had,
No guile did his bosom know; 30
And when Ev'ning clos'd,
His old bones repos'd,
Tho' the wintry blast
O'er his hovel past,
And he slept, while the winds did blow! 35

But his GRANDSON, he could never sleep
'Till the Sun began to rise;
For a fev'rish pain
Oppress'd his brain,
And he fear'd some evil 40
And dream'd of the Devil,
Whenever he clos'd his eyes!

And whenever he feasted the rich and gay,
The Devil still had his joke;
For however rare 45
The sumptutous fare,
When the sparkling glass
Was seen to pass, —
He was fearful the draught would choke!

And whenever, in fine and costly geer,[1] 50
The Squire went forth to ride:
The owl would cry,
And the raven fly
Across his road,
While the sluggish toad 55
Would crawl by his Palfry's side.

---

1 Apparel, attire.

And he could not command the Sunny day,
For the rain would wet him through;
  And the wind would blow
  Where his nag did go,
  And the thunder roar,
  And the torrents pour,
And he felt the chill Evening dew.

And the cramp would wring his youthful bones,
And would make him groan aloud;
  And the doctor's art
  Could not cure the heart,
  While the conscience still
  Was o'ercharg'd with ill;
And he dream'd of the pick-axe and shroud.

And why could Old BARNARD sweetly sleep,
Since so poor, and so old was he?
  Because he could say
  At the close of day,
  "I have done no wrong
  To the weak or strong,
And so, Heaven look kind on me!"

One night, the GRANDSON hied him forth,
To a MONK, that liv'd hard by;
  "O! Father!" said he,
  "I am come to thee,
  For I'm sick of sin,
  And would fain begin
To repent me, before I die!"

"I must pray for your Soul; the MONK replied,
But will see you to-morrow, ere noon:"
  Then the MONK flew straight
  To Old BARNARD's gate,
  And he bade him haste
  O'er the dewy waste,
By the light of the waning Moon.

In the Monkish cell did old BARNARD wait,
And his GRANDSON went thither soon;
    In a habit of grey
    Ere the dawn of day,   95
    With a cowl and cross,
    On the sill of moss,
He knelt by the light of the Moon.

"O! shrive[1] me, Father!" the GRANDSON cried,
"For the Devil is waiting for me!   100
    I have robb'd the poor,
    I have shut my door,
    And kept out the good
    When they wanted food, —
And I come for my pardon, to Thee."   105

"Get home young Sinner," Old BARNARD said,
"And your GRANDSIRE quickly see;
    Give him half your store,
    For he's old, and poor,
    And avert each evil   110
    And cheat the Devil, —
By making him *rich as thee.*"

The SQUIRE obey'd; and Old BARNARD now
Is rescued from every evil:
    For he fears no wrong,   115
    From the weak or strong,
    And the Squire can snore,
    When the loud winds roar,
For he dreams no more of THE DEVIL!

---

1   To hear confession or pardon.

THE HERMIT OF MONT-BLANC[1]

Native imagery

Wordsworth

High, on the Solitude of Alpine Hills,
O'er-topping the grand imag'ry of Nature,
Where one eternal winter seem'd to reign,
An HERMIT's threshold, carpetted with moss,
5   Diversifed the Scene. Above the flakes
Of silv'ry snow, full many a modest flow'r
Peep'd through its icy veil, and blushing ope'd
Its variegated hues; The ORCHIS sweet,
The bloomy CISTUS, and the fragrant branch
10   Of glossy MYRTLE.[2] In his rushy cell,
The lonely ANCHORET[3] consum'd his days,
Unnotic'd, and unblest. In early youth,
Cross'd in the fond affections of his soul
By false Ambition, from his parent home
15   He, solitary, wander'd; while the Maid
Whose peerless beauty won his yielding heart
Pined in monastic horrors! Near his sill
A little cross he rear'd, where, prostrate low
At day's pale glimpse, or when the setting Sun
20   Tissued the western sky with streamy gold,
His Orisons[4] he pour'd, for her, whose hours
Were wasted in oblivion. Winters pass'd,
And Summers faded, slow, unchearly all
To the lone HERMIT's sorrows: For, still, Love
25   A dark, though unpolluted altar, rear'd
On the white waste of wonders!
                                  From the peak
Which mark'd his neighb'ring Hut, his humid Eye

sexual undertones?

---

1   This poem appeared in the *Monthly Magazine* of February 1, 1800. After publication
     in the *Lyrical Tales* it was incorporated into *The Progress of Liberty*. Mont Blanc is the
     highest mountain in the Alps. It is located in France on the border with Italy, near
     Switzerland.
2   Orchis: a plant with an erect stem bearing a spike of flowers. Cistus: a shrub with
     large spotted flowers that last for only a few hours after expansion. Myrtle: a shrub
     with white sweet-scented flowers.
3   Someone who has chosen seclusion from the world for religious reasons.
4   Prayers.

Oft wander'd o'er the rich expanse below;
Oft trac'd the glow of vegetating Spring,   30
The full-blown Summer splendours, and the hue
Of tawny scenes Autumnal: Vineyards vast,
Clothing the upland scene, and spreading wide
The promised tide nectareous; while for him
The liquid lapse of the slow brook was seen   35
Flashing amid the trees, its silv'ry wave!
Far distant, the blue mist of waters rose
Veiling the ridgy outline, faintly grey,
Blended with clouds, and shutting out the Sun.
The Seasons still revolv'd, and still was he   40
By all forgotten, save by her, whose breast
Sigh'd in responsive sadness to the gale
That swept her prison turrets. Five long years,
Had seen his graces wither ere his Spring
Of life was wasted. From the social scenes   45
Of human energy an alien driv'n,   (like alienation)
He almost had forgot the face of Man. —
No voice had met his ear, save, when perchance
The Pilgrim wand'rer, or the Goatherd Swain,
Bewilder'd in the starless midnight hour   50
Implored the HERMIT's aid, the HERMIT's pray'rs;
And nothing loath by pity or by pray'r
Was he, to save the wretched. On the top
Of his low rushy Dome, a tinkling bell
Oft told the weary Trav'ller to approach   55
Fearless of danger. The small silver sound
In quick vibrations echo'd down the dell
To the dim valley's quiet, while the breeze
Slept on the glassy LEMAN.[1] Thus he past
His melancholy days, an alien Man   60
From all the joys of social intercourse,
Alone, unpitied, by the world forgot!

---

1   Lake Geneva, Switzerland, so called because during the period 1798-1814 it was
    annexed to France as the department of Leman.

His Scrip[1] each morning bore the day's repast
Gather'd on summits, mingling with the clouds,
65 From whose bleak altitude the Eye look'd down
While fast the giddy brain was rock'd by fear.
Oft would he start from visionary rest
When roaming wolves their midnight chorus howl'd,
Or blasts infuriate shatter'd the white cliffs,
70 While the huge fragments, rifted by the storm,
Plung'd to the dell below. Oft would he sit
In silent sadness on the jutting block
Of snow-encrusted ice, and, shudd'ring mark
(Amid the wonders of the frozen world)
75 Dissolving pyramids, and threatening peaks,
Hang o'er his hovel, terribly Sublime.

And oft, when Summer breath'd ambrosial gales,
Soft sailing o'er the waste of printless dew
Or twilight gossamer, his pensive gaze
80 Trac'd the swift storm advancing, whose broad wing
Blacken'd the rushy dome of his low Hut;
While the pale lightning smote the pathless top
Of tow'ring CENIS,[2] scatt'ring high and wide
A mist of fleecy Snow. Then would he hear,
85 (While MEM'RY brought to view his happier days)
The tumbling torrent, bursting wildly forth
From its thaw'd prison, sweep the shaggy cliff
Vast and Stupendous! strength'ning as it fell,
And delving, 'mid the snow, a cavern rude!

90 So liv'd the HERMIT, like an hardy Tree
Plac'd on a mountain's solitary brow,
And destin'd, thro' the Seasons, to endure
Their wond'rous changes. To behold the face
Of ever-varying Nature, and to mark
95 In each grand lineament, the work of GOD!

---

1 A small wallet or satchel, especially one carried by a pilgrim, shepherd, or beggar.
2 A mountain in southeast France, five miles northwest of the Italian border.

And happier he, in total Solitude
Than the poor toil-worn wretch, whose ardent Soul
That GOD has nobly organiz'd, but taught,
For purposes unknown, to bear the scourge
Of sharp adversity, and vulgar pride.   100
Happier, O! happier far, than those who feel,
Yet live amongst the unfeeling! feeding still
The throbbing heart, with anguish, or with Scorn.

One dreary night when Winter's icy breath
Half petrified the scene, when not a star   105
Gleam'd o'er the black infinity of space,
Sudden, the HERMIT started from his couch
Fear-struck and trembling! Ev'ry limb was shook
With painful agitation. On his cheek
The blanch'd interpreter of horror mute   110
Sat terribly impressive! In his breast
The ruddy fount of life convulsive flow'd
And his broad eyes, fix'd motionless as death,
Gaz'd vacantly aghast! His feeble lamp
Was wasting rapidly; the biting gale   115
Pierc'd the thin texture of his narrow cell;
And Silence, like a fearful centinel
Marking the peril which awaited near,
Conspir'd with sullen Night, to wrap the scene
In tenfold horrors. Thrice he rose; and thrice   120
His feet recoil'd; and still the livid flame
Lengthen'd and quiver'd as the moaning wind
Pass'd thro' the rushy crevice, while his heart
Beat, like the death-watch, in his shudd'ring breast.

Like the pale Image of Despair he sat,   125
The cold drops pacing down his hollow cheek,
When a deep groan assail'd his startled ear,
And rous'd him into action. To the sill
Of his low hovel he rush'd forth, (for fear
Will sometimes take the shape of fortitude,   130
And force men into bravery) and soon

The wicker[1] bolt unfasten'd. The swift blast,
Now unrestrain'd, flew by; and in its course
The quiv'ring lamp extinguish'd, and again
135   His soul was thrill'd with terror. On he went,
E'en to the snow-fring'd margin of the cragg,
Which to his citadel a platform made
Slipp'ry and perilous! 'Twas darkness, all!
All, solitary gloom! — The concave vast
140   Of Heav'n frown'd chaos; for all varied things
Of air, and earth, and waters, blended, lost
Their forms, in blank oblivion! Yet not long
Did Nature wear her sable panoply,
For, while the HERMIT listen'd, from below
145   A stream of light ascended, spreading round
A partial view of trackless solitudes;
And mingling voices seem'd, with busy hum,
To break the spell of horrors. Down the steep
The HERMIT hasten'd, when a shriek of death
150   Re-echoed to the valley. As he flew,
(The treach'rous pathway yielding to his speed,)
Half hoping, half despairing, to the scene
Of wonder-waking anguish, suddenly
The torches were extinct; and second night
155   Came doubly hideous, while the hollow tongues
Of cavern'd winds, with melancholy sound
Increas'd the HERMIT's fears. Four freezing hours
He watch'd and pray'd: and now the glimm'ring dawn
Peer'd on the Eastern Summits; (the blue light
160   Shedding cold lustre on the colder brows
Of Alpine desarts;) while the filmy wing
Of weeping Twilight, swept the naked plains
Of the Lombardian landscape.
                      On his knees
165   The ANCHORET blest Heav'n, that he had 'scap'd
The many perilous and fearful falls
Of waters wild and foamy, tumbling fast

---

1   All versions of the poem have the word "wicker" in this line, but "wicket" would
make more sense, so this is perhaps an uncorrected error. A wicket is a gate and
thus a wicket bolt is more logical than a bolt made of wicker.

From the shagg'd altitude. But, ere his pray'rs
Rose to their destin'd Heav'n, another sight,
Than all preceding far more terrible,   170
Palsied devotion's ardour. On the Snow,
Dappled with ruby drops, a track was made
By steps precipitate; a rugged path
Down the steep frozen chasm had mark'd the fate
Of some night traveller, whose bleeding form   175
Had toppled from the Summit. Lower still
The ANCHORET descended, 'till arrived
At the first ridge of silv'ry battlements,
Where, lifeless, ghastly, paler than the snow
On which her cheek repos'd, his darling Maid   180
Slept in the dream of Death! Frantic and wild
He clasp'd her stiff'ning form, and bath'd with tears
The lilies of her bosom, — icy cold —
Yet beautiful and spotless.
                                    Now, afar   185
The wond'ring HERMIT heard the clang of arms
Re-echoing from the valley: the white cliffs
Trembled as though an Earthquake shook their base
With terrible concussion! Thund'ring peals
From warfare's brazen throat, proclaim'd th' approach   190
Of conquering legions: onward they extend
Their dauntless columns! In the foremost group
A Ruffian met the HERMIT's startled Eyes
Like Hell's worst Demon! For his murd'rous hands
Were smear'd with gore; and on his daring breast   195
A golden cross, suspended, bore the name
Of his ill-fated Victim! — ANCHORET!
Thy VESTAL[1] Saint, by his unhallow'd hands
Torn from RELIGION's Altar, had been made
The sport of a dark Fiend, whose recreant Soul   200
Had sham'd the cause of Valour! To his cell
The Soul-struck Exile turn'd his trembling feet,
And after three lone weeks, of pain and pray'r,
Shrunk from the scene of Solitude — and DIED!

---

1   Virginal or chaste.

DEBORAH'S PARROT,

A VILLAGE TALE

'Twas in a little western town
    An ancient Maiden dwelt:
Her name was MISS, or MISTRESS, Brown,
    Or DEBORAH, or DEBBY: She
5   Was doom'd a Spinster pure to be,
For soft delights her breast ne'er felt:
Yet, she had watchful Ears and Eyes
    For ev'ry youthful neighbour,
And never did she cease to labour
10   A tripping female to surprize.

And why was she so wond'rous pure,
    So stiff, so solemn — so demure?
Why did she watch with so much care
    The roving youth, the wand'ring fair?
15   The tattler, Fame, has said that she
A Spinster's life had long detested,
But 'twas her quiet destiny,
    Never to be molested! —
And had Miss DEBBY's form been grac'd,
20   Fame adds, — She had not been so chaste; —
But since for frailty she would roam,
She ne'er was taught — *to look at home.*

Miss DEBBY was of mien demure
    And blush'd, like any maid!
25   She could not saucy man endure
    Lest she should be betray'd!
She never fail'd at dance or fair
To watch the wily lurcher's[1] snare;
At Church, she was a model Godly!
30   Though sometimes she had other eyes
Than those, uplifted to the skies,

---

1   Swindler or rogue.

Leering most oddly!
And Scandal, ever busy, thought
She rarely practic'd — what she taught.

Her dress was always stiff brocade,   35
   With laces broad and dear;
Fine Cobwebs! that would thinly shade
   Her shrivell'd cheek of sallow hue,
While, like a Spider, her keen eye,
   Which never shed soft pity's tear,   40
Small holes in others' geer could spy,
And microscopic follies, prying view.
And sorely vex'd was ev'ry simple thing
That wander'd near her never-tiring sting!

Miss DEBBY had a PARROT, who,   45
   If Fame speaks true,
Could prate, and tell what neighbours did,
And yet the saucy rogue was never chid!
Sometimes, he talk'd of roving Spouses
Who wander'd from their quiet houses: 50
Sometimes, he call'd a Spinster pure
By names, that Virtue can't indure!
And sometimes told an ancient Dame
Such tales as made her blush with shame!
Then gabbled how a giddy Miss   55
Would give the boist'rous Squire a kiss!
But chiefly he was taught to cry,
"Who with the Parson toy'd? O fie!"

This little joke, Miss DEBBY taught him,
To vex a young and pretty neighbour;   60
But by her scandal-zealous labour
   To shame she brought him!
For, the Old PARROT, like his teacher,
Was but a false and canting preacher,
And many a gamesome pair had sworn   65
Such lessons were not to be borne.

At last, Miss DEBBY sore was flouted
And by her angry neighbours scouted;
She never knew one hour of rest,
70   Of ev'ry Saucy Boor, the jest:
The young despis'd her, and the Sage
Look'd back on Time's impartial page;
They knew that youth was giv'n to prove
     The season of extatic joy,
75   That none but Cynics would destroy,
     The early buds of Love.

They also know that DEBBY sigh'd
For charms that envious Time deny'd;
That she was vex'd with jealous Spleen
80   That Hymen[1] pass'd her by, unseen.
For though the Spinster's wealth was known,
Gold will not purchase Love — *alone.*
She, and her PARROT, now were thought
The torments of their little Sphere;
85   He, because mischievously taught,
And She, because a maid austere! —
In short, she deem'd it wise to leave
A Place, where none remain'd, to grieve.

Soon, to a distant town remov'd,
90   Miss DEBBY's gold an husband bought;
And all she had her PARROT taught,
(Her PARROT now no more belov'd,)
Was quite forgotten. But, alas!
As Fate would have it come to pass,
95   Her Spouse was giv'n to jealous rage,
For, both in *Person* and in *Age,*
He was the partner of his love,
Ordain'd her second Self to prove!

One day, Old JENKINS had been out
100   With merry friends to dine,

---

1   God of marriage in Greek mythology.

And, freely talking, had, no doubt,
    Been also free with wine.
One said, of all the wanton gay
In the whole parish search it round,
None like the PARSON could be found,   105
    Where a frail Maid was in the way.
Another thought the Parson sure
To win the heart of maid or wife;
And would have freely pledg'd his life
That young, or old, or rich or poor   110
    None could defy
The magic of his roving eye!

JENKINS went home, but all the night
    He dream'd of this strange tale!
Yet, bless'd his stars! with proud delight,   115
    His partner was not young, nor frail.
Next morning, at the breakfast table,
The PARROT, loud as he was able,
Was heard repeatedly to cry,
"Who with the Parson toy'd? O fie!"   120

Old JENKINS listen'd, and grew pale,
    The PARROT then, more loudly scream'd,
And MISTRESS JENKINS heard the tale
    And much alarm'd she seem'd!
Trembling she tried to stop his breath,   125
Her lips and cheek as pale as death!
The more she trembled, still the more
Old JENKINS view'd her o'er and o'er;
And now her yellow cheek was spread
With blushes of the deepest red.   130

And now again the PARROT's Tale
Made his old Tutoress doubly pale;
For cowardice and guilt, they say
    Are the twin brothers of the soul;
So MISTRESS JENKINS, her dismay   135

Could not controul!
While the accuser, now grown bold,
Thrice o'er, the tale of mischief told.

Now JENKINS from the table rose,
140   "*Who with the Parson toy'd?*" he cried.
"So MISTRESS FRAILTY, you must play,
And sport, your wanton hours away.
And with your gold, a pretty joke,
You thought to buy a pleasant cloak;
145   A screen to hide your shame — but know
I will not *blind* to ruin go. —
I am no *modern Spouse*, d'ye see,
Gold will not *gild disgrace*, with me!"
Some say he seiz'd his fearful bride,
150   And came to blows!
Day after day, the contest dire
Augmented, with resistless ire!
And many a drubbing DEBBY bought
For mischief, she her PARROT taught!

155   Thus, SLANDER turns against its maker;
    And if this little Story reaches
     A SPINSTER, who her PARROT teaches,
Let her a better task pursue,
And here, the certain VENGEANCE view
160   Which surely will, in TIME, O'ERTAKE HER.

', very melodramatic (handwritten margin note)

THE NEGRO GIRL

"love story" but in tradition ... abortionism (handwritten margin notes)

I

Dark was the dawn, and o'er the deep
   The boist'rous whirlwinds blew;
The Sea-bird wheel'd its circling sweep,
   And all was drear to view —
5   When on the beach that binds the western shore
The love-lorn ZELMA stood, list'ning the tempest's roar.

II

Her eager Eyes beheld the main,
　　While on her DRACO dear
She madly call'd, but call'd in vain,
　　No sound could DRACO hear,　　　　　　　10
Save the shrill yelling of the fateful blast,
While ev'ry Seaman's heart, quick shudder'd as it past.

III

White were the billows, wide display'd
　　The clouds were black and low;
The Bittern shriek'd, a gliding shade
　　Seem'd o'er the waves to go!　　　　　　　15
The livid flash illum'd the clam'rous main,
While ZELMA pour'd, unmark'd, her melancholy strain.

IV

"Be still!" she cried, "loud tempest cease!
　　O! spare the gallant souls:
The thunder rolls — the winds increase —　　　　20
　　The Sea, like mountains, rolls!
While, from the deck, the storm-worn victims leap,
And o'er their struggling limbs, the furious billows sweep.

V

O! barb'rous Pow'r! relentless Fate!　　　　　25
　　Does Heav'n's high will decree
That some should sleep on beds of state, —
　　Some, in the roaring Sea?
Some, nurs'd in splendour, deal Oppression's blow,
While worth and DRACO pine — in Slavery and woe!　　30

VI

Yon Vessel oft has plough'd the main
　　With human traffic fraught;
Its cargo, — our dark Sons of pain —
　　For wordly treasure bought!
What had they done? — O Nature tell me why —　　35
Is taunting scorn the lot, of thy dark progeny?

VII

Thou gav'st, in thy caprice, the Soul
    Peculiarly enshrin'd;
Nor from the ebon Casket stole
40   The Jewel of the mind!
Then wherefore let the suff'ring Negro's breast
Bow to his fellow, MAN, in brighter colours drest.

VIII

Is it the dim and glossy hue
    That marks him for despair? —
45   While men with blood their hands embrue,
    And mock the wretch's pray'r?
Shall guiltless Slaves the Scourge of tyrants feel,
And, e'en before their GOD! unheard, unpitied kneel.

IX

Could the proud rulers of the land
50   Our Sable race behold;
Some bow'd by torture's Giant hand
    And others, basely sold!
Then would they pity Slaves, and cry, with shame,
Whate'er their TINTS may be, their SOULS are still the same!

X

55 Why seek to mock the Ethiop's face?
    Why goad our hapless kind?
Can features alienate the race —
    Is there no kindred mind?
Does not the cheek which vaunts the roseate hue
60 Oft blush for crimes, that Ethiops never knew?

XI

Behold! the angry waves conspire
    To check the barb'rous toil!
While wounded Nature's vengeful ire —
    Roars, round this trembling Isle!

And hark! her voice re-echoes in the wind —   65
Man was not form'd by Heav'n, to trample on his kind!

XII

Torn from my Mother's aching breast,
   My Tyrant sought my love —
But, in the Grave shall ZELMA rest,
   E'er she will faithless prove —
No DRACO! — Thy companion I will be   70
To that celestial realm, where Negroes shall be free!

XIII

The Tyrant WHITE MAN taught my mind —
   The letter'd page to trace; —
He taught me in the Soul to find   75
   No tint, as in the face:
He bade my Reason, blossom like the tree —
But fond affection gave, the ripen'd fruits to thee.

XIV

With jealous rage he mark'd my love;
   He sent thee far away; —
And prison'd in the plantain grove —   80
   Poor ZELMA pass'd the day —
But ere the moon rose high above the main,
ZELMA, and Love contriv'd, to break the Tyrant's chain.

XV

Swift, o'er the plain of burning Sand
   My course I bent to thee;   85
And soon I reach'd the billowy strand
   Which bounds the stormy Sea. —
DRACO! my Love! Oh yet, thy ZELMA's soul
Springs ardently to thee, — impatient of controul.   90

Handwritten annotations:
- raping of slaves "The Awakening" Kate Chopin
- ← her master
- ← why he sends Draco away
- she ennobles the slave / she makes her a heroine in a drama
- she says that even the best slave owners are rapists (or would be)?

XVI

Again the lightning flashes white —
    The rattling cords among!
Now, by the transient vivid light,
    I mark the frantic throng!
Now up the tatter'd shrouds my DRACO flies —
While o'er the plunging prow, the curling billows rise.

XVII

The topmast falls — three shackled slaves —
    Cling to the Vessel's side!
Now lost amid the madd'ning waves —
    Now on the mast they ride —
See! on the forecastle my DRACO stands
And now he waves his chain, now clasps his bleeding hands.

XVIII

Why, cruel WHITE-MAN! when away
    My sable Love was torn,
Why did you let poor ZELMA stay,
    On Afric's sands to mourn?
No! ZELMA is not left, for she will prove
In the deep troubled main, her fond — her faithful LOVE."

XIX

The lab'ring Ship was now a wreck,
    The Shrouds were flutt'ring wide!
The rudder gone, the lofty deck
    Was rock'd from side to side —
Poor ZELMA's eyes now dropp'd their last big tear,
While, from her tawny cheek, the blood recoil'd with fear.

XX

Now frantic, on the sands she roam'd,
    Now shrieking stop'd to view
Where high the liquid mountains foam'd,
    Around the exhausted crew —

'Till, from the deck, her DRACO's well known form
Sprung mid the yawning waves, and buffetted the Storm.   120

XXI

Long, on the swelling surge sustain'd
  Brave DRACO sought the shore,
Watch'd the dark Maid, but ne'er complain'd,
  Then sunk, to gaze no more!
Poor ZELMA saw him buried by the wave —   125
And, with her heart's true Love, plung'd in a wat'ry grave.

 THE TRUMPETER,

AN OLD ENGLISH TALE

It was in the days of a gay British King
(In the old fashion'd custom of merry-making)
The Palace of Woodstock with revels did ring,
  While they sang and carous'd — one and all:
For the monarch a plentiful treasury had,   5
And his Courtiers were pleas'd, and no visage was sad,
And the knavish and foolish with drinking were mad,
  While they sat in the Banquetting hall.

Some talk'd of their Valour, and some of their Race,
And vaunted, till vaunting was black in the face;   10
Some bragg'd for a title, and some for a place,
  And, like braggarts, they bragg'd one and all!
Some spoke of their scars in the Holy Crusade,
Some boasted the banner of Fame they display'd,
And some sang their Loves in the soft serenade   15
  As they sat in the Banquetting hall.

And here sat a Baron, and there sat a Knight,
And here stood a Page in his habit all bright,

And here a young Soldier in armour bedight[1]
20   With a Friar carous'd, one and all.
Some play'd on the dulcimer, some on the lute,
And some, who had nothing to talk of, were mute,
Till the Morning, awakened, put on her grey suit —
    And the Lark hover'd over the Hall.

25   It was in a vast gothic Hall that they sate,
And the Tables were cover'd with rich gilded plate,
And the King and his minions were toping[2] in state,
    Till their noddles[3] turn'd round, one and all: —
And the Sun through the tall painted windows 'gan peep,
30   And the Vassals[4] were sleeping, or longing to sleep,
Though the Courtiers, still waking, their revels did keep,
    While the minstrels play'd sweet, in the Hall.

And, now in their Cups,[5] the bold topers began
To call for more wine, from the cellar yeoman,
35   And, while each one replenish'd his goblet or can,
    The Monarch thus spake to them all:
"It is fit that the nobles do just what they please,
That the Great live in idleness, riot, and ease,
And that those should be favor'd, who mark my decrees,
40   And should feast in the Banquetting Hall."

"It is fit," said the Monarch, "that riches should claim
A passport to freedom, to honor, and fame, —
That the poor should be humble, obedient, and tame,
    And, in silence, submit — one and all.
45   That the wise and the holy should toil for the Great,
That the Vassals should tend at the tables of state,
That the Pilgrim should — pray for our souls at the gate
    While we feast in our Banquetting Hall.

---

1   Adorned.
2   Drinking hard.
3   Heads (with connotation of dullness).
4   Those who are devoted to the service of someone.
5   In a state of intoxication.

That the low-lineag'd CARLES[1] should be scantily fed —
That their drink should be small, and still smaller their bread;   50
That their wives and their daughters to ruin be led,
　　And submit to our will, one and all!
It is fit, that whoever I choose to defend —
Shall be courted, and feasted, and lov'd as a friend,
While before them the good and enlighten'd shall bend,   55
　　While they sit in the Banquetting Hall."

Now the Topers grew bold, and each talk'd of his right,
One would fain be a Baron, another a Knight;
And another, (because at the Tournament fight
　　He had vanquished his foes, one and all)   60
Demanded a track of rich lands; and rich fare;
And of stout serving Vassals a plentiful share;
With a lasting exemption from penance and pray'r
　　And a throne in the Banquetting Hall.

But ONE, who had neither been valiant nor wise,   65
With a tone of importance, thus vauntingly cries,
"My Liege[2] he knows how a good subject to prize —
　　And I therefore demand — before all —
I this Castle possess: and the right to maintain
Five hundred stout Bowmen to follow my train,   70
And as many strong Vassals to guard my domain
　　As the Lord of the Banquetting Hall!

I have fought with all nations, and bled in the field,
See my lance is unshiver'd,[3] tho' batter'd my shield,
I have combatted legions, yet never would yield   75
　　And the Enemy fled — one and all!
I have rescued a thousand fair Donnas, in Spain,
I have left in gay France, every bosom in pain,
I have conquer'd the Russian, the Prussian, the Dane,
　　And will reign in the Banquetting Hall!"   80

1　Men of low birth, farmers.
2　One to whom allegiance and service are due.
3　Unbroken.

The Monarch now rose, with majestical look,
And his sword from the scabbard of Jewels he took,
And the Castle with laughter and ribaldry shook,
    While the braggart accosted thus he:
85   "I will give thee a place that will suit thy demand,
What to thee, is more fitting than Vassals or Land —
I will give thee, — what justice and valour command,
    For a TRUMPETER bold — thou shalt be!"

Now the revellers rose, and began to complain —
90   While they menac'd with gestures, and frown'd with disdain,
And declar'd, that the nobles were fitter to reign
    Than a Prince so unruly as He.
But the Monarch cried, sternly, they taunted him so,
"From this moment the counsel of fools I forego —
95   And on Wisdom and Virtue will honors bestow
    For such, ONLY, are welcome to Me!"

So saying, he quitted the Banquetting Hall,
And leaving his Courtiers and flatterers all —
Straightway for his Confessor loudly 'gan call
100   "O! Father! now listen!" said he:
"I have feasted the Fool, I have pamper'd the Knave,
I have scoff'd at the wise, and neglected the brave —
And here, Holy Man, Absolution I crave —
    For a penitent now I will be."

105   From that moment the Monarch grew sober and good,
(And nestled with Birds of a different brood,)
For he found that the pathway which wisdom pursu'd
    Was pleasant, safe, quiet, and even!
That by Temperance, Virtue and liberal deeds,
110   By nursing the flowrets, and crushing the weeds,
The loftiest Traveller always succeeds —
    For his journey will lead him to HEAV'N.

THE DESERTED COTTAGE

Who dwelt in yonder lonely Cot,
   Why is it thus forsaken?
It seems, by all the world forgot,
Above its path the high grass grows,
And through its thatch the northwind blows   5
   — Its thatch, by tempests shaken.

And yet, it tops a verdant hill
   By Summer gales surrounded:
Beneath its door a shallow rill
Runs brawling to the vale below,   10
And near it sweetest flowrets grow
   By banks of willow bounded.

Then why is ev'ry casement dark?
   Why looks the Cot so chearless?
Ah! why does ruin seem to mark   15
The calm retreat where LOVE should dwell,
And FRIENDSHIP teach the heart to swell
   With rapture, pure and fearless?

There, far above the busy croud,
   Man may repose in quiet;   20
There, smile, that he has left the proud,
And blest with liberty, enjoy
More than Ambition's gilded toy,
   Or Folly's sick'ning riot.

For there, the ever tranquil mind,   25
   On calm Religion resting,
May in each lonely labyrinth find
The DEITY, whose boundless pow'r
Directs the blast, or tints the flow'r —
   No mortal foe molesting.   30

Stranger, yon spot was once the scene
    Where peace and joy resided:
And oft the merry time has been
When Love and Friendship warm'd the breast,
35   And Freedom, making wealth a jest,
    The pride of Pomp derided.

Old JACOB was the Cottage Lord,
    His wide domain, surrounding,
By Nature's treasure amply stor'd;
40   He from his casement could behold
The breezy mountain, ting'd with gold,
    The varied landscape bounding!

The coming morn, with lustre gay,
    Breath'd sweetly on his dwelling;
45   The twilight veil of parting day
Stole softly o'er his quiet shed,
Hiding the mountain's misty head,
    Where the night-breeze was swelling.

One lovely Girl, Old JACOB rear'd
50   And she was fair, and blooming;
She, like the morning Star, appear'd,
Swift gliding o'er the mountain's crest,
While her blue eyes her soul confess'd,
    No borrow'd rays assuming.

55   'Twas her's, the vagrant lamb to lead,
    To watch the wild goat playing:
To join the Shepherd's tuneful reed,
And, when the sultry Sun rose high,
To tend the Herds, deep-lowing nigh,
60   Where the swift brook was straying.

One sturdy Boy, a younker[1] bold,
    Ere they were doom'd to sever,

---

1   A young nobleman or gentleman.

Maintain'd poor JACOB, sick and old;
But now, where yon tall poplars wave,
Pale primroses adorn the grave —   65
   Where JACOB sleeps, for Ever!

Young, in the wars, the brave Boy fell!
   His Sister died of sadness!
But *one* remain'd their fate to tell,
For JACOB now was left alone,   70
And he, alas! was helpless grown,
   And pin'd in moody madness.

At night, by moonshine would he stray,
   Along the upland dreary;
And, talking wildly all the way,   75
Would fancy, 'till the Sun uprose,
That Heav'n, in pity, mark'd the woes —
   Of which his soul was weary.

One morn, upon the dewy grass
   Poor JACOB's sorrow ended,   80
The woodland's narrow winding pass
Was his last scene of lonely care,
For, gentle Stranger, lifeless there —
   Was JACOB's form extended!

He lies beneath yon Poplar tree   85
   That tops the church yard, sighing!
For sighing oft it seems to be,
And as its waving leaves, around,
With morning's tears begem the ground
   The Zephyr[1] trembles, flying!   90

And now behold yon little Cot
   All dreary and forsaken!
And know, that soon 'twill be thy lot,
To fall, like JACOB and his race,

---

1   Gentle breeze.

95 And leave on Time's swift wing no trace,
 Which way thy course is taken.

 Yet, if for Truth and feeling known,
  Thou still shalt be lamented!
 For when thy parting sigh has flown,
100 Fond MEM'RY on thy grave shall give
 A tear — to bid thy VIRTUES live!
  Then — Smile, AND BE CONTENTED!

THE FORTUNE-TELLER,

A GYPSY TALE

 LUBIN and KATE, as gossips tell,
  Were Lovers many a day;
 LUBIN the damsel lov'd so well,
  That folks pretend to say
5 The silly, simple, doting Lad,
 Was little less than loving mad:
 A malady not known of late —
 Among the little-loving Great!

 KATE liked the youth; but woman-kind
10 Are sometimes giv'n to range.
 And oft, the giddy Sex, we find,
  (They know not why)
 When most they promise, soonest change,
  And still for conquest sigh:
15 So 'twas with KATE; she, ever roving
 Was never fix'd, though always loving!

 STEPHEN was LUBIN's rival; he
  A rustic libertine was known;
 And many a blushing simple She,
20 The rogue had left, — to sigh alone!
 KATE cared but little for the rover,
  Yet she resolv'd to have her way,

For STEPHEN was the village Lover,
  And women pant for Sov'reign sway.
And he, who has been known to ruin, —
Is always sought, and always wooing.

STEPHEN had long in secret sigh'd;
And STEPHEN never was deny'd:
Now, LUBIN was a modest swain,
And therefore, treated with disdain:
For, it is said, in *Love* and *War*, —
The boldest, most successful are!

Vows, were to him but fairy things,
Borne on capricious Fancy's wings;
And promises, the phantoms airy
Which falsehood form'd to cheat th' unwary;
For still deception was his trade,
And though his traffic well was known,
Still, every trophy was his own
  Which the proud Victor, Love, display'd.
In short, this STEPHEN was the bane
Of ev'ry maid, — and ev'ry swain![1]

KATE had too often play'd the fool,
  And now, at length, was caught;
For she, who had been pleas'd to rule,
  Was now, poor Maiden, taught!
And STEPHEN rul'd with boundless sway,
The rustic tyrant of his day.

LUBIN had giv'n inconstant KATE,
  Ten pounds, to buy her wedding geer:
And now, 'tis said, tho' somewhat late,
  He thought his bargain rather dear.
For, Lo! The day before the pair
Had fix'd, the marriage chain to wear,
A GYPSY gang, a wand'ring set,

25

30

35

40

45

50

55

---

1   Shepherd or countryman.

In a lone wood young LUBIN met.
All round him press with canting tale,
And, in a jargon, well design'd
To cheat the unsuspecting mind,
60   His list'ning ears assail.

Some promis'd riches; others swore
  He should, by women, be ador'd;
And never sad, and never poor —
  Live like a Squire, or Lord; —
65 Do what he pleas'd, and ne'er be brought
To shame, — for what he did, or thought;
Seduce men's wives and daughters fair,
Spend wealth, while others toil'd in vain,
And scoff at honesty, and swear, —
70 *And scoff, and trick, and swear again!*

One roguish Girl, with sparkling eyes,
To win the handsome LUBIN tries;
She smil'd, and by her speaking glance,
Enthrall'd him in a wond'ring trance;
75 He thought her lovelier far than KATE,
And wish'd that she had been his mate;
For when the FANCY is on wing,
VARIETY's a dangerous thing:
And PASSIONS, when they learn to stray
80 Will seldom keep the beaten way.
The gypsy girl, with speaking eyes,
Observ'd her pupil's fond surprize;
She begg'd that he her hand would cross
  With Sixpence; and that He should know
85 His future scene of gain and loss,
  His weal[1] and woe. —

LUBIN complies. And straight he hears
That he had many long, long years;

---

1 Wealth, well-being.

That he a maid inconstant, loves,
Who, to another slyly roves.   90
That a dark man his bane will be —
"And poison his domestic hours;
While a fair woman, treach'rously —
    Will dress his brow — with thorns and flow'rs!"
It happen'd, to confirm his care —   95
STEPHEN was *dark*, — and KATE was *fair*!
Nay more that "home his bride would bring
A little, alien, prattling thing
In just six moons!" Poor LUBIN hears
All that confirms his jealous fears;   100
Perplex'd and frantic, what to do
The cheated Lover scarcely knew.
He flies to KATE, and straight he tells
The wonder that in magic dwells!
Speaks of the Fortune-telling crew,   105
And how all things the Vagrants knew;
KATE hears: and soon determines, she
Will know *her* future destiny.

Swift to the wood she hies,[1] tho' late
To read the tablet of her Fate.   110
The Moon its crystal beam scarce shew'd
Upon the darkly shadow'd road;
The hedge-row was the feasting-place
Where, round a little blazing wood,
The wand'ring, dingy, gabbling race,   115
    Crowded in merry mood.
And now she loiter'd near the scene.
Now peep'd the hazle copse[2] between;
Fearful that LUBIN might be near,
The story of *her* Fate to hear. —   120
She saw the feasting circle gay
By the stol'n faggot's yellow light;
She heard them, as in sportive play,

---

1   Hurries.
2   A thicket of small trees or underwood periodically cut for economic purposes.

They chear'd the sullen gloom of night.
125   Nor was sly KATE by all unseen
Peeping, the hazle copse between.

And now across the thicket side
A tatter'd, skulking youth she spied;
He beckon'd her along, and soon,
130   Hid safely from the prying moon,
His hand with silver, thrice she crosses —
"Tell me," said she, "my gains and losses!"

"You gain a *fool*," the youth replies,
"You lose a *lover* too."
135   The false one blushes deep, and sighs,
For well the truth she knew!
"You gave to STEPHEN, vows; nay more
You gave him favors rare:
And LUBIN is condemn'd to share
140   What many others shar'd before!
A false, capricious, guilty heart,
Made up of folly, vice, and art,
Which only takes a wedded mate
To brand with shame, an husband's fate."

145   "Hush! hush!" cried KATE, "for Heav'n's sake be
As secret as the grave —
For LUBIN means to marry me —
And if you will not me betray,
I for your silence well will pay;
150   *Five pounds* this moment you shall have." —
"I will have TEN!" the gypsy cries —
The fearful, trembling girl complies.
But, what was her dismay, to find
That LUBIN was the gypsy bold;
155   The cunning, fortune-telling hind[1]
Who had the artful story told —

---

1   Lad or boy; farm labourer or servant.

Who thus, was cur'd of jealous pain, —
And got his TEN POUNDS *back again!*

Thus, Fortune pays the Lover bold!
    But, gentle Maids, should Fate   160
Have any *secret* yet untold, —
    Remember, *simple* KATE!

POOR MARGUERITE

Swift, o'er the wild and dreary waste
A NUT-BROWN GIRL was seen to haste;
Wide waving was her unbound hair,
And sun-scorch'd was her bosom bare;
For Summer's noon had shed its beams   5
While she lay wrapp'd in fev'rish dreams;
While, on the wither'd hedge-row's side,
By turns she slept, by turns she cried,
"Ah! where lies hid the balsam sweet,
To heal the wounds of MARGUERITE?"   10

Dark was her large and sunken eye
Which wildly gaz'd upon the sky;
And swiftly down her freckled face
The chilling dews began to pace:
For she was lorn, and many a day,   15
Had, all alone, been doom'd to stray,
And, many a night, her bosom warm,
Had throbb'd, beneath the pelting storm,
And still she cried, "the rain falls sweet,
It bathes the wounds of MARGUERITE."   20

Her garments were by briars torn,
And on them hung full many a thorn;
A thistle crown, she mutt'ring twin'd,
Now darted on, — now look'd behind —
And here, and there, her arm was seen   25

Bleeding the tatter'd folds between;
Yet, on her breast she oft display'd
A faded branch, that breast to shade:
For though her senses were astray,
30   She felt the burning beams of day:
She felt the wintry blast of night,
And smil'd to see the morning light,
For then she cried, "I soon shall meet
The plighted love of MARGUERITE."

35   Across the waste of printless snow,
All day the NUT-BROWN GIRL would go;
And when the winter moon had shed
Its pale beams on the mountain's head,
She on a broomy[1] pillow lay
40   Singing the lonely hours away;
While the cold breath of dawnlight flew
Across the fields of glitt'ring dew: —
Swift o'er the frozen lake she past
Unmindful of the driving blast,
45   And then she cried "the air is sweet —
It fans the breast of MARGUERITE."

The weedy lane she lov'd to tread
When stars their twinkling lustre shed;
While from the lone and silent Cot
50   The watchful Cur[2] assail'd her not,
Though at the beggar he would fly,
And fright the Trav'ller passing by:
But she, so kind and gentle seem'd,
Such sorrow in her dark eyes beam'd,
55   That savage fierceness could not greet
With less than love, — POOR MARGUERITE!

Oft, by the splashy brook she stood
And sung her Song to the waving wood;

---

1   Covered with broom, a shrub that bears attractive yellow flowers.
2   Watch-dog or shepherd's dog.

The waving wood, in murmurs low,
Fill'd up the pause of weary woe;   60
Oft, to the Forest tripp'd along
And inly humm'd her frantic Song;
Oft danc'd mid shadows Ev'ning spread
Along the whisp'ring willow-bed.
   And wild was her groan,   65
    When she climb'd, alone —
    The rough rock's side,
    While the foaming tide,
Dash'd rudely against the sandy shore,
And the lightning flash'd mid the thunder's roar.   70

And many a time she chac'd the fly,
And mock'd the Beetle, humming by;
And then, with loud fantastic tone
She sang her wild strain, sad — alone.
And if a stranger wander'd near   75
Or paus'd the frantic Song to hear,
The burthen she would soft repeat,
"Who comes to soothe POOR MARGUERITE?"

And why did she with sun-burnt breast,
So wander, and so scorn to rest?   80
Why did the NUT-BROWN MAIDEN go
O'er burning plains and wastes of snow?
What bade her fev'rish bosom sigh,
And dimm'd her large and hazle eye?
What taught her o'er the hills to stray   85
Fearless by night, and wild by day?
What stole the hour of slumber sweet —
From the scorch'd brain of MARGUERITE?

Soon shalt thou know; for see how lorn
She climbs the steep of shaggy thorn —   90
Now on the jutting cliff she stands,
And clasps her cold, — but snow-white hands.
And now aloud she chaunts her strain

While fiercely roars the troublous main.
95   Now the white breakers curling shew
        The dread abyss that yawns below,
        And still she sighs, "the sound is sweet,
        It seems to say, POOR MARGUERITE!

        Here will I build a rocky shed,
100   And here I'll make my sea-weed bed;
        Here gather, with unwearied hands —
        The orient shells that deck the sands.
        And here will I skim o'er the billows so high,
        And laugh at the moon and the dark frowning sky.
105   And the Sea-birds, that hover across the wide main,
        Shall sweep with their pinions, the white bounding plain. —
        And the shivering sail shall the fierce tempest meet,
        Like the storm, in the bosom of POOR MARGUERITE!

        The setting Sun, with golden ray,
110   Shall warm my breast, and make me gay.
        The clamours of the roaring Sea
        My midnight serenade shall be!
        The Cliff that like a Tyrant stands
        Exulting o'er the wave lash'd sands,
115   With its weedy crown, and its flinty crest,
        Shall, on its hard bosom, rock *me* to rest;
        And I'll watch for the Eagle's unfledg'd brood,
        And I'll scatter their nest, and I'll drink their blood;
        And under the crag I will kneel and pray
120   And silver my robe, with the moony ray:
        And who shall scorn the lone retreat
        Which Heaven has chose, for MARGUERITE?

        Here, did the exil'd HENRY stray,
        Forc'd from his native land, away;
125   Here, here upon a foreign shore,
        His parents, lost, awhile deplore;
        Here find, that pity's holy tear
        Could not an *alien wand'rer* chear;

And now, in fancy, he would view,
Shouting aloud, the rabble crew —   130
The rabble crew, whose impious hands
Tore asunder nature's bands! —
I see him still, — He waves me on!
And now to the dark abyss he's gone —
He calls — I hear his voice, so sweet, —   135
It seems to say — POOR MARGUERITE!"

Thus, wild she sung! when on the sand
She saw her long lost HENRY, stand:
Pale was his cheek, and on his breast
His icy hand he, silent, prest;   140
And now the Twilight shadows spread
Around the tall cliff's weedy head;
Far o'er the main the moon shone bright,
She mark'd the quiv'ring stream of light —
It danc'd upon the murm'ring wave,   145
It danc'd upon — her HENRY's Grave!
It mark'd his visage, deathly pale, —
His white shroud floating in the gale;
His speaking eyes — his smile so sweet
That won the love — of MARGUERITE!   150

And now he beckon'd her along
The curling moonlight waves among;
No footsteps mark'd the slanting sand
Where she had seen her HENRY stand!
She saw him o'er the billows go —   155
She heard the rising breezes blow;
She shriek'd aloud! The echoing steep
Frown'd darkness on the troubled deep;
The moon in cloudy veil was seen,
And louder howl'd the night blast keen! —   160
And when the morn, in splendour dress'd,
Blush'd radiance on the Eagle's nest,
That radiant blush was doom'd to greet —
The lifeless form — of MARGUERITE!

THE CONFESSOR,

A SANCTIFIED TALE

WHEN SUPERSTITION rul'd the land
And Priestcraft shackled Reason,[1]
At GODSTOW[2] dwelt a goodly band,
Grey monks[3] they were, and but to say
5 They were not always giv'n to pray,
    Would have been construed Treason.
Yet some *did* scoff, and some believ'd
That sinners were themselves deceiv'd;
And taking Monks for more than men
10 They prov'd themselves, nine out of ten,
Mere dupes of these Old Fathers hoary;
    But read — and mark the story.

Near, in a little Farm, there liv'd
A buxom Dame of twenty-three;
15 And by the neighbours 'twas believed
    A very Saint was She!
Yet, ev'ry week, for some transgression,
She went to sigh devout confession.
For ev'ry trifle seem'd to make
20   Her self-reproving Conscience ache;

---

1   In 1535 Thomas Cromwell (1488?-1540), Vicar-General for ecclesiastical matters, visited a number of monasteries and declared them to be in evil condition. Parliament a year later approved the suppression of approximately two hundred monasteries with an annual value of less than £200. Many of the larger houses were later persuaded to surrender themselves to the Crown, and Parliament authorized the suppression of those remaining in 1539. This destruction of the monastery system was part of the larger project of the Reformation, a movement that was ostensibly motivated by a desire to cleanse Christianity (for example, do away with corrupt clergy and the practice of selling papal indulgences and pardons), but was fueled practically by King Henry VIII's desire to get a divorce. Papal authority was replaced by kingly authority, and religious identification was inextricably bound to issues of patriotism and nationalism.

2   A village northwest of Oxford, England. It has fragmentary ruins of a nunnery.

3   Monks of the Cistercian order, an offshoot of the Benedictine order (named after Saint Bernard), and aimed at a stricter observance of Benedictine rules.

And Conscience, waken'd, 'tis well known,
Will never let the Soul alone.

At GODSTOW, 'mid the holy band,
Old FATHER PETER held command.
And lusty was the pious man,   25
As any of his crafty clan:
And rosy was his cheek, and sly
The wand'rings of his keen grey eye;
Yet all the Farmers' wives confest
The wond'rous pow'r this Monk possess'd;   30
Pow'r to rub out the score of sin,
    Which SATAN chalk'd upon his Tally;
To give fresh licence to begin, —
    And for new scenes of frolic, rally
For abstinence was not his way —   35
He lov'd to *live* — as well as *pray*;
To prove his gratitude to Heav'n
    By taking freely all its favors, —
And keeping his account still even,
    Still mark'd his best endeavours: 40
That is to say, He took pure Ore
For benedictions, — and was known,
While Reason op'd her golden store, —
    Not to unlock his own. —
And often to his cell went he   45
With the gay Dame of twenty-three:
His Cell was sacred, and the fair
Well knew, that none could enter there,
Who, (such was PETER's sage decree,)
To Paradise ne'er *bought* a key.   50

It happen'd that this Farmer's wife
(Call MISTRESS TWYFORD — alias BRIDGET,)
Led her poor spouse a weary life —
Keeping him, in an endless fidget!
Yet ev'ry week she sought the cell   55
    Where Holy FATHER PETER stay'd,

And there did ev'ry secret tell, —
And there, at Sun-rise, knelt and pray'd.
For near, there liv'd a civil friend,
60   Than FARMER TWYFORD somewhat stouter,
And he would oft his counsel lend,
And pass the wintry hours away
    In harmless play;
But MISTRESS BRIDGET was so chaste,
65   So much with pious manners grac'd,
      That none could doubt her!

One night, or rather morn, 'tis said
The wily neighbour chose to roam,
And (FARMER TWYFORD far from home)
70   He thought he might supply his place;
And, void of ev'ry spark of grace,
Upon HIS pillow, rest his head.
The night was cold, and FATHER PETER,
Sent his young neighbour to entreat her,
75   That she would make confession free —
To Him, — his saintly deputy.
Now, so it happen'd, to annoy
The merry pair, a little boy,
The only Son of lovely Bridget,
80   And, like his *daddy*, giv'n to fidget,
Enquir'd who this same neighbour was
That took the place his father left —
A most unworthy, shameless theft, —
    A sacrilege on marriage laws!

85   The dame was somewhat disconcerted —
    For, all that she could say or do, —
The boy his question would renew,
    Nor from his purpose be diverted.
At length, the matter to decide,
90   "'Tis FATHER PETER" she replied.
"He's come to pray." The child gave o'er,
When a loud thumping at the door
Proclaim'd the Husband coming! Lo!

Where could the wily neighbour go?
Where hide his recreant, guilty head —   95
But underneath the Farmer's bed? —

Now MASTER TWYFORD kiss'd his child;
And straight the cunning urchin smil'd:
"Hush father! hush! 'tis break of day —
And FATHER PETER's come to pray!   100
You must not speak," the infant cries —
"For underneath the bed he lies."

Now MISTRESS TWYFORD shriek'd, and fainted,
And the sly neighbour found, too late,
    The FARMER, than his wife less sainted,   105
For with his cudgel he repaid —
    The kindness of his faithless mate,
And fiercely on his blows he laid,
'Till her young lover, vanquish'd, swore
    He'd play THE CONFESSOR no more!   110

Tho' *fraud* is ever sure to find
Its scorpion in the guilty mind
Yet, PIOUS FRAUD, the DEVIL's treasure,
Is always paid, in TENFOLD MEASURE.

EDMUND'S WEDDING

By the side of the brook, where the willow is waving
    Why sits the wan Youth, in his wedding-suit gay!
Now sighing so deeply, now frantickly raving
    Beneath the pale light of the moon's sickly ray.
Now he starts, all aghast, and with horror's wild gesture,   5
Cries, "AGNES is coming, I know her white vesture![1]
See! see! how she beckons me on to the willow,
Where, on the cold turf, she has made our rude pillow.

---

1   Garment.

Sweet girl! yet I know thee; thy cheek's living roses
10 Are chang'd and grown pale, with the touch of despair:
And thy bosom no longer the lily discloses —
For thorns, my poor AGNES, are now planted there!
Thy blue, starry Eyes! are all dimm'd by dark sorrow;
No more from thy lip, can the flow'r fragrance borrow;
15 For cold does it seem, like the pale light of morning,
And thou smil'st, as in sadness, thy fond lover, scorning!

From the red scene of slaughter thy Edmund returning,
Has dress'd himself gayly, with May-blooming flow'rs;
His bosom, dear AGNES! still faithfully burning,
20 While, madly impatient, his eyes beam in show'rs!
O! many a time have I thought of thy beauty —
When cannons, loud roaring, taught Valour its duty;
And many a time, have I sigh'd to behold thee —
When the sulphur of War, in its cloudy mist roll'd me!

25 At the still hour of morn, when the Camp was reposing,
I wander'd alone on the wide dewy plain:
And when the gold curtains of Ev'ning were closing,
I watch'd the long shadows steal over the Main!
Across the wild Ocean, half frantic they bore me,
30 Unheeding my groans, from Thee, AGNES, they tore me;
But, though my poor heart might have bled in the battle,
Thy name should have echoed, amidst the loud rattle!

When I gaz'd on the field of the dead and the dying —
O AGNES! my fancy still wander'd to Thee!
35 When around, my brave Comrades in anguish were lying
I long'd on the death-bed of Valour to be.
For, sever'd from THEE, my SWEET GIRL, the loud thunder,
Which tore the soft fetters of fondness asunder —
Had only one kindness, in mercy to shew me,
40 To bid me *die bravely*, that thou, Love, may'st *know me!*"

His arms now are folded, he bows as in sorrow,
His tears trickle fast, down his wedding-suit gay;

"My AGNES will bless me," he murmurs, "to-morrow,
    As fresh as the breezes that welcome the day!"
Poor Youth! know thy AGNES, so lovely and blooming,   45
Stern Death has embrac'd, all her beauties entombing!
And, pale as her shroud in the grave she reposes,
Her bosom of snow, all besprinkled with Roses!

Her Cottage is now in the dark dell decaying,
    And shatter'd the casements, and clos'd is the door,   50
And the nettle now waves, where the wild KID is playing,
    And the neat little garden with weeds is grown o'er!
The Owl builds its nest in the thatch, and there, shrieking,
(A place all deserted and lonely bespeaking)
Salutes the night traveller, wandering near it,   55
And makes his faint heart, sicken sadly to hear it.

Then Youth, for thy habit, henceforth, thou should'st borrow
    The Raven's dark colour, and mourn for thy dear:
Thy AGNES for thee, would have cherish'd her Sorrow,
    And drest her pale cheek with a lingering tear: 60
For, soon as thy steps to the Battle departed,
She droop'd, and poor Maiden! she died, broken hearted;
And the turf that is bound with fresh garlands of roses,
Is now the cold bed, where her sorrow reposes!

The gay and the giddy may revel in pleasure, —   65
    May think themselves happy, their short summer-day;
May gaze, with fond transport, on fortune's rich treasure,
    And, carelessly sporting, — drive sorrow away:
But the bosom, where feeling and truth are united —
From folly's bright tinsel will turn, undelighted —   70
And find, at the grave where thy AGNES is sleeping,
That the proudest of hours, is the lone hour of weeping!

The Youth now approach'd the long branch of the willow,
    And stripping its leaves, on the turf threw them round.
"Here, here, my sweet AGNES! I make my last pillow,   75
    My bed of long slumber, shall be the cold ground!

The Sun, when it rises above thy low dwelling,
Shall gild the tall Spire, where my death-toll is knelling.
And when the next twilight its soft tears is shedding,
At thy Grave shall the Villagers — witness *our* WEDDING!

Now over the Hills he beheld a group coming,
    Their arms glitter'd bright, as the Sun slowly rose;
He heard them their purposes, far distant, humming,
    And welcom'd the moment, that ended his woes! —
And now the fierce Comrade, unfeeling, espies him,
He darts thro' the thicket, in hopes to surprize him;
But EDMUND, of Valour the dauntless defender,
Now *smiles*, while his CORPORAL bids him — "SURRENDER!"

Soon, prov'd a DESERTER, Stern Justice prevailing,
    He DIED! and his Spirit to AGNES is fled: —
The breeze, on the mountain's tall summit now sailing
    Fans lightly the dew-drops, that spangle their bed!
The Villagers, thronging around, scatter roses,
The grey wing of Evening the western sky closes, —
And Night's sable pall, o'er the landscape extending,
Is the mourning of Nature! the SOLEMN SCENE ENDING.

80

85

90

95

THE ALIEN BOY

'Twas on a Mountain, near the Western Main
An ALIEN dwelt. A solitary Hut
Built on a jutting crag, o'erhung with weeds,
Mark'd the poor Exile's home. Full ten long years
The melancholy wretch had liv'd unseen
By all, save HENRY, a lov'd, little Son
The partner of his sorrows. On the day
When Persecution, in the sainted guise
Of Liberty, spread wide its venom'd pow'r,[1]

5

---

1   The persecution alluded to here is likely the excesses of the French Revolution: the
     September Massacres of 1792 when over a thousand priests, aristocrats, and crimi-
     nals were publicly executed after mob trials; the beheading of Louis XVI and Marie
     Antoinette in 1793; and the Reign of Terror that followed.

The brave, Saint HUBERT, fled his Lordly home,   10
And, with his baby Son, the mountain sought.
Resolv'd to cherish in his bleeding breast
The secret of his birth, Ah! birth too high
For his now humbled state, from infancy
He taught him, labour's task: He bade him chear   15
The dreary day of cold adversity
By patience and by toil. The Summer morn
Shone on the pillow of his rushy bed;
The noontide, sultry hour, he fearless past
On the shagg'd eminence; while the young Kid   20
Skipp'd, to the cadence of his minstrelsy.

At night young HENRY trimm'd the faggot fire
While oft, Saint HUBERT, wove the ample net
To snare the finny victim. Oft they sang
And talk'd, while sullenly the waves would sound   25
Dashing the sandy shore. Saint HUBERT's eyes
Would swim in tears of fondness, mix'd with joy,
When he observ'd the op'ning harvest rich
Of promis'd intellect, which HENRY's soul,
Whate'er the subject of their talk, display'd.   30

Oft, the bold Youth, in question intricate,
Would seek to know the story of his birth;
Oft ask, who bore him: and with curious skill
Enquire, why he, and only one beside,
Peopled the desart mountain? Still his Sire   35
Was slow of answer, and, in words obscure,
Varied the conversation. Still the mind
Of HENRY ponder'd; for, in their lone hut,
A daily journal would Saint HUBERT make
Of his long banishment: and sometimes speak   40
Of Friends forsaken, Kindred, massacred; —
Proud mansions, rich domains, and joyous scenes
For ever faded, — lost!
                              One winter time,
'Twas on the Eve of Christmas, the shrill blast   45

Swept o'er the stormy main. The boiling foam
Rose to an altitude so fierce and strong
That their low hovel totter'd. Oft they stole
To the rock's margin, and with fearful eyes
50   Mark'd the vex'd deep, as the slow rising moon
Gleam'd on the world of waters. 'Twas a scene
Would make a Stoic[1] shudder! For, amid
The wavy mountains, they beheld, *alone*,
A LITTLE BOAT, now scarcely visible;
55   And now not seen at all; or, like a buoy,
Bounding, and buffetting, to reach the shore!

Now the full Moon, in crimson lustre shone
Upon the outstretch'd Ocean. The black clouds
Flew swiftly on, the wild blast following,
60   And, as they flew, dimming the angry main
With shadows horrible! Still, the small boat
Struggled amid the waves, a sombre speck
Upon the wide domain of howling Death!
Saint HUBERT sigh'd! while HENRY's speaking eye
65   Alternately the stormy scene survey'd
And his low hovel's safety. So past on
The hour of midnight, — and, since first they knew
The solitary scene, no midnight hour
E'er seem'd so long and dreary.
70   While they stood,
Their hands fast link'd together, and their eyes
Fix'd on the troublous Ocean, suddenly
The breakers, bounding on the rocky shore,
Left the small wreck; and crawling on the side
75   Of the rude crag, — a HUMAN FORM was seen!
And now he climb'd the foam-wash'd precipice,
And now the slip'ry weeds gave way, while he
Descended to the sands: The moon rose high —
The wind blast paus'd, and the poor shipwreck'd Man
80   Look'd round aghast, when on the frowning steep

---

1   Someone who practices the repression of emotions.

He marked the lonely exiles. Now he call'd
But he was feeble, and his voice was lost
Amid the din of mingling sounds that rose
From the wild scene of clamour.

                    Down the steep   85
Saint HUBERT hurried, boldly venturous,
Catching the slimy weeds, from point to point,
And unappall'd by peril. At the foot
Of the rude rock, the fainting mariner
Seiz'd on his outstretch'd arm; impatient, wild,   90
With transport exquisite! But ere they heard
The blest exchange of sounds articulate,
A furious billow, rolling on the steep,
Engulph'd them in Oblivion!

                     On the rock   95
Young HENRY stood, with palpitating heart,
And fear-struck, e'en to madness! Now he call'd,
Louder and louder, as the shrill blast blew;
But, mid the elemental strife of sounds,
No human voice gave answer! The clear moon   100
No longer quiver'd on the curling main,
But, mist-encircled, shed a blunted light,
Enough to shew all things that mov'd around,
Dreadful, but indistinctly! The black weeds
Wav'd, as the night-blast swept them; and along   105
The rocky shore the breakers, sounding low
Seem'd like the whisp'ring of a million souls
Beneath the green-deep mourning.

                     Four long hours
The lorn Boy listen'd! four long tedious hours   110
Pass'd wearily away, when, in the East
The grey beam coldly glimmer'd. All alone
Young HENRY stood aghast: his Eye wide fix'd;
While his dark locks, uplifted by the storm
Uncover'd met its fury. On his cheek   115
Despair sate terrible! For, mid the woes,
Of poverty and toil, he had not known,
Till then, the horror-giving chearless hour

Of TOTAL SOLITUDE!

120   He spoke — he groan'd,
But no reponsive voice, no kindred tone
Broke the dread pause: For now the storm had ceas'd,
And the bright Sun-beams glitter'd on the breast
Of the green placid Ocean. To his Hut
125 The lorn Boy hasten'd; there the rushy couch,
The pillow still indented, met his gaze
And fix'd his eye in madness. — From that hour
A maniac wild, the Alien Boy has been;
His garb with sea-weeds fring'd, and his wan cheek
130 The tablet of his mind, disorder'd, chang'd,
Fading, and worn with care. And if, by chance,
A Sea-beat wand'rer from the outstretch'd main
Views the lone Exile, and with gen'rous zeal
Hastes to the sandy beach, he suddenly
135 Darts 'mid the cavern'd cliffs, and leaves pursuit
To track him, where no footsteps but his own,
Have e'er been known to venture! YET HE LIVES
A melancholy proof that Man may bear
All the rude storms of Fate, and still suspire
140 By the wide world forgotten!

 THE GRANNY GREY,

A LOVE TALE

DAME DOWSON, was a granny grey,
   Who, three score years and ten,
Had pass'd her busy hours away,
   In talking of the Men!
5   They were her theme, at home, abroad,
At wake, and by the winter fire,
Whether it froze, or blew, or thaw'd,
In sunshine or in shade, her ire
Was never calm'd; for still she made
10   Scandal her pleasure — and her trade!

A Grand-daughter DAME DOWSON had —
　　As fair, as fair could be!
Lovely enough to make Men mad;
For, on her cheek's soft downy rose
LOVE seem'd in dimples to repose;　　　　　　　　15
Her clear blue eyes look'd mildly bright
Like ether drops of liquid light,
Or sapphire gems, — which VENUS[1] bore,
When, for the silver-sanded shore,
　　She left her native Sea!　　　　　　　　　　20

ANNETTA, was the damsel's name;
A pretty, soft, romantic sound;
Such as a lover's heart may wound;
　　And set his fancy in a flame:
For had the maid been christen'd JOAN,　　　　25
　　Or DEBORAH, or HESTER, —
The little God had coldly prest her,
　　Or, let her quite alone!
For magic is the silver sound —
Which, often, in a NAME is found!　　　　　　　30

ANNETTA was belov'd; and She
　　To WILLIAM gave her vows;
For WILLIAM was as brave a Youth,
As ever claim'd the meed of truth,
　　And, to reward such constancy,　　　　　　35
　　Nature that meed allows.
But Old DAME DOWSON could not bear　　*old v*
A Youth so brave — a Maid so fair.　　　　*young*

The GRANNY GREY, with maxims grave
Oft to ANNETTA lessons gave:　　　　　　　　40
And still the burthen of the Tale
Was, "Keep the wicked Men away,
For should their wily arts prevail

1　Venus or Aphrodite, the goddess of love and beauty, was said to have sprung from
　the foam of the sea.

You'll surely rue the day!"
45 And credit was to GRANNY due,
The truth, she, by EXPERIENCE, knew!
ANNETTA blushed, and promis'd She
Obedient to her will would be.
But LOVE, with cunning all his own,
50 Would never let the Maid alone:
And though she dar'd not see her Lover,
Lest GRANNY should the deed discover,
She, for a woman's weapon, still,
From CUPID's pinion[1] pluck'd a quill:
55 And, with it, prov'd that human art
Cannot confine the Female Heart.

At length, an assignation She
With WILLIAM slily made;
It was beneath an old Oak Tree,
60 Whose widely spreading shade
The Moon's soft beams contriv'd to break
For many a Village Lover's sake.
But Envy has a Lynx's eye
And GRANNY DOWSON cautiously went
65 Before, to spoil their merriment,
Thinking no creature nigh.

Young WILLIAM came, but at the tree
The watchful GRANDAM found!
Straight to the Village hasten'd he
70 And summoning his neighbours round,
The Hedgerow's tangled boughs among,
Conceal'd the list'ning wond'ring throng.
He told them that, for many a night,
An OLD GREY OWL was heard;
75 A fierce, ill-omen'd, crabbed Bird —
Who fill'd the village with affright.
He swore this Bird was large and keen,
With claws of fire, and eye-balls green;

1   Wing.

That nothing rested, where she came;
That many pranks the monster play'd, 80
And many a timid trembling Maid
   She brought to shame
For negligence, that was her own;
Turning the milk to water, clear,
And spilling from the cask, small-beer; 85
Pinching, like fairies, harmless lasses,
And shewing Imps, in looking-glasses;
Or, with heart-piercing groan,
Along the church-yard path, swift gliding,
Or, on a broomstick, witchlike, riding. 90
All listen'd trembling; For the Tale
Made cheeks of Oker,[1] chalky pale;
The young a valiant doubt pretended;
The old believ'd, and all attended.

Now to DAME DOWSON he repairs 95
And in his arms, enfolds the Granny:
Kneels at her feet, and fondly swears
   He will be true as any!
Caresses her with well feign'd bliss
And, *fearfully*, implores a Kiss — 100
On the green turf distracted *lying,*
He wastes his ardent breath, in sighing.
The DAME was silent; for the Lover
   Would, when she spoke,
     She fear'd, discover 105
   Her envious joke:
And she was too much charm'd to be
In haste, — to end the Comedy!

Now WILLIAM, weary of such wooing,
Began, with all his might, hollooing: — 110
When suddenly from ev'ry bush
The eager throngs impatient rush;
With shouting, and with boist'rous glee

---

1   Ochre: a brownish yellow colour.

DAME DOWSON they pursue,
And from the broad Oak's canopy,
O'er moonlight fields of sparkling dew,
They bear in triumph the Old DAME,
Bawling, with loud Huzza's, her name;
"A witch, a witch!" the people cry,
"A witch!" the echoing hills reply:
'Till to her home the GRANNY came,
Where, to confirm the tale of shame,
Each rising day they went, in throngs,
With ribbald jests, and sportive songs,
'Till GRANNY of her spleen, repented;
And to young WILLIAM's ardent pray'r,
To take, for life, ANNETTA fair, —
   At last, — CONSENTED.

And should this TALE, fall in the way
Of LOVERS CROSS'D, or GRANNIES GREY, —
Let them confess, 'tis made to prove —
The wisest heads, — TOO WEAK FOR LOVE!

115
120
125
130

GOLFRE,

A GOTHIC SWISS TALE
In Five Parts

Where freezing wastes of dazzling Snow
   O'er LEMAN's Lake rose, tow'ring;
The BARON GOLFRE's Castle strong
Was seen, the silv'ry peaks among,
   With ramparts, darkly low'ring! —

Tall Battlements of flint, uprose,
   Long shadowing down the valley,
A grove of sombre Pine, antique,
Amid the white expanse would break,
   In many a gloomy alley.

5
10

A strong portcullis[1] entrance show'd,
   With ivy brown hung over;
And stagnate the green moat was found,
Whene'er the Trav'ller wander'd round,
   Or moon-enamour'd Lover.   15

Within the spacious Courts were seen
   A thousand gothic fancies;
Of banners, trophies, armour bright,
Of shields, thick batter'd in the fight,
   And interwoven lances.   20

The BARON GOLFRE long had been
   To solitude devoted;
And oft, in pray'r would pass the night
'Till day's vermillion stream of light
   Along the blue hill floated.   25

And yet, his pray'r was little mark'd
   With pure and calm devotion;
For oft, upon the pavement bare,
He'd dash his limbs and rend his hair
   With terrible emotion!   30

And sometimes he, at midnight hour
   Would howl, like wolves, wide-prowling;
And pale, the lamps would glimmer round —
And deep, the self-mov'd bell would sound
   A knell prophetic, tolling!   35

For, in the Hall, three lamps were seen,
   That quiver'd dim; — and near them
A bell rope hung, that from the Tow'r
Three knells would toll, at midnight's hour,
   Startling the soul to hear them!   40

---

1   An armoured gateway, lowered to block entrance to a fortress.

And oft, a dreadful crash was heard,
   Shaking the Castle's chambers!
And suddenly, the lights would turn
To paly grey, and dimly burn,
45   Like faint and dying embers.

Beneath the steep, a Maiden dwelt,
   The dove-eyed ZORIETTO;
A damsel blest with ev'ry grace —
And springing from as old a race —
50   As Lady of LORETTO![1]

Her dwelling was a Goatherd's poor;
   Yet she his heart delighted;
Their little hovel open stood,
Beside a <u>lonesome</u> frowning wood,
55   To <u>travellers</u> — benighted.

Yet oft, at midnight when the Moon
   Its dappled course was steering,
The Castle bell would break their sleep,
And ZORIETTO slow would creep —
60   To bar the wicket[2] — fearing!

What did she fear? O! dreadful thought!
   The Moon's wan lustre, streaming;
The dim grey lamps, the crashing sound,
The lonely Bittern — shrieking round
65   The roof, — with pale light gleaming.

And often, when the wintry wind
   Loud whistled o'er their dwelling;
They sat beside their faggot fire

---

1 Loreto was a pilgrimage resort in central Italy, famous for the Holy House of the
    Virgin. It was reputed to have been transported to Italy when threatened by the
    Turks in 1791. An alleged appearance by Mary and miraculous cures attested to its
    holiness.
2 A small door or gate.

While ZORIETTO's aged Sire
 A dismal Tale was telling.   70

He told a long and dismal tale
 How a fair LADY perish'd;
How her sweet Baby, doom'd to be
The partner of her destiny
 Was by a peasant cherish'd!   75

He told a long and dismal Tale,
 How, from a flinty Tow'r
A Lady wailing sad was seen,
The lofty grated bars between,
 At dawnlight's purple hour!   80

He told a Tale of bitter woe,
 His heart with pity swelling,
How the fair LADY pin'd and died,
And how her Ghost, at Christmas-tide —
 Would wander, — near her dwelling.   85

He told her, how a lowly DAME
 The LADY, lorn, befriended —
Who chang'd her own dear baby, dead,
And took the LADY's in its stead —
And then — *"Forgive her Heaven!"* He said, 90
 And so, his Story ended.

Golfre, Part Second

As on the rushy floor she sat,
 Her hand her pale cheek pressing;
Oft, on the GOATHERD's face, her eyes
Would fix intent, her mute surprize —   95
 In frequent starts confessing.

Then, slowly would she turn her head,
 And watch the narrow wicket;

And shudder, while the wintry blast
100   In shrilly cadence swiftly past
      Along the neighb'ring thicket.

      One night, it was in winter time,
         The Castle bell was tolling;
      The air was still, the Moon was seen,
105   Sporting, her starry train between,
         The thin clouds round her rolling.

      And now she watch'd the wasting lamp,
         Her timid bosom panting;
      And now, the Crickets faintly sing,
110   And now she hears the Raven's wing
         Sweeping their low roof, slanting.

      And, as the wicket latch she clos'd,
         A groan was heard! — she trembled!
      And now a clashing, steely sound,
115   In quick vibrations echoed round,
         Like murd'rous swords, assembled!

      She started back; she look'd around,
         The Goatherd Swain was sleeping;
      A stagnate paleness mark'd her cheek,
120   She would have call'd, but could not speak,
         While, through the lattice peeping.

      And O! how dimly shone the Moon,
         Upon the snowy mountain!
      And fiercely did the wild blast blow,
125   And now her tears began to flow,
         Fast, as a falling fountain.

      And now she heard the Castle bell
         Again toll sad and slowly;
      She knelt and sigh'd: the lamp burnt pale —
130   She thought upon the dismal Tale —
         And pray'd, with fervour holy!

And now, her little string of beads
    She kiss'd, — and cross'd her breast;
It was a simple rosary,
Made of the Mountain Holly-tree,   135
    By Sainted Father's blest!

And now the wicket open flew,
    As though a whirlwind fell'd it;
And now a ghastly figure stood
Before the Maiden — while her blood   140
    Congeal'd, as she beheld it!

His face was pale, his eyes were wild,
    His beard was dark; and near him
A stream of light was seen to glide,
Marking a poniard, crimson-dyed;   145
    The bravest soul might fear him!

His forehead was all gash'd and gor'd —
    His vest was black and flowing
His strong hand grasp'd a dagger keen,
And wild and frantic was his mien,   150
    Dread signs of terror, showing.

"O fly me not!" the BARON cried,
    "In HEAV'N's name, do not fear me!"
Just as he spoke the bell thrice toll'd —
Three paly lamps they now behold —   155
    While a faint voice, cried, — "HEAR ME!"

And now, upon the threshold low,
    The wounded GOLFRE, kneeling,
Again to HEAV'N address'd his pray'r;
The waning Moon, with livid glare,   160
    Was down the dark sky stealing.

They led him in, they bath'd his wounds,
    Tears, to the red stream adding:
The haughty GOLFRE gaz'd, admir'd!

165 The Peasant Girl his fancy fir'd,
And set his sense, madding!

He prest her hand; she turn'd away,
Her blushes deeper glowing,
Her cheek still spangled o'er with tears;
170 So the wild rose more fresh appears
When the soft dews are flowing!

Again, the BARON fondly gaz'd;
Poor ZORIETTO trembled;
And GOLFRE watch'd her throbbing breast
175 Which seem'd, with weighty woes oppress'd,
And softest LOVE, dissembled.

The GOATHERD, fourscore years had seen,
And he was sick and needy;
The BARON wore a SWORD OF GOLD,
180 Which Poverty might well behold,
With eyes, wide stretch'd, and greedy!

The dawn arose! The yellow light
Around the Alps spread chearing!
The BARON kiss'd the GOATHERD's child —
185 "Farewell!" she cried, — and blushing smil'd —
No future peril fearing.

Now GOLFRE homeward bent his way
His breast with passion burning:
The Chapel bell was rung, for pray'r,
190 And all — save GOLFRE, prostrate there —
Thank'd HEAV'N, for his returning!

Golfre, Part Third

Three times the orient ray was seen
Above the East cliff mounting,
When GOLFRE sought the Cottage Grace

To share the honours of his race,   195
    With treasures, beyond counting!

The Ev'ning Sun was burning red
    The Twilight veil spread slowly;
While ZORIETTO, near the wood
Where long a little cross had stood,   200
    Was singing Vespers holy.

And now she kiss'd her Holly-beads,
    And now she cross'd her breast;
The night-dew fell from ev'ry tree —
It fell upon her rosary,   205
    Like tears of Heav'n twice bless'd!

She knelt upon the brown moss, cold,
    She knelt, with eyes, mild beaming!
The day had clos'd, she heard a sigh!
She mark'd the clear and frosty sky   210
    With starry lustre gleaming.

She rose; she heard the draw-bridge chains
    Loud clanking down the valley;
She mark'd the yellow torches shine
Between the antique groves of Pine —   215
    Bright'ning each gloomy alley.

And now the breeze began to blow,
    Soft-stealing up the mountain;
It seem'd at first a dulcet sound —
Like mingled waters, wand'ring round,   220
    Slow falling from a fountain.

And now, in wilder tone it rose,
    The white peaks sweeping, shrilly:
It play'd amidst her golden hair
It kiss'd her bosom cold and fair —   225
    And sweet, as vale-born Lily!

She heard the hollow tread of feet
  Thridding[1] the piny cluster;
The torches flam'd before the wind —
230   And many a spark was left behind,
    To mock the glow-worm's lustre.

She saw them guard the Cottage door,
  Her heart beat high with wonder!
She heard the fierce and Northern blast
235   As o'er the topmost point it past
    Like peals of bursting thunder!

And now she hied her swift along
  And reach'd the guarded wicket;
But O! what terror fill'd her soul,
240   When thrice she heard the deep bell toll —
    Above the gloomy thicket.

Now fierce, the BARON darted forth,
  His trembling victim seizing;
She felt her blood, in ev'ry vein
245   Move, with a sense of dead'ning pain,
    As though her heart were freezing.

"This night," said he, "Yon castle tow'rs
  Shall echo to their centre!
For, by the HOLY CROSS, I swear," —
250   And straight a CROSS of ruby glare
    Did through the wicket enter!

And now a snowy hand was seen
  Slow moving, round the chamber!
A clasp of pearl, it seem'd to bear —
255   A clasp of pearl, most rich and rare!
    Fix'd to a zone of amber.

---

1   A variant of threading; to make one's way through a narrow place.

And now the lowly Hovel shook,
  The wicket open flying,
And by, the croaking RAVEN flew
And, whistling shrill, the night-blast blew   260
  Like shrieks, that mark the dying!

But suddenly the tumult ceas'd —
  And silence, still more fearful,
Around the little chamber spread
Such horrors as attend the dead,   265
  Where no Sun glitters chearful!

"Now JESU HEAR ME!" GOLFRE cried,
  "HEAR ME," a faint voice mutter'd!
The BARON drew his poniard forth —
The Maiden sunk upon the earth,   270
  And — "Save me Heav'n!" she utter'd.

"Yes, Heav'n will save thee," GOLFRE said,
  "Save thee, to be MY bride!"
But while he spoke a beam of light
Shone on her bosom, deathly white,   275
  Then onward seem'd to glide.

And now the GOATHERD, on his knees,
  With frantic accent cried,
"O! God forbid! that *I* should see
The beauteous ZORIETTO, be   280
  The BARON GOLFRE's bride!

Poor Lady! she did shrink and fall,
  As leaves fall in September!
Then be not BARON GOLFRE's bride —
Alack! in yon black tow'r SHE died —   285
  Full well, I do remember!

Oft, to the lattice grate I stole
  To hear her, sweetly singing;
And oft, whole nights, beside the moat,

290   I listen'd to the dying note —
          Till matin's bell was ringing.

       And when she died! Poor Lady dear!
          A sack of gold, she gave,
       That masses every Christmas day
295   Twelve bare-foot Monks should sing, or say,
          Slow moving round her Grave.

       That, at the Holy Virgin's shrine
          Three Lamps should burn for ever —
       That, ev'ry month, the bell should toll,
300   For pray'rs to save her Husband's soul —
          I shall forget it, never!"

       While thus he spoke, the BARON's eye
          Look'd inward on his soul:
       For He the masses *ne'er* had said —
305   *No* lamps, their quiv'ring light had shed,
          No bell, been taught to toll!

       And yet, the bell *did* toll, self-mov'd;
          And sickly lamps were gleaming;
       And oft, their faintly wand'ring light
310   Illum'd the Chapel aisles at night,
          Till MORN's broad eye, was beaming.

                  Golfre, Part Fourth

       The Maid refus'd the BARON's suit,
          For, well she lov'd another;
       The angry GOLFRE's vengeful rage
315   Nor pride nor reason could assuage,
          Nor pity prompt to smother.

       His Sword was gone; the Goatherd Swain
          Seem'd guilty, past recalling:
       The BARON now his life demands

Where the tall Gibbet skirts the lands
  With black'ning bones appalling!

Low at the BARON's feet, in tears
  Fair ZORIETTO kneeling,
The Goatherd's life requir'd; — but found
That Pride can give the deepest wound   325
  Without the pang of feeling.

That Pow'r can mock the suff'rer's woes
  And triumph o'er the sighing;
Can scorn the noblest mind oppress'd,
Can fill with thorns the feeling breast   330
  Soft pity's tear denying.

"Take me," she cried, "but spare his age —
  Let me his ransom tender;
I will the fatal deed atone,
For crimes that never were my own,   335
  My breaking heart surrender."

The marriage day was fix'd, the Tow'rs
  With banners rich were mounted;
His heart beat high against his side
While GOLFRE, waiting for his bride,   340
  The weary minutes counted.

The snow fell fast, with mingling hail,
  The dawn was late, and louring;
Poor ZORIETTO rose aghast!
Unmindful of the Northern blast   345
  And prowling Wolves, devouring.

Swift to the wood of Pines she flew,
  Love made the assignation;
For there, the sov'reign of her soul
Watch'd the blue mists of morning roll   350
  Around her habitation.

The BARON, by a Spy appriz'd,
　　Was there before his Bride;
He seiz'd the Youth, and madly strew'd
355　　The white Cliff, with his steaming blood,
　　Then hurl'd him down its side.

And now 'twas said, an hungry wolf
　　Had made the Youth his prey:
His heart lay frozen on the snow,
360　　And here and there a purple glow
　　Speckled the pathless way.

The marriage day at length arriv'd,
　　The Priest bestow'd his blessing:
A *clasp of orient pearl* fast bound
365　　A *zone of amber* circling round,
　　Her slender waist compressing.

On ZORIETTO's snowy breast
　　A ruby cross was heaving;
So the pale snow-drop faintly glows,
370　　When shelter'd by the damask rose,
　　Their beauties interweaving!

And now the holy vow began
　　Upon her lips to falter!
And now all deathly wan she grew
375　　And now the lamps, of livid hue
　　Pass'd slowly round the Altar.

And now she saw the clasp of pearl
　　A ruby lustre taking:
And thrice she heard the Castle bell
380　　Ring out a loud funereal knell
　　The antique turrets shaking.

O! then how pale the BARON grew,
　　His eyes wide staring fearful!
While o'er the Virgin's image fair

A sable veil was borne on air   385
    Shading her dim eyes, tearful.

And, on her breast a clasp of pearl
    Was stain'd with blood, fast flowing:
And round her lovely waist she wore
An amber zone; a cross she bore   390
    Of rubies — richly glowing.

The Bride, her dove-like eyes to Heav'n
    Rais'd, calling Christ to save her!
The cross now danc'd upon her breast;
The shudd'ring Priest his fears confest,   395
    And benedictions gave her.

Upon the pavement sunk the Bride
    Cold as a corpse, and fainting!
The pearly clasp, self-bursting, show'd
Her beating side, where crimson glow'd   400
    Three spots, of nature's painting.

Three crimson spots, of deepest hue!
    The BARON gaz'd with wonder:
For on his buried Lady's side
Just three such drops had nature dyed,   405
    An equal space asunder.

And now remembrance brought to view,
    For Heav'n the truth discloses,
The Baby, who had early died,
Bore, tinted on its little side,   410
    Three spots — as red as roses!

Now, ere the wedding-day had past,
    Stern GOLFRE, and his Bride
Walk'd forth to taste the ev'ning breeze
Soft sighing, mid the sombre trees,   415
    That drest the mountain's side.

And now, beneath the grove of Pine,
  Two lovely Forms were gliding;
  A Lady, with a beauteous face!
420   A Youth, with stern, but manly, grace
  Smil'd, — as in scorn deriding.

Close, by the wond'ring Bride they pass'd,
  The red Sun sinking slowly:
  And to the little cross they hied —
425   And there she saw them, side by side,
  Kneeling, with fervour holy.

The little cross was golden ting'd,
  The western radiance stealing;
  And now it bore a purple hue,
430   And now all black and dim it grew,
  And still she saw them, kneeling.

White were their robes as fleecy snow
  Their faces pale, yet chearful.
  Their golden hair, like waves of light
435   Shone lust'rous mid the glooms of night;
  Their starry eyes were tearful.

And now they look'd to Heav'n, and smil'd,
  Three paly lamps descended!
  And now their shoulders seem'd to bear
440   Expanding pinions broad and fair,
  And now they wav'd in viewless air!
  And so, the Vision ended.

Golfre. Part Fifth

Now, suddenly, a storm arose,
  The thunder roar'd, tremendous!
445   The lightning flash'd, the howling blast
  Fierce, strong, and desolating, past
  The Altitudes stupendous!

Rent by the wind, a fragment huge
　　From the steep summit bounded:
That summit, where the Peasant's breast 450
Found, mid the snow, a grave of rest,
　　By GOLFRE's poniard wounded.

Loud shrieks, across the mountain wild,
　　Fill'd up the pause of thunder:
The groves of Pine the lightning past, 455
And swift the desolating blast
　　Scatter'd them wide asunder.

The Castle-turrets seem'd to blaze,
　　The lightning round them flashing;
The drawbridge now was all on fire, 460
The moat foam'd high, with furious ire,
　　Against the black walls dashing.

The Prison Tow'r was silver white,
　　And radiant as the morning;
Two angels' wings were spreading wide, 465
The battlements, from side to side —
　　And lofty roof adorning.

And now the Bride was sore afraid,
　　She sigh'd, and cross'd her breast;
She kiss'd her simple rosary, 470
Made of the mountain holly-tree,
　　By sainted Fathers blest.

She kiss'd it once, she kiss'd it twice;
　　It seem'd to freeze her breast;
The cold show'rs fell from ev'ry tree, 475
They fell upon her rosary
　　Like nature's tears, "twice blest!"

"What do you fear?" the BARON cried —
　　For ZORIETTO trembled —
"A WOLF," she sigh'd with whisper low, 480

"Hark how the angry whirlwinds blow
Like Demons dark assembled.

That WOLF! which did my Lover slay!"
The BARON wildly started.
485 "That Wolf accurs'd!" she madly cried —
Whose fangs, by human gore were died,
Who dragg'd him down the mountain's side,
And left me — Broken hearted!"

Now GOLFRE shook in ev'ry joint,
490 He grasp'd her arm, and mutter'd;
Hell seem'd to yawn, on ev'ry side,
"Hear me!" the frantic tyrant cried —
"HEAR ME!" a faint voice utter'd.

"I hear thee! yes, I hear thee well!"
495 Cried GOLFRE, "I'll content thee.
I see thy vengeful eye-balls roll —
Thou com'st to claim my guilty soul —
The FIENDS — the FIENDS have sent thee!"

And now a Goatherd-Boy was heard —
500 Swift climbing up the mountain:
A Kid was lost, the fearful hind —
Had rov'd his truant care to find,
By wood-land's side — and fountain.

And now a murm'ring throng advanc'd,
505 And howlings echoed round them:
Now GOLFRE tried the path to pace,
His feet seem'd rooted to the place,
As though a spell had bound them.

And now loud mingling voices cried —
510 "Pursue that WOLF, pursue him!"
That guilty BARON, conscience stung,
About his fainting DAUGHTER hung,
As to the ground she drew him.

"Oh! shield me HOLY MARY! shield
    A tortur'd wretch!" he mutter'd.   515
"A murd'rous WOLF! O GOD! I crave
A dark unhallow'd silent grave —"
    Aghast the Caitiff[1] utter'd.

"'Twas I, beneath the GOATHERD's bed
    The golden sword did cover;   520
'Twas I who tore the quiv'ring wound,
Pluck'd forth the heart, and scatter'd round
    The life-stream of thy Lover."

And now he writh'd in ev'ry limb,
    And big his heart was swelling;   525
Fresh peals of thunder echoed strong,
With famish'd WOLVES the peaks among
    Their dismal chorus yelling!

"O JESU Save me!" GOLFRE shriek'd —
    But GOLFRE shriek'd no more!   530
The rosy dawn's returning light
Display'd his corse, — a dreadful sight,
    Black, wither'd, smear'd with gore!

High on a gibbet, near the wood —
    His mangled limbs were hung;   535
Yet ZORIETTO oft was seen
Prostrate the Chapel aisles between —
    When holy mass was sung.

And there, three lamps now dimly burn, —
    Twelve Monks their masses saying;   540
And there, the midnight bell doth toll
For quiet to the murd'rer's soul —
    While all around are praying.

---

1   A villain or wretched person.

For CHARITY and PITY kind,
　　To gentle souls are given;
And MERCY is the sainted pow'r,
Which beams thro' mis'ry's darkest hour,
　　And lights the way — TO HEAVEN!

'Tis on the Prison's flinty floor,
'Tis where the deaf'ning whirlwinds roar,
'Tis when the sea boy, on the mast,
Hears the wave bounding to the blast,
　　　　　　　　And looks below!

Figure 10. Mezzotint engraving after Maria Cosway, illustration No. 6 for "The Wintry Day," 1804. (By courtesy of the Special Collections Department, University of Virginia Library.)

UNCOLLECTED POEMS FROM NEWSPAPERS AND MAGAZINES

TO SIR JOSHUA REYNOLDS[1]

IMMORTAL REYNOLDS! thou, whose art can trace
The glowing semblance of exterior grace;
Whose hand, by GENIUS guided, marks the line
Which stamps perfection on the form divine;
Whose skill unrivall'd, charms the wond'ring heart,   5
Till blushing *Nature* owns the power of *Art*.
What RAPHAEL boasted, and what TITIAN knew,[2]
Immortal REYNOLDS! is excell'd by *You*.
'Tis thine to tinge the lip with vermil dye,
To paint the softness of the *melting eye*;   10
With auburn hair luxuriantly display'd,
The iv'ry shoulder's polish'd fall to shade,
To deck the well-turn'd arm with matchless grace,
To mark the dimpled smile on beauty's face —
With cunning hand, the task is *thine* to throw   15
The *veil transparent* o'er the *breast of snow*;
The *Statesman's* thought, the *Infant's cherub mien*,
The *Poet's fire*, the *Matron's eye serene*,
Alike, with animated colours shine
Beneath thy glowing Pencil's touch divine;   20
As *Britain's Genius* glories in thy *Art*,
Adores thy VIRTUES, and reveres thy HEART;
Nations unborn shall celebrate thy Name,
And stamp thy *Memory* on the page of FAME.

---

1 Published in the *Oracle* of July 9, 1789 where it was attributed to "Laura Maria."
Robinson was an acquaintance of Reynolds (1732-92), one of the most renowned
painters of the day.
    Reynolds wrote to Robinson on December 18, 1790, thanking her for the
"obliging notice" she had taken of him in her "truly excellent poem," possibly this
one. He writes, "I confess I am surprized at the wonderful facility (or *handling*, as we
painters call it) which you have acquired in writing verse, which is generally the
result of great practice." The letter was published in the fourth volume of Robin-
son's 1801 *Memoirs*.

2 Raffaello Sanxio (1483-1520) and Tiziano Vecellio (c. 1487-1576), Italian Renais-
sance painters.

SONNET TO MRS. CHARLOTTE SMITH,

ON HEARING THAT HER SON WAS WOUNDED AT THE SIEGE OF DUNKIRK[1]

FULL many an anxious pang, and rending sigh,
Darts, with keen anguish, through a MOTHER's breast;
Full many a graceful TEAR obscures her eye,
While watchful fondness draws her SOUL from rest.

5   The clang of ARMS! triumphant VALOUR's wreath!
Startle, yet fascinate the glowing mind!
For, ah! too oft the crown by FAME entwin'd,
Conceals the desolating lance beneath!

Yet HOPE for THEE shall bend her soothing wings,
10   Steal to thy breast, and check the rising tear,
As to thy polish'd mind rapt Fancy brings
The GALLANT BOY, to BRITAIN's GENIUS dear!
And, while for HIM a LAUREL'D Couch SHE strews,
Fair TRUTH shall snatch a Wreath, TO DECK HIS PARENT MUSE!

Sept. 15, 1793

STANZAS[2]

IN this vain, busy world, where the Good and the Gay,
By affliction and folly wing moments away;
Where the False are respected, the Virtuous betray'd;
Where Vice lives in sunshine, and Genius in shade;

---

1 Published in the *Oracle* of September 17, 1793 and attributed to "Oberon." There is no evidence that Robinson was personally acquainted with Smith, though they had a mutual friend in William Godwin. In a manuscript letter in the Bodleian Library, Oxford, Smith requests copies of her own works, writing: "These are for a present to the Surgeon who attended him [her son Charles] since the loss of his leg before Dunkirk, with great assiduity and kindness, and who prefers this present to the money he must otherwise have been complimented with." Montagu Ms. d. 10, fol. 68r–v, The Bodleian Library, University of Oxford.
2 Published in the *Gentleman's Magazine*, January 1767. A shorter version of the poem was published in *Walsingham* (3: 65–66).

With a soul-sicken'd sadness all changes I see;   5
For, the world, the base world, has no pleasure for me!

In cities, where wealth loads the coffers of Pride;
Where Talents and Sorrow are ever allied;
Where Dulness is worship'd, and Wisdom despis'd;
Where none but the Empty and Vicious are priz'd;   10
All scenes with disgust and abhorrence I see;
For, the world has no corner of comfort for me!

While pale Asiatics, encircled with gold,
The sons of meek Virtue indignant behold;
While the tithe-pamper'd Churchman reviles at the poor,   15
As the lorn sinking traveller faints at his door;
While Custom dares sanction Oppression's decree —
Oh, keep such hard bosoms, such monsters, from me!

While the flame of a Patriot expires in the breast,
With ribbands, and tinsel, and frippery, dress'd;   20
While Pride mocks the children of Want and Despair,
Gives a sneer for each sigh, and a smile for each pray'r;
Though he triumph his day, a short day it must be —
Heav'n keep such cold tyrants, oh, keep them from me!

While the Lawyer still lives by the anguish of hearts;   25
While he wrings the wrong'd bosom, and thrives as it smarts;
While he grasps the last guinea from Poverty's heir;
While he revels in splendor which rose from Despair;
While the tricks of his office our scourges must be;
Oh, keep the shrewd knave and his quibbles from me!   30

While the court breeds the Sycophant, train'd to ensnare;
While the prisons re-echo the groans of Despair;
While the State deals out taxes, the Army dismay;
While the Rich are upheld, and the Poor doom'd to pay;
Humanity saddens with pity, to see   35
The scale of injustice, and trembles like me!

While Patriots are slander'd, and venal Slaves rise;
While Pow'r grows a giant, and Liberty dies;
While a phantom of Virtue o'er Energy reigns;
40   And the broad wing of Freedom is loaded with chains;
While War spreads its thunders o'er land and o'er sea;
Ah, who but can listen and murmur like me!

While the bosom which loves, and confesses its flame,
By the high-titled Female is branded with shame;
45   While a Coronet hides what the Humble despise;
And the Lowly must fall that the Haughty may rise;
Oh, who can the triumphs of infamy see,
Nor shrink from the reptiles, and shudder like me!

Ah World, thou vile World, how I sicken to trace
50   The anguish that hourly augments for thy race!
How I turn from the Worst, while I honour the Best;
The Enlighten'd adore, and the Venal detest!
And, oh! with what joy to the grave would I flee —
Since the World, the base World has no pleasure for me!

ALL FOR-LORN[1]

LET FASHION and FANCY their beauties display,
And vaunt what they will for the hour, or the day;
Let the WOMEN, with smiles of indiff'rence, declare,
That they soar above sorrow, and laugh at despair;
5   Though the dimples of HEBE[2] their faces adorn,
They are sighing in secret; and *sighing* — FOR-LORN.

At the Play in side boxes simp'ring they sit,
Sigh at KOTZEBUE's pathos, praise SHERIDAN's wit;[3]

---

1   Published in the *Morning Post*, April 4, 1800, and attributed to "T.B."
2   Goddess of youth, the daughter of Zeus and Hera.
3   Popular playwrights of the period — August von Kotzebue (1761-1819) and
      Richard Brinsley Sheridan (1751-1816).

Talk as loud as the Actors, and conquest essay,
And with sweet *prittle prattle* drive anquish away;   10
Though each bosom, in secret, confesses a thorn,
And the wound, which they feel, makes them wretched —

                                                        FOR-LORN.

All the morning in Bond-street they visit the gay,
With their cheeks like the roses just budding in May;
As the Coaches drive on, all confusion and din,   15
Every victor of hearts hopes new trophies to win;
But their eyes' azure lustre, like bright stars of morn,
Through soft tears are seen sparkling, to shew them FOR-LORN.

In Hyde Park, all amaz'd, see the *Citizens* throng,
And exult, once a week, the gay *Nobles* among;   20
As the Coaches move slowly, the Horsemen attend,
With a smile and a nod, and a bow and a bend;
Yet in vain may they hope they for conquest were born,
Since the heart of each woman is throbbing — FOR-LORN.

At the Op'ra in Boxes and Pit now they crowd,   25
And the fairest no longer of fashion are proud;
For they find that the graces of beauty and dress
Have no balsam to soften, no magic to bless;
While in vain they with care ev'ry charm may adorn,
Since the soft sighing bosom is beating — FOR-LORN.   30

Then adieu to the pleasures which FANCY can bring,
And adieu to the *flowrets* and *zephyrs*[1] of SPRING;
Though the season may bloom, still in sadness the day
'Mid the sun-shine of fashion shall linger away,
For no smile can the sweet lip of BEAUTY adorn,   35
While the *victor of hearts* — makes ALL WOMEN FOR-LORN.

---

1   Gentle breezes.

THE CAMP[1]

Tents, *marquees*, and baggage waggons;
Suttling houses,[2] beer in flaggons;
Drums and trumpets, singing, firing;
Girls seducing, *beaux* admiring;
5   Country lasses gay and smiling,
City lads their hearts beguiling;
Dusty roads, and horses frisky;
Many an *Eton boy*[3] in whisky;
Tax'd carts full of farmer's daughters;
10   Brutes condemn'd, and man — who slaughters!
Public-houses, booths, and castles;
Belles of fashion, serving vassals;
Lordly Gen'rals fiercely staring,
Weary soldiers, sighing, swearing!
15   *Petit maitres*[4] always dressing —
In the glass themselves caressing;
Perfum'd, painted, patch'd and blooming
Ladies — manly airs assuming!
Dowagers of fifty, simp'ring
20   Misses, for a lover whimp'ring —
Husbands drill'd to household tameness;
Dames heart sick of wedded sameness.
Princes setting girls a-madding —[5]
Wives for ever fond of gadding —
25   Princesses with lovely faces,
Beauteous children of the Graces!

---

1   Published in the *Morning Post* on August 1, 1800, as the work of "Oberon."
Reprinted with substantial changes as "Winkfield Plain; or A Description of a
Camp in the Year 1800" in *The Wild Wreath* and attributed to M.E.R., the initials of
Robinson's daughter. There was a military camp at Windsor with which Robinson
would have been familiar since she lived nearby. For a vivid treatment of military
camps in Robinson's day, see Gillian Russell's *The Theatres of War: Performance, Poli-
tics, and Society, 1793-1815* (Oxford: Clarendon Press, 1995).

2   Supply stores.

3   Boys from Eton College in Windsor.

4   Dandies or fops.

5   Acting in a mad or frenzied manner.

Britain's pride and Virtue's treasure,
Fair and gracious, beyond measure!
Aid de Camps,[1] and youthful pages —
Prudes, and vestals[2] of all ages! —   30
Old coquets, and matrons surly,
Sounds of distant *hurly burly!*
Mingled voices uncouth singing;
Carts, full laden, forage bringing;
Sociables,[3] and horses weary;   35
Houses warm, and dresses airy;
Loads of fatten'd poultry; pleasure
Serv'd (TO NOBLES) without measure.
Doxies,[4] who the waggons follow;
Beer, for thirsty hinds[5] to swallow;   40
Washerwomen, fruit-girls cheerful,
ANTIENT LADIES — *chaste* and *fearful!*
Tradesmen, leaving shops, and seeming
More of *war* than profit dreaming;
Martial sounds, and braying asses;   45
Noise, that ev'ry noise surpasses!
All confusion, din, and riot —
NOTHING CLEAN — and NOTHING QUIET. —

GREAT AND SMALL![6]

WHEN Nobles live in houses gay,
And pass in splendid ease the day;
When coaches, horses, suits of gold,
In gaudy lustre we behold,
When spendthrifts claim a vast estate —.   5
        They are the GREAT!
But when to ruin they are bow'd,

---

1   An officer who assists a general in his military duties.
2   Virgins or chaste women.
3   Open carriages.
4   Doxy: a mistress, paramour, or prostitute.
5   Hind: lad or boy, often a farm labourer or servant.
6   Published in the *Morning Post*, September 18, 1800, and attributed to "T.B."

When no one marks them in the crowd —
When in a ragged garb they go,
10   And sigh, the sigh of cureless woe —
When spendthrifts hide — when tradesmen call —
    Then — they are SMALL!

When youth and pleasure, on the wing,
A thousand lovely visions bring;
15   When stars and ribbons deck the breast,
And flatt'ry makes its dupe a jest;
When tables groan with massy plate,
    Then — they are GREAT!
But when they knock at friendship's door,
20   Forsaken — hunted, sad, and poor —
When *writs*[1] and *law* pursue their feet —
And taunting scorn they hourly meet;
When bailiffs ev'ry sense appall —
    Then — they are SMALL!

25   When proud, imperious, rich, and bold,
They mount the stage of ill-got gold!
When Fortune lifts the grov'ling soul,
And bids her sunny hour controul —
When Ostentation rolls in state —
30   Then — they are GREAT!
But when, with modest graces dress'd,
The sigh, scarce utter'd, fills the breast;
When slow the tear, indignant, steals,
And CONSCIOUS VIRTUE, silent, feels —
35   When GENIUS flies from SPLENDOUR's hall —
    'Tis then — oh! then! — the *great* are SMALL!

---

1   Orders issued by a court.

Is it beneath the tapers ray,
The banquets luxury to share,
And waste the midnights hours away,
With Fashion's idle vot'ries there.

               Ah! no!

Figure 11. Mezzotint engraving after Maria Cosway, illustration No. 7 for "The Wintry Day," 1804. (By courtesy of the Special Collections Department, University of Virginia Library.)

POEMS THAT WERE INCORPORATED INTO *THE PROGRESS OF LIBERTY*[1]

THE BIRTH-DAY OF LIBERTY[2]

Hail, Liberty! Legitimate of Heav'n!
Who, on a mountain's solitary brow
First started into life; thy Sire, old Time;
Thy mother, blooming, innocent, and gay,
5   The Genius of the scene! Thy lusty form
She gave to Nature; on whose fragrant lap,
Nurs'd by the breath of morn, each glowing vein
Soon throbb'd with healthful streams. Thy sparkling eyes

---

1   The poems that follow, published from April 1798, to August 1800, were ultimately
    incorporated into *The Progress of Liberty*, a long poem in blank verse published after
    Robinson's death in the fourth volume of the 1801 *Memoirs* and in the 1806 *Poetical
    Works*. "The Birth-day of Liberty," "The Progress of Liberty," "The Horrors of Anar-
    chy," "The Vestal," "The Monk," and "The Dungeon" were published anonymously
    under the heading "Poetical Pictures" in the *Morning Post* newspaper between April
    1798 and May 1798. "The African," which appeared in the *Post* over a year after the
    "Poetical Pictures" sequence, was attributed to Mrs. Robinson, and was followed in
    August 1799 by "The Cell of the Atheist," which was attributed to "Laura Maria,"
    by then an easily recognizable Robinson pseudonym. The overall plan for *The
    Progress of Liberty* was in place by this time as "The Cell of the Atheist" was subtitled,
    "From a Poem in Two Books." Finally, in April and August 1800, Robinson pub-
    lished "The Italian Peasantry" (in the *Monthly Magazine*) and "Harvest Home" (in
    the *Morning Post*). "The Hermit of Mont-Blanc," which had appeared in the *Month-
    ly Magazine* in February 1800, as well as being included in Robinson's 1800 *Lyrical
    Tales* (p. 182), also became part of *The Progress of Liberty*. As Robinson neared death –
    she was in poor health in her final years – she apparently felt the need to work on a
    more epic scale, perhaps to serve notice of her artistic ambition. Still, the individual
    poems that she swept into the grand vision of *The Progress of Liberty* are distinctive
    separate entities. The first note to each of the poems that follow gives exact publica-
    tion information.

2   Published in the *Morning Post*, April 7, 1798, as No. I in a series entitled "Poetical
    Pictures." No author's name is given, but the poem was introduced as follows: "We
    have the pleasure of now laying before our readers the first number of Poetical Pic-
    tures, of which we are promised the continuation. It is a flattering circumstance to
    this Paper, that it should be selected for the publication of Lines in honour of Liber-
    ty; and it is still more flattering that it should be selected by a person of so great a
    genius, and splendid an imagination, as the Author of the following Lines."

Snatch'd radiance from the Sun! while ev'ry limb,
By custom unrestrain'd, grew firm and strong.　　　10
Thy midnight cradle, rock'd by howling winds,
Lull'd thee to wholesome rest. Thy bev'rage pure,
The wild brook gushing from the rocky steep,
And foaming, unimpeded, down the vale.
For thee no victim bled: no groan of death　　　15
Stole on the sighing gale to pitying Heav'n!
Thy food the herbage sweet, or wand'ring vine
Bursting its luscious bounds, and scatt'ring wide
The purple stream nectareous. O'er the hills,
Veil'd with an orient canopy sublime,　　　20
'Twas thine to rove unshackl'd, or to weave
Young mountain flow'rs, to deck thy waving hair
But not confine it. Where thy footsteps fell
No vagrant bud was crush'd; for swift and light
As summer breezes, flew thy active limbs,　　　25
Scarce brushing the soft dews. Thy song sublime,
Warbl'd with all the witchery of sound,
Wellcom'd the varied year; nor mark'd the change
Of passing seasons: For to thee THE MORN
(Whether Favonius[1] op'd the sunny East,　　　30
Flaunting its lustrous harbinger of light,
Or slow the paly glimpse of winter's eye
Peer'd on the frozen brow of sickly day),
Still wore an aspect lovely! Ev'ning's star,
Spangling the purple splendours of the West,　　　35
And glowing, 'midst infinity of space,
Temper'd by twilight's tears, still smil'd on THEE,
And bade thee dream of rapture! Nor could night,
With all its glooms opake, its howling blasts —
Thunders, appalling to the guilty soul —　　　40
Or livid fires, winging the shafts of death,
Shake the soft slumbers of thy halcyon home.
The wild was thy domain! as morn's approach
Thy bounding form uprose to meet the Sun,

1　The west wind.

45   Thyself its proud Epitome! For thou,
    Like the vast Orb,[1] wert destin'd to illume
    The mist-encircled world; to warm the soul,
    To call the pow'rs of teeming Reason forth,
    And ratify the laws by Nature made!

THE PROGRESS OF LIBERTY [2]

    LONG didst thou live, unruling and unrul'd,
    The reveller of NATURE's wide domain!
    'Till weary of thy solitude sublime,
    And seeking bliss, beyond the bliss of Heav'n,
5   Thy truant steps the mazy haunts of MEN
    Unheeded trod. Thy mighty voice was heard
    Amidst the groans of anguish and despair,
    The din of revelry, or silence deep
    Of dungeon horrors; while high-bearing Pride,
10 First taught to feel, her ghastly visage wrapp'd
    In Superstition's cowl. Ambition next
    Assum'd the mask of Valour; 'till Revenge
    Mock'd the shrewd spoiler. Terror then rush'd forth;
    Her eyes glar'd wildly thro' the specious tears
15 Of holy sorrow; while her livid lip
    Mutter'd relentless curses, each approv'd
    By FOLLY, CRUELTY, OPPRESSION, VICE:
    Confederate FIENDS, that trampled on the laws
    Of bleeding NATURE. While they stood aghast,
20 Thy bosom bare, and form of God-like mould,
    Burst on their startled gaze! they shrunk appall'd,
    Trembling and pale! But soon the torpid spell
    Of broad-ey'd Horror vanish'd, and each arm

---

1 The sun.
2 Published in the *Morning Post*, April 14, 1798, as No. II in the series "Poetical Pictures." No author's name is given; the poem was introduced as follows: "It is with much pleasure we lay before our readers the Second Number of these beautiful poetical pieces. The description of the Court of Despotism would do honour to the pen of Milton."

Was rais'd for slaughter. Legions bold uprose,
While fierce Despair a frantic phalanx form'd   25
To intercept thy path. The daring host
At thy command gave way. Still urg'd by fate
Onward thou cam'st; o'er cliffs stupendous! where
Dark-brow'd DECEIT hung brooding o'er the wave
That lash'd the sands below. Down the dread gulf,   30
Oblivion's black domain, unnumber'd Fiends
Hurl'd shrieking victims; spirits that rebell'd,
And spurn'd Oppression's chain. Upon a rock
(Which seem'd the top-most beacon of the world),
A lofty fabric stood, whose ebon tow'rs   35
Shadow'd their pond'rous gates. At thy approach
The bolts flew wide, and with a thund'ring crash
The scene disclos'd, where on his iron throne
Terrifically frown'd DESPOTIC POW'R,
A giant strong! his vassals,[1] bound in chains   40
(Artfully twin'd with wreaths of opiate flow'rs,
Thro' which the clanking links sad music made),
Stood trembling at his gaze. Beneath his feet
Pale captives groan'd; while shad'wy spectres dire,
Of persecuted Innocence and Worth;   45
Of GENIUS, bent to an untimely grave; —
Of ETHIOPS,[2] burnt beneath their native sun,
Their countless wounds wide yawning for revenge,
Rose in a mighty host, — and yell'd despair! —

    The flinty fabric shook! the thund'ring spheres   50
Frown'd, dark as Erebus![3] upon its base
The Pandemonium[4] rock'd! while with'ring bolts
From Heav'n's red citadel fell fast around.
The vex'd sea, swoln above its tow'ring walls,
Foam'd madly furious. The gigantic fiend   55
Wav'd high his adamantine[5] wand in vain;

---

1 Servants.
2 An Ethiopian or, more generally, a person with black skin.
3 The region of the underworld where the dead pass as soon as they die.
4 An assembly of all the devils.
5 Like adamant, incapable of being broken.

Thy potent grasp palsy'd the monster's arm,
And hurl'd him fathoms down his native Hell!
All Earth, convulsive yawn'd; while Nature's hand
60 Crush'd the infernal throne, and in its stead,
A thousand temples rose, each dedicate
To Valour, Reason, Liberty, and Fame!

Now from her dark and solitary cell
Suspicion started, vigilant and shrewd,
65 Fear in her eye, and Malice in her breast:
She scowl'd around, trembling, perplex'd, amaz'd,
Scarce daring to believe, yet more afraid
To doubt her startled senses. Ev'ry breeze
That whisper'd peril to the ear of night,
70 Bathing its ebon cheek with humid fears,
Bade her be wary: ev'ry blushing dawn
Beheld a scene of blood. The public streets
(Where needy villains lurk'd in ev'ry turn,
Purchas'd by GUILTY POW'R), at closing day,
75 Flow'd with ensanguin'd streams. The prisons groan'd
With vengeful MINIONS, while their subtle slaves
Aim'd at the breast of Freedom. For a time
Valour withheld the desolating sword,
And Pity offer'd to the lips of Pride
80 The cup capacious, fill'd with essence pure,
Drawn from the fount of REASON. Shrewd Revenge,
With all the restless Demons of her train,
Thirsting for blood, the sacred pledge receiv'd;
And while the eye of PITY turn'd to heav'n,
85 Infus'd a deadly poison! on themselves
The fatal vengeance fell; *they drank* — AND DIED!

THE HORRORS OF ANARCHY[1]

Now ANARCHY roam'd wide, a monster fierce,
Mad as the roaring sea! The dawning hour,
Which welcom'd Liberty, and spread around
A bland effulgence, suddenly grew dark,
And storms of horror blacken'd the broad sun.   5
The highmost hills re-echoed with the shouts
Of yell'd destruction; while the concave vast
Of Heav'n shook horrible! The beaten ways,
By the unwearied foot of Commerce made,
Were wash'd with blood: the holy altar's stain'd   10
With gore of innocents. The good, the wise,
The smiling infant, and the hoary sage,
Sunk in the mass of ruin. Then the eye
Of shudd'ring Liberty was dim with tears,
Haggard and grief-swoln. On his ardent breast   15
Pale NATURE trembled; for infuriate MAN,
Wild with the fateful plenitude of pow'r,
Warr'd 'gainst his desp'rate fellow. Not alone
O'er proud oppression flew the bolts of fate;
Not on the tyrants, or the minion crew,   20
(The locusts that o'er-run the with'ring world),
But all around as the swift summer storm,
Tears from the mountain's brow the sturdy oak,
While the small flowrets and the pois'nous weed
Alike are level'd, so the vengeful shaft   25
Bore down the breathing race: the clang of arms
Deafen'd the ear of reason: the loud shout
Of popular applause was heard to ring
The vaulty arch of Heav'n, while mingling groans
Drown'd the deep sighs of Nature! Liberty,   30
O! pow'r sublime! how was thy sacred name
Profan'd by Cruelty? how many fell

---

1   Published in the *Morning Post*, April 24, 1798, as No. III in the "Poetical Pictures"
    series; a corrected version (reproduced here) was printed the following day. No
    author's name is given; the poem is introduced as follows: "The following beautiful
    Piece is particularly interesting at this period, on account of the subject it treats."

Beneath the arm, in usurpation strong,
Yet recreant in oppression. Not the wise,
35   The virtuous, or the brave, THEN held the scale
Of even Justice: Freedom's sons inspir'd,
In vain, rear'd high their banners 'mid the scene
Of madd'ning slaughter. For a time their zeal
Was mock'd, with barb'rous rage; their great design
40   By frenzy violated, or constrain'd
By spells infernal. Then, O Liberty!
Thy frantic mien, and Heav'n-imploring eye,
Turn'd from the dreadful throng to trace new paths,
And seek, in distant climes, new scenes of woe.

45   Hail'd by the breathing race, O! Child of Time,
Borne on thy parent's wings, thy eagle eyes
Glanc'd o'er the pendent world! Full many a spot
Seem'd dark with misery; and many a wretch
Pin'd in Oppression's chain. Italia's sons,
50   Plac'd in the blooming garden of the world,
A second Athens, Europe's proudest clime,
Pregnant with spicy gales, and balmy dews,
Whose seminaries, rich with treasur'd lore,
Mark'd that emporium, where the classic mind,
55   Gave and receiv'd the pure exchange of thought;
E'en there the sun of intellect was dimm'd
By gloomy tyranny. There Mis'ry's race,
Dark in the centre of expanding light,
Still groan'd beneath the worst of slavery,
60   The spells of SUPERSTITION. Temples vast;
And shrines of massy gold; their prisons were
Replete with numbing chains; while daring hands
Dealt the decrees of Heav'n; and impious tongues
Pronounc'd anathemas, to fright mankind.

THE VESTAL[1]

Dim was the Cloister, where the Vestal sad
Wither'd thro' life's dull hour in ling'ring death;
Her spring of youth chill'd by untimely frost,
And all the warm perceptions of her soul,
Spell-bound by sorrow! What were her pursuits?   5
Fasting and pray'r; long nights of meditation;
And days consum'd in tears. The matin song,
By repetition dull, familiar grown,
Pass'd o'er her lip mechanically cold,
And little mark'd devotion. The wing'd choir,   10
Blithe airy trav'llers of the sphery climes,
Hover'd around the grey and mould'ring spires
Of her dim habitation. Cou'd their songs,
Their dulcet warblings and wild mazy trills,
Soothe the wan mourner's breast, or prompt her thoughts   15
Anticipating Freedom? The cold moon,
Scatt'ring nocturnal incense on the world,
Stole o'er her lonely prison, sadly pale,
Rob'd in a starry vest; her crescent bright
Silver'd the ivy battlements; the haunts   20
Of that lone bird, whose melancholy note,
Breaking the solitude, from fev'rish dreams
Startled her aching breast. The fervid noon
No streamy light bestow'd; to gild the cell,
Where bigot frenzy barr'd the icy grate,   25
And spread perpetual horrors! Day retir'd;
The gaudy monarch of unbounded space,
Furling his ample vest of blushing gold,
Hied to his dusky bed. The vesper bell,

---

1 Published in the *Morning Post*, May 5, 1798, as No. IV in the series entitled "Poetical
Pictures." No author's name is given. The introduction to the poem states: "The fol-
lowing description of desponding Love and resigned Despair, is one of the most
fanciful, accurate, and glowing Pictures of those Passions, that ever was laid before
the Public. The passage respecting 'Love's pure Torch' is particularly beautiful." A
vestal is a nun or chaste woman. The word recalls the vestal virgins, priestesses who
tended the sacred fire in the temple of Vesta at Rome.

30 Pale twilight's peal funereal, rous'd her soul
From transient spells of contemplation sad,
By small and silver sounds; vibrations sweet!
Yet not more sweet than solemn. HAPLESS MAID!
On the cold marble of her cell she knelt,
35 To chant her midnight orisons,[1] and mourn,
The slave confess'd of passion and despair!
'Twas her's to breathe upon her cross the sigh
Of unavailing grief, while Love's pure torch,
In the mild radiance of her humid eyes,
40 Gleam'd like an April sun, thro' passing show'rs,
To shew another idol in her breast!
Her smooth cheek redden'd through the snowy veil
That half conceal'd its bloom; Ah! transient bloom!
The self-reproving flush of conscious love,
45 Which, like the wood-wild rose, unfolds its hues,
And, drest with morning's tears, expires unseen!
Counting her beads, she number'd not her pray'rs,
But only thought of Heav'n, to curse her fate!
Yet who could blame the VESTAL's wand'ring thoughts?
50 Could the day past, to her reflecting mind
Shew consolation? Could the relique cold
Chill the warm pulse that throb'd within her breast,
Or chasten its rebellion, while no gleam
Of peace was her's, save that which hope unfolds,
55 The quiet of THE GRAVE? O! beamless GRAVE!
Thou sombre curtain, which o'er life's dull scene
Throws blank oblivion; while the busy throng
Are bound in apathy, 'till lab'ring time
Dissolves them into nothing! Yet the spark
60 Of Immortality, escap'd the bounds
Of its dark prison-clay, roves, unconfin'd,
Thro' regions infinite, and worlds unknown!
Then joyful is the hour, when, to the wretch
(Whose feet ne'er wander'd from sequester'd haunts,
65 Who, shut from nature's wond'rous scenery,

---

1 Prayers.

Breathes but a living spectre), death shall come,
Robb'd of his terrors, like a Herald gay,
To force the frozen gates of BIGOT Zeal,
Clos'd by OPPRESSION's hand, and barr'd by PRIDE.
Ask the pale VESTAL's meditating soul,   70
Was it for this, her rosy infancy
Was nurs'd with tender care? Her perfect form,
Fashion'd by all the Graces and the Loves,
Rear'd to the op'ning summer of delight,
A model of perfection? Was her mind,   75
Stor'd with the prodigality of nature,
Expanded, warm'd, enlighten'd, and inspir'd,
Unblest to perish? Could the sable vest,
The lawn transparent, or the pendent cross,
Deceive th' OMNISCIENT! While her beating breast   80
Proclaim'd her form'd for rational delight?
Prepost'rous sacrifice! Sweet fading flow'r!
Condemn'd to waste its bloom in one dull speck
Of freezing solitude; to lift its head,
Lovely as Spring! Yet, ere the Summer sun   85
Unfolds its od'rous breast, — to droop, AND DIE!

THE MONK[1]

'MID the grey horrors of his narrow cell,
The wasted MONK is seen. His silv'ry beard
Falls, like Helvetia's[2] snow, half down his breast,
Shading his frozen heart. A torpid spell
Benumbs life's fountain, while the feeble pulse   5
Marks the slow progress of Time's weary course,
With languid circulation. Ev'ry clock

---

1   Published in the *Morning Post*, May 12, 1798, as No.V in the series "Poetical Pic-
    tures." No author's name is given. The introduction to the poem states: "The fol-
    lowing Piece traces out, with great truth and genius, a Picture, which it would
    require the best of the Artists of Somerset House to execute. The alliance between
    Poetry and Painting never was more evident than in these lines." Somerset House
    was home to the Royal Academy of Arts.
2   Switzerland.

That sounds the passing hour, appears the knell
Which warns him to oblivion. A coarse garb
10   Hangs round his meagre frame; his hollow cheek,
Shrivell'd with frequent fasting as with age,
Scarce hides his bony jaws. Beneath his cowl,
His dimly-gleaming eyes, sunk in their cells,
And glaz'd with midnight watching, ask of Heav'n
15   A solitary grave. Poor, breathing Ghost!
Tell that still questioner, thy weary mind,
Was it for cloister'd, visionary glooms,
For castigation and sequester'd hours,
For cold inanity, life's conscious death,
20   That Nature gave thee strength in busy scenes
To act a nobler part? Misguided MONK!
Thou wretched slave of bigotry and fraud!
Was it to gabble o'er a canting tale,
To trim the wasting lamp, to wear away
25   The flinty pavement with thy wounded knees,
To scourge thy quiv'ring flesh, embrace cold Saints,
To starve thy appetites, till ev'ry bone
Shews what a wretched, ghastly thing thou art,
Robb'd of thy outward form! Was it for this
30   That Reason dawn'd upon thy op'ning youth;
And Science smil'd, while Love, with sportive mien,
Danc'd gaily on, leading expectant joys
Which told thee thou wert MAN? O! Did the spark,
Th' electric spark which kindles fancy's Fire,
35   Ne'er in perspective bright unfold such scenes
As bade thy bosom glow, ambition warm'd,
Or melt in rapt'rous visions? What art thou?
Deluded, sad, forgotten! like a tree
Plac'd on a blasted desert, where no Sun
40   Visits the sapless trunk, but all around
One gloom perpetual reigns. Where are thy pow'rs?
Where the perception strong, the active mind,
Th' etherial essence that expands the heart;
The depth of knowledge, and the will to act?
50   Where is the stamp which marks th' immortal soul,

And places THEE above the growling brute?
Shrouded by Superstition, chain'd by Fear,
Benumb'd by long seclusion from the world,
While naught remains, but a lean, wither'd form,
Inert, enfeebl'd, useless, and debas'd!   55
The Indian wild, that roves the pathless steep,
Chasing the famish'd Wolf, or savage Bear,
Anticipates the hour when to his hut
He drags the bleeding spoil, to shout, and sing,
In social feasting with his untaught tribes;   60
The blazing fire encircled, sheds a glow
On the brown cheek, and gilds the gloomy hour
Of wint'ry desolation! Ev'n there
MAN is the friend of MAN! While the rude grasp,
The deaf'ning war-whoop, or the uncouth garb,   65
Shews, with fantastic gestures, the caprice
Of ever-varying Nature. But, for THEE,
O solitary MONK! no chearful hour
Shall mark the Summer morn, or deck the wing
Of Time with sunny lustre! all, yes all,   70
To thee shall seem a blank; a dreadful blank,
Veiling the face of Nature, while her voice
Whispers reproof; reproof that will be heard
Ev'n in the cloister's melancholy gloom;
Till death shall close the tablet of thy fate,   75
Nor leave one friend, to PITY, or to PRAISE.

THE DUNGEON[1]

EXPLORE the Dungeon's gloom, where, all alone,
The HOMICIDE[2] expires; the guilty wretch,
Whose hands are steep'd in gore; whose timid soul
The mild and pitying angel, HOPE, forsakes,

---

1   Published in the *Morning Post*, May 18, 1798, as No. VI in the series now entitled
    "Poetical Pictures, (In France and Italy)." No author's name is given.
2   Murderer.

5   While all the Daemons of Despair and Hell
       Howl in his startled ears! His weary hours
       Have many a season pass'd, since to his cheek
       The breeze of Heav'n gave freshness; since his lip
       Imbib'd th' etherial spirit of the morn,
10   Or balmy sleep, the opiate of the mind,
       Lull'd the sick sense of Sorrow. If his brain
       Snatches a transitory dream of peace;
       If, wearied by perpetual, painful thought,
       A short, but broken slumber, stills the throne
15   Of tott'ring intellect; sudden and fierce
       Some shriek appalling, or some spectre dire,
       Taunts him to waking madness, and again
       The mental fever rages! Down his cheek
       The scalding tear rolls fast. His bloodshot eyes
20   Glare motionless and wide, as if their sense
       Turn'd inward on his soul. His quiv'ring lip,
       Drain'd of the life-stream by the conscious fiend,
       Mutters a brief appeal to angry Heav'n,
       Then freezes into death. What is his crime?
25   Whom did he kill? The minion of his foe;
       The sordid STEWARD, whose infuriate rage
       Snatch'd from his helpless babes the well earn'd store
       Of many a toilsome hour; the pamper'd slave,
       Whose mind, grown callous by Oppression's task,
30   Repell'd compunctuous Pity — Ask thy heart,
       DIVINE PHILANTHROPIST! who rais'd his hand
       Against the Caitiff's[1] life? The CAITIFF'S SELF!
       The petty Tyrant, who, with barb'rous wrongs
       Propell'd him on to sin. For REASON's breast,
35   Arm'd 'gainst Oppression, in resistance strong,
       Can combat giant fierceness; and tho' oft
       By subtle malice vanquish'd or betray'd,
       Still owns the plea of NATURE! In the next cell
       The patient Child of Persecution sits,
40   Pensively sad. His uncomplaining tongue,

---

1   Villain.

His stedfast eye, his lean and pallid cheek,
Grac'd with the stamp of dignified disdain,
Wait the approach of Death. No haggard glance
Ruffles the placid orb, whose lustre, dimm'd
By dungeon vapours, like a dewy star,   45
Gleams 'midst surrounding darkness. On his lip
Smiles Innocence, enthron'd in modest pride,
And eloquently silent! On his breast
His folded arms (shielding his conscious heart
From the damp poisons of a living grave),   50
Are firmly interwoven; while his soul,
Calm as the martyr at the kindling pyre,
Holds strong with resignation. Tell, O TRUTH!
Thou Heav'n-descended Judge! What has he done?
Has he refus'd to bend the flexile knee   55
Before the blood-stain'd foot of ruthless Pow'r?
To fawn upon the bloated, lordly fool,
Who claim'd his vassalage?[1] Has he forgot
To load the groaning altars of the Church;
Libell'd, by Truth, some wanton, courtly dame;   60
Or, like an arrogant, rebellious knave,
Dar'd talk of Freedom? Say, O vengeful MAN,
Are these thy destin'd victims? Is it thus
Thou deal'st the meed of Justice? Dost thou think
Thy petty rage will sever them from HIM,   65
Whose attribute is Mercy, and whose grace
Mocks all distinctions? O! Let NATURE speak,
And with instinctive force inform thy soul,
That LIBERTY, the choicest boon of Heav'n,
Is REASON's birthright, and the gift of GOD!   70

---

1   A state of devotion to another's commands.

THE CELL OF THE ATHEIST[1]

In the worst den of human misery,
Behold the hopeless and forsaken wretch,
Who on the humid pavement naked lies,
Tearing his burning flesh! Then ask thy heart,
5   O! LITTLE GREATNESS! and let Nature's voice,
Piercing the adamantine shield of pride,
Tell thee, thy victim is thy fellow, MAN!
Once Nature's darling, now a maniac wild!
His intellectual treasures scatter'd wide,
10   By Persecution's strong and ruthless arm,
While he, an atom, shrinking from the storm,
Flies to an unbless'd grave! Was it for this
His youth was pass'd in toil — in mental toil —
The hardest labour? Did the classic fount,
15   Such as Athenian sages taught to flow,
For him diffuse its renovated streams,
The Muses bind his brow, the Virtues grace
His bland, instinctive mind, to bow the slave
Of barb'rous IGNORANCE? Did FANCY smile,
20   And bid his fingers smite th' HORATIAN[2] lyre,
His pulses throb with the fine fervour, strong,
His depth of thought explore the wond'rous page,
Which bade LONGINUS[3] live, HIMSELF to die,
Unblest, neglected, indigent, and mad?
25   Did he, for this, with NEWTON climb the stars,[4]
And traverse worlds unknown? Or did the thrill
Of Heav'n-born POESY thro' ev'ry vein
Dart the electric fire, whose vivid glow
Illum'd the darken'd sense of Britain's bard,[5]

---

1 Published in the *Morning Post*, August 19, 1799, as the work of "Laura Maria." The
   poem is subtitled "From a Poem in Two Books, Not Yet Finished."
2 Referring to Horace (65-8 B.C.), sometimes called Rome's greatest poet.
3 Cassius Longinus (*c.* A.D. 213-273): a Greek scholar and Neoplatonic philosopher
   who wrote many books on literature, rhetoric, and philosophy.
4 Isaac Newton (1642-1727): scientist and propounder of a theory of the universe.
5 Milton [M.R.]. John Milton (1608-1674) wrote a sonnet on his blindness.

With full Promethean[1] blaze, while at his touch 30
Immortal themes, embodied, burst to view
Angels, and all the mighty hosts of Heav'n,
Rang'd in tremendous glory! POW'R SUPREME!
   Where is thy justice? VICTIMS such as these
Make REASON stagger; Rouse the thinking soul; 35
And, in the frenzied agony of wrongs,
Present such sceptical and daring thoughts,
That MAN DISOWNS HIS MAKER! Guilty PRIDE,
The crime is THINE, not HIS; thy lofty rage,
Insulting tyranny, and cold disdain 40
Pour'd fell oppression's torrent o'er his sense,
Madden'd his shrinking brain, and WHELM'D HIS SOUL!

THE AFRICAN[2]

   SHALL the poor AFRICAN, the passive Slave,
Born in the bland effulgence of broad day,
Cherish'd by torrid splendours, while around
The plains prolific teem with honey'd stores,
Sink prematurely to a grave obscure, 5
No tear to grace his ashes? Or suspire
To wear Submission's long and goading chain,
To drink the tear that down his swarthy cheek
Flows fast, to moisten his toil-fever'd lip
Parch'd by the noon-tide blaze? Shall HE endure 10
The frequent lash, the agonizing scourge,
The day of labour, and the night of pain;
Expose his naked limbs to burning gales;
Faint in the sun, and wither in the storm;
Traverse hot sands, imbibe the morbid breeze, 15

---

1 Prometheus gave the gift of fire to mankind.
2 Published in the *Morning Post* on August 2, 1798, and attributed to Mrs. Robinson.
   The decade of the 1790s saw fierce debate over slavery that culminated in the pas-
   sage of the 1807 Abolition of the Slave Trade Act. In the mid-1790s abolitionist
   activity was sometimes associated with Jacobin activity in a climate of political
   paranoia.

Wing'd with contagion; while his blister'd feet,
Scorch'd by the vertical and raging beam,
Pour the swift life-stream? Shall his frenzied eyes,
Oh! worst of mortal mis'ries! behold
20   The darling of his heart, his sable love,
Selected from the trembling timid throng,
By the wan TYRANT, whose licentious touch
Seals the dark fiat of the SLAVE's despair!

    OH LIBERTY! From thee the suppliant claims
25   The meed of retribution! Thy pure flame
Wou'd light the sense opake, and warm the spring
Of boundless ecstacy: while Nature's laws,
So violated, plead immortal tongu'd,
For her dark-fated children! Lead them forth
30   From bondage infamous! Bid Reason own
The dignities of MAN, whate'er his clime,
Estate, or colour. And, O sacred TRUTH!
Tell the proud Lords of traffic, that the breast
Thrice ebon-tinted, owns a crimson tide
35   As pure, — as clear, as Europe's Sons can boast.

THE ITALIAN PEASANTRY[1]

TIME WAS, and mem'ry sickens to retrace
The table fraught with wrongs, when seasons roll'd
O'er the small hut of lowly industry
In dim succession of eternal gloom;
5   Though rosy morn upon the eastern cliff
Burst wide her silver gates, and scatter'd round
A bright ethereal show'r! When nature's breast
Unveil'd its fragrance, and its gloomy tints,
Spangl'd by twilight's tears, to weary eyes,
10   Unbless'd with sweet repose! Poor, toil-worn race!

---

1   Published in the *Monthly Magazine*, April 1, 1800, with the heading: "From an unpublished Poem, by Mrs. Robinson."

The hardy blossoms of a fervid soil; —
What was their hapless lot? To sigh, to pant,
To scorch and faint, while from the cloudless sky
The noon-tide beam shot downward. By their hands
The burning ploughshare thro' the Tuscan glebe[1]   15
Pursued its sultry way: The smoking plains,
Refresh'd by tepid show'rs, receiv'd the pledge
Of future luxury. The tangling vine,
Nurs'd by their toil, grew fibrous: the brown rind,
Dried by the parching gale, wove close and firm,   20
Guarded the rich and nect'rous distillation.
The tendrils twin'd, to ev'ry point minute
The od'rous bev'rage stole, till the swoln fruit,
Empurpled by the sun, the labourers prest
To yield its luscious burthen. Yet, for THEM   25
Did summer gild the plain? Did autumn glow?
Did austral[2] breezes fan the tepid show'r,
Scarce whisp'ring as it fell? Did the day's toil
Ensure the night's repose? — sweet recompence,
That well befits the PEASANT's guiltless toil!   30
    Could THEY, when down the crimson plains of light
The lord of day retir'd, when ev'ry bird,
The plumy trav'ller of unbounded space,
Claim'd the short hour of rest, could LABOUR's sons
Shake from their freckled brows the ev'ning dew,   35
And homeward, blithesomely, return to quaff
The honey'd cup of joy? Could THEY suspire
Health's breezy hour; on THEIR OWN cultur'd plains
Reap the full harvest, pen their fleecy store;
Or, as the night-mist gather'd o'er the heath,   40
Call home their wand'ring herds? — O! *suff'ring* CARLE![3]
When the rich vintage heap'd the lordly board,
Moisten'd the feasted lip, or flashing foam'd
Within its crystal prison, amber-dyed;

---

1 Soil.
2 Southern.
3 Man of low birth.

45　　　When nectar, thrice distill'd by burning gales,
　　　　Sated the palate of the pamper'd fool;
　　　　What were THY poor rewards! — A niggard boon!
　　　　Dealt out with freezing scorn, or brutal pride;
　　　　A rushy pillow, and a mountain hut,
50　　　Whose sides of clay, and tempest-shatter'd roof,
　　　　Scarce screen'd thy bosom from the wint'ry blast;
　　　　(The very DOGS of PRINCES warmer housed!)
　　　　While the long hour, 'till morning's dawn, stole on
　　　　In sullen sadness, or in fruitless pray'r!
55　　　　Turn to the marble PALACES of PRIDE,
　　　　The velvet hangings and the golden shows,
　　　　That made their tables groan! Behold their feasts
　　　　Of luscious fruits, and blood-inflaming spice;
　　　　Their oily syrups of ambrosial flow'rs,
60　　　Conserves, thrice essenc'd in Phoenician dews,
　　　　Fit for the sick'ning palate of the wretch
　　　　By luxury unnerv'd! Beneath his feet,
　　　　The polish'd pavement must be sprinkled o'er
　　　　With perfumes of Arabia! From above,
65　　　The lattic'd roof, with summer flow'rs o'er-hung,
　　　　'Midst aromatic sweets, shed cooling airs
　　　　On his feast-fever'd cheek! On ev'ry side,
　　　　In sumptuous colonades of Parian stone,[1]
　　　　Or glitt'ring granite, or the fibrous earth
70　　　Of rich SIENNA's hills; slow-breathing flutes,
　　　　In dulcet strains, take captive the dull sense
　　　　Through the long hour of feasting; cheating time
　　　　With enervating bliss! O! CONTRAST INFINITE!
　　　　Yet WHO, amidst the mortal myriads,
75　　　Most labour'd to embellish NATURE's plan
　　　　Of boundless wonders? WHO, with ceaseless toil,
　　　　Dug from the beamless mazes of the earth
　　　　The boast of varying climes, from LYBIA's groves
　　　　To caves ARMENIAN, guarded by the rocks

1　Parian marble came from the island of Paros (between Greece and Turkey) and was
　prized by the ancients for statuary.

Of wild EUPHRATES? Who, but the SONS OF TOIL, 80
Enrich'd the sculptur'd dome, reviv'd the ARTS,
Sinking, o'erwhelm'd, amidst the wrecks of time?
    Look round the lofty palaces of PRIDE,
Behold the BREATHING CANVAS, wond'rous proof
Of imitative pow'r! where human forms, 85
Colours, and space, miraculously rang'd,
Drew order out of chaos! where the vast
Of bold perception varied hues disclos'd,
From the rich foliage of embow'ring woods
To mountains, azure capp'd, scarce visible 90
Amid the dusk of distance. Trace the lines
That form the graceful STATUE, Grecian born
From rough-hewn quarries! See the rounding limb,
The modest look serene! which marks the nymph
Of MEDICEAN fame:[1] proud monument 95
Of Heav'n-instructed GENIUS! thou shalt charm
When pomp and pride shall mingle in the mass
Of undistinguish'd clay, inanimate,
That, having borne its hour of busy toil,
Shrinks into shapeless nothing! Dreadful thought! 100
To mingle with the cold and senseless earth;
In spells of dull inanity to rest;
The noblest passions, and the living pow'rs
Of intellectual light, the SOUL's pure lamp,
All, all extinguish'd! Tell me, *Nature's* GOD! 105
Then what is the warm magic that supplies
The strong life-loving flame, which fills the breast,
Enliv'ning TIME's slow journey? LIBERTY!
If thou art not the impulse exquisite,
Where does it dwell? What else can teach the wretch 110
(Lab'ring with mortal ills, disease and pain,
Deep-wounding poverty, presumptuous scorn,
High-crested arrogance, affections spurn'd,)
To bear the weight of thought, and linger out

---

1 Robinson is most likely referring to the Medici Venus in the Uffizi Gallery,
Florence. Reportedly, visiting Englishmen kissed the hand of this statue.

115   This weary task of being? Blest with THEE,
The PEASANT were as happy as his LORD —
For NATURE knows no difference! Summer smiles
For the poor cottager, and smiling shews
The vegetating scene, diffusing fair
120   And equal portions for the sons of earth!
But MAN, PROUD MAN, a bold usurper, takes
The law of Nature from its destin'd course,
And fashions it at pleasure! Hence we trace
The gloomy annals of receding time
125   Spotted with gore, and blurr'd by pity's tears,
Where GENIUS, VIRTUE, NATURE's progeny!
Mark'd by th' ETERNAL's hand with ev'ry charm,
Have shrunk beneath Oppression! — bow'd the neck
Before the blood-stain'd shrines of impious fraud,
130   Flouted by fools, the gilded dregs of earth,
And forc'd to hide the gushing tear of scorn,
Till driv'n to moutain caves, and desart glooms,
The godlike wonders fled. The FIRST, sublime,
The darling of his race; majestic! grand!
135   With eyes, whose living lustre beam'd afar
The blaze of intellect, Promethean-touch'd,
And infinitely radiant!——

               By his side,
Beauteous and mild as MORN's returning STAR,
140   The maiden, VIRTUE, mov'd! and who can tell
But in some hovel low, whose rushy roof
The barren cliff defends from wint'ry storms,
The godlike pair, scorning the din of fools,
(Ambition's clamour, which the despot, DEATH,
145   Awhile observes, then, with his iron hand,
Locks in eternal silence!) who can tell,
But the proud pair, by REASON's pow'r sustain'd,
Cherish a glorious race? STATESMEN and CHIEFS,
POETS, and sage PHILOSOPHERS, whose lore
150   Might rival ancient Greece, and nobly prove
The *solitude* of VIRTUE — WISDOM's SCHOOL!

HARVEST HOME[1]

WHO has not seen the chearful HARVEST HOME!
Enliv'ning the scorch'd field, and greeting gay
The slow decline of Autumn? All around
The yellow sheaves, catching the burning beam,
Glow, golden-lustred; and the trembling stem   5
Of the slim oat, or azure corn-flow'r,
Waves on the hedge-rows shady. From the hill
The day-breeze softly steals with downward wing,
And lightly passes, whisp'ring the soft sounds
Which moan the death of Summer. Glowing scene!   10
Nature's long holiday! Luxuriant, rich,
In her proud progeny, she smiling marks
Their graces, now mature, and wonder-fraught!

   Hail! season exquisite! — and hail, ye sons
Of rural toil! — ye blooming daughters! — ye,   15
Who, in the lap of hardy labour rear'd,
Enjoy the mind unspotted! Up the plain,
Or on the sidelong hill, or in the glen,
Where the rich farm, or scatter'd hamlet, shews
The neighbourhood of peace, ye still are found,   20
A merry and an artless throng, whose souls
Beam thro' untutor'd glances. When the dawn
Unfolds its sunny lustre, and the dew
Silvers the outstretch'd landscape, labour's sons
Rise, ever healthful, — ever chearily,   25
From sweet and soothing rest; — for fev'rish dreams
Visit not lowly pallets! All the day
They toil in the fierce beams of fervid noon —
But toil without repining! The blithe song,
Joining the woodland melodies afar,   30
Flings its rude cadence in fantastic sport

---

1   Published in the *Morning Post* August 30, 1800, and attributed to Mrs. Robinson.
    The date August, 1800 is printed at the foot of the poem. Harvest home is the
    occasion of bringing home the last of the harvest.

On Echo's airy wing! The pond'rous load
Follows the weary team: the narrow lane
Bears on its thick-wove hedge the scatter'd corn,
35 Hanging in scanty fragments, which the thorn
Purloin'd from the broad waggon.
                              On the plain
The freckled gleaner gathers the scant sheaf,
And looks, with many a sigh, on the tythe heap
40 Of the proud, pamper'd pastor! To the brook
That ripples, shallow down the valley's slope,
The herds slow measure their unvaried way; —
The flocks along the heath are dimly seen
By the faint torch of Ev'ning, whose red eye
45 Closes in tearful silence. Now the air
Is rich in fragrance! — fragrance exquisite!
Of new-mown hay, of wild thyme dewy wash'd,
And gales ambrosial, which, with cooling breath,
Ruffle the lake's grey surface. All around
50 The thin mist rises, and the busy tones
Of airy people, borne on viewless wings,
Break the short pause of Nature. From the plain
The rustic throngs come chearly, their loud din
Augments to mingling clamour. Sportive hinds,[1]
55 Happy! — more happy than the Lords ye serve! —
How lustily your sons endure the hour
Of wintry desolation; and how fair
Your blooming daughters greet the op'ning dawn
Of love-inspiring Spring!
                              Hail! harvest home!
60 To thee, the Muse of Nature pours the song,
By instinct taught to warble; instinct pure,
Sacred, and grateful to that POW'R ADOR'D,
Which warms the sensate being, and reveals
65 The Soul self-evident! — beyond the dreams
Of visionary sceptics! Scene sublime!
Where Earth presents her golden treasuries;

---

1   Hind: lad or boy; often refers to farm laborer.

Where balmy breathings whisper to the heart
Delights unspeakable! Where seas, and skies,
And hills and vallies, — colours, odours, dews,   70
Diversify the work of Nature's GOD!

'Tis on the cheerless naked room,
Where mis'ry's victims wait their doom,
Where a fond Mother famish'd dies,
While forth a frantic Father flies
                            Man's desp'rate foe!

Figure 12. Mezzotint engraving after Maria Cosway, illustration No. 8 for "The Wintry Day,"
1804. (By courtesy of the Special Collections Department, University of Virginia Library.)

FROM *THE POETICAL WORKS OF THE LATE MRS. MARY ROBINSON* (1806)

ODE TO THE SNOW-DROP[1]

The Snow-drop, Winter's timid child,
   Awakes to life, bedew'd with tears,
And flings around its fragrance mild;
And where no rival flow'rets bloom,
Amidst the bare and chilling gloom,   5
   A beauteous gem appears!

All weak and wan, with head inclin'd,
   Its parent-breast the drifted snow,
It trembles, while the ruthless wind
Bends its slim form; the tempest lowers,   10
Its em'rald eye drops crystal show'rs
   On its cold bed below.

Poor flow'r! on thee the sunny beam
   No touch of genial warmth bestows!
Except to thaw the icy stream   15
   Whose little current purls along,
And whelms thee as it flows.

The night-breeze tears thy silky dress,
   Which deck'd with silv'ry lustre shone;
The morn returns, not thee to bless. —   20
   The gaudy *Crocus* flaunts its pride,
   And triumphs where *its rival* — died
   Unshelter'd and unknown!

---

1   From "Walsingham," a Novel, in 4 vols. by the same Author [M.R.]. This poem,
   published in the *Morning Post* of 26 December 1797, inspired Samuel Taylor
   Coleridge's poetic rejoinder, "The Apotheosis, or the Snow-Drop," published in
   that same newspaper on January 3, 1798. See Appendix B. David Erdman's "Lost
   Poem Found" recounts the search for Coleridge's poem. A snowdrop is one of the
   earliest blooming flowers of spring.

No sunny beam shall gild thy grave,
25   No bird of pity thee deplore:
There shall no verdant branches wave,
        For spring shall all her gems unfold,
        And revel 'midst her beds of gold,
    When thou art seen no more!

30   Where'er I find thee, gentle flow'r,
        Thou still art sweet, and dear to me!
For I have known the cheerless hour,
        Have seen the sun-beams cold and pale,
        Have felt the chilling, wint'ry gale,
35   And WEPT, and SHRUNK LIKE THEE!

ODE INSCRIBED TO THE INFANT SON OF S.T. COLERIDGE, ESQ.[1]

Born Sept. 14, 1800, at Keswick, in Cumberland

SPIRIT OF LIGHT! whose eye unfolds
    The vast expanse of Nature's plan!

---

1 Robinson and Coleridge were in each other's company, according to William God-
    win's diary, in January and February of 1800. Coleridge moved his family to Gretna
    Green in the Lake District town of Keswick in July of that year. In an undated
    manuscript letter to Mrs. Coleridge, Robinson expresses regret that she has been
    too ill to visit, but looks forward to visiting Buttermere, a town near Keswick.
    Uncatalogued letter, ALS box 80, Harvard Theatre Collection, Nathan Marsh Pusey
    Library, Harvard University, Cambridge, Massachusetts. The version of this poem
    that was published in the *Morning Post* on October 17, 1800, follows:

    Ode, Inscribed to the Infant Son of S. T. Coleridge, Esq.
    Born Sept. 14, at Keswick, in Cumberland

    SPIRIT OF LIGHT! Whose eye unfolds
        The vast expanse of NATURE's plan!
    And from thy Eastern throne beholds
        The paths of the lorn trav'ller Man!
    To thee I sing! *Spirit of Light!* to thee
    Attune the varying strain of wood-wild harmony.

    I sing to thee! on Skiddaw's heights upborne —
    Painting with Heav'n's own tint the brows of morn!

And from thy eastern throne beholds
  The mazy paths of the lorn traveller — Man!
To thee I sing! *Spirit of Light*, to thee   5
Attune the varying strain of wood-wild minstrelsy!

O Pow'r Creative! — but for Thee
  Eternal Chaos all things would enfold;
And black as Erebus this system be,
  In its ethereal space — benighted — roll'd.   10
But for thy influence, e'en *this day*

I sing to thee! while down the breezy steep
Thy broad wing rushes with impetuous sweep!
While far and wide the roseate ray
Flushes the dewy breast of day: —
Hope fost'ring Day! which Nature bade impart
A Parent's transport to a Parent's heart!
Day! that *first* saw the smiling BABY prest
Close to its beauteous Mother's throbbing breast:
While his clear, laughing eyes foretold
The mind susceptible — the spirit bold; —
The soul enlighten'd — virtues, prone to grace
With Pity's holy tear Man's woe-bewilder'd race!

Ye Mountains! from whose crests sublime
  Imagination might to frenzy turn;
Or to the starry realms impatient climb,
  Scorning this low world's solitary bourne.
Ye Cat'racts! on whose headlong tide
The midnight whirlwinds howling ride; —
Ye silent Lakes! that trembling hail
The cold breath of the morning gale;
And on your lucid mirrors wide display,
In colours bright, in dewy lustre gay,
Fantastic woodlands, while the dappled dawn
Scatters its pearl-drops on the sunny lawn;
And thou, meek Orb, that lift'st thy silver bow
O'er frozen vallies, and o'er hills of snow; —
Ye all shall lend your wonders — all combine
To greet the Babe, with energies divine!
While his rapt soul, Spirit of Light! to thee
Shall raise the magic song of wood-wild harmony!

Yet, who can tell, in this dread scene,
  What sorrows thou art born to know?
Whether thy days content, serene —
  Shall in one even tenour flow;

Would slowly, sadly, pass away;
Nor proudly mark the Mother's tear of joy,
The smile seraphic of the baby boy,
15   The Father's eyes, in fondest transport taught
To beam with tender hope — to speak the enraptur'd thought.

To thee I sing, Spirit of Light! to thee
Attune the strain of wood-wild minstrelsy.
Thou sail'st o'er SKIDDAW's heights sublime,
20   Swift borne upon the wings of joyous time!
The sunny train, with widening sweep,

Or, plung'd in passion's whelming wave —
Despair shall mark an early grave; —
Or false ambition's scorpion brood
Lure thee to tread the fields of blood?
Who knows but fortune's frown may chase
From thy warm heart affection's grace —
And sordid Nature bid thee flee —
From the soft voice of wood-wild harmony!

Ye Rocks! coeval with the birth of TIME, —
   Bold summits, link'd in chains of rosy light!
Ere long your whisp'ring breezes shall invite
   Your NATIVE SON the loftiest paths to climb, —
Where, in majestic pride of solitude,
Silent and grand, the *Hermit* THOUGHT shall trace
Far o'er the wide infinity of space,
The mid-day horrors of the black'ning wood;
The misty glen, the torrent's foamy way,
The parting blush of summer's ling'ring day;
The wintry storm, with rushing clouds combin'd,
To seize the broad wings of th' unfetter'd wind;
Then, INFANT BOY! thy unchain'd tongue
Shall sing the song thy father sung,
And he shall listen, rapture fraught, to THEE,
And bless the dulcet tone of wood-wild harmony!

Then, hand in hand, together ye shall tread,
In converse sweet, the mountain's head,
   Or on the river's will'wy bank,
Gather the wild-flow'rs budding near,
And often, with a pitying tear,
   Bathe their soft leaves, so sweet, so dank,
     Leaves, doom'd to fade,
     In solitude's oblivious shade!
   Emblems of GENIUS, taught to fear,

Rolls blazing down the misty-mantled steep;
And far and wide its rosy ray
Flushes the dewy-silver'd breast of day!
HOPE-FOST'RING DAY! which NATURE bade impart   25
Heav'n's proudest rapture to the parent's heart.
DAY! first ordain'd to see the baby prest
Close to its beauteous mother's throbbing breast;
While instinct, in its laughing eyes, foretold
The mind susceptible — the spirit bold —   30
The lofty soul — the virtues prompt to trace
The wrongs that haunt mankind o'er life's tempestuous space.

———————————

————O! fate severe!————
E'en in the shades of life, the thorn
Of cold neglect — or smiling scorn;
Save when a kindred soul in thee —
Pours the soft plaint of wood-wild harmony!

Then through thy breast thy parent shall diffuse
The mightier magic of his loftier muse!
Then shall each sense, legitimate, expand,
The proud lyre throb beneath thy glowing hand!
While WISDOM, chast'ning pleasure's smile,
Shall listen, and applaud the while;
And REASON (pointing to the sky,
Bright as the morning star, her "*broad, bright eye!*")
Shall ope the page of NATURE's book sublime —
The lore of ev'ry age, the boast of ev'ry clime!

SWEET BOY! accept a STRANGER's song,
    Who joys to sing of thee,
Alone, her forest haunts among,
    The haunts of wood-wild harmony!
A stranger's song, by falsehood undefil'd,
Hymns thee, O! INSPIRATION's darling child!
In thee it hails the GENIUS of thy SIRE
Her sad heart sighing o'er her feeble lyre,
And, whether on the breezy height,
Where Skiddaw greets the dawn of light,
Ere the rude sons of labour homage pay
To summer's flaming eye, or winter's banner grey;
Whether, by bland religion early taught,
To track the devious pilgrimage of thought;
Or, borne on FANCY's variegated wing,
    A willing vot'ry to that shrine,
Where ART and SCIENCE all their flow'rs shall bring
    Thy temples to entwine:

ROMANTIC MOUNTAINS! from whose brows sublime
Imagination might to frenzy turn!
35 Or to the starry worlds in fancy climb,
Scorning this low earth's solitary bourn —
Bold CATARACTS! on whose headlong tide
The midnight whirlwinds howling ride —
Calm-bosom'd LAKES! that trembling hail
40 The cold breath of the morning gale;
And on your lucid mirrors wide display,
In colours rich, in dewy lustre gay,
Mountains and woodlands, as the dappled dawn
Flings its soft pearl-drops on the summer lawn;
45 Or paly moonlight, rising slow,
While o'er the hills the ev'ning zephyrs[1] blow: —
Ye all shall lend your wonders — all combine
To bless the BABY BOY with harmonies divine.

O BABY! when thy unchain'd tongue
50 Shall, lisping, speak thy fond surprise;
When the rich strain thy father sung,
Shall from thy imitative accents rise;
When thro' thy soul rapt Fancy shall diffuse
The mightier magic of his loftier Muse;
55 Thy waken'd spirit, wond'ring, shall behold
Thy native mountains, capp'd with streamy gold!
Thy native Lakes, their cloud-topp'd hills among,
O! hills! made sacred by thy parent's song!
Then shall thy soul, legitimate, expand,
60 And the proud LYRE quick throb at thy command!

Whether LODORE for thee its white wave flings,
The brawling herald of a thousand springs;
Whether smooth BASENTHWAITE, at eve's still hour,
Reflects the young moon's crescent meekly pale,
Or MEDITATION seeks her silent bow'r
Amid the rocks of lonely BORRO-DALE;
Still may THY FAME survive, SWEET BOY, till time
Shall bend to KESWICK's vale thy SKIDDAW's brow sublime.

October 12, 1800

1   Light breezes

And WISDOM, ever watchful, o'er thee smile,
His white locks waving to the blast the while;
And pensive REASON, pointing to the sky,
Bright as the morning star her clear broad eye,
Unfold the page of NATURE's book sublime,   65
The lore of ev'ry age — the boast of ev'ry clime!

SWEET BABY BOY! accept a STRANGER's song;
   An untaught Minstrel joys to sing of thee![1]
And, all alone, her forest haunts among,
   Courts the wild tone of mazy harmony!   70
A STRANGER's song! BABE of the mountain wild,
Greets thee as Inspiration's darling child!
O! may the fine-wrought spirit of thy sire
Awake thy soul and breathe upon thy lyre!
And blest, amid thy mountain haunts sublime,   75
   Be all thy days, thy rosy infant days,
And may the never-tiring steps of time
   Press lightly on with thee o'er life's disastrous maze.

Ye hills, coeval with the birth of time!
   Bleak summits, link'd in chains of rosy light!   80
   O may your wonders many a year invite
Your native son the breezy path to climb;
Where, in majestic pride of solitude,
   Silent and grand, the hermit THOUGHT shall trace,
   Far o'er the wild infinity of space,   85
The sombre horrors of the waving wood;
The misty glen; the river's winding way;
The last deep blush of summer's ling'ring day;
The winter storm, that, roaming unconfin'd,
Sails on the broad wings of the impetuous wind.   90

O! whether on the breezy height
Where SKIDDAW[2] greets the dawn of light,
Ere the rude sons of labour homage pay

---

1   See Coleridge's poem to Robinson, "A Stranger Minstrel," in Appendix B.
2   A mountain north of where Coleridge lived in Keswick.

To Summer's flaming eye or Winter's banner grey;
95 Whether LODORE[1] its silver torrent flings —
The mingling wonders of a thousand springs!
Whether smooth BASENTHWAITE,[2] at EVE's still hour,
    Reflects the young moon's crescent pale;
Or meditation seeks her silent bow'r,
100   Amid the rocks of lonely BORROWDALE.[3]
Still may thy name survive, SWEET BOY! till TIME
Shall bend to KESWICK's vale — thy SKIDDAW's brow sublime!

TO THE POET COLERIDGE[4]

RAPT in the visionary theme!
    SPIRIT DIVINE! with THEE I'll wander,
Where the blue, wavy, lucid stream,
    'Mid forest glooms, shall slow meander!
5 With THEE I'll trace the circling bounds
    Of thy NEW PARADISE extended;
And listen to the varying sounds
    Of winds, and foamy torrents blended.

Now by the source which lab'ring heaves
10   The mystic fountain, bubbling, panting,
While Gossamer its net-work weaves,
    Adown the blue lawn slanting!
I'll mark thy *sunny dome*, and view
Thy *Caves of Ice*, thy fields of dew!
15 Thy ever-blooming mead, whose flow'r
Waves to the cold breath of the moonlight hour!
    Or when the day-star, peering bright

---

1   A waterfall near Keswick.
2   A lake northwest of Keswick.
3   A valley on the opposite side of Derwentwater lake from Keswick.
4   This poem, which is signed SAPPHO in the 1806 *Poetical Works*, is a response to Samuel Taylor Coleridge's "Kubla Khan," which Robinson saw in manuscript. The "sunny dome" and "caves of ice" allude to images in Coleridge's poem, and Robinson's nymph with a dulcimer recalls Coleridge's damsel with a dulcimer.

On the grey wing of parting night;
While more than vegetating pow'r
Throbs grateful to the burning hour,
As summer's whisper'd sighs unfold   20
Her million, million buds of gold;
Then will I climb the breezy bounds,
    Of thy NEW PARADISE extended,
And listen to the distant sounds
    Of winds, and foamy torrents blended!   25

SPIRIT DIVINE! with THEE I'll trace
Imagination's boundless space!
With thee, beneath thy *sunny dome*,
    I'll listen to the minstrel's lay,
    Hymning the gradual close of day;   30
In *Caves of Ice* enchanted roam,
Where on the glitt'ring entrance plays
The moon's-beam with its silv'ry rays;
        Or, when glassy stream,
            That thro' the deep dell flows,   35
        Flashes the noon's hot beam;
            The noon's hot beam, that midway shows
Thy flaming Temple, studded o'er
With all PERUVIA's lustrous store!
There will I trace the circling bounds   40
    Of thy NEW PARADISE extended!
And listen to the awful sounds,
    Of winds, and foamy torrents blended!

And now I'll pause to catch the moan
    Of distant breezes, cavern-pent;   45
Now, ere the twilight tints are flown,
Purpling the landscape, far and wide,
On the dark promontory's side
    I'll gather wild flow'rs, dew besprent,
And weave a crown for THEE,   50
GENIUS OF HEAV'N-TAUGHT POESY!
While, op'ning to my wond'ring eyes,

Thou bidst a new creation rise,
55   I'll raptur'd trace the circling bounds
            Of thy RICH PARADISE extended,
        And listen to the varying sounds
            Of winds, and foaming torrents blended.

        And now, with lofty tones inviting,
60   Thy NYMPH, her dulcimer swift smiting,
        Shall wake me in ecstatic measures!
        Far, far remov'd from mortal pleasures!
            In cadence rich, in cadence strong,
        Proving the wondrous witcheries of song!
65   I hear her voice! thy *sunny dome*,
            Thy *caves of ice*, loud repeat,
            Vibrations, madd'ning sweet,
                Calling the visionary wand'rer home.
        She sings of THEE, O favour'd child
70   *Of Minstrelsy*, SUBLIMELY WILD!
        Of thee, whose soul can feel the tone
        Which gives to airy dreams *a magic* ALL THY OWN!

THE SAVAGE OF AVEYRON[1]

        'TWAS in the mazes of a wood,
        The lonely wood of AVEYRON,
        I heard a melancholy tone: —
            It seem'd to freeze my blood!
5   A torrent near was flowing fast,

---

1   On July 25, 1799, three hunters captured a feral boy who had been previously spot-
    ted living in the woods of Lacaune, in south central France. He became known as
    the "enfant sauvage de l'Aveyron," a misnomer, according to Harlan Lane, since he
    was from Tarn not Aveyron, was between twelve and fifteen years of age, and did
    not deserve to be described as savage, a term usually applied to wild animals, prim-
    itive people, or original man, such as Rousseau's noble savage. See Harlan Lane, *The
    Wild Boy of Aveyron* (Cambridge: Harvard University Press, 1976) 11. Newspaper
    accounts of the boy appeared regularly in England, and Robinson seems to draw
    her details from the *Morning Post*. The poem exhibits the metrical influence of
    Coleridge's "Kubla Khan." "The Savage of Aveyron" was included in the third vol-

And hollow was the midnight blast
As o'er the leafless woods it past,
  While terror-fraught I stood!
O! mazy woods of AVEYRON!
  O! wilds of dreary solitude!   10
  Amid thy thorny alleys rude
I thought myself alone!
  I thought no living thing could be
  So weary of the world as me, —
While on my winding path the pale moon shone.   15

  Sometimes the tone was loud and sad,
And sometimes dulcet, faint, and slow;
And then a tone of frantic woe:
  It almost made me mad.
The burthen was "Alone! alone!"   20
And then the heart did feebly groan; —
Then suddenly a cheerful tone
  Proclaim'd a spirit glad!
O! mazy woods of AVEYRON!
  O! wilds of dreary solitude!   25
  Amid your thorny alleys rude
I wish'd myself — a traveller alone.

---

ume of Robinson's 1801 *Memoirs* with the following preface: "The following
Poem, which by the *date* the Reader will perceive to have been written a very
short time previous to the dissolution of its excellent Author, will require no apol-
ogy for its insertion in this publication. The correctness of the metre, and the plain-
tive harmony which pervades every stanza, clearly evinces the mild philosophy
with which a strong mind can smooth its journey to the grave. This LAST offspring
of Mrs. ROBINSON's Muse was produced at intervals of favourable symptoms of
her fatal malady. The *subject* was *interesting to her heart*. She adopted it with all the
enthusiasm of mournful ANTICIPATION. The story first suggested itself to her after
perusing various accounts of a SAVAGE BOY, lately discovered in the *Forest* of *Avey-
ron*, in the department of *Tarn*, and said to be then existing at PARIS. Frequent
instances of this kind have occurred in the history of Man, and conjecture has
almost uniformly been bewildered respecting the origin of such fugitives. In coun-
tries where BANDITTI have been known to reside, imagination may be allowed the
exercise of its powers; and Reason may ruminate on the possibility, as well as the
probability, of such an interesting history as that of "THE SAVAGE OF AVEYRON"
(*Memoirs* 3:173-74).

"*Alone!*" I heard the wild boy say, —
And swift he climb'd a blasted oak;
30   And there, while morning's herald woke,
        He watch'd the opening day.
Yet dark and sunken was his eye,
Like a lorn maniac's, wild and shy,
And scowling like a winter sky,
35   Without one beaming ray!
Then, mazy woods of AVEYRON!
        Then, wilds of dreary solitude!
        Amid thy thorny alleys rude
I sigh'd to be — a traveller alone.

40   "*Alone, alone!*" I heard him shriek,
'Twas like the shriek of dying man!
And then to mutter he began, —
        But, O! *he could not speak!*
I saw him point to Heav'n, and sigh,
45   The big drop trembl'd in his eye;
And slowly from the yellow sky,
        I saw the pale morn break.
I saw the woods of AVEYRON,
        Their wilds of dreary solitude:
50   I mark'd their thorny alleys rude,
And wish'd to be — a traveller alone!

His hair was long and black, and he
From infancy *alone* had been:
For since his fifth year he had seen,
55   None mark'd his destiny!
No mortal ear had heard his groan,
For him no beam of Hope had shone:
While sad he sigh'd — "*alone, alone!*"
        Beneath the blasted tree.
60   And then, O! woods of AVEYRON,
        O! wilds of dreary solitude,
        Amid your thorny alleys rude
I thought myself a traveller — alone.

And now upon the blasted tree
He carv'd *three* notches, broad and long,   65
And all the while he sang a song —
    Of nature's melody!
And though of words he nothing knew,
And, though his dulcet tones were few,
Across the yielding bark he drew,   70
    Deep sighing, notches THREE.
O! mazy woods of AVEYRON,
    O! wilds of dreary solitude,
    Amid your thorny alleys rude
Upon this BLASTED OAK no sun beam shone!   75

And now he pointed one, two, three;
Again he shriek'd with wild dismay;
And now he paced the thorny way,
    Quitting the blasted tree.
It was a dark December morn,   80
The dew was frozen on the thorn:
But to a wretch so sad, so lorn,
    All days alike would be!
Yet, mazy woods of AVEYRON,
    Yet, wilds of dreary solitude,   85
    Amid your frosty alleys rude
I wish'd to be — a traveller alone.

He follow'd me along the wood
To a small grot[1] his hands had made,
Deep in a black rock's sullen shade,   90
    Beside a tumbling flood.
Upon the earth I saw him spread
Of wither'd leaves a narrow bed,
Yellow as gold, and streak'd with red,
    They look'd like streaks of blood!   95
Pull'd from the woods of AVEYRON,
    And scatter'd o'er the solitude
    By midnight whirlwinds strong and rude,

---

1   A grotto or cave-like space.

To pillow the scorch'd brain that throbb'd alone.

100   Wild berries were his winter food,
With them his sallow lip was dy'd;
On chestnuts wild he fed beside,
    Steep'd in the foamy flood.
Chequer'd with scars his breast was seen,
105 Wounds streaming fresh with anguish keen,
And marks where other wounds had been
    Torn by the brambles rude.
Such was the boy of AVEYRON,
    The tenant of that solitude,
110   Where still, by misery unsubdued,
He wander'd *nine long winters*, all alone.

        Before the step of his rude throne,
The *squirrel* sported, tame and gay;
The *dormouse* slept its life away,
115   Nor heard his midnight groan.
About his form a garb he wore,
Ragged it was, and mark'd with gore,
And yet, where'er 'twas folded o'er,
    Full many a spangle shone!
120 Like little stars, O! AVEYRON,
    They gleam'd amid thy solitude;
    Or like, along thy alleys rude,
The summer dew-drops sparkling in the sun.

        It once had been a lady's vest,
125 White as the whitest mountain's snow,
Till ruffian hands had taught to flow
    The fountain of her breast!
Remembrance bade the WILD BOY trace
Her beauteous form, her angel face,
130 Her eye that beam'd with Heavenly grace,
    Her fainting voice that blest, —
When in the woods of AVEYRON,
    Deep in their deepest solitude,
    Three barb'rous ruffians shed her blood,

And mock'd, with cruel taunts, her dying groan.   135

   Remembrance trac'd the summer bright,
When all the trees were fresh and green,
When lost, the alleys long between,
   The lady past the night:
She past the night, bewilder'd wild,   140
She past it with her fearless child,
Who raised his little arms, and smil'd
   To see the morning light.
While in the woods of AVEYRON,
   Beneath the broad oak's canopy,   145
   She mark'd aghast the RUFFIANS THREE,
Waiting to seize the traveller alone!

   Beneath the broad oak's canopy
The lovely lady's bones were laid;
But since that hour no breeze has play'd   150
   About the blasted tree!
The leaves all wither'd ere the sun
His next day's rapid course had run,
And ere the summer day was done
   It winter seem'd to be: 155
And still: O! woods of AVEYRON,
   Amid thy dreary solitude
   The oak a sapless trunk has stood,
To mark the spot where MURDER foul was done!

   From HER the WILD BOY learn'd "ALONE,"   160
She tried to say, *my babe will die!*
But angels caught her parting sigh,
   The BABE her *dying tone.*
And from that hour the BOY has been
Lord of the solitary scene,   165
Wand'ring the dreary shades between,
   Making his dismal moan!
Till, mazy woods of AVEYRON,
   Dark wilds of dreary solitude,
   Amid your thorny alleys rude   170

I thought myself alone.
　And could a wretch more wretched be,
　More wild, or fancy-fraught than he,
Whose melancholy tale would pierce AN HEART
　OF STONE.

THE BIRTH-DAY[1]

HERE bounds the gaudy gilded chair,
　Bedeck'd with fringe, and tassels gay;
The melancholy Mourner there
　Pursues her sad and painful way.

5　Here, guarded by a motley train,
　The pamper'd Countess glares along;
There, wrung by poverty and pain,
　Pale Mis'ry mingles with the throng.

Here, as the blazon'd[2] chariot rolls,
10　And prancing horses scare the crowd,
Great names, adorning little souls,
　Announce the empty, vain, and proud.

Here four tall lacquies slow precede
　A painted dame, in rich array;
15　There the sad shiv'ring child of need
　Steals barefoot o'er the flinty way.

"Room, room! stand back!" they loudly cry,
　The wretched poor are driv'n around

1　The birthday celebration is that of Queen Charlotte. A version of this poem was first published in the *Morning Post* of January 21, 1795 (with the title "St. James's Street, on the Eighteenth of January, 1795") as the work of "Portia," and again in that same newspaper on January 19, 1798 (again entitled "St. James's Street," but this time as the work of "T.B."). The *Morning Post* regularly carried accounts of the festivities attending royal birthdays, and, especially, of the extravagant costumes of the members of the royal retinue.
2　Painted with a heraldic device.

On ev'ry side, they scatter'd fly,
　　And shrink before the threat'ning sound.　　20

Here, amidst jewels, feathers, flow'rs,
　　The senseless Duchess sits demure;
Heedless of all the anguish'd hours
　　The sons of modest worth endure.

All silver'd, and embroider'd o'er,　　25
　　She neither knows nor pities pain;
The Beggar freezing at her door
　　She overlooks with nice disdain.

The wretch whom poverty subdues
　　Scarce dares to raise his tearful eye;　　30
Or if by chance the throng he views,
　　His loudest murmur is a sigh!

The poor wan mother, at whose breast
　　The pining infant craves relief,
In one thin tatter'd garment drest,　　35
　　Creeps forth to pour the plaint of grief.

But ah! how little heeded here
　　The fault'ring tongue reveals its woe;
For high-born fools, with frown austere,
　　Contemn the pangs they never know.　　40

"Take physic,[1] Pomp!" let Reason say,
　　"What can avail thy trappings rare?
The tomb shall close thy glitt'ring day,
　　The BEGGAR prove thy equal there!"

1　Medical treatment, more particularly a cathartic or purge. Mental, moral, or spiritu-
　al remedy.

THE SUMMER DAY

Ah! who beneath the burning ray
Can bear the long, long summer's day?
Who, 'mid the dust and scorching sun,
Content, his daily race will run?
5   And yet, when winter's icy breath
Flies o'er the white and frozen heath,
The wand'rer shudders to behold
The dreary scene, and shrinks with cold.

When drifted snow across the plain
10   Spreads desolation's chill domain,
The Trav'ller, sighing, seems to say,
"Ah! wou'd it were a SUMMER'S DAY!"
Yet when the sun flames far and wide,
He hastens to the wood's dark side,
15   And, shelter'd by embow'ring trees,
Sighs for the fresh and cooling breeze!

When dusty roads impede his way,
And all around the fervid ray
Scorches the dry and yellow heath,
20   Unvisited by Zephyr's breath:
Or, when the torrent wildly pours,
When the fierce blast impetuous roars,
Man, still on changes fondly bent,
Still murmurs, sad and discontent!

THE WINTRY DAY[1]

Is it in mansions rich and gay,
On downy beds, or couches warm,
That Nature owns the wintry day,

---

1   This poem exists in at least three versions found in the 1806 edition (printed here),
the *Morning Post* of January 4, 1800, and *The Wild Wreath* (1804). It was also reprint-
ed in the captions to Maria Cosway's illustrations of the poem. Caroline Watson's

And shrinks to hear the howling storm?
  Ah! No!   5

'Tis on the bleak and barren heath,
  Where Mis'ry feels the ice of death,
As to the dark and freezing grave
  Her children, not a friend to save,
    Unheeded go!   10

Is it in chambers silken drest,
  At tables which profusions heap,
Is it on pillows soft to rest,
  In dreams of long and balmy sleep?
    Ah! No!   15

'Tis in the rushy hut obscure,
  Where Poverty's low sons endure,
And, scarcely daring to repine,
  On a straw pallet, mute, recline,
    O'erwhelm'd with woe!   20

Is it to flaunt in warm attire,

---

engravings of these drawings, reprinted in this edition, were published by Rudolph Ackermann in 1804, preceded by an introduction which states: "Mrs. Robinson's poetry is before the public, and the sanction given to her genius in the rapid sale of the late publication of her works, is a decided proof of the estimation in which her talents are held. Mrs. Cosway's designs, it must be admitted, are sometimes eccentric, but it is the eccentricity of *genius*, and we have seen instances where she has '*snatch'd a grace beyond the reach of art.*' That extravagance carried to excess is an error, cannot be denied; but we prefer the artist who rather overcharges his figure, to him who touches the canvas with a timid feeble pencil, and leaves the imagination of the spectator to supply what he cannot or dares not express." The introduction goes on to provide a brief gloss on each engraving, explaining that in Number 10 (here Figure 14) an allegorical figure of Genius contemplates the base of a column "on which we may suppose there will be inscribed a false panegyric upon some opulent but despicable character." Number 12 (here Figure 16) portrays "*Hope* recumbent, leaning on her broken anchor, totally exhausted, and on the point of expiring; *Virtue*, kneeling on one knee, and hiding her face with her clasped hands, deploring her fate, while *Pride*, represented by the emblem of a peacock, is proudly exalting itself above her, and rendered resplendent by its gaudy and glittering plumage, rising still higher, and screaming out its triumphant song in discordant and unharmonious notes." *The Winter Day* (London: R. Ackermann's Repository of Arts), 1804.

To laugh, to feast, and dance, and sing;
To crowd around the blazing fire,
    And make the roof with revels ring?
        Ah! No!

25

'Tis on the prison's flinty floor,
    'Tis where the deaf'ning whirlwinds roar;
'Tis when the Sea-boy, on the mast,
    Hears the wave bounding to the blast,
        And looks below!

30

'Tis in a cheerless naked room,
    Where Mis'ry's victims wait their doom,
Where a fond mother famish'd dies,
    While forth a frantic father flies,
        Man's desp'rate foe!

35

Is it where gamesters thronging round,
    Their shining heaps of wealth display?
Where fashion's giddy tribes are found,
    Sporting their senseless hours away?
        Ah! No!

40

'Tis in the silent spot obscure,
    Where, forc'd all sorrows to endure,
Pale Genius learns — oh! lesson sad!
    To court the vain, and on the bad
        False praise bestow!

45

Where the neglected Hero sighs,
    Where Hope, exhausted, silent dies,
Where Virtue starves, by Pride oppress'd,
    'Till ev'ry stream that warms the breast
        Forbears to flow!

50

ON LEAVING THE COUNTRY FOR THE WINTER SEASON, 1799[1]

YE leafless woods, ye hedge-rows bare,
    Farewel! awhile farewel!
Now busy scenes, my thoughts must share
    Scenes of low guile,
Where shrewd Hypocrisy shall smile,   5
    And empty Folly dwell!

Ye rising floods, ye mountains bleak,
    Farewel! awhile farewel!
The din of mingling tones I seek;
    The midnight gloom   10
I change, for the light taper'd room
    Where sounds unmeaning swell.

Ye meadows wide, that skirt the stream,
    Farewel, awhile farewel!
Ye green banks, where the summer beam,   15
    So rich and gay,
Among the fragrant buds would play
    Adown the silent dell.

Now dark and dreary hours I see,
    I hear the deaf'ning noise;   20
The troublous scene returns to me,
    Who sick'ning sigh
For the soft breeze, and summer sky,
    With all their glowing joys!

Yet, yet, where'er my course I bend,   25
    May ev'ry hour be blest
With the sweet converse of A FRIEND!
    The smile that shows

---

1   The winter social season was timed to coincide with the opening of Parliament.
The nobility and gentry began coming to London sometime around Christmas.

A calm contempt for human woes:

30   Then, Splendour take the rest!

OBERON'S INVITATION TO TITANIA[1]

OH! come, my pretty love! and we
    Will climb the dewy hill together;
An acorn shall our goblet be,
    A ROSE our couch in sunny weather;
5   Amidst its fragrant leaves we'll lie,
    List'ning the zephyrs passing by!

Come, come, my pretty love, and sip
    The dew that from each herb is flowing;
And let the insects round thy lip
10   With envy hover while 'tis glowing!
Beneath a spring-flow'r's bell we'll sing,
While southern gales shall fragrance bring.

Then haste, my pretty queen, and dress
    Thy snowy breast with pearls of morning;
15 Thy smiles shall charm, thy voice shall bless,
    Thy beauty ev'ry grace adorning!
By dawn-light o'er the daisied ground
We'll sport, while fairies gambol round.

Ah! why delay, my pretty love!
20   The sun is sinking in the ocean,
    The clear green waters slowly move;

---

1   Oberon and Titania are the names of Shakespeare's fairy king and queen in *A Mid-summer Night's Dream*. Robinson often used the name Oberon as a pseudonym under which she published poems in newspapers. "Oberon's Invitation to Titania" was published under the heading "Fairy Rhymes," and followed by "Titania's Invitation to Oberon" in Robinson's 1806 *Poetical Works*. These poems are printed under the heading of "Fairy Visions" in the 1804 *Wild Wreath*, an anthology edited by Robinson's daughter, Maria Elizabeth Robinson. The *Wild Wreath* version has numerous alterations.

The weary zephyrs scarce have motion!
Soon, soon the gloomy shades of night
Will want those eyes of starry light.

I've made thee, love, a canopy   25
    Of tulips tinted rich — a cluster
Of golden cups is waving nigh,
    Bath'd in the moon-beams' dewy lustre!
The softest turf shall be our floor,
    With twinkling dew-drops spangled o'er!   30

Thy curtains are of insect's wings,
    With feather-grass festoon'd and corded;
And, for their tassels, zephyr brings
    The thistle's down, in winter hoarded.
Thy pillow is of swan-down fair,   35
    "Which floats upon the summer air."

Now, OBERON, thy love attends,
    His heart with doubt and terror swelling;
While low his brow with sorrow bends,
    To mark of LOVE the *lonely dwelling!*   40
Oh! come! or ere night's shadows fly,
    The chilling breeze shall *bid me* DIE!

TITANIA'S ANSWER TO OBERON

IN vain, for me, thy gifts display'd,
    Meet the red eye of smiling morning;
I still will court the lonely shade,
    Alike thy vows and splendours scorning!
Inconstant! ev'ry fairy knows   5
Thy love is like the gale that blows!

Thy oaths are like the summer flow'rs,
    No sooner made than quickly faded;

Thy home, like April's transient show'rs,
10   Now gay — and now by storms invaded!
Thy song is like the vagrant bird,
That sweet in ev'ry clime is heard!

Thy couch, so fragrant, rich, and gay,
     Will fade ere love has learnt to sicken;
15 And thou wilt wander far away,
     While hope declines, by falsehood stricken:
And o'er the moonlight dewy space
A thousand rivals fear shall trace!

False lover! to the shaggy steep
20   Titania flies, from thee and sorrow!
There, while, beneath, the waters sleep,
     From night a sable veil I'll borrow,
And on a thorny pillow rest,
Beside the bird of pity's nest.

25 Yes, the lorn nightingale shall be
     My only friend in hopeless anguish;
And to the star of ev'ning we
     Will tell, how faithful love can languish!
The owl shall watch us all night long,
30 Hooting the dreary cliffs among!

Go! vagrant lover! 'mid the throngs
     Of fairy rovers seek a dwelling;
While I in silence mourn my wrongs,
     My sighs upon the cold breeze swelling:
35 Go! sport in wanton, idle play,
While moonlight scatters mimic day.

Go, where the sun its splendour throws
     Upon the crest of yon tall mountain —
Go, drink oblivion to love's woes,
40   Where ev'ning gilds the lucid fountain:
Go, where inconstant zephyrs flee —
But think, ah! think, no more of me!

JASPER[1]

I

THE night was long, 'twas winter time,
   The moon shone pale and clearly;
The woods were bare, the nipping air
Across the heath, as cold as death,
   Blew shrilly and severely.   5

II

And awful was the midnight scene!
   The silent river flowing,
The dappled sky, the screech-owl's cry,
The blackning tow'r, the haunted bow'r,
   Where pois'nous weeds were growing!   10

III

With footsteps quick, and fev'rish heart,
   One tatter'd garment wearing,
Poor JASPER, sad, alone, and MAD,
Now chaunted wild, and now he smil'd,
   With eyes wide fix'd and glaring.   15

IV

His cheek was wan, his lip was blue,
   His head was bare and shaggy;
His limbs were torn by many a thorn;
For he had pac'd the pathless waste,
   And climb'd the steep rock craggy.   20

V

An iron window in the tow'r
   Slow creek'd as it was swinging;
A gibbet[2] stood beside the wood,

---

1   An unfinished novel by Robinson, published as part of the 1801 *Memoirs*, bears this
same title.
2   A gallows or an upright post with projecting arm from which the bodies of crimi-
nals were hung.

The blast did blow it to and fro,
25   The rusty chains were ringing.

VI

His voice was hollow as the tone
        Of cavern'd winds, and mournful;
No tears could flow, to calm his woe;
Yet on his face sat manly grace,
30   And grief, sublimely scornful!

VII

Twelve freezing nights poor JASPER's breast
        Had brav'd the tempests yelling;
For mis'ry keen *his* lot had been
Since he had left, of sense bereft,
35   A tyrant father's dwelling.

VIII

That father, who with lordly pride,
        Saw him from MARY sever;
Saw her fair cheek in silence speak,
Her eyes blue light, so heav'nly bright,
40   Grow dim, and fade for ever!

IX

"How hot yon sun begins to shine!"
The maniac cried, loud laughing:
"I feel the pain that burns my brain;
Thy sulphur beam bids ocean steam,
45   Where all the fiends are quaffing.

X

Soft! soft! the dew begins to rise,
        I'll drink it while 'tis flowing;
Down ev'ry tree the bright rills[1] see,
Quick let me sip, they'll cool my lip,
50   For now my blood is glowing.

---

1   Small streams

XI

Hark! the she-wolf howling by!
   Poor JASPER smiles to hear thee;
For he can hide by the hedge-row's side,
While storms shall sweep the mountain's steep;
   Then, she-wolf, can he fear thee?   55

XII

Pale moon! thou spectre of the sky![1]
   I see thy white shroud waving:
And now behold thy bosom cold —
Oh! mem'ry sad, it made me mad!
   Then wherefore mock my raving?   60

XIII

Yes! on my MARY's bosom cold
   Death laid his bony fingers.
Hark! how the wave begins to lave[2]
The rocky shore! — I hear it roar —
   The whirling pilot lingers!   65

XIV

Oh! bear me, bear me o'er the main!
   See the white sails are flying:
Yon glitt'ring star shall be my car,
And by my side shall MARY glide,
   Mild as the south wind sighing.   70

XV

My bare-foot way is mark'd with blood —
   Well — what care I for sorrow?
The sun shall rise to cheer the skies,
The wintry day shall pass away,
   And summer smile to-morrow!   75

---

1 Coleridge particularly admired this line, singling it out in a letter to Robert
   Southey, then editor of the *Annual Anthology.* See Introduction, pp. 57-58. "Jasper"
   and Robinson's "Haunted Beach" (p. 217) were published in the 1800 *Annual*
   Anthology.
2 Wash.

XVI

The frosted heath is wide and drear,
    And rugged is my pillow;
Soon shall I sleep beneath the deep —
How calm to me that sleep will be,
    Rock'd by the bounding billow!

80

XVII

The village clock strikes mournfully,
    It is my death-bell tolling;
But though yon cloud begins to shroud
The gliding moon, the day-stream soon
    Shall down yon steep come rolling.

85

XVIII

Roll down yon steep, broad flood of light!
    Drive hence that spectre! JASPER
Remembers now, her snowy brow —
'Tis MARY! see — she beckons me —
    O! let me, let me clasp her!

90

XIX

She fades away! I feel her not, —
    She's gone! — 'tis dark and dreary:
The drizzling rain now chills my brain,
The bell, for me, tolls mournfully!
    Come, death! for I am weary.

95

XX

I'll steal beneath yon haunted tow'r,
    And wait the day-star's coming;
The bat shall flee at sight of me,
The ivy'd wall shall be my pall —
    My priest, the night-fly humming.

100

XXI

Yon spectre's iron shroud I'll steal,
    With frozen drops bespangled!

The night-shade too, besprent with dew,
With many a flow'r of healing pow'r,
   Shall cool my bare-feet mangled.   105

XXII
Is it the storm that JASPER feels!
   Ah, no! 'tis passion blighted!
The owlet's shriek makes white my cheek,
The dark toads stray across my way,
   And sorely am I frighted.   110

XXIII
Amid the broom my bed I'll make,
   Dry fern shall be my pillow;
And, MARY, dear! wert thou but here,
Blest should I be, sweet maid, with thee,
   To weave a crown of willow.   115

XXIV
The church-yard path is wet with dew,
   Hence, ravens! for I fear ye!
Fall, gentle show'rs, revive the flow'rs
That feebly wave on MARY's grave;
   But whisper — she will hear you!   120

XXV
Beneath the yew-tree's shadow long,
   I'll hide me and be wary;
But I shall weep when others sleep!
Is it the dove that calls its love?
   No! 'tis the voice of MARY!   125

XXVI
How merrily the lark is heard!
   The ruddy dawn advancing:
JASPER is gay! his wedding-day
To-morrow's sun shall see begun,
   With music and with dancing!   130

XXVII

How sullen moans the midnight main![1]
How wide the dim scene stretches!
The moony light all silver white,
Across the wave, illumes the grave
135   Of heav'n-deserted wretches!

XXVIII

The dead-lights[2] gleam, the signal sounds!
Poor bark! the storm will beat thee!
What spectre stands upon the sands?
'Tis MARY dear! Oh! do not fear —
140   Thy JASPER flies to meet thee!"

XXIX

Now to the silent river's side
Poor JASPER rush'd unwary;
With frantic haste the green bank pac'd,
Plung'd in the wave — no friend to save,
145   And, sinking, call'd — ON MARY!

LONDON'S SUMMER MORNING[3]

WHO has not wak'd to list the busy sounds
Of summer's morning, in the sultry smoke
Of noisy London? On the pavement hot
The sooty chimney-boy, with dingy face
5   And tatter'd covering, shrilly bawls his trade,
Rousing the sleepy housemaid. At the door
The milk-pail rattles, and the tinkling bell
Proclaims the dustman's office;[4] while the street
Is lost in clouds impervious. Now begins
10   The din of hackney-coaches, waggons, carts;

---

1   An expanse of water.
2   A deadlight is a luminous appearance seen over dead bodies, for example, in grave-yards.
3   In its subject and details, this poem recalls Jonathan Swift's "A Description of the Morning" (1709).
4   Someone who collects and carts away dust and refuse.

While tinmen's shops, and noisy trunk-makers,
Knife-grinders, coopers, squeaking cork-cutters,
Fruit-barrows, and the hunger-giving cries
Of vegetable venders, fill the air.
Now ev'ry shop displays its varied trade,   15
And the fresh-sprinkled pavement cools the feet
Of early walkers. At the private door
The ruddy housemaid twirls the busy mop,
Annoying the smart 'prentice, or neat girl,
Tripping with band-box[1] lightly. Now the sun   20
Darts burning splendour on the glitt'ring pane,
Save where the canvas awning throws a shade
On the gay merchandize. Now, spruce and trim,
In shops (where beauty smiles with industry,)
Sits the smart damsel; while the passenger   25
Peeps thro' the window, watching ev'ry charm.
Now pastry dainties catch the eye minute
Of humming insects, while the limy snare[2]
Waits to enthral them. Now the lamp-lighter
Mounts the tall ladder, nimbly vent'rous,   30
To trim the half-fill'd lamp; while at his feet
The pot-boy[3] yells discordant! All along
The sultry pavement, the old-clothes man cries[4]
In tone monotonous, and side-long views
The area for his traffic: now the bag   35
Is slily open'd, and the half-worn suit
(Sometimes the pilfer'd treasure of the base
Domestic spoiler), for one half its worth,
Sinks in the green abyss. The porter now
Bears his huge load along the burning way;   40
And the poor poet wakes from busy dreams,
To paint the summer morning.

---

1 A box of cardboard or thin chip and covered with paper; it was used to hold collars, caps, hats, and millinery.
2 Probably a reference to bird-lime, a sticky substance spread upon twigs to catch birds. Perhaps here a more general reference to a substance used to catch insects.
3 Boy employed at tavern to carry beer to outside customers.
4 There was an active trade in second-hand clothes in the London of Robinson's time.

THE POET'S GARRET

COME, sportive fancy! come with me, and trace
The poet's attic home! the lofty seat
Of the heav'n-tutor'd nine! the airy throne
Of bold imagination, rapture fraught
Above the herds of mortals. All around
A solemn stillness seems to guard the scene,
Nursing the brood of thought — a thriving brood
In the rich mazes of the cultur'd brain.
Upon thy altar, an old worm-eat board,
The pannel of a broken door, or lid
Of a strong coffer, plac'd on three-legg'd stool,
Stand quires of paper, white and beautiful!
Paper, by destiny ordain'd to be
Scrawl'd o'er and blotted; dash'd, and scratch'd, and torn;
Or mark'd with lines severe, or scatter'd wide
In rage impetuous! Sonnet, song, and ode,
Satire, and epigram, and smart charade;
Neat paragraph, or legendary tale,
Of short and simple metre, each by turns
Will there delight the reader.
                  On the bed
Lies an old rusty[1] suit of "solemn black," —
Brush'd thread-bare, and, with brown, unglossy hue,
Grown somewhat ancient. On the floor is seen
A pair of silken hose, whose footing bad
Shews they are trav'llers, but who still bear
Marks somewhat *holy*. At the scanty fire
A chop turns round, by packthread strongly held;
And on the blacken'd bar a vessel shines
Of batter'd pewter, just half fill'd, and warm,
With Whitbread's bev'rage pure.[2] The kitten purs,
Anticipating dinner; while the wind
Whistles thro' broken panes, and drifted snow
Carpets the parapet with spotless garb,

---

1   Faded or shabby.
2   Beer from the brewery of Samuel Whitbread.

Of vestal[1] coldness. Now the sullen hour   35
(The fifth hour after noon) with dusky hand
Closes the lids of day. The farthing light[2]
Gleams thro' the cobwebb'd chamber, and the bard
Concludes his pen's hard labour. Now he eats
With appetite voracious! nothing sad   40
That he with costly plate, and napkins fine,
Nor china rich, nor fork of silver, greets
His eye or palate. On his lyric board
A sheet of paper serves for table-cloth;
An heap of salt is serv'd, — oh! heav'nly treat!   45
An ode Pindaric![3] while his tuneful puss
Scratches his slipper for her fragment sweet,
And sings her love-song soft, yet mournfully.
Mocking the pillar Doric, or the roof
Of architecture Gothic, all around   50
The well-known ballads flit, of Grub-street fame![4]
The casement, broke, gives breath celestial
To the long dying-speech; or gently fans
The love-inflaming sonnet. All around
Small scraps of paper lie, torn vestiges   55
Of an unquiet fancy. Here a page
Of flights poetic — there a dedication —
A list of dramatis personae, bold,
Of heroes yet unborn, and lofty dames
Of perishable compound, light as fair,   60
But sentenc'd to oblivion!
                          On a shelf,
(Yclept a mantle-piece) a phial stands,[5]
Half fill'd with potent spirits! — spirits strong,

---

1   Pure or chaste; usually applied to virginal women.
2   A coin worth a quarter of a penny. A farthing light is presumably a very small
    amount of light.
3   An ode in the manner of Pindar, the Greek lyric poet.
4   Grub-street was the name of a street in London (now known as Milton Street)
    inhabited by writers of histories, dictionaries, and occasional poetry. The name
    came to be synonymous with hack writers.
5   Yclept: called. A literary archaism in Robinson's time. Phial: a vessel for holding liq-
    uid, especially medicine.

65 Which sometimes haunt the poet's restless brain,
And fill his mind with fancies whimsical.
Poor poet! happy art thou, thus remov'd
From pride and folly! for in thy domain
Thou can'st command thy subjects; fill thy lines;
70 Wield th'all-conqu'ring weapon heav'n bestows
On the grey goose's wing![1] which, tow'ring high,
Bears thy sick fancy to immortal fame!

JANUARY, 1795[2]

I

PAVEMENT slip'ry; People sneezing;
Lords in ermine, beggars freezing;
Nobles, scarce the Wretched heeding;
Gallant Soldiers — fighting! — bleeding!

II

5 Lofty Mansions, warm and spacious;
Courtiers, cringing and voracious:
Titled Gluttons, dainties carving;
Genius, in a garret, starving!

III

Wives, who laugh at passive Spouses;
10 Theatres, and Meeting-houses;
Balls, where simpring Misses languish;
Hospitals, and groans of anguish.

IV

Arts and Sciences bewailing;
Commerce drooping, Credit failing!

---

1 Quill pens were made from goose feathers.
2 The poem printed here is from the *Morning Post*, January 29, 1795, where it appeared as the work of "Portia." In the 1806 version, the stanzas are not numbered, some lines are rearranged, and, in the third line, misers, rather than nobles, are heedless of the wretched (a somewhat softening alteration).

Placemen,[1] mocking subjects loyal;   15
Separations; Weddings Royal!

V

Authors, who can't earn a dinner;
Many a subtle rogue, a winner!
Fugitives, for shelter seeking;
Misers hoarding, Tradesmen breaking!   20

VI

Ladies gambling, night and morning;
Fools, the works of Genius scorning!
Ancient Dames for Girls mistaken,
Youthful Damsels — quite forsaken!

VII

Some in luxury delighting;   25
More in talking than in fighting;
Lovers old, and Beaux decrepid;
Lordlings, empty and insipid.

VIII

Poets, Painters, and Musicians;
Lawyers, Doctors, Politicians;   30
Pamphlets, Newspapers, and Odes,
Seeking Fame, by diff'rent roads.

IX

Taste and Talents quite deserted;
All the laws of Truth perverted;
Arrogance o'er Merit soaring!   35
Merit, silently deploring!

X

Gallant Souls with empty purses;
Gen'rals, only fit for Nurses!

---

1   Office holders, or those who held an appointment in the service of a sovereign. The
term has derogatory connotations.

Schoolboys, smit with Martial spirit,
40   Taking place of vet'ran merit!

XI

Honest men, who can't get place;
Knaves, who shew unblushing faces;
Ruin hasten'd. Peace retarded!
Candour spurn'd, and Art rewarded!

IMPROMPTU

SENT TO A FRIEND WHO HAD LEFT HIS GLOVES, BY MISTAKE,
AT THE AUTHOR'S HOUSE ON THE PRECEDING EVENING

YOUR gloves I send,
My worthy friend,
With no *gallant* intent:
With gauntlet I
5   No knight defy;
So take it as 'tis meant.

In merry mood,
'Tis understood,
That frolic *fancy* loves,
10   When eye-lids close
In sweet repose,
To *steal* a pair of gloves.

But neither here
(I vow and swear)
15   My sportive measures rule;
Too *weak* to wield
The daring shield,
Too *old* to play the fool.

Tho' dark their hue,
20   Their semblance true,

Like fortune's frowns appear;
   By absence torn,
   Like me, they mourn
For *him* — who thought them *dear.*

   Then take the pair,   25
   And let them share
The warmth that from your breast
   On all bestows,
   The balm of woes,
Which gives to sorrow — rest!   30

   These truant twins,
   To mend their sins,
Shall wait your kind command;
   And ev'ry day,
   Or sad, or gay,   35
Shall — take you by the hand.

   In solitude,
   'Mid sorrows rude,
Or passion's wildest storm,
   Where'er you go,   40
   Thro' weal or woe,
You'll find them ever warm.

   So fare you well;
   This pair shall tell,
And tell with lungs of leather,   45
   That friends who part,
   Must know the smart
They never feel *together.*

MODERN MALE FASHIONS[1]

CROPS,[2] like *Hedge hogs*, high-crown'd Hats,
    Whiskers like *Jew* Moses;
Collars padded, thick Cravats,
    And Cheeks as red as roses.

5   Faces painted deepest brown,
    Waistcoats strip'd and gaudy;
Sleeves, thrice doubled, thick with down,
    And Straps, to brace the body!

Short Great Coats, that reach the knees,
10   Boots like French *Postillion*;[3]
Meant the *lofty race* to please,
    But laugh'd at by the million.

Square to'd Shoes, with silken Strings;
    Pantaloons, tight fitting;
15   Fingers, deck'd with golden Rings,
    And Small-cloaths,[4] made of Knitting.

Bludgeons,[5] like a Pilgrim's Staff,
    Or Canes, as slight as Osiers;[6]
Doubled Hose, to shew THE CALF,
20   *And swell* the *bills* of HOSIERS!

Curricles,[7] so low that they
    Along the earth are dragging;

---

1   The version of the poem printed here was published in the *Morning Post* on January 3, 1800, as the work of "Tabitha Bramble." The 1806 version of the poem was entitled "Male Fashions for 1799" and is lacking stanzas 5, 8, and 9.
2   A style of wearing the hair cut conspicuously short.
3   One who rides the near horse of the horses pulling a carriage.
4   Small-clothes: short trousers fastened below the knee.
5   Short, stout sticks or clubs.
6   A species of willow with tough pliant branches used for basket work.
7   Light, two-wheeled carriages usually drawn by two horses.

Hacks, that weary half the day,
    In *Rotten Row* are fagging![1]

Bull-dogs fierce, and *Boxers* bold,   25
    In their train attending;
Beauty, which is bought with *Gold*,
    And *Flatt'rers, vice* commending!

Married Women, who have seen
    The fiat of the *Commons*;[2]   30
Tradesmen, with terrific mien,
    And Bailiffs, with a Summons!

TAILORS, with their Bills unpaid;
    Parasites, high feeding;
Letters, from a Chamber maid,   35
    And *Billets*, not worth reading!

Perfumes; *Wedding rings*, to shew
    Many a LADY's favour, —
Bought by ev'ry vaunting *Beau*,
    With mischievous endeavour!   40

Such is giddy *Fashion's* SON,
    Such a *modern* LOVER!
Oh! wou'd their *reign* had ne'er begun,
    And *may it* SOON BE OVER!!

---

1 Rotten Row is a road in Hyde Park that was much used as a fashionable resort for
   horse or carriage exercise. To fag is to droop or decline, or to do something that
   wearies one.
2 Doctors' Commons: buildings that housed the Doctors of Civil Law. Divorce suits,
   which were often based on accusations of adultery, were deliberated there.

MODERN FEMALE FASHIONS[1]

A FORM, as lank as taper[2] fine,
   A head like half pint bason;[3]
Where golden cords and band entwine,
   As rich as fleece of JASON![4]

5   A pair of shoulders, strong and wide,
   Breast-works of size resisting;
Bare arms, long dangling by the side,
   And shoes, of ragged listing.[5]

Cravats, like towels thick and broad,
10   Long tippets[6] made of bear skin;
Muffs, that a RUSSIAN might applaud,
   And *rouge* to tint a fair skin.

Long petticoats, to hide the feet,
   Silk hose, with clocks[7] of scarlet;
15   A load of perfumes, sick'ning sweet,
   Made by *Parisian* VARLET.

A bowl of straw to deck the head,
   Like porringer, unmeaning;
A bunch of *poppies*, flaming red,
20   With tawdry ribbands, streaming.

A bush of hair, the brow to shade,
   Sometimes the eye to cover;

---

1   The version of the poem reprinted here was published in the *Morning Post*, December 28, 1799, and attributed to "Tabitha Bramble." An 1806 version, entitled "Female Fashions for 1799," is lacking stanza 7.
2   A long wick coated with wax.
3   Basin.
4   In classical mythology, Jason had to retrieve a golden fleece, guarded by a dragon, in order to become ruler of Iolcos, a position that had been usurped by his uncle Pelias.
5   Fabric made from list, the selvage or edge of a piece of cloth.
6   A cape or cloak, often with hanging ends.
7   Ornamental patterns worked on the side of a stocking in silk thread.

A necklace, such as is display'd
  By OTAHEITIAN[1] lover!

Long chains of gold about the neck,   25
  Like a *Sultana* shining;
Bracelets, the snowy arms to deck,
  And cords the body twining.

Bare ears on either side the head,
  Like wood-wild savage SATYR![2]   30
Tinted with deep vermillion red,
  To mock the flush of nature.

Red elbows, gauzy gloves, that add
  An icy cov'ring merely;
A wadded coat, the shape to pad,   35
  Like *Dutch woman* — or nearly.

Such is CAPRICE! but, LOVELY KIND,
  Oh! let each *mental* feature
Proclaim, the labours of the MIND,
  And leave your *charms* to NATURE!   40

---

1   Tahitian.
2   A woodland god or demon, part human and part beast, associated with lust.

Is it to lavish fortune's store,
In vain fantastic empty joys?
To scatter round the glit'ring ore,
And worship folly's gilded toys?

                              Ah! no!

Figure 13. Mezzotint engraving after Maria Cosway, illustration No. 9 for "The Wintry Day,"
1804. (By courtesy of the Special Collections Department, University of Virginia Library.)

Appendix A: Three letters of Mary Robinson

1. To John Taylor,[1]

Salt Hill, October 5, 1794

I was really happy to receive your letter. Your silence gave me no small degree of uneasiness, and I began to think some *demon* had broken the links of that chain, which I trust has united us in *friendship* for ever. Life is such a scene of trouble and disappointment that the sensible mind can ill endure the loss of any consolation that renders it supportable. How then can it be possible that we should resign without a severe pang, the first of all human blessings, the friend we love. Never give me reason again, I conjure you, to suppose you have wholly *forgot me.*

Now I will impart to you a secret, which must not be revealed. I think that before the 10th of December next I shall quit England *for ever.* My dear and valuable brother, who is now in Lancashire, wishes to persuade me, and the unkindness of the *world* tends not a little to forward his hopes. I have no relations in England except my darling girl, and, I fear, few friends. Yet, my dear Juan, I shall feel a very severe struggle in quitting those paths of fancy I have been childish enough to admire — false prospects. They have led me into the vain expectation that fame would attend my labours, and my country be my pride. How have I been treated? I need only refer you to the critiques of last month, and you will acquit me of unreasonable instability. When I leave England — adieu to the *muse* for *ever!* — I will never publish another line while I exist, and even those manuscripts now finished I WILL DESTROY.

Perhaps this will be no loss to the world, yet I may regret the many fruitless hours I have employed to furnish occasions for malevolence and persecution.

---

1   This letter was first printed in *Collection of Autograph Letters and Historical Documents, Formed Between 1865 and 1882 by A. Morrison,* ed. A. W. Thibaudeau, 6 vols. (London: Strangeways and Sons, 1883-92) 5: 286. Robinson dedicated her poem, "Sight," to John Taylor. See note 2 on page 116.

In every walk of life I have been equally unfortunate, but here shall end my complaints.

I shall return to St. James's Place for a few days this month to meet my brother, who then goes to York for a very short time, and after his return (the end of November) I DEPART. This must be *secret*, for to my other misfortunes pecuniary derangement is not the least. Let common sense judge how I can subsist upon £500 a year when my carriage (a necessary expense) alone costs me £200. My mental labours have failed through the dishonest conduct of my publishers. My works have sold handsomely, but the profits have been theirs.

Have I not reason to be disgusted when I see him, to whom I ought to look for better fortune, lavishing favours on unworthy objects, gratifying the *avarice* of *ignorance* and *dullness*; while I, who sacrificed reputation, an advantageous profession, friends, patronage, the brilliant hours of youth, and the conscious delight of correct conduct, am condemned to the scanty pittance bestowed on every indifferent page who holds up his ermined train of ceremony!

You will say, "why trouble me with all this." I answer because when I am *at peace* you may be in possession of my real sentiments and defend my cause when I shall not have the power of doing it.

My comedy has been long in the hands of *a* manager, but whether it will ever be brought forward time must decide.[1] You know, my dear friend, what sort of authors have lately been patronized by managers; their pieces ushered to public view, with all the advantages of splendour; yet I am obliged to wait two long years without a single hope that a trial would be granted. Oh, I am TIRED *of the* WORLD and all its mortifications. I promise you this shall close my *chapters* of *complaint*; keep them and remember how ill I have been treated.

I believe I may thank the author of the BAVIAD[2] for the critique in *Hamilton's Review*. Mr. Hamilton told *Peter*[3] that he should '*cut up my work*' *before* he had *read* it. My poor little Mary, too — what had she done to injure those

---

1   Robinson is likely referring to her play *Nobody*, a satire of female gamesters, which was staged on November 29, 1794 at Drury Lane with Mrs. Jordan in the starring role.

2   William Gifford's *Baviad* (1791) was a poetic attack on Della Cruscan poets.

3   Probably Peter Pindar, pen name of John Walcot (1738-1819), poetic satirist.

Self-named monarchs of the laurelled crown,
Props of the press — and tutors of the town.[1]

Adieu, my dear Juan. I hope to pass a few pleasant hours in your society before I am EXILED for the *remainder of my days*.

Faithfully and always yours, &c.

2. To William Godwin[2]

Cottage, Monday August 24: 1800

Why, my dear Philosopher, why will you continue to think me unworthily capricious? If you believe that I am insensible to the severity, which even Friendship sometimes evinces, you know but little of my heart, or of its too sensitive organization. Self love should tell you *minute "Enquirer,"*[3] that we seldom take the trouble to resent, or have the inclination to be offended, where the heart is wholly indifferent or where the good or bad opinion of the offender, is not of importance to our feelings. I really wish to cultivate your esteem, to deserve your approbation; — But I know not how it is. I have always feared more than I have hoped, when I have anticipated the acquirement of either the one or the other. I had, before I even saw you, formed an Idea, — that you were fastidious, stern, austere, and abstracted from worldly enjoyments. I was to contemplate the Philosopher; the enlightened, studious observer of mankind; —. I ventured to know you, rather to wonder at your wisdom, than to idolize your heart; I met you as a tutor of the *mind*, and I never expected to find you, an associate of the *soul*. — What was my surprize when I beheld in you a thousand amiable qualities! And how much have I admired since the period of our first interview, the progress of fine feeling which has distinguished and [illumined] your

---

1 Robinson quotes from her own poem, *Modern Manners*. In her reference to poor little Mary, she is probably referring to the reviews of her daughter's novel, *The Shrine of Bertha*, which was published in the year Robinson wrote this letter.
2 Mary Robinson to William Godwin, August 24, 1800, [Abinger Deposit] Dep. b. 215/2, The Bodleian Library, University of Oxford.
3 A reference to Godwin's *An Enquiry Concerning Political Justice* (1793).

domestic journey. I have, from time to time, seen you in new points of view. I have *wondered*, — pardon the expression, at your *sensibility*! Why have I wondered? Because your life has been a life of mental occupation, — of secluded study. — You have, in the very bosom of meditation, cherished the warm and graceful offspring of sentiment and feeling: you have scattered sweets, even in the thorny paths of intellectual labour; — for however they may lead to fame, they are not without their anguish. All this I acknowledge, — yet I have *feared more than I have hoped*. I have permitted an Idea to take root in my imagination, that you held, both me and my humble Talents in slender estimation; and that the thin [texture] of toleration, (for I did not once think of Esteem,) was sustained by a thread so feeble, that every breath had power to destroy it. I observed, in mixed societies, that you *appeared to* feel pleasure, in humbling *my* vanity: — for I am *vain* — I am not without ambition, growing out of a [rooted], and I once hoped, a distinguished adoration of Superior talents. You love Sincerity, my dear Philosopher, and yet you are not pleased when, even in womanish resentment, I have dared to be Sincere! Would you not despise a servile, fawning Hypocrite? Would you not think me less worthy of regard, were I more capable of Falshood? There have been periods when I have almost idolized you, — there have also been others when I hated even some of your best qualities. I name those of *Sincerity, Judgment*, — *penetration*, — *Wisdom*! and why have I hated them? because they have blighted the feeble blossoms of *self-love*, that have begun to chear my heart, by severe, though perhaps not unmeritted, disapprobation.

I am not *capricious*: new associates do *not* charm me from those that I have ever loved. But, since I first felt the power of discrimination, since I adored the excellent part of mankind, and [execrated] the base, I have been a wanderer in search of something, approaching to *my idea* of a perfect being. I have found many objects who, on an early intercourse, have presented the semblance of the creature I longed to idolize! — I have fancied that I found the graces of feeling and sincerity, in woman; the fascinations of Truth, Genius, and Sensibility, in Man. — Alas! if I were deceiv'd, — am I to blame in shrinking under the painful [pressure] of disappointment? I have, it is True, seen a few, a *very few*, in my journey through life, whose minds and sentiments, whose feelings and affections, have been such as I almost instinctively idolize. — But they have not honoured *me* with the title of Friend; — They have not been drawn towards *me*, by congenial, sympathetic [intuition]. — They have mistaken both my taste and my discernment; and in the person of what they have considered a "fine *Lady*" they have wounded the Being of all others, perhaps, *least* meritting the appellation. If I am vain, — If I appear to be trifling, I have to thank the world for its foolish, fond indulgence; I have to reproach such men as Fox and Sheridan,[1] for having professed, more than I had strength of mind to credit, without some little portion of self love. You accuse me, — yes, Philosopher, *you accuse* me of withdrawing my regard, without a cause for such apostacy. I deny the charge — from you I never have withdrawn it. You have vexed me; you have tormented me by your severity. You have evinced at times, a species of contemptuous indifference when I have sought, and *laboured* to obtain your approbation, that has made me peevish. — perhaps uncivil. But I cannot, I never could dissemble; whatever feeling actuates my soul, that feeling is instantaneously visible, even to less discerning Eyes than *Yours*. In the broad circle of society it is frequently convenient, some will maintain that it is justifiable, to assume a character, rather than to sustain one. I am a living proof that such artifice is advantageous, and that to be impervious, is to ensure a long succession of pains and disappointments! Had I been an artificial creature — I might have been in wealth and vulgar estimation, a creature to be envied! But the impetuosity of my temper; the irritability of my feelings; — the proud, [indifferent],[resentful] energy of my soul, placed a barrier between me and Fortune, which has thrown a gloom on every hour of my existence[.] So much for *Self*. If I am an egotist, *you* must bear the blame; for I had rather be anything, than the insensible mortal who can patiently endure such reproof as *yours*, without attempting some sort of vindication.

I wish that you had honored our hovel with a visit. I still hope that you *will*, notwithstanding my deep [impulsion] of disgust respecting young children. I am indeed too irritable, as well as too feeble, to bear the smallest fatigue and I confess that my anxieties are so poignant, my fears so easily awakened, my mind so bewildered by vexation, and

---

1   Charles Fox, Whig politician, and Richard Brinsley Sheridan, playwright. Both were friends of Robinson.

my *heart* so oppressed by *sorrows*, that nothing which is not calm and soothing to the senses, — can delight me. I am strongly impressed with a presentiment, that my days are nearly numbered: and I am, as that opinion takes root in my mind, more tranquil, more gay, than when I dreaded a long life of suffering.

The kind, the unexampled interest, which Mr Marshal[1] has displayed, — (not ostentatiously, but involuntarily,) for my welfare, demands my admiration and Esteem. — To you, my dear *cross cross* Philosopher, I am indebted for the introduction to this excellent mortal! — and I thank you, thank you, most sincerely.

Come and accept the *olive branch* — if you think I ever acted, or felt, in any degree, with hostility towards you. Allow me on all occasions to be *Sincere*; and rest assured that though I may sometimes dare to *disapprove*, I never shall have either *inclination* or *courage* to be any thing less *distinguished*, than

Your affectionate Friend —
and obliged servant —
Mary Robinson

P.S. You never will pardon my troubling you with such a long stupid letter! I write in great *haste*, and with a most excruciating head-ache. —

3. To Jane Porter[2]

Englefield Cottage 27th August 1800
near Egham Surrey. —

Lovely, and amiable Friend! What will you think of our shameful silence? What will you say of our good manners? and how justly will you condemn that, which must appear a want of Taste and feeling; in not answering your letter and cultivating your affection! Indeed I have in my tedious journey through life found so few estimable women, [(]particularly where I beheld handsome ones) that I not

---

1 James Marshall, Godwin's friend.
2 Mary Robinson to Jane Porter, August 27, 1800, Misc. Ms. 2295, The Carl H. Pforzheimer Collection of Shelley & His Circle; The New York Public Library; Astor, Lenox and Tilden Foundations.

only admire but value you, excessively. If I do not enter into the true spirit of Friendship for my own Sex, it is because I have almost universally found that Sex unkind and hostile towards *me*. I have seen the most miserable and degrading [reserve], the most contemptible *traits* of false delicacy, glaring through the thin veil of artificial virtue. I have found those women the most fastidiously severe, whose own lives have been marked by *private follies* and *assumed propriety*. The women whom I have most admired, have been the least prone to condemn, while they have been themselves the most *blameless*. — Of this distinguished class I consider you. — I lament that our poor Friend, Thomas continues so ill. I have been confined lately by two unpleasant companions, the one a swelled ancle, that by a violent degree of inflamation, (which thank Heaven has disappeared for I should not admire a mutilated leg) alarmed me considerably. The other torment was the German work of Doctor Hager, the History of Palermo, a *little* Volume, which I have finished translating, and which is now in the press. I have also [something] at Bristol (in the beautiful press of Biggs and Cottle)[1] a volume of Lyrical Tales; my favourite offspring. — The *distinction* you mentioned, I have taken care to make, in the M. Post. You will see it shortly. Great Genius is not to be restrained — and therefore your truant Brother,[2] has braved the winds and waves — wisely sparing you the inquietude of absence, or the pain of parting. I am here fixed for some months. I have one large spare bed, — or two small ones, (in one room) — disposed of either as you think proper; and contrive to pass a few days with us before the Camp breaks up.[3] I will give you Cottage fare, and the greeting of a warm heart, too sensitively organized ever to be happy — and too severely wrung by a vile world's persecution ever to be tranquil. Come, Come, — and tell your dear good — nay *excellent* mother, that I will embrace her sincerely, and warmly, *malgre* the dislike I *once* entertained for the Society of my own Sex, but which my intercourse with a few, like *yourselves*, has nearly over come. I have received a long letter from my old friend Mrs Parsons, who wished to present Mrs Bennet to me before she

---

1 Biggs and Company. printed *Lyrical Tales* for the publisher T. N. Longman and O. Rees.

2 Robert Ker Porter (1777-1842) was the much beloved brother of Jane and Anna Maria Porter. He was an artist renowned for his vast historical paintings, such as his panorama "Storming of Seringapatam" which was exhibited in 1800.

3 See note 1 to "The Camp" on page 294.

departed for Scotland. Mrs Fenwick is gone. — Mrs Parson's will I believe make me a short visit soon.[1] I am sorry that all hope vanishes of seeing Mrs Thomas, at least for the present: my earnest prayers are offered up for her *sufferer*; and, whatever a malignant world may suppose to the contrary, my soul fervently worships that *God* — who has power to heal the wounded, as he [is] *Omniscient* to know that I address him *sincerely*. —

I find little benefit from the change of air. I work too hard, and too incessantly, at my pen, to recover rapidly: and, to say truly, I very little value life, therefore, perhaps, am neglectful of those attentions which are calculated to prolong it. My adored girl is an indefatigable nurse, — and *in her* I shall *live* — I trust, as I now exist *by her affectionate solicitudes.* What a long *slovenly* letter!!! But I am so accustomed to scribbling for printers *Devils*,[2] that I am now incapable of transcribing a single page for the perusal of *Angels*! — Forgive me therefore, and instead of fine writing or fine phrases, accept the unadorned transcript of the heart subscribing *affectionate friend*, to the name of —

Mary Robinson

ps.

My Maria sends her love (united with mine,) to all your family. *She* will write next: But at present she is busied in the sublime occupation of watching her sister *Spinsters*, through the warm and fatiguing progress of — *Great Wash*!! She therefore hopes that she may *wash her hands* of all blame, and that she shall not be in the *suds* of disgrace, but come clean out of the scrape; If not she has fire, water, and a line — with a winding sheet — to complete her desperation!! She therefore hopes you will not [be] *stiff* or she must look *blue* on the occasion!

Miss Porter
 Gerrard Street
  Soho
  London
No. 6
postmark: Aug. 28 1800

---

1 See Introduction, note 54 on page 44.
2 Printer's devil: errand boy in a printing office; youngest apprentice.

'Tis in the silent spot obscure,
Where forc'd all sorrows to endure,
Pale Genius turns, O! lesson sad!
To court the vain & on the bad,
                    False praise bestow!

Figure 14. Mezzotint engraving after Maria Cosway, illustration No. 10 for "The Wintry Day,"
1804. (By courtesy of the Special Collections Department, University of Virginia Library.)

Appendix B: Samuel Taylor Coleridge's poems in response to Robinson

The Apotheosis, or the Snow-Drop[1]

FEAR no more, thou timid flower!
    Fear thou no more the Winter's might;
The whelming thaw; the ponderous shower;
    The silence of the freezing night!
Since LAURA murmur'd o'er thy leaves
    The potent sorceries of song,
To thee meek flow'ret! gentler gales
    And cloudless skies belong.

On thee with feelings unreprov'd
    Her eye with tearful meanings fraught,
She gaz'd till all the body mov'd
    Interpreting the spirit's thought:
Now trembled with thy trembling stem;
    And, while thou drooped'st o'er thy bed,
With imitative sympathy
    Inclin'd the drooping head.

She droop'd her head, she stretch'd her arm,
    She whisper'd low her witching rhymes;
FAME unrebellious heard the charm,
    And bore thee to Pierian climes.[2]
Fear thou no more the matin frost
    That sparkled on thy bed of snow:

---

1   This poem apparently appeared in the *Morning Post* on January 3, 1798, but no copy of the newspaper for that date is known to exist. Lucyle Werkmeister discovered a reprinting of the poem in the *Express and Evening Chronicle* for January 6-9, 1798. The poem was attributed to "Francini." David Erdman describes the cooperative effort that led to the discovery of the poem in "Lost Poem Found." Coleridge's poem was published in response to Robinson's "Ode to the Snow-Drop" (p. 323), which appeared in the *Morning Post* on December 26, 1797.

2   Belonging to Pieria, the reputed home of the muses.

For there, mid laurels ever green,
　　Immortal thou shalt blow.

Thy petals boast a white more soft —
　　The spell hath so perfumed thee,
That careless LOVE shall deem thee oft
　　A blossom from his myrtle-tree:
Then laughing at the fair deceit
　　Shall race with some Etesian wind[1]
To seek the woven arboret,
　　Where LAURA lies reclin'd!

For them, whom LOVE and FANCY grace,
　　When human eyes are clos'd in sleep,
Them oft the spirits of the place
　　Waft up that strange unpathway'd steep;
On whose vast summit, smooth and broad,
　　His nest the phoenix bird conceals,
And where by cypresses o'erhung
　　A heavenly Lethe[2] steals.

A sea-like sound the branches breathe,
　　Stirr'd by the breeze that loiters there;
And all, who stretch their limbs beneath,
　　Forget the coil of mortal care.
Such mists along the margin rise,
　　As heal the guests, who thither come;
And fit the soul to re-endure
　　It's earthly martyrdom.

That marge, how dear to moonlight elves!
　　There zephyr-trembling lilies blow,
And bend to kiss their softer selves
　　That tremble in the stream below!
There, nightly borne, does LAURA lie —

1　Etesian winds are those which blow from the northwest for about forty days during
　summer in the region of the Mediterranean.
2　Mythological river in Hades that induced forgetfulness in those who drank from its
　waters.

A magic slumber heaves her breast!
Her arm, white wanderer of the harp,
    Beneath her cheek is prest!

The harp, uphung by golden chains,
    Of that low wind which whispers round,
With coy reproachfulness complains
    In snatches of reluctant sound!
The music hovers half-perceiv'd,
    And only moulds the slumberer's dreams;
Remember'd loves light up her cheek
    With youth's returning gleams.

The LOVES trip round her all the night;
    And PITY hates the morning's birth,
That rudely warns the ling'ring SPRITE
    Whose plumes must waft her back to earth!
Meek PITY, that foreruns relief,
    Yet still assumes the hues of woe;
Pale promiser of rosy Spring,
    A SNOW-DROP mid the snow.

Alcaeus to Sappho[1]

How sweet, when crimson colours dart
    Across a breast of snow,
To see that you are in the heart
    That beats and throbs below!

All Heav'n is in a Maiden's blush,
    In which the soul doth speak,
That it was you who sent the flush
    Into the Maiden's cheek!

---

1   Coleridge submitted this poem to Daniel Stuart, editor of the *Morning Post*, where it
was published on November 24, 1800, but the poem was apparently the work of
William Wordsworth. In a 1798 letter to Coleridge, Wordsworth referred to the
poem as his own work and said he did not care a farthing for it. Coleridge apparent-
ly gave the poem its title and added the name Sappho in the second to last stanza.

Large stedfast eyes, eyes gently roll'd
  In shades of changing blue,
How sweet are they, if they behold
  No dearer sight than you!

And, can a lip more richly glow,
  Or be more fair than this?
The world will surely answer, No!
  I, SAPPHO! answer, Yes!

Then grant one smile, tho' it should mean
  A thing of doubtful birth;
That I may say these eyes have seen
  The fairest face on earth!

A Stranger Minstrel[1]

Written to Mrs. Robinson a few weeks before her Death

As late on Skiddaw mount[2] I lay supine
Midway th' ascent, in that repose divine,
When the soul, center'd in the heart's recess,
Hath quaff'd its fill of Nature's loveliness,
Yet still beside the fountain's marge will stay,
  And fain would thirst again, again to quaff; —
Then, when the tear, slow travelling on its way,
  Fills up the wrinkle of a silent laugh;
In that sweet mood of sad and humorous thought —
A form within me rose, within me wrought
With such strong magic, that I cry'd aloud,
Thou ancient SKIDDAW! by thy helm of cloud,

---

1   The text here is taken from the fourth volume of Robinson's 1801 *Memoirs*.
    Coleridge apparently gave the poem to her in manuscript after reading her "Ode
    Inscribed to the Infant Son of S.T. Coleridge," which was published in the *Morning
    Post* on October 17, 1800. In a letter to Maria Elizabeth Robinson, dated Decem-
    ber 27, 1802, Coleridge called this poem "excessively silly" and said he regretted its
    publication. *Collected Letters of Samuel Taylor Coleridge*, 6 vols., ed. Earl Leslie Griggs
    (Oxford: Clarendon Press, 1966-71) 2: 904. See page 324 for the revised 1806 ver-
    sion of Robinson's poem and note 1 to that poem for the *Post* version.
2   Skiddaw is a mountain north of Coleridge's town of Keswick in the Lake District.

And by thy many-colour'd chasms so deep;
And by their shadows, that for ever sleep;
By yon small flaky mists, that love to creep
Along the edges of those spots of light,
Those sunshine islands on thy smooth green height;
 And by yon shepherds with their sheep,
 And dogs and boys, a gladsome crowd,
 That rush even now with clamour loud
 Sudden from forth thy topmost cloud;
 And by this laugh, and by this tear,
 I would, old Skiddaw! SHE were here!
 A Lady of sweet song is she,
 Her soft blue eye was made for thee!
 O ancient Skiddaw! by this tear,
 I would, I would, that she were here!

Then ancient Skiddaw, stern and proud,
 In sullen majesty replying,
Thus spake from out his helm of cloud,
 (His voice was like an echo dying!)
"She dwells, belike, by scenes more fair,
And scorns a mount so bleak and bare!"

I only sigh'd, when this I heard,
Such mournful thoughts within me stirr'd,
That all my heart was faint and weak,
 So sorely was I troubled!
No laughter wrinkled now my cheek,
 But O! the tears were doubled.

But ancient Skiddaw, green and high,
Heard and understood my sigh:
And now in tones less stern and rude,
As if he wish'd to end the feud,
Spake he, the proud response renewing:
(His voice was like a monarch wooing!)

"Nay, but thou dost not know her might,
    The pinions of her soul how strong!
But many a stranger in my height
    Hath sung to me her magic song,
        Sending forth his extacy
        In her divinest melody;
And hence I know, her soul is free,
She is, where'er she wills to be,
        Unfetter'd by mortality!
Now to the 'haunted beach' can fly,[1]
    Beside the threshold scourg'd with waves,
    Now to the maniac while he raves,
Pale moon! thou spectre of the sky![2]
No wind that hurries o'er my height
Can travel with so swift a flight.
    I too, methinks, might merit
    The presence of her spirit!
    To me too might belong
The honour of her song, and witching melody,
    Which most resembles me,
    Soft, various, and sublime,
    Exempt from wrongs of Time!"
Thus spake the mighty Mount: and I
Made answer with a deep-drawn sigh,
Thou ancient Skiddaw! by this tear
I would, I would, that she were here!

---

1   A reference to Robinson's "The Haunted Beach" (p. 217).
2   A line from the twelfth stanza of Robinson's "Jasper" (p. 347).

Is it where Gamesters thronging round,
Their shining heaps of wealth display?
Where vice's fashion'd tribes are found,
Sporting their senseless hours away?

Ah! no!

Figure 15. Mezzotint engraving after Maria Cosway, illustration No. 11 for "The Wintry Day," 1804. (By courtesy of the Special Collections Department, University of Virginia Library.)

Appendix C: Reviews of Robinson's poetry

Review of *Poems* (1791) in the *Critical Review* n.s. 2 (July 1791): 309-314.

However the present age may be censured for want of originality and invention, in several departments of polite literature, it is certain that the animadversion does not extend to Poetry. Within very few years, a race of versifiers has sprung up, determined to claim at least the merit of novelty in expression, in unusual figure and striking combination. Rejecting the accustomed modes of description and phraseology, these fastidious writers seem fond of introducing uncommon terms and ideas, to provoke attention and excite admiration. We hardly know how to decide on this new species of Poetry. Sometimes we are charmed by the splendor of some particular passages, and at other times are so dazzled by the brilliancy of its images, that they are rendered "dark with excess of light." This perpetual search after somewhat new is as old as the days of Longinus, who deems this propensity the parent of almost every vice in style and composition, and mentions its votaries as labouring under a sort of insanity.[1] Its tendency to produce affected singularity of thought and obscurity of diction, cannot be doubted. The attempt at originality is in all pursuits laudable. Invention is the noble attribute of the mind. But the danger is, lest, by pursuing it too intensely, we deviate so far from ease and nature, that the grand object of Poetry, that of touching the heart, be lost. In short, there is danger, lest, in carrying this propensity too far, we fall into the same error with Cowley,[2] and the rest of those abstract metaphysical poets, who striving to leave the common herd of mankind at humble distance, both in thought and expression, have at different times soared so high or dived so low, that, to the generality of readers, their works constitute a sort of perpetual puzzle or enigma, which is not to be solved without a competent share of erudition.

It is not meant to apply these observations peculiarly to the Poems before us; but chiefly to point out the blemishes incidental to this

---

1   Longinus, *On the Sublime*, section V.
2   Abraham Cowley (1618-1667).

species of Poetry, and which, without attention, it will infallibly incur. On the contrary, making occasional allowance for the already noticed aim at novelty and even singularity of expression, we scruple not to affirm that these compositions abound with vivid exertions of genius, pathos, and sentiment; not such as merely "circum praecordia ludunt," but those which, besides affording delight to the fancy, sooth or pierce the heart. — The work consists of seventy-six detached pieces; odes, elegies, sonnets, stanzas, and a variety of non-descript addresses: most of which originally appeared in the News-papers under fictitious signatures, and were distinguished by such general attention and applause that the author was induced to collect and present them, with many others, to the public. From so beautiful a garden it may not appear difficult to select a bouquet for the gratification of our readers: but in truth, the choice is distracted by the competition of rival sweets. Without any distinct motive for preference, we select the following extract.

[Review reprints Robinson's "Ode to Health" in its entirety]

Amongst several others is an ode inscribed to colonel Tarleton, and next to it are "Lines to him who will understand them." They are of a valedictory nature, were written when the author was about to quit the kingdom for the restoration of her health, and imply an unexpected dissolution of friendship in very tender and delicate language. The mutable character of this friend is likewise touched in the following lines:

> Where'er my lonely course I bend,
> Thy image shall my steps attend;
> Each object I am doom'd to see
> Shall bid remembrance picture thee,
>
> Yes; I shall view thee in each flow'r,
> That changes with the transient hour;
> Thy wand'ring fancy I shall find
> Borne on the wings of every wind:
> Thy wild impetuous passions trace
> O'er the white wave's tempestuous space:
> In every changing season prove,
> An emblem of thy wav'ring love.

In the elegy to the memory of Mr. Boyle, and in another to the memory of Mr. Garrick, we find allusions to a want of humanity to the dying, and of respect to the dead, which in plain prose have often met our ears before. Mr. B. was son of the hon. Mrs Walsingham; who *happened* not to be at Clifton when he was languishing and died there in 1788.

The lines to Loutherbourg demonstrate no mean talents in the sublime of poetry. But the ingenious author descends with ease to its familiar provinces. In the lines on hearing it declared that no women were so handsome as the English, are the following neat and just remarks.

> Beauty, the attribute of heaven!
> In various forms to mortals given,
> With magic skill enslaves mankind,
> As sportive fancy sways the mind.
> Search the wide world, go where you will,
> Variety pursues you still;
> Capricious nature knows no bound,
> Her unexhausted gifts are found
> In ev'ry clime, in ev'ry face,
> Each has its own peculiar grace.

> To Gallia's frolic scenes repair,
> There reigns the tiny debonnaire;
> The mincing step — the slender waist,
> The lip with bright vermillion grac'd;
> The short pert nose — the pearly teeth,
> With the small dimpled chin beneath, —
> The social converse, gay and free,
> The smart bon mot — and repartee.

> Italia boasts the melting fair,
> The pointed step — the haughty air,
> Th' empassion'd tone, the languid eye,
> The song of thrilling harmony;
> Insidious love conceal'd in smiles
> That charms, and as it charms beguiles.

View Grecian maids, whose finish'd forms
The wond'ring sculptor's fancy warms!
There let thy ravish'd eye behold
The softest gems of nature's mould;
Each charm that Reynolds learnt to trace,
From Sheridan's bewitching face.

Imperious Turkey's pride is seen
In beauty's rich luxuriant mien;
The dark and sparkling orbs that glow
Beneath a polish'd front of snow:
The auburn curl that zephyr blows
About the cheek of brightest rose:
The shorten'd zone, the swelling breast,
With costly gems profusely drest;
Reclin'd in softly-waving bow'rs;
On painted beds of fragrant flow'rs;
Where od'rous canopies dispense
Arabia's spices to the sense;
Where listless indolence and ease
Proclaim the sovereign wish to please.

'Tis thus, capricious fancy shows
How far her frolic empire goes!
On Asia's sands, on Alpine snow,
We trace her steps where'er we go;
The British maid with timid grace;
The tawny Indian's varnish'd face;
The jetty African; the fair
Nurs'd by Europe's softer air;
With various charms delight the mind,
For Fancy governs all mankind.

But we must not deal so liberally in quotation. — We have
endeavored to give some idea of this poetical collection. It is certainly
an elegant and original work; which coming from the pen of one
person, and that person a woman, is entitled to singular approbation.

The work is elegantly printed on superfine paper, exhibits a
numerous list of subscribers from the first ranks of title and fashion,

and is decorated with a copper-plate of the fair author, from an original painting by Sir Joshua Reynolds.

Review of *Sappho and Phaon. In a Series of Legitimate Sonnets; with Thoughts on Poetical Subjects, and Anecdotes of the Grecian Poetess* (1796) **in the** *English Review* **(Dec. 1796): 583–584.**

Mrs. Robinson's address to the reader will explain her design: "The story of the Lesbian muse, though not new to the classical reader, presented to my imagination such a lively example of the human mind enlightened by the most exquisite talents, yet yielding to the distractive control of ungovernable passions, that I felt an irresistible impulse to attempt the delineation of their progress; mingling with the glowing picture of her soul such moral reflections as may serve to excite that pity which, while it proves the susceptibility of the heart, arms it against the danger of indulging a too luxuriant fancy."

Although we have never professed an admiration for the Della Crusca school, the pupils of which appear to us to be no other than a kind of imitators of poets, yet it is due to Mrs. Robinson to say, that she possesses great fertility of imagination, delicacy of sentiment, and a just ear for harmony and varied modulation of numbers. There is a stiffness, constraint, and affectation, in the models on which our British Sappho studies to form her style and manner: but in these, as in her other poems, she gives proofs of a genius capable of producing greater excellence, if it had been better directed.

The following is an extract, not crowded with imagery, nor set at variance with itself by a mixture of metaphors, but giving a natural description of the feelings of a mind wrapped in despair:

[Review reprints Sonnet XLI]

We repeat it once more, Mrs. Robinson is most unfortunate in having adopted, as a model, the contortions and dislocations of Della Crusca. If she had followed nature, seldom more justly or elegantly represented than in her own mind, free from the shackles of imitation, she would have produced sonnets nearer akin to the natural, pathetic, and passionate Sappho.

By a profusion of incongruous images, or mixture of metaphors, Mrs. Robinson, in many instances, renders her poetry absolutely unintelligible. Her course would be more graceful, if she would not so often start aside to hunt after flowers.

Review of *Lyrical Tales* (1800) in the *Monthly Review* 36 (Sept. 1801): 26–30.

In order to excel in lyric poetry, a happy combination of genius and taste must be formed; since this kind of composition ought not only to display a considerable degree of dignity and elevation, but also those charms and subordinate graces which we admire in the most finished literary productions. Mrs. Robinson, then, may be said to have made a bold attempt; and the critic will not take up this volume with the expectation of finding her completely successful. Her lyre, however, is harmonious, and she has displayed the power of touching the chords with pathos. As her life, though in some periods gay and dazzling, was deeply tinctured with sorrow, her muse is of the sombre cast; and though, being desirous of giving variety to her tales, she sometimes endeavours to be sprightly, her efforts are evidently forced, and she soon relapses into the dark and fearful region of tragic invention. She takes her harp from the willow on which it hung, to attune it to sounds of woe, to harrow up the soul, and to impress on the imagination the melancholy truth that human life is indeed a *vale of tears*. If she described it as she found it, we must not only forgive her, but lament her unfortunate destiny; yet we do not recommend it to our readers to cherish these gloomy representations of our present state, which the wounded mind feels a satisfaction in delineating.

Of the twenty-two tales which compose this volume, those intitled *All Alone* — *The Lascar* — *The Widow's Home* — *The Shepherd's Dog* — *The Fugitive* — *The Hermit of Mont Blanc* — *The Negro Girl* — *The Deserted Cottage* — *Poor Marguerite* — *Edmond's Wedding* — *The Alien Boy* — and *Golfre*, — are calculated to touch the soul with pity, and to fill the eye with tears. Some of them are composed in blank verse; a kind of measure not strictly *lyrical*, which is an epithet usually applied to a poem adapted to music. In general, however, Mrs. R. has attended to this circumstance; and it must be allowed that the work is no contemptible monument of her poetic genius. As she is now beyond the reach of human advice, we shall not minutely examine these tales: but, for the benefit of young writers, we must point out an instance or two in which she has violated the truth of nature.

In the tale of *The Lascar*, she thus makes him describe his situation in Asia;

> Oft I the stately camel led
> And sung the *short-hour'd* night away;

forgetting that, in the East Indies, the days and nights are nearly of an equal length throughout the year.

In *Golfre*, we find this couplet:

> So the pale *snow-drop* faintly glows,
> When sheltered by the *damask rose*.

Mrs. Robinson must have known that the snow drop and the damask rose never blow together; and that the latter never *sheltered* the former. This is therefore a singular inadvertency.

A line in *The Widow's Home* shews the same inattention to Nature:

> Of the *tame* sparrow and the red-breast *bold*:

it should be,

> Of the bold sparrow and the red-breast tame.

As a specimen of the blank verse, we extract a part of the tale intitled *The Fugitive*:

[Reprints third, fourth, and fifth verse stanzas of the poem]

Instead of copying Mrs. R.'s heart-breaking or terrific descriptions, we shall bring our readers acquainted with the ability which she displays in the line of playful satire, by quoting *The Mistletoe, a Christmas Tale*:

[Reprints the poem in its entirety]

Some Memoirs of the Life of Mrs. Robinson have lately appeared, which were partly written by herself. We shall pay farther attention to them, at a future opportunity.

Review of *The Poetical Works of the Late Mrs. Mary Robinson* (1806) in the *Annual Review* 5 (1806): 516–19.

This ample collection of the versified effusions of the late Mrs. Robinson claims at our hands just such a share of notice as may exempt us from the charge of careless, oversight, or contemptuous omission. It is ushered into the world by a preface, or prefatory memoir, which appears to us sufficiently objectionable to call for a few remarks. "The principal, and, in *some estimation*," says the Prefacer, "perhaps the most interesting events of the Author's days have already been given from her own memoirs, yet it may be no unreasonable supposition that this brief account which accompanies the *most excellent part of her character* may be justly appreciated when the mere annals of a beautiful woman are no more remembered."

Does the following sentence refer to *the most excellent part of her character?* and is there no effrontery in this easy manner of laying the blame on destiny. "At this, perhaps most unfortunate moment of her destiny, it was her fate to attract the attention of a distinguished personage, whose *unceasing importunities* obliged her, with reluctance, *to quit a profession*, by which she might have secured, to her latest hour, both independence and admiration."

After relating, that at an early age Mrs. R. was deprived, by disease, of the use of her limbs, the narrator proceeds: "To the MUSE, as the only solace to a mind of the most exquisite sensibility, blended with more than female fortitude, did this lovely and unfortunate being retire for consolation. The strain of plaintive tenderness which pervades her earlier productions fully exemplified the impressions of an afflicted mind, striving to wander from itself; and, in the mazes of fiction, lose for a time the melancholy objects which fate had so early presented before her." Again: "Of Mrs. Robinson's general character, it can only be added that she possessed a sensibility of heart and tenderness of mind which very frequently led her to form hasty decisions, while more mature deliberation would have tended to promote her interest and worldly comfort; she was liberal to a fault!"

These sentences irresistibly remind us of an admirable passage in a work which we have the pleasure of noticing in our present volume, the "Leonora" of Miss Edgeworth. "Pray what brings hundreds and thousands of women to the Piazzas of Covent Garden but sensibility? What does the colonel's and the captain's and the ensign's mistress talk of, but *sensibility?* And are you to be duped by this hacknied word?" Sensibility is a most bewitching power, and when sensibility, under the form of "lovely woman," complains of the perfidy of false friends, the ingratitude of fickle lovers, the nothingness of pomp and pleasure, and the variety of nameless miseries that assail from every quarter the generous and feeling heart — who but must melt with compassion towards the charming sufferer, and glow with indignation against a base unfeeling world? But let us stop a moment, to enquire from what description of people these pathetic lamentations most frequently proceed. Why from these very mistresses of colonels, captains, and ensigns — from that guilty, but much enduring class of women, who rashly bartering away the good opinion of the world, the respect of friends, and the care of legal protectors, receive nothing in exchange but some vague and ineffectual claims on the gratitude, tenderness, or pity, of the most base, selfish, and profligate portion of mankind! Such a one was poor Mrs. Robinson, and as an impressive lesson of the effects of such a course of conduct upon the mind, temper, and fortune, her prolix, and querulous effusions, her "miserable strain," may be recommended to the attention of thoughtless and inexperienced youth. But let not juvenile ignorance be deceived by sentimental misrepresentations and unprincipled concealments. Before a tender-hearted young lady has committed to memory the invocation to "Apathy," or learned to recite with tragic emphasis the "Ode to Ingratitude," let her at least be aware from *what reflections* the author wished to take shelter in insensibility, and for *what favours* her lovers had proved ungrateful.

It has sometimes been weakly enough pretended, that the private character of an author signifies nothing to his works; but can it be supposed safe for the *herd* of readers, that they should remain in doubt whether high-wrought effusions which claim their admiration, their sympathy, even their esteem, for the Queen of France, the Duchess of D., Chatterton, and Werter,[1] proceed from the pen of vice or virtue? Can the kind of apotheosis which Mrs. Robinson so liberally bestows on characters such as these, and the confident hope of heaven which she expresses for herself, be tamely viewed by the friends of religion?

---

1 Georgiana, Duchess of Devonshire (1757-1806); Thomas Chatterton (1752-1770); Werter was the fictional hero of Johann Wolfgang von Goethe (1749-1832) in *The Sorrows of Werter* (1774). All were subjects of Robinson poems.

With regard to the poetical merits of these volumes, it will be almost sufficient to remind our readers, that Mrs. R. was one of the chief disciples of what was called the Della Cruscan School; a sect of harmonious drivellers, who bewitched the idle multitude for a time with a sweet sound which passed for fine poetry, and an extravagant and affected cant which was mistaken for the language of exquisite feeling. Longer had they sung, and longer, perhaps, had the wreath flourished on their brows, but "with a frown arose" the doughty author of the Baviad and Maeviad;[1] their pseudo-laurels could not withstand the lightning of his wrath, and the vain pretenders were glad to shelter their "diminished heads" amid the gloom of snug obscurity.

From the numerous odes of our author we extract one, in which, if in any, we might expect to be gratified by the genuine expression of feeling, but which affords in fact only that kind of unmeaning exaggeration and decorated inanity which are the miserable resource of a cold heart, a vitiated taste, and a defective genius.

[Reprints Robinson's "Ode to the Memory of My Lamented Father, Who died in the Service of the Empress of Russia, December 5, 1786" in its entirety]

It is not by the artifice of italics and capitals that such lines as these can be taught to outface the judgment of a discerning reader, or to arrest the feelings of an impressible one. There is such a sameness of sentiment, and equality of execution in the productions of this author, that we shall excuse ourselves from farther quotation; as to criticism, it would be mere mockery to employ it on such objects.

---

1   William Gifford (1756-1826)

'Tis where neglected Merit sighs,
Where Hope, exhausted, silent dies;
Where Virtue starves by pride oppress'd,
    'Till ev'ry stream that warms the breast
                    Forbears to flow!

Figure 16. Mezzotint engraving after Maria Cosway, illustration No. 12 for "The Wintry Day," 1804. (By courtesy of the Special Collections Department, University of Virginia Library.)

Appendix D: Publication histories of Robinson's poems

Key to Symbols and Abbreviations

Works in which Robinson's poems appear

1775	*Poems.* London: C. Parker, 1775.
1791	*Poems.* London: J. Bell, 1791.
1793	*Poems.* London: J. Evans and T. Becket, 1793.
1800	*Lyrical Tales.* London: Longman and Rees, 1800.
1804	M. E. Robinson, ed. *The Wild Wreath.* London: Richard Phillips, 1804.
1806	*The Poetical Works of the Late Mrs. Mary Robinson.* 3 vols. London: Richard Phillips, 1806.
Ainsi	*Ainsi va le Monde.* London: J. Bell, 1790.
Angelina	*Angelina; a Novel.* 3 vols. London: Hookham and Carpenter, 1796.
Captivity	*Captivity, a Poem and Celadon, a Tale.* London: T. Becket, 1777.
Lucky	*Songs, Chorusses, &c. in the Lucky Escape, a Comic Opera.* London: Printed for the author, [1778].
MMLQ	*Monody to the Memory of the Late Queen of France.* London: J. Evans, 1794.
Memoirs	*Memoirs of the Late Mrs. Robinson, Written by Herself.* 4 vols. London: R. Phillips, 1801.
Mistletoe	Laura Maria. *The Mistletoe. A Christmas Tale.* London: Laurie and Whittle, 1800.
MMJR	*Monody to the Memory of Sir Joshua Reynolds.* London: J. Bell, 1792.
Modern	*Modern Manners; A Poem in Two Cantos.* London: J. Evans, 1793.
Nat. D.	*The Natural Daughter.* 2 vols. London: T. N. Longman & O. Rees, 1799.
Ode	*Ode to the Harp of the Late Accomplished and Amiable Louisa Hanway.* London: J. Bell, 1793.

Progress	*The Progress of Liberty*. Published in *Memoirs* (1801) and *Poetical Works* (1806).
Sicilian	*The Sicilian Lover. A Tragedy*. London: Printed for the author by Hookham and Carpenter, 1796.
Sight	*Sight, The Cavern of Woe, and Solitude*. London: Evans and Becket, 1793.
Sappho	*Sappho and Phaon, in a Series of Legitimate Sonnets*. London: Hookham and Carpenter, 1796.
Shrine	Maria Elizabeth Robinson, *The Shrine of Bertha*. 2 vols. London: Printed for the author by W. Lane at the Minerva Press, 1794.
Vanc.	*Vancenza; or the Dangers of Credulity, a Moral Tale*. 3rd ed. 2 vols. London: J. Bell, 1792.
Wals.	*Walsingham; or the Pupil of Nature*. 4 vols. London: T. N. Longman, 1797.
Widow	*The Widow, or a Picture of Modern Times*. 2 vols. London: Hookham and Carpenter, 1794.

Newspapers, journals, and anthologies

AA	*Annual Anthology* (Bristol)
BA	*British Album. Containing the Poems of Della Crusca, Anna Matilda, Arley, Benedict, The Bard, &c*, 2nd ed. (London: J. Bell, 1790.
CG	*Calcutta Gazette or Oriental Advertiser* (Calcutta)
EM	*European Magazine* (London)
GM	*Gentleman's Magazine* (London)
LM	*Ladies Magazine* (London)
LMM	*Lady's Monthly Museum* (London)
MM	*Monthly Magazine and British Register* (London)
MP	*Morning Post and Fashionable World*, later *Morning Post and Gazeteer* (London)
NAR	*New Annual Register, or General Repository of History, Politics, and Literature* (London)
Oracle	*Oracle and Public Advertiser* (London)
Scots	*Scots Magazine* (Edinburgh)
T & C	*Town and Country Magazine or Universal Repository* (London)
W	*World. Fashionable Advertiser* (London)

Each poem title is given in italics, followed by the poem's first line in parentheses and then the publication history for each poem, with individual publications separated by semicolons. Poem titles and first lines are, when possible, taken from the 1806 *Poetical Works* since this collection is more readily available (particularly given Caroline Franklin's 1996 facsimile edition) than earlier editions. Variant titles and author pseudonyms are given in parentheses after a publication entry when necessary. If no pseudonym is given, the poem was published under (or above) Robinson's own name. For example, "The Admonition" (see listing below) was published first in the *Morning Post* on October 25 1800 as the work of "T.B.," and then reprinted in the 1806 *Poetical Works of the Late Mrs. Mary Robinson*. For untitled poems, the first line is listed (and is not italicized). The sonnets in *Sappho and Phaon* are listed by their first lines with sonnet number following *Sappho*. There is a notation after each of the many short poems that were eventually incorporated into *The Progress of Liberty* indicating this fact. The publication history of *The Progress of Liberty* completes the publication history of each of the shorter pieces eventually included in this long poem. Finally, for those poems interpolated into Robinson's novels and *Memoirs*, the volume and page number of the edition listed above is provided.

I would appreciate being informed of new Robinson publication discoveries so that I can update this listing. I can be contacted by e-mail: judith-pascoe@uiowa.edu.

Absence — see *To Absence*
The Adieu to Fancy. Inscribed to the Same
    ("When first I knew thee, Fancy's aid")
       1793 (*The Adieu to Fancy. Inscribed to a Friend*); 1806
The Adieu to Love ("Love, I renounce thy tyrant sway")
    1791
The Admonition. After the Manner of the Ancient Poets
    ("Lady! 'tis somewhat strange to find")
       MP 25 Oct. 1800 (T.B.); 1806
Admonitory. Ode VIII ("Peter! Thou son of whim and satire")
    MP 23 July 1799
The African ("Shall the poor African, the passive slave")
    MP 2 Aug. 1798; incorporated into *Progress*

After Successive and Melancholy Dreams — see *Stanzas Written After Successive Nights of Melancholy Dreams*

Agnes, a story — see *Edmund's Wedding*

Ainsi va le Monde ("O thou, to whom superior worth's allied")
      Ainsi; 1791; *Memoirs* 2: 179–80 (excerpt); 1806

The Alien Boy ("'Twas on a mountain, near the western main")
      1800; 1806

All Alone ("Ah! wherefore by the Church-yard side")
      MP 18 Dec. 1800; 1800; 1806

All For-Lorn ("Let Fashion and Fancy their beauties display")
      MP 4 April 1800 (T.B.)

Anacreontic ("Bring me the flowing cup, dear boy")
      MP 11 July 1800 (Sappho); 1804; 1806

Anacreontic ("The day is past! the sultry west")
      MP 11 Jan. 1800 (*Anacreontic, To Henry,* Sappho); 1804; 1806

Anacreontic ("You say, my love, the drifted snow")
      MP 25 Oct. 1799 (variant, L.M.); 1804 (*Winter*); 1806

Anacreontic. To Bacchus ("Is it the purple grape that throws")
      MP 1 Feb. 1800 (*Sappho to Bacchus,* Sappho); 1804 (*To Bacchus*); 1806

Anacreontic. To Cupid ("Hither, god of pleasing pain")
      1793; 1806

And now my friend, to peaceful scenes I'll fly
      Angelina 3: 409–11

Another ("Ye myrtles and woodbines so green")
      1775

Anselmo, the Hermit of the Alps
      ("Where, mingling with Helvetia's skies")
      1793; 1806

The Answer ("O Peter! since thy sportive Muse")
      MP 15 May 1799 (*Mrs. Robinson's Impromptu Answer to Peter Pindar*); *Memoirs* 4: 104–5; 1806

As o'er the world, by sorrow prest — see *Stanzas* ("As o'er the world, by sorrow prest")

Aunt Bridget to her Sister Margaret, Mother of Simkin and Simon
      ("My dear sister Maggie, this letter I write")
      W 25 Jan. 1789 (Bridget)

The Beau's Remonstrance ("Fair dames, of fickle man you say")
MP 1 April 1800 (T.B.)

Beauty's Grave ("Unhappy has the traveller been")
MP 23 Oct. 1800 (*Beauty's Grave, Inscribed to the Memory of the Late Countess of Tyrconnel*, Sappho); 1806

The Bee and the Butterfly ("Upon a garden's perfum'd bed")
1791

The Birth-day ("Here bounds the gaudy gilded chair")
MP 21 Jan. 1795 (*St. James's Street, on the Eighteenth of January, 1795*, Portia); MP 19 Jan. 1798 (*St. James Street. The Birth-Day*, T.B.); 1806

The Birth-day of Liberty ("Hail Liberty! legitimate of Heav'n")
MP 7 April 1798 (no author); incorporated into *Progress*

Blest as the gods! Sicilian maid is he
Sappho XXXII; 1806

Blush, blush, ye dull, ye insolently great
The Widow 2: 109

Bosworth Field ("Gliding o'er the moonlight heath")
1793; 1806

Bring, bring, to deck my brow, ye sylvan girls
Sappho XIII; 1806

Bring me the flowing cup, dear boy! — see *Anacreontic* ("Bring me the flowing cup")

The Camp ("Tents, marquees, and baggage wagons")
MP 1 Aug. 1800 (Oberon); 1804 (*Winkfield Plain; or A Description of a Camp in the Year 1800*, M.E.R.)

Can'st thou forget, O! Idol of my soul!
Sappho XXV; 1806

Canzonet ("Slow the limpid currents twining")
1791

Captivity, a Poem
("While bright-ey'd Science crowns this favor'd Isle")
Captivity

The Cavern of Woe ("As Reason, fairest daughter of the skies")
1793; *Sight*; 1806

Celadon and Lydia. A Tale ("Secluded from the world's ignoble strife")
Captivity

The Cell of the Atheist ("In the worst den of human misery")
>MP 19 Aug. 1799 (Laura Maria); incorporated into
>*Progress*

A Character ("Generous, and good, sincere, and void of art")
>1775

A Character ("How very rare my gen'rous friend we find")
>1775

A Character ("If a perfect form can please")
>1775

Come, reason, come! each nerve rebellious bind
>*Sappho* VII; 1806

Come, soft Aeolian harp, while zephyr plays
>*Sappho* XIV; 1806

The Complaint ("Ye verdant greens, ye shady woods")
>1775

The Confessor. A Sanctified Tale ("When superstition rul'd the land")
>MP 20 March 1800 (Tabitha Bramble); 1800; 1806

Cupid Sleeping ("Close in a woodbine's tangled shade")
>T & C Oct. 1791; 1791; 1806

A Cure for Love ("Oft have I said my love's smile")
>MP 15 April 1800 (Sappho)

Dang'rous to hear is that melodious tongue
>*Sappho* X; 1806

The day is past; the sultry west — see *Anacreontic* ("The day is past")

Deborah's Parrot. A Village Tale ("'Twas in a little western town")
>MP 4 March 1800 (*The Tell Tale; Or Deborah's Parrot*,
>Tabitha Bramble); 1800; 1806

Delusive hope! more transient than the ray
>*Sappho* XVI; 1806

The Deserted Cottage ("Who dwelt in yonder lonely Cot?")
>MP 13 March 1800; 1800; 1806

The Dippers ("Since dipping's the fashion with old and with young")
>MP 5 Sept. 1800 (T.B.)

Domestic Beverage ("A little acid, now and then")
>MP 21 Aug. 1800

Donald and Mary ("On Scotia's Hills a gentle Maid")
>1793; 1806

The Doublet of Grey ("Beneath the tall turrets that nod o'er the dell")
Wals. 3: 197-202; *MP* 15 Feb. 1798
The Dungeon ("Explore the dungeon's gloom, where all alone")
MP 18 May 1798 (no author); incorporated into *Progress*
Echo to Him Who Complains ("O fly thee from the shades of night")
1791
Edmund's Wedding
("By the side of the brook, where the willow is waving")
MP 28 Feb. 1800 (*Agnes, a story*) 1800; 1806
Elegiac Ode to the Memory of My Lamented Father — see *Ode to the Memory of My Father*
Elegy on the Death of Lady Middleton
("The knell of death, that on the twilight gale")
Oracle 18 July 1789 (Laura Maria); 1791
Elegy to the Memory of Garrick
("Dear Shade of him who grac'd the mimic scene")
Oracle 26 Sept. 1789 (*Lines Inscribed to the Memory of David Garrick, Esq.*); 1791; 1806
Elegy to the Memory of Mrs. Gunning, Inscribed to Her Accomplished Daughter (The hour is past! the hour of mortal pain")
MP 3 Sept. 1800 (M.R.)
Elegy to the Memory of Werter. Written in Germany in the Year 1786
("When from day's closing eye the lucid tears")
W 15 July 1789 (*To the Memory of Werter*, Laura); 1791; 1806
Epigram ("Pride puffs up ignorance, says pompous Joe")
MP 17 March 1800 (T.B.)
Epigram, on seeing it announced that Mr. Cumberland has nine dramatic pieces ready for representation
("Nine pieces, and each quite complete for the town")
MP 31 July 1799 (Tabitha)
Epilogue: Supposed to Have Been Spoken After the Play of Fontainville Forest ("So long, by solitude, by grief oppress'd")
Oracle 1 July 1794
An Epistle to a Friend ("Permit me dearest girl to send")
1775
Ere ye condemn, let Conscience be your guide
MP 2 Jan. 1800 (interpolated into *The Sylphid*, No. IX);
Memoirs 3: 79-80

Evening Meditations on St. Anne's Hill, Inscribed to the Right Honourable
Charles James Fox
("Day's glory fades! and now the rustic swain")
1793
Every blessing crowns this wedding
Lucky
The Exile ("Lost on a rock of dreadful height")
Wals. 4: 64-65; *MP* 4 Jan. 1798; *Express and Evening*
Chronicle 6-9 Jan. 1798; 1806
Extempore, Sent with a Pair of Gloves to S. J. Pratt, Esq. — see
Impromptu Sent to a Friend
The Faded Bouquet — see *Written on a Faded Bouquet*
Farewel, Sir, farewel, depend on my care
Lucky
Fairy Rhymes — see *Oberon's Invitation to Titania* and *Titania's Answer*
to Oberon
Farewel to Glenowen
("Farewel, dear Glenowen! adieu to thy mountains")
Wals. 1: 106-7; 1806
Farewell, ye coral caves, ye pearly sands
Sappho XIX; 1806
Farewell, ye tow'ring cedars, in whose shade
Sappho XXIX; 1806
Far o'er the waves my lofty bark shall glide
Sappho XXXI; 1806
Favour'd by Heav'n, are those, ordain'd to taste
Sappho I; 1806
Female Fashions for 1799 ("A form, as any taper, fine")
MP 28 Dec. 1799 (*Modern Female Fashions*, Tabitha
Bramble); 1806
The Fisherman ("Along the smooth and glassy stream")
MP 26 July 1800 (Oberon); 1804; 1806
Fly swift, ye tardy, mournful hours
Widow 1: 179
For oft where high the tree of genius springs
Wals. 2: 298-99
For the Morning Post and Fashionable World ("So, Mr. Editor, in troth")
MP 11 Oct. 1794 (Bridget)

The Fortune Teller. A Gypsy Tale ("Lubin and Kate, as gossips tell")
>   *MP* 12 April 1800 (Tabitha Bramble); 1800; 1806

For what is life? — a Summer day
>   *Wals.* 1: 259

The Foster-Child ("'Mid Cambria's hills a lowly cottage stood")
>   1804, 1806

A Fragment ("I love the labyrinth, the silent glade")
>   *T&C* Aug. 1794 (*Seclusion*); *Widow* 1: 154; 1806

*A Fragment, Supposed to Be Written Near the Temple, at Paris, on the
Night Before the Murder of Louis XVI*
>   ("Now Midnight spreads her sable vest")
>   *Oracle* 27 Feb. 1793 (Laura Maria); 1793; *EM* April 1794
>   (Laura Maria); 1806

The Fugitive ("Oft have I seen yon solitary man")
>   1800; 1806

The Gamester ("Say, what is he, whose haggard eye")
>   *MP* 15 Jan. 1800 (Laura Maria); 1804; 1806

The gauzy rock, while round its purple side
>   *Wals.* 2: 246.

Golfre. A Gothic Swiss Tale
>   ("Where freezing wastes of dazzl'ing snow")
>   1800; 1806

The Granny Grey ("Dame Dowson, was a granny grey")
>   *MP* 10 June 1800 (Tabitha Bramble); 1800; 1806

Great and Small! ("When Nobles live in houses gay")
>   *MP* 18 Sept. 1800 (T.B.)

The Grey Beard ("Myrtilla was a lady gay")
>   *MP* 24 June 1800 (T.B.)

Harvest Home ("Who has not seen the chearful Harvest Home!")
>   *MP* 30 Aug. 1800; 1804; incorporated into *Progress*

The Haunted Beach ("Upon a lonely desart Beach")
>   *MP* 26 Feb. 1800; 1800; *AA* 1800; *Memoirs* 4: 179–83;
>   1806

Here droops the Muse! while from her glowing mind
>   *Sappho* XLIV; 1806 (XLIII)

Hermit of Mont Blanc ("High, on the Solitude of Alpine Hills")
>   *MM* 1 Feb. 1800; 1800; incorporated into *Progress*

High on a rock, coeval with the skies
>   *Sappho* II; 1806

Hope, thou source of every blessing
    Lucky
Horatian Ode ("Say, when the captive bosom feels")
    Oracle 19 Nov. 1793 (*Stanzas to Fate*, Laura Maria); 1793
    (*Stanzas to Fate, in the Manner of Sappho*); 1806
The Horrors of Anarchy
    ("Now Anarchy roam'd wide, a monster fierce")
    MP 24 April 1798 (no author); incorporated into *Progress*
A Hue and Cry ("O Yez! pray who has lately seen")
    MP 27 Aug. 1800 (Oberon)
Hymn to Virtue ("Divine inhabitant of heaven")
    1775
Impromptu ("Humdrum complains his giddy wife")
    MP 28 July 1800 (T.B.)
Impromptu ("Says Time to Love, "Thou idle boy!"")
    MP 22 Aug. 1799 (*Time and Love*, L.M.); 1806
Impromptu ("Tho' beauty may charm, and tho' youth may invite")
    MP 27 Aug. 1799 (L.M.)
Impromptu on **** ("When Myra bloom'd at gay fifteen")
    1793 (*Impromptu on an Antiquated and Splenetic Beauty*);
    Scots Dec. 1793 (*Myra*); 1806
Impromptu on an antiquated and splenetic Beauty — see *Impromptu*
    on ****
Impromptu on Mr. Merry's Marriage with Miss Brunton
    ("Tho' beauty may charm the fond heart with a smile")
    Oracle 29 Oct. 1791 (Julia)
Impromptu Sent to a Friend Who Had Left His Gloves, by Mistake, at the
    Author's House on the Preceding Evening
    ("Your gloves I send")
    MP 29 Dec. 1797 (*To a Gentleman Who Had Left a Pair of*
    Gloves at Her House); *Memoirs* 4: 164-166 (*Extempore Sent*
    with a Pair of Gloves to S.J. Pratt, Esq.); 1806
Ingratitude — see *The Worst of Ills*
The Ingredients Which Compose Modern Love
    ("Twenty glances, twenty tears")
    MP 14 Jan. 1800 (Tabitha Bramble, Spinster)
Inscribed to a Once dear Friend ("Say not the moments swiftly move")
    1804

Inscribed to Maria, My Beloved Daughter
  ("The Rose that hails the morning")
  1793 (*Song. Inscribed to Maria, My Beloved Daughter*); 1806
Invocation to Oberon, Written on the Recovery of My Daughter from
  Inoculation
  ("Lightly on the breath of morn")
  Oracle 15 March 1792 (*Invocation*, Oberon); 1793
  (*Invocation, Written on the Recovery of My Daughter from*
  Inoculation, and First Published with the Signature of Oberon;
  Memoirs 4: 126-9 (*Lines by Mrs. Robinson Written on the*
  Recovery of her Daughter from Illness); 1806
Is it to love, to fix the tender gaze
  Sappho VI; 1806
The Italian Peasantry ("Time was, and mem'ry sickens to retrace")
  MM 1 April 1800; incorporated into *Progress*
I wake! delusive phantoms, hence, away!
  Sappho XXXIII; 1806
January, 1795 ("Pavement slipp'ry, people sneezing")
  MP 29 Jan. 1795 (Portia); 1806
Jasper ("The night was long, 'twas winter time")
  AA 1800; 1806
Julia to ——— ("Oh, cease the sad prophetic song")
  Oracle 3 April 1793
Julia to Arno ("Arno, where steals thy dulcet lay?")
  Oracle 19 Oct. 1793 (Julia)
Julia to Arno ("Oh! had I thought, that from the tuneful train")
  Oracle 28 Oct. 1793 (Julia); 1793 (*To Arno*)
Julia to Carlos — see *To Carlos*
Justifiable Apostacy ("When Edwin first my heart possess'd")
  MP 24 July 1800 (Lesbia)
A Kiss — see *To a Friend Who Asked the Author's Opinion of a Kiss*
The Lady of the Black Tower ("Watch no more the twinkling stars")
  1804; 1806
The Lascar ("Another day, Ah! me, a day")
  1800; 1806
Laura Maria, on Seeing the Crayon Landscapes of Peter Pinder — see *On*
  Seeing the Crayon Landscapes of Peter Pindar

Laura Maria, to Peter Pindar, Esq.
>   ("Since malice, dear Peter, has ventur'd to mention")
>   *MP* 29 July 1799 (Laura Maria)

Laura To Anna Matilda — see *To Anna Matilda*

Laura, to Arno
>   ("When the bleak blast of winter howls o'er the blue
>   hill")
>   *Oracle* 5 December 1792 (Laura)

Lead me, Sicilian maids, to haunted bow'rs,
>   *Sappho* XXXVI

Lesbia and Her Lover ("Lesbia upon her bosom wore")
>   *MP* 3 March 1800 (Tabitha Bramble); 1804; 1806

Lesbia's Dream ("Lesbia believ'd her ardent mind")
>   *MP* 17 April 1800 (no author given)

Lesbia, to Him Who Complains ("In vain, thy timid love would hide")
>   *MP* 15 July 1800 (Lesbia)

Letter to a Friend on Leaving Town
>   ("Gladly I leave the town, and all its care")
>   1775

Let your passion still be guarded
>   *Lucky*

Lewin and Gynneth — see *Llwhen and Gwyneth*

Life ("Love, thou sportive fickle boy")
>   *W* 15 June 1789 (no title, Laura); 1791; 1806

Lines ("Bid me the ills of life endure")
>   *MP* 30 Jan. 1800 (*Sappho to her Lover*); 1806

*Lines, Addressed By a Young Lady of Fashion to a Small Green Fly, Which
>   Had Pitched on the Left Ear of Lady Amaranth's Little White
>   Barbet, Fidelio; on a Summer Evening, After a Shower, Near
>   Sunset*
>   ("Little, barb'rous cruel fly")
>   *Wals.* 3: 248

Lines Addressed to a Beautiful Infant Inscribed to Mrs Fenwick
>   ("Orlando! when the dawn of grace")
>   *MP* 29 July 1800 (Oberon)

Lines Addressed to Earl Moira
>   ("In these degenerate times the Muses blend")
>   *MP* 3 July 1800 (*Sappho — To the Earl of Moira*, Sappho);
>   1804

Lines Addressed to Miss Wortley, on Her Attachment to Colonel
   Cunningham
   ("Transcendent maid! while fashion's race")
   MP 10 Mar. 1800 (Julia); *LMM* April 1800 (Julia)
Lines Addressed to the Hon. Mrs. Meynel. On the Death of Her Husband
   ("Oh! check the tear, which mem'ry bids to flow")
   MP 8 July 1800 (M.R.)
Lines by Mrs. Robinson, Now Engraven on Her Monument in Old Windsor
   Church-yard — see *Penelope's Epitaph*
Lines by Mrs. Robinson. Written on the Recovery of Her Daughter from
   Illness — see *Invocation to Oberon*
Lines, Dedicated to the Memory of a Much-Lamented Young Gentleman
   ("If virtues rarely known to grace mankind")
   W 24 Oct. 1788 (Laura)
Lines from "Angelina" ("I wake from dreams of proud delight")
   Oracle 28 Jan. 1794 (*Lines Written on Monday, January 27,*
   1794); *Angelina* 3: 323-26; 1806 (printer's error in title:
   Lines from "Angelica")
Lines Inscribed to P. de Loutherbourg, Esq. R.A.
   ("Where on the bosom of the foamy Rhine")
   1791; *Shrine* 2: 100 (excerpt); 1806
Lines Inscribed to the Memory of David Garrick
   ("Dear shade of him, who grac'd the mimic scene")
   Oracle 26 Sept. 1789
Lines on Beauty — see *Ode to Beauty*
Lines on Hearing a Gentleman Declare, That No Women Were So
   Handsome as the English
   ("Beauty, the attribute of heav'n")
   1791 (*Lines on Hearing It Declared That No Women Were So*
   Handsome as the English; 1806
Lines on Reading Mr. Pratts Volume "Gleaning Through England"
   ("Thrice welcome, lib'ral gleaner! to whose lore")
   MP 25 July 1799 (Laura Maria); *LMM* Sept. 1799 (Laura
   Maria)
Lines on Seeing the Duchess of Devonshire in Her New and Splendid
   Carriage
   ("The jewel, which a casket holds")
   MP 8 March 1800 (Oberon)

*Lines Supposed to be Written Near the Monument of the Rev. John
      Parkhurst, at Epsom, in Surrey*
   ("When memory, led by resignation strays")
   MM July 1800
Lines to an Infant Sleeping, Inscribed to Mrs. Fenwick — see *To an Infant
      Sleeping*
Lines to Him Who Will Understand Them
   ("Thou art no more my bosom's Friend")
   W 31 Oct. 1788 (*To Him Who Will Understand It*, Laura);
   BA (*To Him Who Will Understand It*); 1791; *NAR* 1791;
   Memoirs 2: 117-20; 1806
Lines to Maria, My Beloved Daughter
   ("To paint the lust'rous streaks of morn")
   Oracle 22 Oct. 1793 (*Lines to Maria, Written on Her Birth-
   day, Oct. 18, 1793*, Julia); 1793 (*Lines to Maria, Written on
   Her Birthday*); 1806
Lines to Maria, Written on Her Birthday — see *Lines to Maria, My
      Beloved Daughter*
Lines to Spring — see *To Spring. Written After a Winter of Ill Health*
Lines to the Memory of a Young Gentleman
   ("If worth, too early to the grave consign'd")
   1806
Lines to the Memory of My Brother
   ("If 'tis the lot of mortal eye to scan")
   1793 (*To the Memory of My Beloved Brother*); *Memoirs* 2:
   171-174 (*To the Memory of My Beloved Brother*)
Lines to the Memory of Richard Boyle, Esq.
   ("Near yon mountain's dizzy height")
   1791
Lines to the Rev. J. Whitehouse
   ("In this dread Era! when the Muse's train")
   GM Nov. 1794; *Wals.* 2: 298 (excerpt); 1806
Lines Written by the Side of a River ("Flow soft River, gently stray")
   1791; 1806
Lines Written on a Day of Public Rejoicing!
   ("While shouts and acclamations rend the skies")
   1806
Lines Written on a Sick Bed, 1797 ("Another night of fev'rish pain")
   MP 16 Oct. 1800 (*Written on a Sick Bed*, M.R.); 1806

The Misanthrope ("There was a cave, o'er hung with thorn")
        MP 5 Jan. 1801 (M.R.)
The Miser ("Miser, why countest thou thy treasure")
        MP 23 Dec. 1799 (Laura Maria); 1804; 1806
The Mistletoe, a Christmas Tale
        ("A Farmer's Wife, both young and gay")
        MP 31 Dec. 1799 (Laura Maria);1800; *The Mistletoe*
Mistress Gurton's Cat. A Domestic Tale
        ("Old Mistress Gurton had a cat")
        MP 8 Jan. 1800 (Tabitha Bramble); 1800; 1806
Modern Female Fashion — see *Female Fashions for 1799*
Modern Manners ("In these enlightened times, when critic elves")
        Modern; *Oracle* 6 Aug. 1793 (excerpt)
The Monk ("Mid the grey horrors of his narrow cell")
        MP 12 May 1798 (no author); incorporated into *Progress*
Monody to the Memory of Chatterton
        ("If Grief can deprecate the wrath of Heav'n")
        Oracle 11 May 1791; 1791; *Wals.* 2: 64 (excerpt); 1806
Monody to the Memory of Marie Antoinette, Queen of France
        ("When, the dread scene of death and horror o'er")
        Oracle 18 Dec. 1793 (*Mrs. Robinson's Monody*); *MMLQ*;
        1806
Monody to the Memory of Sir Joshua Reynolds, Late President of the Royal
        Academy
        ("When Resignation, bending from the sky")
        MMJR; 1793; *Memoirs* 2: 181-3 (excerpt); 1806
The Moralist ("Hark! the hollow moaning wind")
        Oracle 23 Nov. 1791 (Laura Maria); *CG* 14 June 1792
        (Laura Maria); 1793; 1806
Morning ("O'er fallow plains and fertile meads")
        1791; 1806
Morning. Anacreontic ("The sun now climbs the eastern hill")
        MP 8 Nov. 1799 (*Anacreontic*, L.M.); 1804; 1806
Mrs. Robinson's Impromptu Answer to Peter Pindar — see *The Answer*
Mrs. Robinson to the Poet Coleridge — see *To the Poet Coleridge*
The Murdered Maid ("High on the solitude of Alpine Hills")
        1806

My Lord, at a dinner, was lying and swearing
> *MP* 24 Dec. 1799 (interpolated into *The Sylphid* XVIII);
> *Memoirs* 3: 45

My Native Home ("O'er breezy hill and woodland glade")
> *Wals.* 4: 226-8; 1806

Myra — see *Impromptu on* ****

Neglect ("Ah! cold Neglect! more chilling far")
> *Wals.* 2: 290-91; *MP* 20 Dec. 1797; 1806

The Negro Girl ("Dark was the dawn, and o'er the deep")
> *LM* 1 Feb. 1796 (*The Storm*); *MP* 3 Feb. 1796 (*The Storm*); 1800; 1806

The Nettle and the Daisy ("Drench'd by a fiercely beating show'r")
> *MP* 22 Jan. 1800 (Laura Maria)

Ne wealth had I; ne garland of renown
> *Wals.* 1: 72-74; *MP* 4 Dec. 1797

A New Song ("Since quacking is grown into fashion and taste")
> *MP* 19 Feb. 1798 (T.B.)

A New Song, To an Old Tune
> ("O! rare ***** ****! he's the wonder of nature!")
> *MP* 12 Jan. 1798 (T.B.)

Nimrod. A Tale for Sportsmen
> ("Nimrod, of sportsmen the most fond of sport")
> *MP* 17 Jan. 1800 (Tabitha Bramble)

Now, o'er the tesselated pavement strew
> *Sappho* XII; 1806

Now round my favour'd grot let roses rise,
> *Sappho* XV; 1806

The Nun's Complaint ("Within this drear and silent gloom")
> *Vanc.* 2: 47-8; 1793

Oberon's Invitation to Titania ("Oh! Come, my pretty love! and we)
> *MP* 28 Aug. 1800 (*Oberon to Titania*); 1804 (*Oberon to Titania*); 1806

Oberon to Maria, on Seeing Her Gather Some Pensees — see *Stanzas to My Beloved Daughter*

Oberon to the Queen of the Fairies
> ("Sweet Mab! at thy command I flew")
> *Oracle* 3 June 1790 (Oberon); 1791

Oberon to Titania — see *Oberon's Invitation to Titania*

Ode for the 18th of January, 1794
>   ("The Muse who pours the votive strain")
>   *Oracle* 18 Jan. 1794 (different first line and other
>   variations); 1806

Ode for the New Year ("While in the misty-mantled spheres")
>   *MP* 7 Jan. 1794

Ode Fourth, For New Years Day
>   ("O ye! who basking in the sunny sphere")
>   *MP* 1 Jan. 1798 (Tabitha Bramble)

Ode in Imitation of Pope ("How blest is he who, born to tread")
>   *Wals.* 3: 164-5; 1806

Ode Inscribed to the Infant Son of S. T. Coleridge, Esq.
>   ("Spirit of light! whose eye unfolds")
>   *MP* 17 Oct. 1800; 1806

Ode: Oberon to Mrs. Jordan
>   ("Why, from those scenes, the passions paint")
>   *MP* 5 March 1800 (Oberon)

Ode. The Eagle and the Flock of Geese
>   ("How rarely, by the outward show")
>   1806

Ode on Adversity
>   ("Where o'er my head, the deaf'ning Tempest blew")
>   1791

Ode to Apathy — see *To Apathy*

Ode to Beauty ("Exulting Beauty! — phantom of an hour")
>   *Oracle* 24 June 1789 (*Lines on Beauty*, Laura Maria); 1791;
>   1806

An Ode to Charity ("Hail meek-eyed daughter of the sky")
>   1775

An Ode to Contentment ("Celestial maid, if on my way")
>   1775

Ode to Della Crusca ("Enlighten'd Patron of the sacred Lyre!")
>   1791; 1806

Ode to Despair ("Terrific Fiend! thou Monster fell!")
>   1791; 1806

Ode to Eloquence ("Hail! Goddess of persuasive art!")
>   *Oracle* 15 Sept. 1789 (Laura Maria); 1791; 1806

Ode to Envy ("Deep in th' abyss where frantic horror 'bides")
>   1791; 1806

Ode to the Moon ("Pale Goddess of the witching hour!")
        1791; 1806
Ode to the Muse ("O, let me seize thy pen sublime")
        W 13 Nov. 1788 (*The Muse*, Laura); 1791; 1806
Ode to the Nightingale ("Sweet bird of sorrow! — why complain")
        Oracle 11 Dec. 1789 (*To the Nightingale*, Laura Maria);
        1791; *Shrine* 2: 22-3 (excerpt); 1806
Ode to the Snow-Drop ("The Snow-drop, Winter's timid child")
        Wals. 1: 53-5; *MP* 26 Dec. 1797; 1806
Ode to the Spirit of Chivalry
        ("From antique courts and banner'd halls")
        MP 15 March 1800 (Sappho)
Ode to the Sun-Beam ("Thou dazzling beam of fervid light")
        MP 13 Aug. 1800; 1806
Ode to Valour ("Transcendent Valour! godlike Pow'r!")
        1791; 1806
Ode to Vanity ("Insatiate tyrant of the mind")
        1791; 1806
Ode to Virtue ("Hail daughter of th' etherial sky")
        1775
Ode to Winter ("Hail! Tyrant of the gloomy season, hail!")
        MP 10 Dec. 1799 (Laura Maria); 1806
An Ode to Wisdom ("Hail wisdom, goddess of each art")
        1775
O'er the tall cliff that bounds the billowy main
        Sappho XXX; 1806
Oh! can'st thou bear to see this faded frame
        Sappho XLII; 1806 (XLI)
Oh! I could toil for thee o'er burning plains;
        Sappho XX; 1806
O! How can Love exulting reason quell!
        Sappho V; 1806
O, how to bid my love adieu
        Lucky
O! many are the pangs and keen the woes
        Wals. 1: 321
Oh Sigh! thou steal'st, the herald of the breast,
        Sappho XXXVIII; 1806

Oh! ye bright stars! that on the ebon fields
      Sappho XXVII; 1806

Old Barnard. A Monkish Tale ("Old Barnard was still a lusty hind")
      MP 28 Jan. 1800 (Tabitha Bramble); 1800; 1806

The Old Beggar ("Do you see the Old Beggar who sits at yon gate")
      MP 25 July 1800 (M.R.); *Memoirs* 4: 167-72; 1806

The Old Shepherd and the Squire ("Deep in a solitary glen")
      MM 1 Sept. 1800 (*The Old Shepherd. A Tale*, author
      identified as Mrs. Robinson, but printed over name of
      Tabitha Bramble); *Memoirs* 4: 172-7 (*The Old Shepherd*);
      1804

The Old Soldier ("O Pity! if thy holy tear")
      MP 31 Aug. 1799; *Nat. D* 1: 36-7

On a Friend ("A gentle soul, a beauteous form")
      1775

On Leaving the Country for the Winter Season, 1799
      ("Ye leafless woods, ye hedge-rows bare")
      MP 10 Feb. 1800 (Laura Maria); 1806

On Seeing the Countess of Yarmouth at Her Window in Picadilly on
      Sunday Last
      ("Is it the early smile of Spring")
      MP 25 March 1800 (Oberon)

On Seeing the Crayon Landscapes of Doctor Walcot
      ("Now the grey wing of Twilight o'er the plain")
      MP 12 Aug. 1799 (*On Seeing the Crayon Landscapes of*
      Peter Pindar, Laura Maria); 1806 (listed in table of
      contents but omitted in text)

On the Birth-day of a Lady ("To hail Louisa, this auspicious day")
      1775

On the Death of a Friend
      ("Adieu, dear Emma; — and now, alas! no more")
      1775

On the Death of Lord George Lyttelton
      ("Ye chrystal streams, ye murm'ring floods")
      1775

On the Death of Mr. Fortune, of Pembrokeshire
      ("Time, with his wing, has stopp'd this mortal's breath")

MP 5 Feb. 1800 (T.B.)
On the low margin of a murm'ring stream
    Sappho XL; 1806 (XXXIX)
O! Reason! vaunted sov'reign of the mind!
    Sappho XI; 1806
Original Sketches from Nature — see *Twilight*
The Origin of Cupid ("On Ida's mount the gods were met")
    1791
O! Thou! meek orb! that stealing o'er the dale
    Sappho XXIV; 1806
O where shall I run, which way shall I fly
    Lucky
O woman! greatest friend or foe
    Wals. 2: 161
A Pastoral Ballad ("Ye Shepherds who sport on the plain")
    1775
A Pastoral Elegy ("Ye nymphs, ah! give ear to my lay")
    1775
Pastoral Stanzas
    ("By the side of a mountain, o'er-shadow'd with trees")
    1791
Pastoral Stanzas. Written at Fifteen Years of Age
    ("When Aurora's soft blushes o'erspread the blue hill")
    1791; 1806
Penelope's Epitaph ("O thou! whose cold and senseless heart")
    Wals. 1: 46; *MP* 2 Dec. 1797; *Memoirs* 2: 166 (*Lines by
    Mrs. Robinson, Now Engraven on Her Monument at Old
    Windsor Churchyard*)
Petrarch to Laura ("Ye Sylvan haunts, ye close embow'ring shades")
    1791; *Shrine* 2: 19 and 35 (excerpts); 1806
The Pilgrim's Farewell. From the Romance of "Vancenza"
    ("O'er desarts untrodden, o'er moss-cover'd hills")
    1793; 1806
Pity's Tear ("What falls so sweet on Summer flow'rs")
    MP 8 Aug. 1800 (Sappho); 1806
The Poet's Garret ("Come, sportive fancy! come with me, and trace")
    MP 6 Sept. 1800 (M.R.); 1804; 1806
Poor Marguerite ("Swift o'er the wild and dreary waste")
    MP 8 April 1800; *LMM* Sept. 1800; 1800; 1806

The Poor Singing Dame
  ("Beneath an old wall, that went round an old castle")
  MP 25 Jan. 1800; 1800; 1806
Prepare your wreaths, Aonian maids divine
  Sappho XXXIX
Pretty Susan ("Near the top of yonder meadow")
  MP 31 July 1800 (T.B.)
The Progress of Liberty ("Hail, Liberty sublime! hail godlike pow'r")
  Memoirs 4: 1-96; 1806. See poems that were incorporated
  into *Progress of Liberty*, as well as notes to these poems, for
  precursor publications (p.298-321)
The Progress of Melancholy ("O! Melancholy! parent of Despair")
  Angelina 1: 227-32; 1806
The Recantation. To Love ("Tell not me of silv'ry sands")
  1793; 1806
A Receipt for Modern Love — see *The Way to Keep Him*
A Reflection ("The loathsome toad, whose mis'ry feeds")
  Wals. 2: 222-3; 1806
Reflections ("Ah! who has pow'r to say")
  Oracle 21 Sept. 1793 (*Reflections, Which With a Power So
  Pleasing, at Least Cheer the Condition of Life They Are
  Unable to Change*, Laura Maria); 1793; 1806
The Reply to Time ("O Time! forgive the mournful song")
  1791; 1806
A ruby lip, a dimpled cheek,
  Lucky
St. James Street. The Birth-Day — see *The Birth-day*
Sappho to Bacchus ("Is it the purple grape that throws")
  MP 1 Feb. 1800 (Sappho)
Sappho — To Night ("What! though thy crystal lamp, dull night")
  MP 27 Feb. 1800 (Sappho)
Sappho and Phaon — see individual sonnets listed by first lines
Sappho, to Phaon ("If deep in gloom the day has past")
  MP 6 March 1800 (Sappho)
Sappho — To the Earl of Moira — see *Lines Addressed to Earl Moira*
Sappho — To Time ("Steal softly on. O! ruthless Time!")
  MP 22 July 1800 (Sappho)
The Savage of Aveyron, a Poem ("'Twas in the mazes of a wood")
  Memoirs 3: 173-84; 1806

Seclusion — see *A Fragment* ("I love the labyrinth")

Second Ode to the Nightingale ("Blest be thy song, sweet Nightingale")
    1791; 1806

The shepherd boy, on yonder mountain's crest — see *Sonnet*
    ("The shepherd boy on yonder mountain's crest)

The Shepherd's Dog ("A Shepherd Dog there was; and he")
    1800; 1806

The Sicilian Lover ("It shall be so! Think not, my honour'd liege")
    Sicilian; *MP* 17 Feb. 1796 (excerpts); *MP* 18 Feb. 1796
    (excerpts); *Wals.* 3: 257 and 3: 318-19 (excerpts); 1806

Sight. Inscribed to John Taylor, Esq.
    ("O thou! all wonderful, all glorious Pow'r!")
    Sight; 1793; 1806

The silence of the solitary tomb
    Memoirs 3: 92 (interpolated into *Jasper*, an unfinished
    novel)

The silver moon shall light the hills to dance,
    Wals. 2: 243

A Simple Tale (Addressed to the Most Expert of Jugglers,) in the Form of
    Ode Second
    ("A juggler, at a village fair")
    MP 13 Dec. 1797 (Tabitha Bramble)

Sir Joshua Reynolds ("The arts, that thro' dark centuries have pin'd")
    Oracle 3 March 1792 (Laura Maria)

Sir Raymond of the Castle ("Near Glaris, on a mountain side")
    1791; 1806

The Snake and the Linnet. A Fable
    ("Beside a Wood, whose lofty shade")
    1793; 1806

Solitude ("Hail, Solitude serene! thou nurse of thought!")
    Sight; 1793; 1806

A Song ("Chloe, 'tis not thy graceful air")
    1775

Song ("As Cupid wanton, giddy child")
    1775

Song ("Ye crystal fountains, softly flow")
    1775; *Lucky*

Song, Inscribed to Maria, My Beloved Daughter — see *Inscribed to Maria,*
    My Beloved Daughter

Sonnet ("The gauzy rock, while round its purple side")
　　　　Wals. 2: 246

Sonnet ("In early youth, blithe Spring's exulting day")
　　　　1791

Sonnet ("In the lone valley, on its verdant bed")
　　　　Oracle 25 Sept. 1792 (Julia)

Sonnet ("Night's dewy orb, that o'er yon limpid stream")
　　　　Oracle 29 July 1789 (Laura Maria); 1791; 1806

Sonnet ("O busy world! since ev'ry passing day")
　　　　Wals. 3: 277; 1806

Sonnet ("O gold, thou poisonous dross, whose subtile pow'r")
　　　　MP 1 Oct. 1799; *Nat. D* 1: 242-3; 1806

Sonnet ("Pale twilight! wrapp'd in melancholy grey")
　　　　1806

Sonnet ("Say, stern oppression! Thou, whose iron chain")
　　　　MP 3 Feb. 1798 (T.B.)

Sonnet ("The shepherd boy on yonder mountain's crest")
　　　　Oracle 21 April 1794 (Miss Robinson); *Shrine* 1: 133

Sonnet ("Slow sail the vapours o'er the mountain's crest")
　　　　Wals. 1: 286

Sonnet ("'Tis Night's dull reign! — The silver-mantled queen")
　　　　Wals. 4: 239

Sonnet ("When the loud torrent rushing from the rock")
　　　　1791

Sonnet ("Where, thro' the starry curtains of the night")
　　　　Oracle 3 Oct. 1789 (Laura Maria); 1791; 1806

Sonnet. Inscribed to Her Grace the Dutchess of Devonshire
　　　　("'Tis not thy flowing hair of orient gold")
　　　　1791

Sonnet in the Manner of Metastasio
　　　　("Days pass, o'ershadow'd! mournful! and unblest!")
　　　　Oracle 12 Nov. 1793 (Julia); 1793

Sonnet. Laura to Petrarch ("O solitary wand'rer! whither stray")
　　　　MP 3 April 1800 (Laura); 1806

Sonnet, to the Prince of Wales
　　　　("From courtly crowds and empty joys retir'd")
　　　　Oracle 20 Oct. 1792 (Julia)

Sonnet. The Mariner ("The sea-beat mariner, whose watchful eye")
        Oracle 7 Nov. 1789 (Laura Maria); 1791; 1806
Sonnet. The Peasant
        ("Wide o'er the barren plain the bleak wind flies")
        1791; 1806
Sonnet. The Snow Drop ("Thou meekest emblem of the infant tear")
        1791
Sonnet. The Tear ("Ah! lust'rous gem, bright emblem of the heart")
        1791; 1806
Sonnet. To Amicus
        ("When, o'er the darkened globe, the wings of night")
        1793; 1806
Sonnet to Amicus ("When the poor Exile, who the live-long night")
        Oracle 3 Sept. 1791 (Laura Maria); 1793; 1806
Sonnet to Amicus ("Whoe'er thou art, whose soul enchanting song")
        1791
Sonnet to a Rose
        ("Come, glowing Rose! unfold thy blushing breast!")
        Oracle 1 Oct. 1793 (Julia); 1793
Sonnet to a Sigh ("Go, Sigh! go viewless herald of my breast")
        Oracle 25 Sept. 1793 (Julia); 1793
Sonnet to a Tear
        ("Stay, sparkling wand'rer! whither wouldst thou rove")
        Oracle 27 Sept. 1793 (Julia); 1793
Sonnet. To Evening
        ("Sweet balmy hour! — dear to the pensive mind")
        1791; 1806
Sonnet to Hope ("Ah! Beauteous Syren! Shall I still believe")
        1793
Sonnet to Fame ("Proud Child of Genius! whose immortal hand")
        1793
Sonnet to Independence
        ("Supreme, enchanting pow'r! from whose blest source")
        Oracle 13 April 1792 *(To Independence*, Laura Maria); *MP* 9
        Jan. 1794; 1793; 1806
Sonnet. To Ingratitude ("I could have borne affliction's sharpest thorn")
        1791; 1806

Sonnet to Lesbia ("False is the youth, who dares by thee recline")
    Oracle 5 Oct. 1793 (Sappho)
Sonnet. To Liberty ("Ah! liberty! transcendent and sublime!")
    MP 10 Jan. 1795 (Portia); *MP* 20 Jan. 1796; *Angelina* 3: 30
Sonnet to Memory ("O Thou! whose vivid Tablet still retains")
    1793
*Sonnet to Mrs. Charlotte Smith, On Hearing That Her Son Was Wounded
    at the Siege of Dunkirk*
    ("Full many an anxious pang, and rending sigh")
    Oracle 17 Sept. 1793 (Oberon)
Sonnet. To My Beloved Daughter
    ("When Fate in ruthless rage assail'd my breast")
    1791; 1806
Sonnet. To Philanthropy ("First blessing frail mortality can know!")
    MP 23 Jan. 1795 (*To Philanthropy. Sonnet II*, Portia);
    Angelina 3: 356-7; 1806
Sonnet to Sympathy ("Oh! Sympathy! Thou pleasing source of pain")
    MP 29 Mar. 1796
Sonnet to the Memory of Miss Maria Linley
    ("So bends beneath the storm yon balmy flow'r")
    Oracle 26 Nov. 1789; 1791
Sonnet to Time ("Insatiate Despot! whose resistless aim")
    1793
*Sonnet. Written Among the Ruins of an Ancient Castle in Germany, in the
    Year 1786*
    ("Ye mould'ring walls, where Titian colours glow'd")
    1791; 1806
Sonnet. Written at Sea, Sept. 1, 1792
    ("While o'er the waste of waters, loud and deep")
    1793; 1806
Sonnet Written on the Sea-shore
    ("You smooth expanse, that woos the parting ray")
    EM June 1793; 1793
The Sorrows of Memory ("In vain to me the howling deep")
    MP 26 Jan. 1798 (L.M.); 1804; 1806
The Spinster ("Says Lady Jane, 'So scant is fame'")
    MP 16 April 1800 (Bridget)
Stanzas ("As o'er the world, by sorrow prest")
    MP 9 Sept. 1799; *Nat. D.* 2: 58-9; 1806

Stanzas ("Hark! 'tis the merry bells that ring")
> *Oracle* 9 June 1794; *Nat. D.* 1: 218; 1806

Stanzas ("In this vain busy world, where the good and the gay")
> *GM* Jan. 1797; *Wals.* 3: 65-6

Stanzas ("Since Fortune's smiles too often give")
> *Wals.* 4: 15-16; *MP* 9 Jan. 1798; *Express and Evening*
> *Chronicle* 6-9 Jan. 1798; 1806

Stanzas ("Teach me, love, since thy torments no precepts can cure")
> *Wals.* 2: 235-36; *MP* 5 Feb. 1798; 1806

Stanzas ("Tell me, that nature welcomes rosy spring")
> *Oracle* 12 Dec. 1793 (Laura Maria); 1793; 1806

Stanzas ("The chilling gale that nipp'd the Rose")
> *Vanc.* 1: 89-90; 1793; *Memoirs* 4: 118-19; 1806

Stanzas ("The savage hunter, who afar")
> *Wals.* 2: 49-50; 1806

Stanzas ("When fragrant gales and summer show'rs)
> *Oracle* 13 Aug. 1789 (Laura Maria); 1791; 1806

Stanzas ("When the bleak blast of Winter howls o'er the blue hill")
> *Oracle* 5 Dec. 1792 (*To Arno*, Laura); 1793; 1806

Stanzas ("Why, if perchance thy gaze I meet")
> 1791; 1806

Stanzas from "The Natural Daughter"
> ("'Tis night! and o'er the barren plain")
> *MP* 6 Sept. 1799; *Nat. D.* 2: 182-3; 1806

Stanzas from "The Natural Daughter" ("Unhappy is the Pilgrim's lot")
> *Nat. D.* 1: 286-7; 1806

Stanzas. From "The Shrine of Bertha"
> ("Farewell! dear haunts of pleasing woes!")
> *Shrine* 1: 203-6; 1806

Stanzas, From Walsingham — See *Stanzas to Rest*

Stanzas Inscribed to a Once Dear Friend, When Confined By Severe
> *Indisposition, in March 1793*
> ("Ye glades that just open to greet the blue sky")
> 1793 (*Stanzas Inscribed to a Friend, When Confined by*
> *Severe Indisposition, in March, 1793*); 1806

Stanzas Inscribed to Lady William Russell
> ("Nature, to prove her heav'n-taught pow'r")
> 1791

Stanzas on Jealousy — see *To Jealousy*

Stanzas on the Duchess of Devonshire — see *To the Duchess of Devonshire*

Stanzas on the Duchess of Devonshire's Indisposition
>("If, while the sky, by storms o'ercast")
>
>*MP* 5 April 1800 (Oberon)

Stanzas on May 1799
>("Sweet May! once the parent of love, we behold")
>
>*MP* 11 May 1799; *LMM* June 1799

Stanzas Presented with a Gold Chain Ring to a Once Dear Friend
>("Oh! take these little easy chains")
>
>1793 (*Stanzas, Presented with a Gold Chain Ring*); 1806

Stanzas Supposed to Be Written Near a Tree, Over the Grave of an Officer,
>*Who Was Killed at Lincelles, in Flanders, in August 1793*
>
>("Ah! pensive trav'ller, if thy tear")
>
>1793 (*Stanzas Supposed to Be Written Near a Tree, Over the Grave of Colonel Bosville, Who Was Killed at Lincelles, in Flanders, in August 1793*); *Oracle* 7 Sept. 1793 (Laura Maria); *EM* Sept. 1793; *Scots* Oct. 1793 (*Stanzas*); 1806

Stanzas to a Friend ("Ah! think no more that Life's delusive joys")
>*T&C* May 1790 (*To a Friend*, Laura Maria); 1791; 1806

Stanzas to a Friend, Who Desired to Have My Portrait — see *Stanzas to a Friend Who Wished to Have My Portrait*

Stanzas to a Friend Who Wished to Have My Portrait
>("E'en from the early days of youth")
>
>1793 (*Stanzas to a Friend, Who Desired to Have My Portrait*); 1806 (shorter version)

Stanzas to Fate — see *Horatian Ode*

Stanzas to Flora ("Let others wreaths of roses twine")
>1791; 1806

Stanzas to Him Who Said, "What is Love"
>("'Say, what is Love?' I heard the sound")
>
>*Oracle* 21 June 1791 (*Laura Maria to Arno*, Laura Maria); 1793; 1806

Stanzas to Julius — see *To Julius*

Stanzas to Love
>("Tell me, Love, when I rove o'er some far distant plain")
>
>1791; 1806

Stanzas to My Beloved Daughter, On Seeing Her Gather Some Pensées
  ("Forbear, rash Maid! thy hand restrain")
  Oracle 27 Mar. 1792 (*Oberon: To Maria On Seeing Her
  Gather Some Pensées*, Oberon); 1793; 1806
Stanzas to Rest ("When hidden fears the bosom tears")
  Wals. 3: 11-12; *MP* 1 Feb. 1798 (*Stanzas from Walsingham*);
  1806
Stanzas to the Author of a Celebrated Tragedy
  ("The Rainbow glows with orient dyes")
  1793
Stanzas to the Memory of a Young Lady
  ("As Heav'n's own Beam awakes the gentle flow'r")
  1793
Stanzas to the Rose ("Sweet Picture of Life's chequer'd hour!")
  1791; 1806
Stanzas to Time ("Capricious foe to human joy")
  1791; 1806
Stanzas Written After Successive Nights of Melancholy Dreams
  ("Ye airy Phantoms, by whose pow'r")
  Oracle 30 Nov. 1792 (*Stanzas Written After Successive and
  Melancholy Dreams*, Laura); 1793; *Memoirs* 4: 134-7 (*After
  Successive and Melancholy Dreams*); 1806
Stanzas Written at the Shrine of Bertha — see *Stanzas from "The Shrine
  of Bertha"*
Stanzas Written Between Dover and Calais, in July 1792
  ("Bounding billow, cease thy motion")
  Oracle 2 Aug. 1792 (Julia); *EM* Oct. 1792; 1793; *Memoirs*
  2: 134-7; 1806
Stanzas Written for "The Shrine of Bertha"
  ("Pleas'd with the calm bewitching hour")
  Shrine 1:70-72; 1806
Stanzas Written in Hyde-Park on Sunday Last
  ("This gay *parterre*, of motley hue")
  MP 7 Mar. 1800 (Oberon)
Stanzas Written on the 14th of February 1792, to My Once Dear Valentine
  ("Come, Hope, and sweep the trembling string")
  1793; *Scots* Feb. 1794 (*Stanzas to My Valentine*); 1806
Stanzas Written Under an Oak in Windsor Forest — see *To Pope's Oak*
The Storm — see *The Negro Girl*

The Summer Day ("Ah! who beneath the burning ray")
    MP 7 Aug. 1800 (T.B.); 1806

The Swan ("Majestic bird! who lov'st to glide")
    MP 30 July 1800 (*To the Swan*, M.R.); 1806

Sweet Madeline of Aberdeen — A Comical Elegy!
    ("So fair a maid was never seen")
    MP 27 Sept. 1800 (Oberon)

Tabitha Bramble, Ode Fifth ("Candour, our sages say, is most divine")
    MP 14 Feb. 1798

Tabitha Bramble, to Her Cousins in Scotland. Ode the Third
    ("Again I smite the bounding string")
    MP 25 Dec. 1797

Tabitha Bramble Visits the Metropolis By Command of Her Departed
    Brother. Ode First
    ("From mountains, barren, bleak, and bare")
    MP 8 Dec. 1797 (Tabitha Bramble)

Taste and Fashion ("Says Fashion to Taste, 'I am strangely perplex'd'")
    MP 4 July 1800 (T.B.); 1806

Tell me, that Nature welcomes rosy Spring — see *Stanzas* ("Tell me,
    that nature welcomes rosy spring")

The Tell Tale; or Deborah's Parrot — see *Deborah's Parrot*

Think on the pangs that must rend the soft breast
    Lucky

Thoughts on Retirement ("Hence pining grief, and black despair")
    1775

Time and Love — see *Impromptu* ("Says Time to Love, 'Thou idle
    boy")

'Tis night, and o'er the barren plain — see *Stanzas from "The Natural*
    Daughter"

Titania's Answer to Oberon ("In vain, for me, thy gifts display'd")
    MP 29 Aug. 1800; 1804; 1806

To ——— ("'Tis past! and now, remorseless Fate")
    Oracle 13 Dec. 1791 (Julia); 1793; 1806

To ——— . ("Ah! Cease thy sad prophetic song")
    1793

To Absence ("When from the craggy mountain's pathless steep")
    1791; 1806

To Aetna's scorching sands my Phaon flies!
    Sappho XXIII; 1806

To a False Friend. In Imitation of Sappho
> ("The Seasons, lover false! are changing slow")
> *MP* 12 Sept. 1800 (*Sappho to Her Lover*, Sappho); 1806

To a Friend ("Cold blows the wind upon the mountain's brow")
> 1806

To a Friend Who Asked the Author's Opinion of a Kiss
> ("'What is a kiss?' 'tis but a seal")
> *MP* 20 June 1800 (*Sappho, To a Gentleman Who Asked Her Opinion of a Kiss*, Sappho); *LMM* July 1799 (*Stanzas by Mrs. Robinson, to a Gentleman Who Asked Her Opinion of a Kiss*); 1804 (*A Kiss*); 1806

To a Friend, With Some Painted Flowers
> ("Oh! had the little hand that trac'd these flow'rs")
> 1804

To a Gentleman Who Had Left a Pair of Gloves at Her House — see *Impromptu Sent to a Friend*

To an Infant Sleeping ("Sweet Baby Boy! thy soft cheek glows")
> *MP* 9 July 1800 (*Lines to an Infant Sleeping. Inscribed to Mrs. Fenwick*, Oberon); 1804; 1806

To Anna Matilda ("O Anna, since thy graceful song)
> *W* 6 Mar. 1789 (*Laura, To Anna Matilda*); *BA*

To Apathy ("Welcome, thou petrifying pow'r!")
> *MP* 1 July 1800 (*Ode to Apathy*);1806

To Arabella! After the Manner of the English Poets
> ("My love, when'er those radiant eyes")
> *MP* 11 Sept. 1800 (*To Arabelle! In the Manner of the Antient English Poets*, Oberon); 1806

To Arno — see *Stanzas* ("When the bleak blast of winter howls")

To Aurelia on Her Going Abroad
> ("Farewell, my friend, good angels waft thee o'er")
> 1775

To Bacchus — see *Anacreontic. To Bacchus*

To Carlos ("When Day's retiring glow was spread")
> *Oracle* 9 July 1792 (*Julia*); 1793

To Cesario ("Cesario, thy lyre's dulcet measure")
> 1791; 1806

To Georgiana, on the Morning of Her Birthday
> ("Last night, as musing on a lay")
> 1804

To Him Who Complains — see *Lesbia, to Him Who Complains*

To Him Who Lamented Seeing a Beautiful Woman Weep
> ("The tear that falls from Lesbia's eye")
> *EM* April 1793; 1793; 1806

To Him Who Will Understand It — see *Lines to Him Who Will Understand Them*

To Jealousy ("A thousand torments wait on love")
> *MP* 2 Dec. 1797 (*Stanzas on Jealousy*); *Wals.* 1: 290; 1806

To John Taylor, Esq.
> ("To the heart that has feeling, what gift is so rare")
> 1806

To Julius ("The dusky veil of night was thrown")
> 1793; 1806

To Leonardo ("And dost thou hope to fan my flame")
> *W* 6 Dec. 1788 (*Laura*); 1791; 1806

To Leonardo ("Chill blows the blast")
> *W* 28 Feb. 1789 (*Laura*)

To Liberty. Sonnet I — see *Sonnet. To Liberty*

To live by mental toil; e'en when the brain
> *Wals.* 2: 64

To Lisardo, on His Recovering from a Long Indisposition, in May 1793 — see *To the Same, on His Recovering from a Long Indisposition*

To Love: Written Extempore ("Resistless power, ah! wherefore reign")
> 1775

To Matilda ("Pure and divine, without a fault")
> 1775

To Meditation — see *Ode to Meditation*

To Miss Maria Porter, as Roxalana
> ("So sportive! so lovely! so witty! so chaste!")
> *MP* 16 June 1800

To Miss Porter, in the Character of a Nun
> ("The Persian, at the dawn of day")
> *MP* 16 June 1800

To Mrs. Hanway on the Death of Her Lovely and Accomplished Daughter
> ("Sad, pensive hour! now let Reflection see")
> *Oracle* 26 Dec. 1792 (*Laura Maria*)

To Peace: From the "Shrine of Bertha
    ("O Peace! thou nympth of modest mien")
    Shrine 2: 193-4; 1806

To Pope's Oak ("'Here Pope first sung!' o hallow'd tree!")
    1791 (*Stanzas Written Under an Oak in Windsor Forest*);
    1806

To Rinaldo ("Soft is the balmy breath of May")
    1791

To Simplicity ("Sweet blushing Nymph, who loves to dwell")
    T&C Oct. 1791; 1791; 1806

To Sir Joshua Reynolds
    ("Immortal Reynolds! thou, whose art can trace")
    Oracle 9 July 1789 (Laura Maria)

To Spring. Written After A Winter of Ill Health in the Year 1800
    ("Life-glowing season! odour-breathing Spring!")
    MP 30 April 1800; *Memoirs* 2: 149 (*Ode to Spring*); 1804
    (*Lines to Spring*); 1806

To Summer ("Thy golden hour returns! The Sun")
    MP 7 July 1800 (M.R.)

To the Aspin Tree ("Why tremble so, broad Aspin Tree?")
    MP 13 May 1800 (*Sappho to the Aspen Tree*, Sappho);
    1804; 1806

To the Author of "The Secret Tribunal"
    ("Let the Muse, who with classical taste can impart")
    Oracle 20 October 1795 (Julia)

To the Blue Bell ("Blue Bell! how gayly art thou drest")
    MP 5 April 1799; *Nat. D.* 2: 109-10; 1806

To the Duchess of Devonshire ("The Nightingale with mourning lay")
    LMM June 1799 (Oberon); 1806

To the Editor of the Morning Post and Fashionable World. Letter II
    ("Dear Mister Editor, again")
    MP 5 Nov. 1794 (Bridget)

To the May Fly ("Poor insect! what a little day")
    MP 8 May 1800 (*Oberon, to the May Fly*, Oberon); 1806

To the Memory of My Beloved Brother — see *Lines to the Memory of My Brother*

To the Memory of My Lamented Father — see *Ode to the Memory of My Lamented Father*

To the Memory of Werter — see *Elegy to the Memory of Werter*

To the Mole ("Thou creep'st in darkness, busy thing!")
   MP 12 Aug. 1800; 1806

To the Muse of Poetry ("Exult, my Muse! exult to see")
   1791; 1806

To the Myrtle ("Unfading branch of verdant hue")
   1791; 1806

To the New Type of the Morning Post
   ("Ye sable legions, here you stand")
   MP 27 Jan. 1800 (M.R.)

To the Poet Coleridge ("Rapt in the visionary theme!")
   Memoirs 4: 145-9 (*Mrs. Robinson to the Poet Coleridge*,
   Sappho); 1806

To the Queen of the Fairies — see *Oberon to the Queen of the Fairies*

To the Same ("Ah! Tell me not that jealous fear")
   1793

To the Same ("On the base shrine of sordid Love")
   1793

To the Same ("Say not, that minutes *swiftly* move")
   1793

To the Same, on His Recovering From a Long Indisposition, in May 1793
   ("Go, balmy gales, and tell Lisardo's ear")
   1793 (*Stanzas to Lisardo*); 1806

To the Wanderer ("Welcome! once more, to this sad breast")
   1806

To the Wild Brook ("Unheeded emblem of the mind")
   MP 6 Aug. 1799 (Laura Maria); *Memoirs* 3: 102-3
   (interpolated into *Jasper*); 1806

To Time — see *Sappho — To Time*

To Zephyrus, Written in August 1793
   ("Light Zephyrus! gay child of Spring")
   1793; *Oracle* 7 Jan. 1794 (Laura Maria)

The Trumpeter. An Old English Tale
   ("It was in the days of a gay British King")
   1800; 1806

Turn to yon vale beneath, whose tangled shade
   Sappho III; 1806

Twilight ("How placid is thy hour, O Twilight pale")
   MP 20 April 1798

Venus! to thee, the Lesbian Muse shall sing,
    Sappho XXXIV; 1806
The Vestal ("Dim was the cloister, where the vestal sad")
    MP 5 May 1798 (no author); incorporated into *Progress*
The Vision ("As lately musing in a lonely shade")
    1775
The Way to Keep Him ("A lover, when he first essays")
    LMM May 1800 (Bridget); 1804 (*A Receipt for Modern
    Love*); 1806
Weak is the sophistry, and vain the art
    Sappho XXVIII; 1806
The Weeping Willow ("Beneath a spreading WILLOW")
    1793; *Scots* April 1794
What means the mist opake that veils these eyes
    Sappho XXXV; 1806
When hidden fears the bosom tear — see *Stanzas to Rest*
When I Was Young ("Old Lady Dinah, peevish grown")
    MP 16 June 1800 (Tabitha Bramble)
When, in the gloomy mansion of the dead
    Sappho XXXVII; *MP* 26 Nov. 1796; 1806
When winter o'ershadows the scene
    Lucky
When women are suffer'd to ramble at large
    Lucky
Where antique woods o'er-hang the mountain's crest
    Sappho XXVI; 1806
While from the dizzy precipice I gaze
    Sappho XLIII; 1806 (XLII)
Why art thou chang'd? O Phaon! tell me why?
    Sappho XVIII; 1806
Why do I live to loath the cheerful day
    Sappho XXI; 1806
Why, through each aching vein, with lazy pace
    Sappho VIII; 1806
Why, when I gaze on Phaon's beauteous eyes
    Sappho IV; 1806
The Widow's Home ("Close on the margin of a brawling brook")
    1800; 1806

Wild is the foaming sea! the surges roar!
>*Sappho* XXII; 1806

Winkfield Plain — see *The Camp*

Winter — see *Anacreontic* ("You say, my love, the drifted snow")

The Wintry Day ("Is it in mansions rich and gay")
>*MP* 4 Jan. 1800; *EM* Jan. 1800; 1804 (The Wint'ry Day);
>1806

A Wish ("Heav'n knows I never would repine")
>*MP* 5 Jan. 1796; *Angelina* 2: 263-4; 1806

The Wish ("All I ask of bounteous heav'n")
>1775

Within this drear and silent gloom — see *The Nun's Complaint*

The Worn-out Mariner ("O Pride! behold where, at thy lofty gate")
>*MP* 16 Sept. 1799 (Laura Maria); *LMM* Oct. 1800 (Laura
>Maria)

The Worst of Ills ("What wounds more deep than arrows keen")
>*MP* 21 June 1800 (Sappho); 1804 (*Ingratitude*); 1806

Written at Brighton ("The evening sun now sinks serene")
>*MP* 9 Oct. 1800 (*Written on the Sea-Shore*, Oberon);
>*Memoirs* 3: 94-5 (interpolated into *Jasper*); 1806

Written During the Late Stormy Weather
>("Far and wide the tempest howls")
>*MP* 18 Oct. 1800 (T.B.)

Written Extempore on the Picture of a Friend
>("Within this narrow compass is confin'd")
>1775

Written Near an Old Oak, in Windsor Forest
>("Old tree! how yellow are thy leaves")
>*MP* 31 Oct. 1800 (Oberon)

Written on a Faded Bouquet ("Fair was this blushing rose of May")
>*T&C* July 1790 (*On a Faded Bouquet*, Laura Maria); 1791
>(*The Faded Bouquet*); 1806

Written on the Outside of an Hermitage
>("Stranger beware who'ere thou art")
>1775

Written on Richmond Hill
>("From Richmond's verdant hills and flow'ry plains")
>*T&C* Jan. 1776

Written on Seeing a Rose Still Blooming at a Cottage Door on Egham
  Hill, the 25th of October, 1800
    ("Why dost thou linger still, sweet flow'r?")
    MP 4 Nov. 1800 (M.R.); 1806
Written on the Sea-Shore — see *Written at Brighton*
Ye crystal fountains softly flown — see *Song* ("Ye crystal fountains,
    softly flow")
Ye powers, ah! wherefore decree
    Lucky
Yes, I will go, where circling whirlwinds rise
    Sappho XLI; 1806 (XL)
Ye, who in alleys green and leafy bow'rs
    Sappho IX; 1806
Your blooming face, and gait so smart
    Lucky

Bibliography

Adams, R. Ray. *Studies in the Literary Backgrounds of English Radicalism*. London: Franklin and Marshall P, 1947.

Bass, Robert D. *The Green Dragoon: The Lives of Banastre Tarleton and Mary Robinson*. London: Alvin Redman, 1957.

Behrendt, Stephen C., and Harriet Kramer Linkin, eds. *Approaches to Teaching British Women Poets of the Romantic Period*. New York: The Modern Language Association, 1997.

Bolton, Betsy. "Romancing the Stone: 'Perdita' Robinson in Wordsworth's London." *ELH* 64 (1997): 727-59.

Cullens, Chris. "Mrs. Robinson and the Masquerade of Womanliness." *Body and Text in the Eighteenth Century*. Ed. Veronica Kelly and Dorothea Von Mücke. Stanford: Stanford UP, 1994. 266-89.

Curran, Stuart. "The I Altered." *Romanticism and Feminism*. Ed. Anne K. Mellor. Bloomington: Indiana UP, 1988. 185-207.

———. "Mary Robinson's *Lyrical Tales* in Context." *Re-Visioning Romanticism: British Women Writers, 1776-1837*. Eds. Carol Shiner Wilson and Joel Haefner. Philadelphia: University of Pennsylvania P, 1994. 17-35.

Davenport, Hester. "Mary 'Perdita' Robinson 1758-1800: A Royal Scandal." *Windlesora* no. 15 (1997): 4-8.

Erdman, David V. "Lost Poem Found: The cooperative pursuit & recapture of an escaped Coleridge 'sonnet' of 72 lines." *Bulletin of the New York Public Library* 65 (1961): 249-68.

Favret, Mary. "Telling Tales about Genre: Poetry in the Romantic Novel." *Studies in the Novel* 26 (1994): 153-72.

Fergus, Jan, and Janie Farrar Thaddeus. "Women Publishers and Money, 1790-1820." *Studies in Eighteenth-Century Culture* 17 (1987): 191-207.

Ford, Susan Allen. "'A name more dear': Daughters, Fathers, and Desire in *A Simple Story*, *The False Friend*, and *Mathilda*." *Re-Visioning Romanticism: British Women Writers, 1776-1837*. Ed. Carol Shiner Wilson and Joel Haefner. Philadelphia: University of Pennsylvania P, 1994. 51-71.

Griggs, Earl Leslie. "Coleridge and Mrs. Mary Robinson." *Modern Language Notes* 45 (1930): 90-95.

Kelly, Gary. *The English Jacobin Novel, 1780-1805.* Oxford: Clarendon P, 1976.

Labbe, Jacqueline M. "Selling One's Sorrows: Charlotte Smith, Mary Robinson, and the Marketing of Poetry." *Wordsworth Circle* 25 (1994): 68-71.

Levy, Martin J. "Coleridge, Mary Robinson and *Kubla Khan.*" *Charles Lamb Bulletin* ns 77 (1992): 156-66.

———. "Gainsborough's *Mrs. Robinson:* A Portrait and its Context." *Apollo* ns 136 (1992): 152-55.

Luther, Susan. "A Stranger Minstrel: Coleridge's Mrs. Robinson." *Studies in Romanticism* 33 (1994): 391-409.

McGann, Jerome J. *The Poetics of Sensibility: A Revolution in Literary Style.* Oxford: Clarendon P, 1996.

Miskolcze, Robin L. "Snapshots of Contradiction in Mary Robinson's *PoeticalWorks.*" *Papers on Language and Literature* 31 (1995): 206-19.

Mellor, Anne K. "British Romanticism, gender and three women artists." *The Consumption of Culture 1600-1800.* Ed. Ann Bermingham and John Brewer. New York: Routledge, 1995. 121-42.

Pascoe, Judith. *Romantic Theatricality: Gender, Poetry, and Spectatorship.* Cornell UP, 1997.

Peterson, Linda H. "Becoming an Author: Mary Robinson's *Memoirs* and the Origins of the Woman Artist's Autobiography." *Re-Visioning Romanticism: British Women Writers, 1776-1837.* Ed. Carol Shiner Wilson and Joel Haefner. Philadelphia: University of Pennsylvania P, 1994. 36-50.

Robinson, Daniel. "Coleridge, Mary Robinson, and the Prosody of Dreams." *Dreaming: Journal of the Association for the Study of Dreams* 7 (1997): 119-40.

———. "From 'Mingled Measure' to 'Ecstatic Measures': Mary Robinson's Poetic Reading of 'Kubla Khan.'" *Wordsworth Circle* 26 (1995): 4-7.

———. "Reviving the Sonnet: Women Romantic Poets and the Sonnet Claim." *European Romantic Review* 6 (1995): 98-127.

Setzer, Sharon M. "Mary Robinson's Sylphid Self: The End of Feminine Self-Fashioning." *Philological Quarterly* 75 (1996): 501-20.

———. "Romancing the Reign of Terror: Sexual Politics in Mary Robinson's *The Natural Daughter.*" *Criticism* 39 (1997): 531-55.

Shaffer, Julie. "Illegitimate Female Sexualities in Romantic-Era Women-Penned Novels in Corvey." *Corvey Journal* 5.2-3 (1993): 44-52.

Ty, Eleanor. "Engendering a Female Subject: Mary Robinson's (Re)Presentations of the Self." *English Studies in Canada* 21 (1995): 407-31.

———. *Unsex'd Revolutionaries: Five Women Novelists of the 1790s.* Toronto: University of Toronto P, 1993.

Vargo, Lisa. "The Claims of "real life and manners": Coleridge and Mary Robinson." *Wordsworth Circle* 26 (1995): 134-37.

Walker, John. "Maria Cosway: An Undervalued Artist." *Apollo* ns 123 (May 1986): 318-24.

Woof, R.S. "Wordsworth's Poetry and Stuart's Newspapers: 1797-1803." *Studies in Bibliography* 15 (1962): 149-89.

List of Changes

Occasional changes to spelling and punctuation have been made, usually based on revision that occurred in the 1806 *Poetical Works*. The changes listed below are found in the 1806 edition unless the alteration is attributed to the editor in brackets.

Ainsi va le Monde
line 331   "lovers tears" changed to "lovers' tears" [editor's alteration]

The Alien Boy
line 96   "stood;" changed to "stood,"

All Alone
line 33   "yewtree-shades" changed to "yew-tree shades"
line 64   "yew-tree's shadowy row" changed to "yew-trees'
            shadowy row"

The Confessor, a Sanctified Tale
line 29   "Farmers wives" changed to "Farmers' wives"
line 78   "little boy" changed to "little boy,"

Deborah's Parrot, a Village Tale
line 58   opening quotation mark added
line 63   "teacher" changed to "teacher,"
line 120   opening quotation mark added
line 147   "dy'e" changed to "d'ye"

The Fortune-Teller, a Gypsy Tale
line 33,   "fairy things" changed to "fairy things,"
line 35   "Phantom's Airy" changed to "phantoms airy"
line 67   "mens wives" changed to "men's wives"
line 82   "fond surprize," changed to "fond surprize;"
line 83   "cross," changed to "cross"
line 119   "near" changed to "near,"
line 132   "losses?" changed to "losses!"

A Fragment, Supposed to Be Written Near the Temple
line 75   "awhile" changed to "a while"

Golfre, a Gothic Swiss Tale
line 1   "dazzl'ing snow" changed to "dazzling snow" [editor's
           alteration]
line 40,   "Start'ling" changed to "Startling"
line 220   "round" changed to "round,"
line 427   "ting'd" changed to "ting'd,"

The Granny Grey, a Love Tale
line 58   "made," changed to "made;"

The Haunted Beach
line 20   "Ocean;" changed to "Ocean,"
line 21   "scene," changed to "scene"

The Lascar
line 248   "care;" changed to "care?"
line 268   "boy" changed to "Boy"
line 276   "boy" changed to "Boy"

Lines Inscribed to P. de Loutherbourg
line 29   "Or mingling" changed to "Or, mingling"

The Maniac
line 5   "speak!" changed to "speak?"
line 84   "Chain?" changed to "Chain!"
line 88   "warriors hearts" changed to "warriors' hearts"

Marie Antoinette's Lamentation, in her Prison of the Temple
lines 31 and 40 "awhile" changed to "a while"
line 78   "Despair!" changed to "Despair?"

Mistress Gurton's Cat
line 39   "menanc'd" changed to "menac'd"
line 57   "emral'd" changed to "em'rald" [editor's alteration]

The Monk

line 71   "beam" changed to "seem" [as in Memoirs (1801)]

The Negro Girl

line 23   "storm worn" changed to "storm-worn"

Oberon's Invitation to Titania

line 11   "spring-flow'rs bell" changed to "spring-flow'r's bell"
            [editor's alteration]

Ode to Della Crusca

line 1   "Lyre?" changed to "Lyre!"

Poor Marguerite

line 78,   quotation mark added to end of line
line 123   "stray" changed to "stray,"
line 145   "wave" changed to "wave,"
line 88   "Marguerite." changed to "Marguerite?" [editor's
            alteration]

The Poor, Singing Dame

line 15   "or goblin or fairy" changed to "nor goblin nor fairy"

The Shepherd's Dog

line 97   "Sea" changed to "Sea,"
line 110   "seen," changed to "seen;"

Sonnet XI

line 3   "Can'st thou, the soul's" changed to "Can'st thou the
            soul's"

Sonnet XIII

line 2   "wreathe" changed to "wreath"

Sonnet XXVI

line 2   "lour;" changed to "lour,"

Sonnet XL

line 13   "end," changed to "end;"

Sonnet XLIV. Conclusive

line 4   "flowr's" changed to "flow'rs"

The Trumpeter, an Old English Tale

line 90   "menanc'd" changed to "menac'd"

The Widow's Home

line 94   "The meek flow'r" changed to "the meek flow'r"

Index of first lines

High on a rock, coeval with the skies 157
High, on the Solitude of Alpine Hills 224
I wake! delusive phantoms hence, away! 174
Immortal Reynolds! thou, whose art can trace 289
In the worst den of human misery 312
In this vain, busy world, where the Good and the Gay 290
In vain, for me, thy gifts display'd 345
Is it in mansions rich and gay 340
Is it to love, to fix the tender gaze 160
It was in the days of a gay British King 239
Lead me, Sicilian Maids, to haunted bow'rs 175
Let Fashion and Fancy their beauties display 292
Let others wreaths of Roses twine 99
Long didst thou live, unruling and unrul'd 300
Love steals unheeded o'er the tranquil mind 165
Love, I renounce thy tyrant sway 94
Lubin and Kate, as gossips tell 246
Mid the grey horrors of his narrow cell 307
My Portrait you desire! and why? 139
Nature, with colours heav'nly pure! 138
Now Anarchy roam'd wide, a monster fierce 303
Now Midnight spreads her sable vest 127
Now, o'er the tessellated pavement strew 163
Now, round my favour'd grot let roses rise 164
O Thou! all wonderful, all glorious Pow'r! 116
O Thou! meek Orb! that stealing o'er the dale 169
O Thou, to whom superior worth's allied 103
O! How can Love exulting Reason, quell! 159
O! Reason! vaunted Sov'reign of the mind! 162
O'er the tall cliff that bounds the billowy main 172
O, let me seize thy pen sublime 76
Oft have I seen yon Solitary Man 215
Oh Sigh! thou steal'st, the herald of the breast 176
Oh! can'st thou bear to see this faded frame 178
Oh! come, my pretty love! and we 344
Oh! I could toil for thee o'er burning plains 167
Oh! ye bright Stars! that on the Ebon fields 171
Old Barnard was still a lusty hind 220

Index of titles